T0327017

Ilex Foundation Series 19

THE STUDY OF AL-ANDALUS

Also in the Ilex Foundation Series

Dreaming across Boundaries: The Interpretation of Dreams in Islamic Lands
edited by Louise Marlow

Strī: Women in Epic Mahābhārata
by Kevin McGrath

Persian Literature and Judeo-Persian Culture: Collected Writings of Sorour S. Soroudi
edited by H. E. Chehabi

The Rhetoric of Biography: Narrating Lives in Persianate Societies
edited by L. Marlow

Jaya: Performance in Epic Mahābhārata
by Kevin McGrath

The History *of Beyhaqi (The History of Sultan Masʿud of Ghazna, 1030–1041) by Abu'l-Fażl Beyhaqi*
translated and with commentaries by Clifford Edmund Bosworth
fully revised and with further commentary by Mohsen Ashtiany

The Last of the Rephaim: Conquest and Cataclysm in the Heroic Ages of Ancient Israel
by Brian R. Doak

Ruse and Wit: The Humorous in Arabic, Turkish, and Persian Narrative
edited by Dominic Parvis Brookshaw

Kṛṣṇa: Friendship in Epic Mahābhārata
by Kevin McGrath

On the Wonders of Land and Sea: Persianate Travel Writing
edited by Roberta Micallef and Sunil Sharma

Poet and Hero in the Persian Book of Kings
third edition
by Olga M. Davidson

Comparative Literature and Classical Persian Poetics
second edition
by Olga M. Davidson

Ferdowsi's Shāhnāma*: Millennial Perspectives*
edited by Olga M. Davidson and Marianna Shreve Simpson

Mirror of Dew: The Poetry of Ālam-tāj Zhāle Qā'em-Maqāmi
translated with an introduction by Asghar Seyed-Gohrab

Global Medieval: Mirrors for Princes Reconsidered
edited by Regula Forster and Neguin Yavari

Erin and Iran: Cultural Encounters between the Irish and the Iranians
edited by H. E. Chehabi and Grace Neville

THE STUDY OF AL-ANDALUS

THE SCHOLARSHIP AND LEGACY OF JAMES T. MONROE

Edited by
Michelle M. Hamilton
and
David A. Wacks

Ilex Foundation
Boston, Massachusetts

Center for Hellenic Studies
Trustees for Harvard University
Washington, D.C.

Distributed by Harvard University Press
Cambridge, Massachusetts, and London, England

The Study of al-Andalus: The Scholarship and Legacy of James T. Monroe
Edited by Michelle M. Hamilton and David A. Wacks

Published by Ilex Foundation, Boston, Massachusetts and The Center for Hellenic Studies, Trustees for Harvard University, Washington, D.C.

Distributed by Harvard University Press, Cambridge, Massachusetts and London, England

Production editor: Christopher Dadian
Cover design: Joni Godlove

Cover image: Plaster relief carving (detail). Alhambra. Granada, Spain. Photo by: Mary Celeste Holm

Printed in the United States of America

Library of Congress Cataloging-in-Publication Data

Names: Hamilton, Michelle, 1969- editor. | Wacks, David A., editor. | Monroe, James T., honoree.
Title: The study of al-Andalus : the scholarship and legacy of James T. Monroe / edited by Michelle M. Hamilton and David A. Wacks.
Description: Boston, Massachusetts : Ilex Foundation ; Washington, D.C. : The Center for Hellenic Studies, Trustees for Harvard University, 2018. | Series: Ilex Foundation series ; 19 | Includes bibliographical references and index.
Identifiers: LCCN 2018017721 | ISBN 9780674984462 (alk. paper)
Subjects: LCSH: Arabic literature--Spain--Andalusia--History and criticism. | Arabic literature--750-1258--History and criticism.
Classification: LCC PJ8417.A5 S78 2018 | DDC 892.7/09946--dc23
LC record available at https://lccn.loc.gov/2018017721

To James, a great mentor and teacher and an excellent scholar

CONTENTS

The Study of al-Andalus: The Scholarship and Legacy of James T. Monroe

Michelle M. Hamilton and David A. Wacks

THIS COLLECTION OF ESSAYS recognizes and explores the impact of the scholarship of James T. Monroe. Among his students and colleagues (several of whom have contributed to the present volume) James T. Monroe is recognized as a pioneer in a variety of fields, including Andalusī, Iberian, and Spanish studies and Arabic and comparative literatures. The studies in this volume underscore the impact of Monroe's work on these fields and bring it into focus within the larger scholarly discourses that (arguably) define the modern academy (cultural studies, Orientalism, identity, postcolonial studies, etc.). Monroe's work has made accessible to generations of English-speaking scholars works from the medieval Andalusī tradition (including al-Saraqusṭī's *maqāmāt*; Ibn Shuhayd's *Risālat at-tawābiʿ wa z-zawābiʿ*; Ibn Garcia et al.'s Andalusī *shuʿūbiyya* treatises; the *muwashshaḥāt* and the *kharjas*; and the poetry of Ibn Quzmān), as well as one of the earliest studies on the phenomenon of Orientalism: *Islam and the Arabs in Spanish Scholarship* from 1970. His bilingual anthology of Andalusī poetry has become the de facto textbook for college courses, not only within departments of Spanish, Romance languages and Arabic, but in fields such as creative writing and political science. This small sampling of his scholarship, the product of some fifty years of work as a scholar, the majority of which has been spent as a professor at the University of California, Berkeley, reveals the importance of Monroe's work in establishing the place of Andalusī literature and culture in the study of the Iberian traditions, from which, in the academy of the United States, it had been almost wholly absent.

Monroe's body of work reveals some constant theoretical imperatives, including an emphasis on exploring literary works within their broader cultural context and on examining how factors such as literary patronage, race and political change impact forms of the cultural production, particularly literature. His studies on Hispano-Arabic poetry, the *maqāmāt* of al-Hamadhānī (d. 1007 CE) and al-Saraqusṭī (d. 1143 CE) and the *zajals* of Ibn Quzmān (d. 1160 CE) reveal that, contrary to the inherited narrative that Andalusī literature went into decline after the disintegration of the Umayyad caliphate, the record shows instead that political fragmentation and weakness often resulted in "literary innovation and excellence."[1] The Arabic lyric and prose forms such as the *muwashshaḥāt, zajals*, and *maqāmāt* that dominated the Iberian Peninsula after the fall of the caliphate of Cordoba, are innovative, hybrid genres that are, as Monroe has explored in most of his scholarship over the past fifty years, the unique products of Arabic and European cultures in contact. Monroe's insistence on examining the broader cultural context as integral to these forms and modes of literary production makes him one of the earliest scholars of cultural studies and its methodological approach, evident especially in his perspective toward Andalusī cultural production as part of the larger context of the Arab Mediterranean, Western Europe, and of the Arabic-speaking world. One of the most important contributions of Monroe's work for scholars of Spanish studies has been his portrayal of Iberia and Iberian cultural production as both part of Europe and of the "Muslim East." In his studies of Andalusī and medieval Spanish literature, Monroe explores how works such as Ibn Quzmān's zajals and the Spanish rhymed prose narrative, the *Libro de buen amor*, are hybrid works produced combining literary structures from one tradition and material or themes from another by people living at the crossroads of various cultures and literary traditions.[2]

This comparative mode is one of the cornerstones of Monroe's work. His 1983 study of al-Hamadhānī's *maqāmāt*, the *Art of Badīʿ al-Zamān al-Hamadhāni* (= *Art*), shows how productive such a comparative frame can be. It allows scholars of vernacular Romance and English literature to begin to approach the Arabic literature of al-Andalus as something other than wholly alien. In this study Monroe explores how the *maqāmāt* can be read as an inversion of the heroic values and moral lessons of such genres as *hadith*, classical Arabic poetry and epic, much as the Spanish picaresque can be read as a satire of the epic and romances of chivalry.[3] Like his 1974 anthology of *Hispano-Arabic Poetry*, this study of the *maqāmāt* is an early contribution to his larger mission of shifting the field of comparative literature away from its Eurocentric focus. Monroe states this clearly in the introduction of the *Art:*

> If the discipline of Comparative Literature is to achieve the goal of becoming the "Poetics" of the twenty-first century, it must assimilate hitherto neglected non-Western traditions into its theoretical

1. Monroe and Pettigrew 2003, 139.
2. Monroe 2011a; Monroe 2017, 11 and 1309–1312.
3. Monroe's student, Douglas Young, explores the connection between the *maqāmāt* and Spanish works such as *La Lozana andaluza* and the *Guzmán de Alfarache* (Young 2004).

constructions, in order to eliminate the bias in favor of Western literature that now dominates it.[4]

Monroe has contributed to this shift in focus not only through his book-length studies like the *Art, Islam and the Arabs in Spanish Scholarship,* and over sixty articles exploring the intersection of Arabic and Romance literary traditions, but also in the production of translations of such works as the *diwan* of ibn Quzmān's *zajals* (*The Mischievous Muse*), al-Saraquṣṭī's collection of *maqāmāt* (*Al-Maqāmāt al-Luzūmīyah*), the anthology of Andalusī poetry (*Hispano-Arabic Poetry*), Ibn Shuhayd's treatise on Arab poetry and poets (*Risālat at-tawābiʿ wa z-zawābiʿ*), and Ibn Garcia's *shuʿubiyya* treatise and its responses (*The Shuʿubiyya in al-Andalus*), all of which allow scholars to include this literature in their own theories and models of literary development, and in so doing "eliminate the bias in favor of [traditionally accepted] Western literature."[5]

The studies included in the present volume (discussed in detail below) show how scholars are responding to this project, not only by expanding the horizons of traditional medieval comparative literary frames that have focused on the comparison of various European traditions such as French, English, and German to include the Andalusī-Arabic and Hebrew as part of this larger European or Western tradition, but that also explore how Andalusī literature and realities – the most western (Maghribi) of Arabic-speaking peoples and cultural production – impacted and was impacted by the Arabic traditions of the Muslim East.

One can see in Monroe's pioneering role as founder of Andalusī studies in the United States the important legacy of his mentor, Américo Castro, the

4. Monroe 1983, 15.

5. Monroe 1983, 15. Arguably all of Monroe's subsequent work has contributed to addressing these needs: providing translations that can be used as "tools" by scholars, as well as analytic studies showing the interconnectedness of Spanish and other vernacular literary traditions with medieval Arabic and Andalusī literature. Monroe's corpus of scholarly work includes hundreds of articles and books – far too many to list in their entirety here; however, a few that can be recommended as exemplary in showing the type of study that brings the literature of the Arab world into dialogue with that of Europe, that allows for a truly comparative frame, includes his comparative study of the *maqāmāt*, with the Spanish picaresque and *Don Quijote* (1983; 2002); his analysis of Ibn Quzmān's *zajal* 12 as perhaps the earliest testimony to the Arab shadow puppet tradition, which he then shows must be read as a precursor to the popular *Romancero* tradition as well as to later popular Spanish theatrical performances such as those described in *Don Quijote* and in the plays of Tirso de Molino (2017 2:1033–43); the study of both *muwashshaḥāt* and *zajals* as hybrid forms indebted to the European lyric traditions for their form and the Arabic tradition for their material or content (1974; 1975; 1977; 1989; 2011b; 2017).

Spanish exile who, as a professor of Spanish at Princeton, trained a generation of scholars, and whose now iconic concept of *convivencia* has become a touchstone for reframing not only the ways in which the role of Jewish and Arabic traditions of medieval Spain are considered, but the very nature of Iberian studies in the Americas.[6] While several of Castro's students (Stephen Gilman, Samuel Armistead, Albert Sicroff) became leaders in Spanish studies, Monroe is unique among them in having pursued Castro's legacy in the field of Arabic studies. In fact, Monroe's encounter with Castro was not as a graduate student, but first as an undergraduate when the latter was a visiting professor at the University of Houston. They reunited some years later when Monroe was a junior colleague of Castro's at the University of California, San Diego, where Castro was a professor of Spanish in his final years of teaching. Castro, thus, was fortunate to have as a colleague at the end his career a highly trained Arabist and young assistant professor (Monroe), a former student whom he launched into a career in Arabic literature, who had been educated and brought up in the Spanish-speaking world, in Chile.[7] While Castro may not have approved of Monroe's decision to study Arabic (warning the young James that "the study of Arabic was a bottomless pit"), Monroe went on to study with others, such as the professor he encountered while studying abroad at the University of Toulouse, Stanislas de Benda, who insisted that if students who had enrolled in his Arabs in Spain class (among them Monroe) wanted to understand the course material they must learn Arabic. Monroe also pursued graduate studies with Sir Hamilton Gibb, the legendary Arabist, at Harvard, where he received his PhD in Romance Languages in 1963.[8]

Even as scholarship exploring European representations of the "East" has proliferated in the last ten years among historians/literary critics (see, for example, the work of Suzanne Akbari, John Tolan, and Jeremy Cohen) as well as part of a cottage industry of crusade studies that has followed in the wake of the wars in Iraq, Afghanistan, and Syria (Jonathan Riley-Smith, Thomas

6. Castro 1948. In his introduction to the translations and editions of Ibn Quzmān's *diwan*, Monroe uses Castro's theoretical approach as a useful lens for understanding Ibn Quzmān's creation of a hybrid literary form out of European and Arabic traditions (2017 1:9–11). Other scholars that have revisited Castro's work and theory of *convivencia* include María Menocal, Ryan Szpiech, and Brian Catlos.

7. Although born in Texas, Monroe moved with his parents at the age of three months to Rancagua, Chile. His mother, Ethel Florence Cooke, had been born in Chile and his father worked as chief supplier for the Braden Copper Company (an American subsidiary of the Kennecott Copper Corporation). Monroe attended La Grange in Santiago, an English school for boys, for nine years.

8. Monroe, acknowledgements to the *Maqāmāt al-Luzūmīyah of al-Saraquṣṭī*, xxi–xxii.

Madden, Giles Constable, Christopher Tyerman, and others), a discussion of the complex realities of medieval Iberia as part of what constitutes "Europe" continues to be, in large part, absent. It is still the unspoken rule that English and French culture are defining traditions of Europe.[9] In this volume we bring the Andalusī culture made visible to an English-speaking audience by Monroe's work into greater relief as a complement to other non-Western literary cultures (among them Persian, Egyptian, and Iraqi), as well as to the current debates about Muslims and the cultures and traditions of the Arabic-speaking world. This volume further explores the legacy of Andalusī culture in both East and West, and the ways we choose to remember the Andalusī past has become an important mode of critical inquiry.

The first essay in the volume reflects on the legacy of Monroe's scholarship in the Spanish academy. Manuela Marín's contribution, "Revisiting *Islam and the Arabs in Spanish Scholarship*," shows us that while Monroe's pioneering 1970 study may have elicited little response among contemporary Spanish Arabists, who worked in the long shadow of such figures as Miguel Asín Palacios and Emilio García Gómez, as well as within the complex realities of Franco's Spain, an emerging generation of scholars such as Bernabé López García show that Monroe's work has made inroads in Spanish Arabism and is now instrumental in shaping the ways in which Spanish Arabists (and Arabists in Spain) think about not only their own field, but also the nature of Andalusī cultural production. Marín shows that in *Islam and the Arabs* Monroe highlights the birth of Spanish Arabism in the progressivism of the late eighteenth century, but that by the early twentieth century its leaders, Asín Palacios, Ángel González Palencia, and García Gómez negotiated and at times were even complicit with the political Right.[10] Marín also explores the role that Monroe's intellectual indebtedness to Américo Castro and Krausism plays in the way in which he presents the history of Spanish Arabism and in the reception his own work has received in Spain. While Marín offers Bernabé López García as exemplary of the new critical turn in Spanish Arabism, we can add to this list the work of Marín herself, as well as Teresa Garulo and Maribel Fierro, whose essays are also included in this collection, and whose work has been similarly shaped by Monroe's scholarship on al-Andalus (as discussed below).

Monroe's legacy rests on a cornerstone of his research on Andalusī

9. Akbari 2009; Tolan 2002; Cohen 1996, 2003; Riley-Smith 2002; Madden 1999; Constable 2008; Tyerman 2009. Studies that do seek to explore al-Andalus as part of Europe include those of Menocal 2002, Wacks 2007, Hamilton 2007 and González Ferrín 2006.

10. See García Sanjuán 2016 for the "persistence of this phenomenon" in contemporary Spain.

poetry, made accessible to English-speaking audiences first in *Hispano-Arabic Poetry*. Over the subsequent decades Monroe developed a theory of Andalusī poetics that positioned the Andalusī poetic form par excellence, the *muwashshaḥāt*, vis-à-vis not only the Arabic poetic traditions of the East, but also the emerging vernacular poetry of Europe. While Monroe has long encouraged scholars to consider the emergence and popularity of a strophic rhymed poetic form in eleventh- to thirteenth-century al-Andalus and Iberia when considering the rise and popularity of vernacular poetry in the Romance traditions, he has further stressed that such poetry was "intended primarily for singing."[11] This aspect of the poetry may in large part be lost because this poetry – *muwashshaḥāt* and *zajals* – was passed on primarily through a tradition with no system for recording melodies. Monroe has worked with both Benjamin Liu and David Switatlo tracing the survival of Andalusī *muwashshaḥāt* and *zajals* in subsequent North African and Eastern musical traditions, from the time of the Almoravids to twentieth-century Morocco and Palestine.[12] This work is the springboard for the studies of Reynolds and Garulo in the present collection.

In "From *Ṣawt* to *Muwashshaḥ*: A Musical Revolution," Dwight Reynolds encourages us to consider the musical character of Arabic strophic poetry, arguing that failing to do so misses the point entirely, for this was – and remains – primarily a song tradition, and not merely a poetic form. These songs and their form, strophes of alternating rhymes, were so original (and hitherto unknown in the Arabic literary tradition) that Arabic scholars and musicians were forced to develop a new vocabulary to describe them. Reynolds explores how Abū al-Faraj al-Iṣbahānī's tenth-century *Kitāb al-Aghānī* contains descriptions of the composition process that often involved the adaptation or borrowing (*muʿāraḍa* or *contrafactum*) of another song's melody. In this tradition, classical Arabic songs were normally short compositions designed to be used by professionally trained singers to build complex, sophisticated melodic constructions (they are therefore, as Reynolds puts it, "melocentric"). Reynolds explains how the simple melodies of the Andalusī *muwashshaḥāt* and *zajals*, whose end-rhymes made them relatively easy to memorize and thus more accessible to a wide audience, transformed the Arabic musical tradition in the Middle Ages, and that the rhymed strophic form of both the *muwashshaḥāt* and the *zajal* continued to be a respected and widespread song form in the early modern Arabic-speaking world.

Teresa Garulo's essay "Some Andalusī *Muwashshaḥāt* and their Eastern Imitations" takes as its point of departure how the Eastern authors

11. Liu and Monroe 1989, 1.
12. Liu and Monroe 1989; Monroe and Swiatlo 1977, 160.

al-Ṣafadī (d. 1363 CE) and Ibn Sanāʾ al-Mulk (d. 1211 CE) continued the Andalusī *muwashshaḥāt* tradition. Both authors composed *muʿāraḍāt* (*contrafacta*), poems inspired by the form (rhyme and meter) of earlier Andalusī *muwashshaḥāt*. The testimonies of Ibn Sanāʾ al-Mulk and al-Ṣafadī offer valuable insights into how Andalusī metrics were adopted in the Muslim East, as well as to the large number of Andalusī poems that were circulating and familiar to Eastern readers and musicians. Garulo focuses on a few examples from both Ibn Sanāʾ al-Mulk's *Dār al-ṭirāz*, a work designed to instruct its reader on how to compose *muwashshaḥāt*, and from al-Ṣafadī's *Tawshīʿ al-tawshīḥ*, a work in which the poet includes his original compositions and the Andalusī models on which they are based. Garulo shows the complex rhymes and meters used by Andalusī authors, and how the Eastern authors adopted and transformed these meters and rhymes in their original compositions, and in so doing introduced change based on the vernacular elements of the Hispano-Arabic poetic tradition into the Eastern tradition. Garulo's study is important because it gives English-speaking readers access to and a sense of the importance of sound in this Arabic poetry, which was fundamental to the importance and novelty of the Andalsui *muwashshaḥāt*. In addition, Ibn Sanāʾ al-Mulk and al-Ṣafadīʾ both provide valuable observations about the poetic process, such as Ibn Sanāʾ al-Mulk's comments about how the *muwashshaḥāt* were "adapted to Arabic meters." Such testimonies should be taken into account by anyone examining the poetic origins of the *muwashshaḥāt*.

The process of adapting poetic forms popular in non-Arabic languages and cultures to the Khalilian poetic meters of the classical Arabic tradition is also the subject of Olga M. Davidson's study, "Monroe's Methodology in Analyzing Andalusī Meters and Its Relevance to a Comparative Analysis of a Classical Persian Meter, the *mutaqārib*." Davidson takes as her point of departure Monroe's 1989 article "Which Came First, the *zajal* or the *muwashshaḥa*?" one of the studies in which Monroe presents evidence to support the idea that the *muwashshaḥāt* and *zajal*s developed from Hispano-Romance poetic traditions. Davidson's focus, though, is not the vernacular traditions of the Muslim West, but the poetic tradition of the Persian East. Davidson explores how the metrical form used in the composition of the Persian epic, the *mutaqārib*, like the *muwashshaḥāt*, is the vestige of an older, pre-existing regional metric system not found in classical Arabic poetry. While in the case of the *muwashshaḥāt*, as Reynolds and Garulo explore in their essays, this difference is defined by the use of both meter and a strophic rhyme form, in the case of the *mutaqārib*, a stichic form defined by the use of internal rhyme within the verse, the difference originates in the manner in which Persian authors adapted quantitative meter foreign to the accentual patterns of the classical Arabic tradition. Davidson's comparative approach and her focus on poetic forms echo the foci of Monroe's studies on the Andalusī poetic tradition and his call to expand the scope of comparative literature beyond the Western tradition.

Raymond Farrin's essay, "Seville, Where Miḥrābs Weep and Pulpits Lament: Al-Rundī's Elegy in the Classical Poetic Tradition," rounds out this group of essays on the medieval poetic traditions of al-Andalus and the broader Arabic-speaking world. Farrin offers a careful reading of al-Rundī's elegy, written after the city of Seville was conquered by Castilian forces in 1248. Farrin explores how this Andalusī poet adopts poetic imagery from the Arabic poetic tradition. Al-Rundī (d. 1285) crafts a *qaṣīda* expressing nostalgia, anger, and a muted call for vengance for the loss and destruction of Arabo-Islamic culture in Seville. Farrin shows how al-Rundī's poem is intellectually indebted not only to the earliest city elegies in the Arabic tradition, namely al-Khuraymī, Ibn al-Rūmī and Ibn al-Muʿtazz's laments for Baghdad, Basra, and Samarra, but also to those of the Andalusī poets Ibn Jahwar and Ibn Shuhayd, who composed elegies bemoaning the destruction of the Umayyad palace city *Medināt al-Zahrāʾ*. Farrin further shows, in a close reading of al-Rundī's elegy, that the latter adopts the rhymes and several motifs of an elegy composed upon the destruction of Qayrawan in 1057 by the Zirid poet Ibn Rashīq (d. c.1091). Al-Rundī tells us (in Farrin's translation) that monotheism (religion itself), along with the sites of faith – mosques – weep over the loss of Seville, and he then chastises his fellow Muslims, asking who will come to the aid of the city and its inhabitants. The elegy is a valuable Arabic testimony to the loss of Muslim-controlled Seville. Farrin provides an English translation of al-Rundī's poem as well as a cogent contextualization of the poem in a larger and older Arabic literary tradition, thus furthering Monroe's goal of making such texts (in languages other than the dominant Western European languages) accessible to scholars of comparative literature. The city elegy genre and this *qaṣīda* in particular will be of much interest to scholars exploring historical memory and trauma in the pre-modern world.

While Farrin dedicates much of his study to the literary elegy as genre, he also notes that the fall of Seville to Christian forces in 1248 followed in relatively close succession the political and social upheaval precipitated by the Almoravid invasion/transition to power in al-Andalus. Almoravid rule implied a series of changes in Andalusī cultural production that Monroe has studied in detail over the last twenty years. The Almoravids arrived in the 1080s as political and social outsiders at the invitation of the Taifa king of

Seville, al-Muʿtamid (d. 1095). They came to assist their Muslim coreligionists in resisting the aggression of Alfonso VI of Castile. They were Berbers who had established control over the Maghrib, ruling most of what is today Morocco and Mauritania, with their capital in Marrakech. Once in the Peninsula they established their rule, based on Māliki law and a bellicose ethos, over the prior Taifa states. Almoravid rule precipitated formal and thematic changes in Peninsular Arabic literature.

As Monroe has shown in his studies of the literary production of both Ibn Quzmān and al-Saraqusṭī, in al-Andalus the Almoravids replaced the various Andalusī Taifa kings, along with their courts and jurists (the upper and middle classes that had been the literary patrons of generations of Andalusī poets). These Almoravid rulers of Berber origins who spoke a dialect of Arabic and lacked an education in *adab* did not value or commission the compositions of the traditional classical Arabic tradition, such as the *qaṣīda*, that had previously been composed for and financed by the powerful, aristocratic patrons of the Taifa kingdoms. Instead, poets like Ibn Quzmān composed panegyrics in vernacular Cordoban Arabic using the popular strophic form of the Peninsula and dedicated them to members of the middle class – merchants and local officials. These poems are defined by an indecorous humor, scatological in nature.[13] In his studies of the *zajals* of Ibn Quzmān and the *maqāmāt* of al-Saraqusṭī, Monroe focusses on the broader social and cultural context, including patrons and patronage, race and identity, forces important in shaping literary production, particularly in the adoption of non-classical genres and the use of the vernacular. He further examines how this process works against the grain of accepted discourses prevalent in Arabic literary studies, namely the idea that political upheaval and the disappearance of the caliphate led to the decline or decadence of Arab literature and culture. On the contrary, Monroe shows that in al-Andalus, "political decline often led to literary innovation and excellence."[14]

In the case of al-Saraqusṭī, whose collection of fifty *maqāmāt* Monroe made available in English translation in 2002 (*Al-Maqāmāt al-Luzūmīyah*), the use of the rhymed prose *maqāmāt* with poetry embedded in it is an example of how new patrons and political situations can be catalysts for new literary forms and topics.[15] The *maqāmāt* had its origins in the Arabized culture of former Persian territories of the East. In both his study on al-Hamadhānī and al-Saraqusṭī's collection of *maqāmāt,* Monroe asserts that while the *maqāma* is in many ways a unique product of the Arabic literary tradition, it

13. See Monroe 1996; Monroe 2017, 2:1088–1089.
14. Monroe and Pettigrew 2003, 139.
15. Monroe 2002, 9–13.

is nevertheless also one branch of a larger, more global literary genre, the picaresque, that transcends individual and national literary traditions: "a counter-genre to noble literary genres such as epics, romances of chivalry, sermons, holy scriptures, etc."[16] While these genres may exalt and uphold the values and ideals of their society, the picaresque invites the reader to evaluate those values and ideals through the use of negative examples – tricksters and morally bankrupt characters who cynically invoke ideals and social norms to justify reprehensible behavior.[17]

In his collection of *maqāmāt*, al-Saraqusṭī often uses the unreliable narrator to question accepted discourses. Michelle M. Hamilton, "Astrology, *Jinn* and Magical Healing in al-Saraqusṭī's Forty-sixth *Maqāma*," explores not al-Saraqusti's parodic representation of the chivalric or epic, but rather of popular beliefs and practices associated with astrology, folk medicine, and spirits or *jinn*. In this *maqāma*, the trickster al-Sāʾib takes the guise of a popular healer who can not only exorcise *jinns*, but also cast horoscopes with what was then the most advanced of science, astronomical tables. Hamilton's focus on material culture and science echoes such a focus in various of Monroe's studies, including his examination of the Arab origins of the thirteenth-century Castilian go-between, Trotaconventos's spell-casting materials, and the importance of gold, mantles, or musical instruments in Ibn Quzmān's poetry.[18] In al-Saraqusṭī's *maqāma*, belief in *jinn* possession echoes the depiction of familiar *jinn* or spirits as literary muses for the poets of the Arabic tradition in Ibn Shuhayd's treatise, *Risālat at-tawābiʿ wa z-zawābiʿ*, which Monroe translated into English in 1971.

Shamma Boyarin ("The Triple Bound Cord": On Hebrew and Arabic in the Work and Identity of Judah al-Ḥarīzī") further picks up Monroe's insight into the unreliable narrator of the *maqāmāt* as a vehicle for social commentary and literary innovation. Boyarin turns to the Hebrew *maqāmāt* of Judah al-Ḥarīzī (d. 1225 CE), the *Sefer Tahkemoni*, arguing that the attitudes expressed toward Hebrew and Arabic in them must be taken with a grain of salt. While most scholars have long accepted al-Ḥarīzī's assertions in the introductory chapter that he composed the work in part to revive Hebrew among Jews who have long favored Arabic, Boyarin reminds us of Monroe's dictum that the *maqāmāt* are defined as a genre by logical contradictions and untrustworthy narrators. Boyarin asserts that this is in fact the case with al-Ḥarīzī, the diegetic author (who is one and the same with the fiction-

16. Monroe 2002, 2–3.

17. Monroe 2002, 3–8.

18. Monroe and Márquez Villanueva 1973; Monroe 2006, Monroe 2007; Monroe 2017, 2:1018–1022.

al narrator) of the introduction. Boyarin argues that al-Ḥarizi's collection of Hebrew *maqāmāt* have a complex relationship with the Arabic tradition, and most importantly reflect al-Ḥarīzī's response to the crisis in patronage felt among Andalusī Jewish authors forced into exile in Christian Spain and beyond. The Andalusī style literary courts of the elite, in which poets such as al-Ḥarīzī could make a living, disappeared after the Almoravids and Almohads conquered the Muslim kingdoms of Iberia and, just as Ibn Quzmān and al-Saraquṣṭī's work (discussed above) reflect the emergence of new genres and systems of patronage, so too does al-Ḥarizi's *Tahkemoni.* In the latter, a further innovation, unique to the Jewish literary milieu, is al-Ḥarīzī's use (and ambivalent attitude toward) Hebrew. Just as Monroe has stressed that far from ushering in literary decadence, the political and social upheavals of the eleventh and twelfth centuries produced literary innovation and an outpouring of creativity – this is the case, as Boyarin shows, with al-Ḥarīzī's *Tahkemoni.*

Another case study of how political and social change precipitate the adoption of new literary forms and usher in new periods of cultural flourishing is Samuel England's "Drama and Multiculturalism in Crisis: Ibn Dāniyāl's Shadow Play." Muḥammad ibn Dāniyāl (d. 1311 CE), an Iraqi scholar making a living in Mamluk Cairo as a medical doctor, wrote works catering to the literary tastes of second-generation, Arabic-speaking Mamluk minor officials and nobility. England argues that rather than rejecting the literary norms and conventions of the Arab *adab* tradition as scholars such as Li Guo and Elliot K. Rowson have asserted, Ibn Dāniyāl's shadow puppetry librettos should be read in the subgenre of the Banū Sāsān, a medieval class of beggars, thieves, and rogues, an element of classical Arabic poetry for at least the preceding 250 years. England's study of how Ibn Dāniyāl brings the popular dialect of the Banū Sāsān into dialogue with classical Arabic literary motifs such as the panygeric, the *qaṣīda* and the epic echoes the process – evident in al-Andalus in the work of Ibn Quzmān and al-Saraquṣṭī as studied by Monroe (and discussed above). In the case of the Egyptian shadow play, England argues that the often obscene, humorous narratives told by rogues and ne'er-do-wells are not satirical indictments of classical Arabic culture, but rather a nostalgic reaffirmation of lost Arab ethnic, religious, and linguistic/rhetorical values.

Maribel Fierro's essay, "Heraclius in al-Andalus," returns us to al-Andalus and explores how the Andalusī scholar Ibn Ḥubaysh revived a figure from the classical Arabic tradition, the Byzantine Emperor Heraclius, as a clever way to gain his freedom. According to al-Maqarrī, Alfonso VII released Ibn Hubaysh from the newly conquered Almería after the latter traced Alfonso's family line back to Heraclius. Alfonso is flattered and allows Ibn Hubaysh to take his family and resettle in Muslim-controlled Murcia. Fierro explores how in the Quran, *hadith* and subsequent Islamic tradition Heraclius is depicted as a Christian who exchanges letters with and subsequently accepts Muhammad as the *Mahdī* predicted in the New Testament. He is also portrayed as a Christian ruler who attempts to convert his own subjects to Islam, and Ibn Hubaysh probably presented Alfonso VII in hopes that the latter too would accept Islam. Alfonso, unaware of the Muslim legends about the figure of Heraclius, found Ibn Hubaysh's genealogy flattering because from his perspective it connected him to the "First Crusader," famed in the West for retaking Jerusalem and recovering the Holy Cross. Fierro argues that while Ibn Hubaysh's invocation of Heraclius, in spite of his intended message, worked in his favor because it struck chords (for the Christian Alfonso VII) of which Ibn Hubaysh was wholly unaware. Fierro does, however, point out that the figure of Heraclius was popular among Muslims on the Peninsula. In the face of increased Christian military strength and expansion, Andalusīs found solace in this story of a powerful Christian ruler who, at least in the Muslim versions of the legend, came to recognize the truth of Islam through the use of logic and persuasion.

David Wacks similarly explores how a particular figure and the discourses associated with it shift across cultures/traditions. While Fierro focuses on the historical figure of Heraclius, in "Ziyad ibn 'Āmir al-Kinānī: Andalusī Muslim Crusade Literature," Wacks focuses on how a chivalrous Christian knight is reimagined as a Muslim hero for a thirteenth-century Granadan Arabic-speaking audience. Wacks shows that the fictional narrative of Ziyad ibn 'Āmir, while evocative of Arabic *sirat* or popular heroic epics, also reflects certain conventions of the Western European romances of chivalry, including an aristocratic hero bent on conquest and religious conversion. Wacks argues that the tale of Ziyad ibn 'Āmir al-Kinānī – the tale of a Muslim hero who conquers and converts whole civilizations to Islam – is aspirational fiction and offers an imagined world that would have been appealing to the Muslims of Granada faced with increased Christian bellicosity and an uncertain future on the Peninsula. Like so many of the studies in this volume, including those of Davidson, Garulo, Boyarin, England, and Fierro, Wacks' study shows that the comparative ethos advocated by Monroe and embodied in his work is essential to understanding not only Andalusī literature and culture, but also its reception and legacy in the medieval Arabic-speaking world.

The final study in this collection, Nabil Matar's "The Expulsion of the Andalusīs in Arab Memory, 1609/1614–2014," carries the exploration of the impact of Andalusī people and culture in the rest of the Arabic-speaking world through the early modern until the present, showing how the fate of the Moriscos who were expelled from the Peninsula between 1609 and 1614 has become a productive and conflictive source of inspiration for a series of contemporary scholars and fiction writers writing in Arabic. According to Matar, while early modern authors such as al-Qafṣī (d. 1622) and al-Maqarrī (d. 1632) frame the expulsion of the Moriscos in religious terms, since 1948 it has been presented within the larger discourses of activist Arab nationalism. Al-Qafsī and al-Maqarrī frame the expulsion and forced relocation of the Moriscos in Quranic terms, as a form of *hijra* or migration and as part of God's plan, while for twentieth-century novelists such as Raḍwā ʿAshūr and Ṣubḥī Mūsa the fate of the Morsicos is a tragedy and historical trauma compared to that of other modern phenomena, such as the dislocation of the Palestinians or the anti-Mubarak revolution of 2011. Matar's study includes the testimony of various early modern writers, particularly diplomats from North Africa who published their first-hand accounts of encounters with Morisco immigrants in North Africa, as well as with descendants of the Moriscos still living in Iberia. In addition, Matar explores how al-Andalus and the fate of the Moriscos figures prominently in twentieth-century historical novels in Arabic, such as those of Jurjī Zaydān, Amin Maalouf, and Raḍwā ʿAshūr, and in those of Ṣubḥī Mūsa from the twenty-first century.

Matar's study, like all in this collection, reflects the ethos Monroe articulated early in his career, namely making texts written in languages other than those of Western Europe available to scholars of literature and history and raising awareness of these texts among scholars in the anglophone academy. In addition, all of the essays that scholars have contributed to this volume show the richness that such an expanded scope holds for the study of literature, whether premodern or modern. These essays display not only the richness, vibrancy, and complexity of Andalusī literature and culture and its legacy among subsequent peoples and cultures, but also the legacy of Monroe's critical insights and literary translations as keys to helping unlock this tradition in ways that allow it to continue to speak to and dialogue with the various traditions of the premodern world. In a time when listening to other voices and other peoples is more important than ever, the windows into how medieval Iberian cultures in contact, as well as those in other parts of the world (Persia, Iraq, Egypt, Tunis, Palestine, etc.) have much to offer those who the study the Middle Ages, the Mediterranean, the East and the West.

Bibliography

Akbari, Suzanne. 2009. *Idols in the East: European Representations of Islam and the Orient, 1100–1450*. Ithaca.

Catlos, Brian. 2015. "Christian-Muslim-Jewish Relations, Medieval 'Spain,' and the Mediterranean: An Historiographical Op-Ed." In *In and of the Mediterranean*, edited by Michelle M. Hamilton and Nuria Silleras-Fernández, 1–16. Nashville.

Castro, Américo. 1948. *España en su historia*. Argentina.

Cohen, Jeffrey Jerome. 1999. *Monster Theory: Reading Culture*. Minneapolis.

——. 2003. *Medieval Identity Machines*. Minneapolis.

Constable, Giles. 2008. *Crusaders and Crusading in the Twelfth Century*. Burlington.

García Sanjuán, Alejandro. 2016. "Rejecting al-Andalus, Exalting the *Reconquista*: Historical Memory in Contemporary Spain." *Journal for Medieval Iberian Studies* 8:1-19. http://dx.doi.org.ezp1.lib.umn.edu/10.1080/17546559.2016.1268263.

González Ferrín, Emilio. 2006. *Historia general de al-Andalus*. Córdoba.

Guo, Li. 2012. *The Performing Arts in Medieval Islam: Shadow Play and Popular Poetry in Ibn Daniyal's Mamluk Cairo*. Leiden.

Hamilton, Michelle M. 2007. *Representing Others in Medieval Iberia*. New York.

Ibn Shuhayd. 1971. *Risālat at-tawābiʿ wa z-zawābiʿ: The Treatise of Familiar Spirits and Demons.* Translated by James T Monroe. Berkeley.

Liu, Benjamin M. and James T. Monroe. 1989. *Ten Hispano-Arabic Strophic Songs in the Oral Tradition. Music and Texts*. Modern Philology 125. Berkeley.

Madden, Thomas F. 1999. *A Concise History of the Crusades. Critical Issues in History*. Lanham, MD.

Menocal, María Rosa. 2002. *The Ornament of the World: How Muslims, Jews, and Christians Created a Culture of Tolerance in Medieval Spain*. Boston.

Monroe, J. T. 1970a. *Islam and the Arabs in Spanish Scholarship (Sixteenth Century to the Present)*. Leiden.

——. ed. and trans. 1970b. *The Shuʿūbiyya in al-Andalus. The Risāla of Ibn García and Five Refutations*. Berkeley.

———. ed. and trans. 1974. *Hispano-Arabic Poetry: A Student Anthology*, Berkeley.

——. 1975. "Formulaic Diction and the Common Origins of Romance Lyric Traditions." *Hispanic Review* 43, no. 4:341–350.

——. 1983. *The Art of Badīʿ az-Zamān al-Hamadhānī as Picaresque Narrative.* Papers of the Center for Arab and Middle East Studies 2. Beirut.

——. 1989. "Which Came First, the *zajal* or the *muwaššaḥa*? Some Evidence for the Oral Origins of Hispano-Arabic Strophic Poetry." *Oral Tradition* 4, nos. 1–2:38–74.

——. 1996. "The Underside of Arabic Panegyric: Ibn Quzman's (unfinished) 'zajal no. 84'." *Al-Qantara: Revista de Estudios Árabes* 17, no. 1:79–116.

——. 2002. Introduction and translation of *Maqāmāt al-Luzūmīyah* by al-Saraqusṭī ibn al-Aštarkūwī, 1-110. Leiden.

——. 2006. "The Mystery of the Missing Mantle: The Poet as Wittol? (Ibn Quzmān's Zajal 20)." *Journal of Arabic Literature* 35, no. 1:1–45.

——. 2007. "Literary Hybridization in the *Zajal*: Ibn Quzmān's *Zajal* 88, the Visit of Sir Gold." *Journal of Arabic literature* 38, no. 3:324–351.

——. 2011a. "Arabic Literary Elements in the Structure of the *Libro de buen amor*." *Al-Qantara: Revista de Estudios Arabes* 32 no. 1:27–70.

——. 2011b. "Its Maṭla' and Ḫarja are Twofold in Function: Form and Content in Ibn Quzmān's 'Zajal 59' and '138'." *Boletín de Literatura Oral* 1:14–39.

——, ed. and trans. 2017. *The Mischievous Muse: Extant Poetry and Prose by Ibn Quzmān of Córdoba (d. AH 555/AD 1160).* 2 vols. Leiden.

Monroe, J. T. and Francisco Márquez Villanueva. 1973. "Nuevos arabismos en un pasaje del *LBA* (941ab)." In *Actas del I Congreso Internacional sobre el Arcipreste de Hita*, edited by M. Criado de Val, 202-207. Barcelona.

Monroe, J. T. and Mark F. Pettigrew. 2003. "The Decline of Courtly Patronage and the Emergence of New Genres in Arabic Literature." *Journal of Arabic Literature* 34, nos. 1–2:138–177.

Monroe, J. T. and David Swiatlo. 1977. "Nintey-Three Ḫarǧas in Hebrew Muwaššaḥs: Their Hispano-Romance Prosody and Thematic Features." *Journal of the American Oriental Society* 97, no. 2:141–63.

Riley-Smith, Jonathan. 2008. *The Crusades, Christianity and Islam*. New York.

Rowson, Everett K. 1997. "Two Homoerotic Narratives from Mamluk Literature: Al-Safadi's *Law'at al-shaki* and Ibn Daniyal's *al-Mutayyam*." In *Homoeroticism in Classical Arabic Literature*, edited by J. W. Wright and Everett K. Rowson, 158–191. New York.

Szpiech, Ryan. 2013. "The Convivencia Wars: Decoding Historiography's Polemic with Philology." In *A Sea of Languages*, edited by Suzanne Akbari and Karla Mallette, 135-161. Toronto.

Tolan, John V. 2002. *Saracens: Islam in the Medieval European Imagination*. New York.

Tyerman, Christopher. 2009. *God's War: A New History of the Crusades*. Cambridge, MA.

Wacks, David. 2007. *Framing Medieval Iberia:* Maqāmāt *and Frametale Narratives in Medieval Spain*. Leiden.
Young, Douglas C. 2004. *Rogues and Genres: Generic Transformation in the Spanish Picaresque and Arabic Maqāma*. Newark, DE.

Revisiting *Islam and the Arabs in Spanish Scholarship*, by James T. Monroe

Manuela Marín
Consejo Superior de Investigaciones Científicas (Madrid)

> Occasionally, and always unsuccessfully, I have suggested that graduate students choose the development of Spanish Arabism, from the Middle Ages to our present times, as a subject for their doctoral dissertation. It would have been, in my opinion, a fruitful exploration into our scientific thought, as well as an exceedingly enertaining history.
>
> -- Emilio García Gómez[1]

This wish of Emilio García Gómez (1905–1995), recorded in 1950, was fulfilled twenty years later, when James T. Monroe published his *Islam and the Arabs in Spanish Scholarship (Sixteenth Century to the Present)*.[2] Nowadays, the book has attained the status of an indispensable and masterful study. It has not been superseded by later contributions on the same subject; in fact, it remains the only work covering such a long historical period and with so ambitious an objective: that of understanding the intellectual milieu in which Spanish Arabists worked and discussing to what extent this milieu could have been influenced by their work.[3]

At the time of its publication, however, the impact of Monroe's book in Spain was limited because, after 1967, no book reviews were published in the journal of the "Spanish school of Arabists," that is, *Al-Andalus*, which was directed by García Gómez. No exception was made for a book which did not really conform to the "canonical" narrative of the history of Spanish Arabism as established by García Gómez – the latter probably being what he had in mind when he suggested it as a topic for a doctoral dissertation. There have been other approaches to the subject, usually limited to a descriptive approach[4] or, in more recent times, to concentrating on specific subjects,

1. García Gómez 1950, 266 ("Algunas veces, y siempre sin éxito, he recomendado a los aspirantes al doctorado que eligiesen como asunto de su tesis la evolución del arabismo español, arrancando de la Edad Media para llegar a nuestros días, pues sería, a mi juicio, una calicata fecunda en nuestro pensamiento científico a la vez que una historia por extremo divertida.").
2. Henceforth referred to as *IASS*.
3. Monroe 1970, x.
4. Cortabarría 1968. For an updated overview, see Penelas 2004.

periods, or distinguished Spanish Arabists.[5] But the characteristics of Monroe's study are such that it is impossible for any scholar interested in this subject to ignore it. It became, and still is, the indispensable point of departure for those interested in the complex history of Arab studies in Spain and its relationship with the construction of national and collective identities.

Two years after the publication of *IASS*, another study on Spanish Arabism appeared, this time published in Spain, by an Arabist who had long been a resident in the USA, Manuela Manzanares de Cierre (she was forced into exile with her husband after the Civil War).[6] Manzanares focused on Arabists living in the nineteenth century, and her work is usually quoted after that of Monroe, as a sequel or complement to it, although they are very different in scope, methodology, and ambition.[7] But an interesting feature of this book was the introduction, written by Pedro Chalmeta, by then a rising star in the universe of Spanish Arabism and a scholar critical of the history of the discipline (and of many other things).

This introduction represents a reevaluation of Arabic studies in Spain, from the Middle Ages to the present. Despite its short length, the text opened new fields of discussion and proposed new interpretations of a century-long history of relationships between Spain and the Islamic world. Chalmeta emphasized the "vital" factor dominating this relationship: contrary to the English or French, Spaniards had "lived" within Islam, thus having an intimate knowledge of this "alien" world and, therefore, being in a better position to understand it.[8] Without acknowledging it explicitly, Chalmeta was following a theoretical path already explored by García Gómez: the study of Islamic Spain was the privileged field of insiders, that is, Spaniards. This is more clearly formulated when Chalmeta discussed *IASS*: Monroe could not understand properly the school founded by Francisco Codera, because he had studied it "from outside." Therefore, his work may "accumulate data, sketch a history, but is not able to analyze evolution" and could not capture the "spirit" of Spanish Arabism.[9] This negative appraisal of Monroe as a scholar lacking the necessary credentials for understanding his chosen

5. As in Rivière Gómez 2000, Viguera 2004, Marín 2009, and López García 2011.

6. Amo 2003.

7. Manzanares 1972; the book was originally a Ph.D. dissertation (University of Michigan, 1958). The publication was not updated.

8. Chalmeta 1972, 14.

9. Chalmeta 1972, 17. In this assessment, Chalmeta is referring both to Monroe and to the Spanish Arabist Ángel Cortabarría, who did not really belong to the "school" founded by Codera. Cortabarría (1919–2008), a Dominican friar who specialized in Islamic philosophy, was a student of Arabic with García Gómez, but spent practically the whole of his career in the Dominican Institute of Oriental Studies in Cairo.

subject of research scarcely deserves to be commented upon, as its logical inference would be that only Russians or Germans, for instance, could write the history of Russian or German oriental/Arabic studies and, more specifically, only those belonging to the "official" tradition of such studies.

A more meaningful objection concerning *IASS* was made by Chalmeta (and followed by others), when he asserted that Monroe exaggerated the role of Krausism in the development of Arabic studies in Spain.[10] In doing so – and his arguments are quite relevant, if not totally convincing – Chalmeta was also reducing the impact of liberal thinking in the shaping of Spanish Arabism, something that he, however, suggests tentatively in another part of his text. The question, then, remained open, and it will surface in other comments and reflections on *IASS*.[11]

At the time of their publication, Chalmeta's remarks were unique as the only reaction by a Spanish Arabist to *IASS*. Hidden in the preface to another author's work, they were nevertheless significant, because their author was a prominent member of the new generation of Spanish Arabists. The 1970s were a crucial period in the history of Spain, and fundamental changes were brewing under the surface during the last years of Francoism, but Chalmeta's opinions betray the difficulties implied in assuming that there could have been an intimate link between liberal political trends and the rise of Arabic studies in Spain.

A proper review of *IASS* was also published in 1972 by Francisco Marcos Marín, then a promising young scholar trained as a Hispanist and with an interest in Arabic.[12] The review appeared in the *Revista de Occidente*, addressed, as is well known, to a cultivated general audience. For Marcos Marín, the book is "excellent" and indispensable for those interested not only in the history of Arabic studies, but also in the history of Spanish culture. In contrast with Chalmeta, Marcos Marín agrees with Monroe on the connection of Spanish Arabism with liberal thought and Krausism, and emphasizes the intellectual links of the author of *IASS* with Américo Castro. The only criticism in this review is Marcos Marín's disagreement with Monroe's appraisal of Asín Palacios: "the work and the example of Asín are more positive than what Monroe says," concludes Marcos Marín.[13]

10. Chalmeta 1972, 15. Krausism was an important intellectual trend in nineteenth-century Spain, inspired by the ideas of the German philosopher Karl Krause; see the classic study by J. López Morillas (1980).

11. Goytisolo 1982, 186.

12. His Ph.D. dissertation was published under the title *Poesía narrativa árabe y épica hispánica* (Madrid, 1971).

13. Marcos Marín 1972, 93.

Due to his research on contacts between Islamic and Christian cultures in medieval Iberia, it is not surprising to observe how enthusiastically Marcos Marín writes about the "brilliant intuitions" of Américo Castro, which were sustained by the well-documented work of his disciples, such as Monroe.[14] Spanish Arabists, for their part, had a long history of research in cross-cultural areas – as Marcos Marín observes in his review – but as a whole, they remained impervious to Castro's theories, and only very occasionally did they aknowledge their existence.[15]

In an article published in Spain about the same time as *IASS*, Monroe remarked that, while Castro's views had been well received in the United States and Europe by competent specialists, Spanish scholars reacted with an almost complete indifference to his insights. Monroe alludes in a veiled form to the conservative political position adopted by Arabists after the Civil War as an explanation for their silence on a subject that was so intimately linked to their professional pursuits, and expresses his hope of a better understanding of Castro by a future generation of Arabists, after "Spanish life will attain a more normal condition" – that is, when freedom of expression would be restored.[16]

Political positions were undoubtedly important, and Monroe was right when he pointed them out as a cause for the silence surrounding Castro's interpretation of Spanish history in the academic milieu of Francoist Spain. But there were other elements, more personal and related to the inner history of Spanish Arabism, that might explain the refusal of allowing "strangers" to intervene into the secluded field of interpreting al-Andalus. No review of the works by Claudio Sánchez Albornoz, the most critical opponent of Américo Castro, was ever published in *Al-Andalus*, although the Spanish historian made a point of sending copies of his books to the journal.[17] The Arabists, that is, the self-appointed representative body of Arab studies in Spain, headed by Emilio García Gómez in postwar times, chose to remain in their ivory towers and establish clear boundaries to preserve their field of research from any outsider's intrusion.[18] Moreover, they maintained a safe distance from theoretical discussions, historical interpretations, and works of synthesis; in fact, they could have recognized themselves in the portrait of British orientalists drawn by Roger Owen in 1973:

14. Marcos Marín 1972, 91.

15. In a few instances, they mention Castro's theories, such as in García Gómez 1957, xxvi; see Monroe 1970, 212.

16. Monroe 1971, 351, 363.

17. Marín 2009, 291. The polemic between Castro and Sánchez Albornoz has generated an enormous bibliography; see, for instance, Glick 1979, 6–13, 314–316; Álvarez Junco and de la Fuente Monge 2013, 385–396; Hertel 2015, 17, 30–31.

18. García Gómez 1983.

> Based on the knowledge of a number of difficult languages, and focused on the examination of the historical development of a complex religion, they have assumed the character of an esoteric rite in which only a few are skilled enough to take part. They proceed according to their own, often hidden, rules; each new publication is a tactful reminder to the uninitiated that his role is to listen, to wonder, but never to ask questions or to suggest that there might be an alternative way of doing things.[19]

Although *IASS* was publicly received in Spain in this more than subdued way – two paragraphs in the introduction to another book on a similar subject, and a review by a Hispanist in a cultural journal – the work was circulating and comments by Arabists on its contents and orientation reached Américo Castro (who by then was living in Spain). In a letter to writer Juan Goytisolo, Castro explained that "here, among the *harcas*, it [the book] went down badly."[20] According to Castro, while Spanish Arabists' criticisms centered on trifles ("menudencias"), they had never seriously considered the larger problem dealt with by Monroe for the first time in his book.[21]

Other important works on Arab studies published in the '70s were similarly ignored by García Gómez's disciples, and for similar reasons. This was the case of Pierre Guichard and his fundamental study on the social structures of al-Andalus, published in Spanish in 1976, or the groundbreaking *Orientalism* by Edward Said (1978).[22] It was also during this period that the bitter controversy over the *kharjas* exploded, creating a yawning abyss between García Gómez and anglophone scholarship. Philology in its more

19. Quoted in Lockman 2004, 163.

20. Escudero 1997, 121–122. The letter is dated June 26, 1971. The word "harcas" is a transliteration of an Arabic term, used in Morocco for armed irregular forces and popular in Spain during the colonial period. Spanish Arabists used it in the first decades of the twentieth century to refer to their own group (Marín 2009, 159); it is probable that Castro was familiar with it from the time he and the Arabists Ribera and Asín were members of the Centro de Estudios Históricos. The whole paragraph is quoted in Martínez Montávez 2010.

21. In a previous letter to Goytisolo (Escudero 1997, 94), dated December 2, 1969, Castro rebukes García Gómez's opinions on the Arabs ("Moors") as predatory invaders of Spain, as published in 1966. Castro's letter on the reception of IASS by Arabists alludes to this "unbearable" ("intolerable") assessment.

22. See Guichard 2002, 202. The early translation of Guichard's work was due to medievalist Miquel Barceló (1939–2013), author of many controversial and provocative analyses of the history of al-Andalus. The "silence" over Guichard's work was interrupted by Joaquín Vallvé (1978), opening a controversy over Berbers in the early history of al-Andalus that ended years later when new documents were published supporting Guichard's interpretation (Marín 1999, 548). Subsequently, Víctor Morales Lezcano, a historian working on Spanish-Moroccan relations in the nineteenth-twentieth centuries, drew attention to the impact of Edward Said's work (Morales Lezcano 1984). See also González Alcantud 2006 and 2011.

narrow definition restricted the exchange of scientific opinions to an "undignified dispute,"[23] which represented one of the worst known examples of scholarly debates. In this rarefied space, the old school of Arab studies in Spain was reduced to defensive moves and a gradual loss of public presence (the last issue of *Al-Andalus* appeared in 1978). Meanwhile, the emergence of new academic generations and the social changes associated with the establishment of the democratic state in 1978 brought the necessary conditions for a renovation of Arab studies for which the opening to other disciplines was as essential as it was to think about the past and the future of the field from a totally new perspective.

In this respect, the doctoral dissertation by Bernabé López García (University of Granada, 1973) was a pioneering work. Only recently published (2011), its author has contributed to the history of Spanish Arab studies with a long series of monographs, and his views and perspectives have been influential for anyone working in this field. In the preface of his dissertation, López García agrees with Monroe on the significance of Krausism in the development of Spanish Arabism, although he also points out to what he thinks are the limitations of *IASS*, a work, nonetheless, that he qualifies as "masterful."[24] It has to be noted that the very fact that a doctoral dissertation on this subject was accepted by a Spanish University was a sign of how things were changing: for, despite García Gómez's wish that such a study be written (as mentioned above), any student of Arabic at this time knew that his/her doctoral dissertation should prove his/her deep knowledge of Arabic and, preferably, deal with the edition and translation of an Arabic manuscript. In breaking with this unwritten but well-established norm, López García was making a major contribution to the necessary changes in the field of Arabism. In this way, he was also recognizing his debt to *IASS* – and underscoring his own contribution to the field.[25]

In 1976, Pedro Martínez Montávez, a specialist in contemporary Arabic literature, gave a lecture at the Instituto Hispano-Árabe de Cultura, Madrid – an institution pertaining to the Spanish Ministry of Foreign Affairs – on Arab studies in Spain in the nineteenth century.[26] The subject of the lecture gave Martínez Montávez the occasion of discussing parts of *IASS*, especially

23. Monroe 1981–82, 122.

24. The 2011 edition of López García's dissertation includes footnotes updating the forty year-old text. Two of these footnotes (López García 2011, 24–25) explain the changes in the author's appreciation of *IASS* ("masterful" being one of the innovations in the published text).

25. For instance, he used documentary materials not used by Monroe, like the articles published by Spanish Arabists in cultural journals and newspapers, which allowed a more nuanced understanding of the evolution of their thought. López García 2011, 26.

26. The lecture was later published in Martínez Montávez 1977.

the controversial question of the influence of Krausism in the development of Arab studies. Following Chalmeta's opinion on this issue, Martínez Montávez concludes that one of the problems of Monroe's interpretation was precisely the reduction of his analysis to a narrow intellectual framework – Krausism – thus missing the potential of a wider scope. Martínez Montávez denies that Krausism played a significant role in nineteenth-century Arabism, giving as a proof the scarcity of references to Arab studies in the more notable and recent studies on Krausism.[27]

This last statement is as faulty as Chalmeta's on the same matter: Krausist thinkers were mainly interested in institutions while nineteenth-century Spanish Arabists were not.[28] Both Martínez Montávez and Chalmeta shared a very positivist approach to a question demanding perhaps a broader perspective. The specific cases of Arabists influenced by Krausism are well documented in *IASS*, but it is also evident that, from the time of Codera on, no direct link between Krausists and Arabists exists. This said, Krausism and its liberal attitudes and new scientific interests opened the way for Arab studies to acquire a more relevant place in the academic milieu. The most significant expression of this trend happened in 1907, when the Junta para Ampliación de Estudios (JAE) was created. It was inspired by the Krausist Institución Libre de Enseñanza. Julián Ribera, then the leading Arabist of the "school," was asked to be a member of the Board of Directors of the JAE, and in 1910, when the Centro de Estudios Históricos, a body depending on the JAE, began its activities, Miguel Asín Palacios and Julián Ribera headed two different sections of research on Arab studies.[29] The conservative positions of Ribera and Asín did not prevent their joining the new institution, which had attracted the foremost scientists of the time and contributed crucially to the renovation of the academic field in Spain. These same positions, however, played a significant role in 1916, when the Arabists left the JAE, after a conflict between them and the secretary of the institution.[30]

To sum up, the role of Krausism in the development of Arab studies in Spain was indeed emphasized by Monroe, who throughout *IASS* tries to identify a continuous line of liberal thought in the Arabists' school. The link between Arab studies and Krausism is best exemplified by the figure of Fran-

27. Martínez Montávez 1977, 3–4. Other and shorter references to IASS in Martínez Montávez 1983–84; see also Martínez Montávez 2010, on this author's other works on Américo Castro.

28. Chalmeta 1972, 15.

29. Marín 2009, 107–119.

30. There were other reasons, as explained in Marín 2009, 125–137 and Peiró Martín 2010, 150–152. Curiously, Monroe does not explore this point.

cisco Fernández y González (1833–1917).[31] But the Arabists of Codera's school never acknowledged him as one of their "ancestors," and some of them even denied to the liberal-minded Pascual de Gayangos (1809–1897), Codera's own teacher, the qualities of professionalism and scientificism that defined the "true" Arabist.[32] The liberal/Krausist trend was abandoned by Codera and his disciples, who belonged to the conservative and Catholic political right. They never advocated ultra-right political positions, with the exception of Francisco J. Simonet (1829–1897), but it would be an exaggeration to consider them as members of a "progressive" trend of thought in Spain.

In the 80's, it was the medievalist Miquel Barceló who drew new attention to *IASS* in a short but substantial article on Arabism in Spain. Barceló applied the model established by Edward Said to define Spanish Arabism as an Orientalism tinged by the peculiarity of Spanish history: the object of Spanish Orientalism/Arabism was located in the same territorial space that was occupied by the Spanish state in modern times. Annihilation of al-Andalus was thus necessary for the very existence of this state, and this was achieved during the "Reconquista."[33] For Barceló, Monroe's study of Spanish Arabism was "a fundamental book" in which the author identifies two constrasting trends, the traditionalist and the liberal. Both trends, asserts Barceló, reduced al-Andalus to an accidental and Islamized part of Spain; traditionalists saw it as an "oriental" interference that should be, and ultimately was, surgically removed from the Spanish political body, while for liberals, al-Andalus was recovered because, in fact, its inhabitants were basically Spaniards. In both cases, the historical reality of al-Andalus was wiped out, and this, says Barceló, was something that Monroe did not properly understand. The idea of the annihilation of al-Andalus as a necessary condition for the existence of Spain was subsequently used by Barceló and, in fact, it became the foundation of much of his research, to such an extent that he styled himself as an "historian of exterminations."[34] Although not devoid of historical meaning, this was a highly personal choice, and it seems unfair to blame others for not sharing it, or even being suspicious about its existence.

Reading *IASS* from the vantage point of the present, more than forty years after its publication, one is surprised at how kind Monroe is toward his subject of study. His characterization of the two trends in Arab studies

31. Monroe 1970, 112–118; Viñes Millet 1995, 81; López García 2011, 59–61, 88–100, 108–110, 118–124.

32. García Gómez 1950, 266. On Gayangos, see Álvarez Millán and Heide 2008.

33. Barceló 1980, 28.

34. Manresa 2013.

– traditionalist and liberal – is inclined to privilege the latter over the former, and even when he analyzes the figure of Simonet, admittedly a fervent far-rightist, he took care to rescue his more important contributions and to highlight some of his more valuable insights.[35] But it is probably at the end of *IASS* where Monroe, drawing his findings to a conclusion, displays his deep conviction that Spanish Arabism is defined by a progressive character:

> [it is] largely a product of the victims of Golden Age intolerance, of the reforming ideals of the Spanish Enlightenment, of nineteenth-century Spanish liberalism. The lesson it had to offer is one of international understanding. One of the main contributions made by Spain to the scholarly world during the past five hundred years has thus been humane and tolerant. It has taught Europe to broaden its cultural perspectives and has therefore contributed to the decline of nationalism and the birth of the multinational world of the twentieth century. In this sense, Spanish Arabism, an outgrowth of progressive forces, has had a generous contribution to offer the world of scholarship.[36]

Any Spanish Arabist reading this last paragraph of *IASS* would be grateful to its author for the very favorable view he presents of his/her scholarly tradition. Well inscribed in Américo Castro's understanding of the Spanish Islamic past, Monroe broadens Spanish Arabism to include its contemporary interpreters, Arabists, and predicts it will result in a future multiculturalism and decline of nationalisms. History has not been kind to this prognosis, especially in present times. But it contributed to the understanding of the history of al-Andalus as a weapon in the struggle for a more open-minded and inclusive world – a Western world, indeed, that in the '70s needed to be reminded that other worlds existed.

To what extent the use of al-Andalus as a metaphor for this better world corresponds to a historical reality is another and very debatable question. As to the role of Spanish Arabists in the "outgrowth of progressive forces," it requires a lot of good will to accept it without a more nuanced assessment. The first criticisms by Arabists to *IASS* and its political stance in favor of Krausism have been replaced more recently by other opinions that challenge Monroe's characterization of Arabists as liberal and progressive.[37] Monroe asserts that the Civil War and its consequences provoked a change in orientation among Arabists, who felt obliged to take a more conservative political

35. Monroe 1970, 85–100.
36. Monroe 1970, 270.
37. Rivière 2000, 54–56; Manzano Moreno 2000, 27–28, and Manzano Moreno 2009, 214.

position to preserve their place in the academic world under Francoism. Advances in the history of Spanish historiography – a nearly unknown discipline in Monroe's times – and the unearthing of new documentary evidence, such as the collected letters of Julián Ribera and Miguel Asín Palacios, have made it possible to reach other conclusions, namely, that the core of the "school" – Codera, Ribera, Asín – belonged to the political right well before the Civil War.[38] Obviously, this position did not prevent them from rescuing the Islamic past of the Iberian Peninsula and giving it a new meaning inside the academic milieu of their time, challenging the traditional position, which was very reluctant to accept anything related to Arabs and Islam as a part of the Hispanic past.

These efforts on the part of Arabists are well documented and analyzed in *IASS*, and are among the many parts of the book that remain valid. One is somewhat surprised, nevertheless, when the quality of the analysis, of great refinement and accuracy for the period concerning the nineteenth century, undergoes a change in the chapters of *IASS* describing the Arabists' school in the twentieth and, especially, after the Spanish Civil War (1936–1939). In contrast with the previous advocacy for a prevailing "liberal" trend and the influence of Krausism among Arabists, a much more neutral tone – from an ideological point of view – characterizes the picture of later Arabists. The lack of commentary on the cataclysmic break of Arabists (Ribera and Asín) with the JAE, mentioned above, is noticeable, as this was probably the event that most affected the development of Arab studies in Spain in the first third of the twentieth century, with consequences that are still felt today: in leaving the JAE, the Arabists abandoned the most serious attempt to renovate the humanities in Spain, a collective endeavour that transformed the field up to the moment when the Civil War interrupted it – as it did so many other things.

Also striking is the silence of *IASS* on the changes brought about by the war. The JAE was inmediately suppressed after the end of the war and was replaced by the still extant Consejo Superior de Investigaciones Científicas, of which Asín Palacios was appointed vice-president. By this time, the "presumed" heir to Asín Palacios as head of the Arabists' school was Ángel González Palencia (1889–1949);[39] after his untimely death in a car accident, it was Emilio García Gómez who took over the task of steering Arabists through the murky waters of Francoist times.

Monroe highlights the contributions of González Palencia "in favour of accepting the impact of Arabic culture on Spain,"[40] linking his proposals in

38. Marín 2009, 259.
39. Monroe 1970, 196–202.
40. Monroe 1970, 198, 201.

this respect to Simonet's legacy and the search for the essence of an eternal Spain, a subject that had been central to the discussions on Spanish history during the nineteenth and the first part of the twentieth century. While this interpretation of González Palencia's work is adequate, the fact is that, on an other level, his political role during the war and in the post-war period is completely omitted in *IASS*. As is now well documented, not only was González Palencia a prominent member of the "Comisión de depuración," which forced university lecturers and professors to submit to a process of purging to remain in their jobs (or be expelled from them), but he also participated in publications in which the JAE was accused of the worst sins against the "new order" of the victorious fascist Spain.[41]

It would be unfair, however, to assume that Monroe chose to ignore the role of González Palencia in the repression of his university colleagues who had not adhered to Franco's regime or who had a liberal or left-wing past. By the time he did his research for *IASS*, any reference to González Palencia's political stance and his activities during the war and in post-war times had been expurgated from all the available evidence – biographies, obituaries, homages, etc. – for his biography. The silence over this subject and over the political position of Arabists reflects the silence that prevailed throughout Spain for decades, and that is mirrored in *IASS*, whose author was not provided such information and could not find it in the publications available to him.[42]

A field of research was opened in *IASS* that had not been cultivated before. As stated in a recent publication, Monroe was "one of the few historians of Spanish Arabism who had shown the intimate relationship between political ideologies and Arabist production;"[43] and it should be added that he was the first to take this step. Moreover, despite the date of its publication, *IASS* still provides the reader with a comprehensive overview that cannot be discarded – although it should obviously be updated on several points, as many studies have been added to this pioneering work since 1971. But *IASS* is valuable not only as a document of what could be written on Spanish Arabism in the '70s and of the difficulties that had to be dealt with, but also of the evolution of the idea of al-Andalus as a part of the history of Spain. As Monroe follows the life and works of Spanish Arabists, this becomes the leitmotiv that gives substance to the whole structure of the book.

As a disciple of Américo Castro, Monroe's interpretation of this vexed

41. Marín 2009, 268–293; Peiró 2010, 161–162; Gil Cremades, 2010. On the "depuration" processes and how they affected the Spanish university, see Claret Miranda 2006.

42. It is more surprising to find that no mention is made to this question in a doctoral dissertation dedicated to the study of the personality and works of González Palencia, dated as late as 1991. Ágreda 1991 and 1998.

43. Molina López 2007, xv.

question is subtly situated in the context of the search for individual and national identities in contemporary Spain, and the shared cultures of medieval Iberia.[44] He cannot but sympathize with the efforts of Arabists for including their subject of study within the canonical narrative of Spanish history, and rightly points out that, unlike other Arabists in Europe, Spaniards were "caught up in a struggle with [their] own feelings, ideals and national pride which directly coloured [their] thought and [their] scholarship."[45] Not only that: "By the very nature of his subject, the Spanish Arabist has tended to focus his attention on problems of cultural contacts between East and West perhaps more than his colleagues in the rest of Europe. Spain is a rich laboratory for the scholar interested in this peculiar historical phenomenon."[46] But the record of Spanish Arabists on this matter – as in others – was open to criticism, and Monroe did not hesitate to express his difference of opinion with some of them. Perhaps the most significant case is that of Miguel Asín Palacios. In contrast to the nearly hagiographic reverence with which he was treated by the Arabists' school, Monroe manifested in *IASS* his disagreement with Asín's methodological approach, which he qualified as "ahistorical."[47] Monroe recognized Asín's great intellectual stature, yet nevertheless found that Asín placed religion and spirituality in empty spaces devoid of social, political and economic contexts, thus denying the possibility of a Muslim mystical tradition independent of other religions. That Asín's very valuable studies on Muslim spirituality were lacking in historical meaning is now accepted, and it is one of the many insights in *IASS* that make the book such a rewarding read.[48]

As indicated above, Castro's theories on the Semitic substratum of Spanish history and the crucial role played by Muslims and Jews in the construction of Spanish national identity were not taken into account by contemporary Arabists. Several reasons for this intellectual chasm have already been given, but to them it should be added the fact that, while Castro shared with Arabists a common interest in cultural contacts and mutual influences between Semitic and Christian societies, their objectives differed radically. While Castro emphasized Arab culture as the building block of al-Andalus, and its unavoidable weight in the subsequent history of Spain, for Arabists the inhabitants of al-Andalus were really Spaniards *avant la lettre*, and the best features of Andalusi culture, the result of a unique hybridation

44. Monroe 1970, 258–263 and Monroe 2013.
45. Monroe 1970, 3.
46. Monroe 1970, 69.
47. Monroe 1970, chapter 7.
48. Manzano 2000, 36. See also Rodríguez Mediano 2002. A harsh criticism of Asín's competence in Arabic linguistics is in Corriente 1999, 69–74.

that infused this culture with the essential characteristics of Spanishness. The breach between Arabists and other disciplines, especially medieval studies, pushed the interpretation of al-Andalus by Arabists, with few exceptions, out of the historical framework of analysis prevalent in Spain until the last decades of the twentieth century.[49]

In the wake of Castro's theories, cultural contacts beyond the religious and political frontiers of medieval Iberia has become a favorite subject of research in North American universities. The reasons for this popularity are varied, and have been related to the history of American society, the development of area studies and the various associated disciplines, the evolution of philological traditions, or even the personal trajectory of individual scholars.[50] In any case, the dissemination of Castro's theories and the academic prestige attained by many of his students were not comparable to what happened in Spain, where changes in the academic milieu after the '70s did not contribute to a better appraisal of Castro's thought. By then, new historiographical trends, in medieval studies as in Arab studies, were dominating a panorama in which the search for the historical essence of Spain or of al-Andalus was considered obsolete. In North America, by contrast, cultural and literary studies, with their growing interest for the study of frontier and multicultural societies, continued and enlarged the tradition initiated by Américo Castro.[51]

In the conclusions to *IASS*, Monroe expresses the hope that in the future, Romance language departments will produce Romanists "who are at the same time competent Orientalists," in order to produce a new "Hispanism" that will provide an integrated picture of the three religions – Christianity, Judaism, and Islam – and of the medieval history of Spain and Europe. This renovated vision would also contribute "to a better understanding of our own age."[52] Historical changes since the publication of *IASS* have been dramatic and no one in the '70s could have foreseen them. But the implications of Monroe's words are still valid, insofar as they argue in favor of overcoming existing boundaries in scientific disciplines and intellectual approaches, and propose an "integrated picture" of the three Abrahamic religions as a tool for understanding past and present.

The school of Arab studies headed by Emilio García Gómez was not receptive to this program. The bitter polemic on the *kharjas*, in which García

49. Manzano 2009.

50. Surtz, Ferrón, and Testa 1988; Doubleday 2011; Szpiech 2013; Manzano Moreno 2013; Wacks 2014.

51. A critical assessment of this trend of research can be found in Soravia 2009.

52. Monroe 1970, 269–270.

Gómez played so prominent a role, "abandoning the usual norms of professional decorum and scholarly restraint,"[53] deepened the chasm between Spanish and anglophone Arabists.[54] It was a lost battle, and the inheritors of García Gómez, although preserving their institutional and academic power in late Francoist Spain, would never recover the international prestige of their predecessors. It is interesting to note, in this respect, how the work of Miguel Asín was recovered and reappraised by scholars such as Maria Rosa Menocal and Luce López-Baralt, themselves inheritors of Castro's tradition, who have seen in Asín a pioneer of the studies on medieval cultural hybridity.[55]

Today, the history of al-Andalus is still a controversial matter in Spain, where the more traditional historians see it as a period unrelated to the "true" essence of "Spanish" national identity.[56] The debate is contaminated with current and very polemical issues, such as immigration, jihadism, terrorism, etc., and the wish expressed by Monroe forty years ago, pleading for a comprehensive understanding of medieval Iberian societies and religions, still waits to be fulfilled. His work, however, opened a path that many scholars, Spaniards among them, have fruitfully followed to this day. The history of Arab studies in Spain owes to James T. Monroe its first and most important step, and all those who belong to this scholarly tradition should be grateful to him.

53. Monroe 1981–1982, 122. García Gómez alluded malevolently to Monroe, without naming him, in an article published in the conservative newspaper *ABC*. García Gómez 1984; see also Menocal 2003, 275.

54. See Mallette 2010, 173, on García Gómez's belief that *kharja* studies should be the exclusive field of Spanish scholars.

55. See especially Menocal 1996.

56. Fierro 2004; Marín 2013–2014; Wacks 2014. A recent addition to this clearly Islamophobic stance is that of Dario Fernandez Morera, 2016, who is the author of a previous book denouncing the survival of Marxism in the American academy.

Bibliography

Ágreda Burillo, F. de. 1991. *La personalidad y la obra de don Ángel González Palencia*. PhD diss, Universidad Autónoma, Madrid.

——. 1998. "Don Ángel González Palencia:1889–1949. Apuntes biográficos." *Anaquel de Estudios Árabes* 9:215–238.

Álvarez Junco, J. and G. de la Fuente Monge. 2013. "La evolución del relato histórico." In *Las historias de España. Visiones del pasado y construcción de identidad. Historia de España*, vol. 12, edited by J. Álvarez Junco, J. Fontana, and R. Villares, 1–437. Barcelona.

Álvarez Millán, C. and C. Heide, eds. 2008. *Pascual de Gayangos. A Nineteenth-Century Spanish Arabist*. Edinburgh.

Amo, M. del. 2003. "Una mañana con la arabista Manuela Manzanares de Cirre." *Aljamía. Revista de la Consejería de Educación de la Embajada de España en Rabat* 15:11–16.

Barceló, M. 1980. "L'orientalisme i la pecularietat de l'arabisme espanyol." *L'Avenç* June, 405–408.

Chalmeta, P. 1972. "A guisa de prólogo." In *Arabistas españoles del siglo XIX*, edited by M. Manzanares de Cirre, 7–17. Madrid.

Claret Miranda, J. 2006. *El atroz desmoche. La destrucción de la Universidad española por el franquismo (1936–1945)*. Barcelona.

Corriente, F. 1999. "Las etimologías árabes en la obra de Joan Coromines." In *L'obra de Joan Coromines: cicle d'estudi i homenatge*, edited by J. Solà, 67–87. Sabadell.

Cortabarría, Á. 1968. "El arabismo en la España contemporánea." *Estudios Filosóficos* 17:5–56, 207–248.

Doubleday, S. R. 2011. "Hacia la descolonización del concepto de *convivencia*: algunos apuntes sobre el contexto norteamericano." In *La influencia de la historiografía española en la producción histórica americana*, edited by A. Guiance, 59–75. Valladolid.

Escudero, J., ed. and intr. 1997. *El epistolario (1968–1972). Cartas de Américo Castro a Juan Goytisolo*. Valencia.

Fernández Morera, D. 2016. *The Myth of the Andalusian Paradise. Muslims, Christians, and Jews under Islamic Rule in Medieval Spain*. Wilmington, DE.

Fierro, M. 2004. "Idealización de al-Andalus." *Revista de Libros* 94:4.

García Gómez, E. 1950. "Homenaje a don Francisco Codera (1836–1917)." *Al-Andalus* 15:263-274.

——. 1957. "Introducción." In *España musulmana hasta la caída del califato de Córdoba, Historia de España dirigida por Ramón Menéndez Pidal*, vol. 4, edited by E. Lévi-Provençal, ix–xxxvi. Madrid.

——. 1983. "En el cincuentenario de la Escuela de Estudios Árabes de Madrid." *Al-Qantara* 3: v–xii.
——. 1984. "Arabistas, romanistas y anfibios." *ABC*, August 8.
Gil Cremades, J. J. 2010. "Los detractores aragoneses del institucionismo: el libro *Una poderosa fuerza secreta: la Institución Libre de Enseñanza* (1940)." In *El Centro de Estudios Históricos (1910) y sus vinculaciones aragonesas, Con un homenaje a Rafael Lapesa*, edited by J. C. Mainer, 115–130. Zaragoza.
Glick, Thomas F. 1979. *Islamic and Christian Spain in the Early Middle Ages*. Princeton.
González Alcantud, J. A. 2006. "El orientalismo: génesis topográfica y discurso crítico." In *El orientalismo desde el sur*, edited by J. A. González Alcantud, 7–34. Barcelona.
——. 2011. "*Orientalismo* de Edward W. Said 32 años después. Entre el dédalo teórico, el compromiso político-moral y la proyección poscolonial." *Awraq* 4:128–145.
Goytisolo, J. 1982. *Crónicas sarracinas*. Barcelona.
Guichard, P. 2002. "De l'Espagne musulmane à al-Andalus." In *La historiografía francesa del siglo XX y su acogida en España*, edited by B. Pellistrandi, 191–215. Madrid.
Hertel, P. 2015. *The Crescent Remembered. Islam and Nationalism on the Iberian Peninsula*. Sussex.
Lockman, Z. 2004. *Contending Visions of the Middle East: the History and Politics of Orientalism*. Cambridge.
López García, B. 2011. *Orientalismo e ideología colonial en el arabismo español (1840-1917)*. Granada.
López Morillas, J. 1980. *El krausismo español. Perfil de una aventura intelectual*. México.
Mallette, K. 2010. *European Modernity and the Arab Mediterranean. Toward a New Philology and a Counter-Orientalism*. Philadelphia.
Manresa, A. 2013. "Miquel Barceló Perelló, cronista de la destrucción de la España islámica." *El País*, November 24.
Manzanares de Cirre, M. 1972. *Arabistas españoles del siglo XIX*. Madrid.
Manzano Moreno, E. 2000. "La creación de un esencialismo: la historia de al-Andalus en la visión del arabismo español." In *Orientalismo, exotismo y traducción*, edited by G. Fernández Parrilla and M. C. Feria García, 23–37. Cuenca.
——. 2009. "«Desde el Sinaí de su arábiga erudición». Una reflexión sobre el medievalismo y el arabismo recientes." In *Al-Andalus/España. Historiografías en contraste. Siglos XVII-XXI*, edited by M. Marín, 213–230. Madrid.

——. 2013. "Qurtuba: algunas reflexiones críticas sobre el califato de Córdoba y el mito de la convivencia." *Awraq* 7:225–246. http://www.awraq.es/blob.aspx?idx=5&nId=96&hash=ac20943d589408c5a0a3cd2c1e0908a4.

Marcos Marín, F. 1971. "Elementos árabes en los orígenes de la épica hispánica." PhD diss., Universidad Complutense de Madrid.

——. 1972. "James T. Monroe. Islam and the Arabs in Spanish Scholarship." *Revista de Occidente* 112:91–94.

Marín, M. 1999. "El "halcón maltés" del arabismo español: el volumen II/1 de *al-Muqtabis* de Ibn Hayyan." *Al-Qantara* 20:543–549.

——. 2009. "Arabismo e historia de España (1886–1944). Introducción a los epistolarios de Julián Ribera Tarragó y Miguel Asín Palacios." In *Los epistolarios de Julián Ribera Tarragó y Miguel Asín Palacios. Introducción, catálogo e índices*, edited by M. Marín, C. de la Puente, F. Rodríguez Mediano, J. I. Pérez Alcalde, 11–434. Madrid.

——. 2013–2014. "Reflexiones sobre el arabismo español: tradiciones, renovaciones y secuestros," *Hamsa. Journal of Judaic and Islamic Studies* 1:1–17.

Martínez Montávez, P. 1977. "Sobre el aún "desconocido" arabismo español del siglo XIX." *Ensayos marginales de arabismo*, 3–22. Madrid.

——. 1983–84. "Lectura de Américo Castro por un arabista: apuntes e impresiones." *Revista del Instituto Egipcio de Estudios Islámicos* 22:21–42.

——. 2010. "Américo Castro y los moriscos." Biblioteca Virtual. Miguel de Cervantes. Alicante. http://www.cervantesvirtual.com/obra-visor/el-pensamiento-de-americo-castro-la-tradicion-corregida-por-la-razon--0/html/59a331f7-5fa5-495f-a76b-5faaf159cfbf_70.html.

Menocal, M. R. 1996. "An Andalusianist's Last Sigh." *La Corónica* 24:3–12.

——. 2003. "The Myth of Westernness in Medieval Literary Historiography." In *The New Crusades. Constructing the Muslim Enemy*, edited by E. Qureshi and M. A. Sells, 249–287. New York.

Molina López, E. 2007. "Estudio preliminar." In *Juan de Segovia y el problema islámico*, edited by D. Cabanelas, xiii–cxlv. Granada.

Monroe, James T. 1970. *Islam and the Arabs in Spanish Scholarship (Sixteenth Century to the Present)*. Leiden.

——. 1971. "Américo Castro y los estudios arabistas." In *Estudios sobre la obra de Américo Castro*, 349–364. Madrid.

——. 1981–1982. "¿Pedir peras al olmo? On Medieval Arabs and Modern Arabists." *La Corónica* 10:121–147.

——. 2013. "Remembering Francisco Márquez Villanueva." *eHumanista Journal of Iberian Studies*. http://www.ehumanista.ucsb.edu/sites/secure.lsit.ucsb.edu.span.d7_eh/files/sitefiles/cervantes/HOMENAJE_F.%20M.V.2.pdf.

Morales Lezcano, V. 1984. "El islam en la palestra occidental." *Revista de Occidente* 35:78–86.

Peiró Martín, I. 2010. "Los aragoneses en el Centro de Estudios Históricos: historia de una amistad, historia de una "escuela," historia de una profesión." In *El Centro de Estudios Históricos (1910) y sus vinculaciones aragonesas, Con un homenaje a Rafael Lapesa,* edited by J. C. Mainer, 131–168. Zaragoza.

Penelas, M. 2004. "Hispano-Arabic Studies in the New Millenium: Spain." *Al-Masaq* 16:227–239.

Rivière Gómez, A. 2000. *Orientalismo y nacionalismo español. Estudios árabes y hebreos en la Universidad de Madrid (1843–1868).* Madrid.

Rodrígez Mediano, F. 2002. *Pidal, Gómez-Moreno, Asín. Humanismo y progreso. Romances, monumentos y arabismo.* Madrid.

Szpiech, R. 2013. "The Convivencia Wars: Decoding Historiography's Polemic with Philology." In *A Sea of Languages. Rethinking the Arabic Role in Medieval Literary History*, edited by S. C. Akbari and K. Mallette, 135–161. Toronto.

Soravia, B. 2009. "Al-Andalus au miroir du multiculturalisme. Le mythe de la *convivencia* dans quelques essais nord-américains récents." In *Al-Andalus/España. Historiografías en contraste. Siglos XVII-XXI*, edited by M. Marín, 351–365. Madrid.

Surtz, R. E., J. Ferrón, and D. P. Testa, eds. 1988. *Américo Castro: The Impact of His Thought.* Madison.

Vallvé, J. 1978. "España en el siglo VIII: ejército y sociedad." *Al-Andalus* 43:1–112.

Viguera, M. J. 2004. "Al-Andalus prioritario. El positivismo de Francisco Codera." In *Decadencia y desaparición de los almorávides en España,* edited by F. Codera y Zadín, ix–cxxxvii. Pamplona.

Viñes Millet, C. 1995. *Granada y Marruecos. Arabismo y africanismo en la cultura granadina.* Granada.

Wacks, D. A. 2014. "Medieval Iberian Literary Studies in the US: Challenges Past and Present." http://davidwacks.uoregon.edu/2014/05/02/les-treilles/.

From *Ṣawt* to *Muwashshaḥ*: A Musical Revolution[1]

Dwight Reynolds,
University of California, Santa Barbara

IN THE LATE TENTH/EARLY ELEVENTH CENTURY, an artistic revolution took place in al-Andalus. A new song-form emerged that broke away from the traditional models previously adhered to in classical Arabic poetry and in the courtly musical traditions of Mecca, Medina, Damascus, Baghdad, and Cordoba. This new musico-poetic form had two different linguistic registers, referred to in Arabic with separate terms: it was referred to as a *muwashshaḥ* if it was composed in high literary Arabic and a *zajal* if it was composed in more colloquial Andalusī Arabic.[2] Musically, however, the *muwashshaḥ* and *zajal* are indistinguishable and will therefore be treated as a single song-form here. In the eleventh and twelfth centuries this new musical genre swept across the Arabic-speaking Middle East from Morocco to Yemen to Iraq, and it survives into the present day in multiple regional traditions clustered around urban centers throughout the modern Arab world.

Wherever it went, the new song-form was recognized as having originated in al-Andalus. It was *not*, however, received as a fixed corpus of compositions from Iberia, but rather as a new genre in which local poets and composers almost immediately began to try their hand. In fact, the very first text to treat the composition of the new genre, Ibn Sanāʾ al-Mulk's twelfth-century treatise *Dār al-Ṭirāz* (*The House of Brocade*), is accompanied by a collection of thirty-four Andalusī *muwashshaḥāt* and thirty-five *muwashshaḥāt* that the Egyptian author himself composed in imitation of the Andalusī examples he had encountered in Cairo (see below).[3] Thus, even the earliest historical

1. It is my great pleasure to dedicate this essay to James T. Monroe as thanks for his tremendous intellectual generosity over the years. His work on musical aspects of the muwashshaḥ forms the basis of the arguments put forward in this modest contribution. I hope here to have reconfirmed and strengthened arguments that he first made nearly thirty years ago.

2. As Monroe noted (1988, 25–26), the portrayal of the *zajal* as a form separate from that of the *muwashshaḥ* is a modern Western idea and is a misleading anachronism. Medieval Arabic sources differentiate between the two purely and solely by their different linguistic registers, not by their form.

3. Ibn Sanāʾ al-Mulk (1155–1211 CE), *Dār al-ṭirāz*; translations and a study of these poems are found in Compton 1976.

documentation demonstrates that poets/composers saw the new song-form as one in which they could compose new repertory. Indeed, Ibn Sanāʾ al-Mulk's treatise and its accompanying collection of examples pre-date the earliest known collections that contain *only* Andalusī *muwashshaḥāt* by over a century.[4] The *muwashshaḥ/zajal* song-form, and the large body of songs that it encompasses, should therefore be understood historically to be *in the Andalusian style*, and not as a fixed body of compositions from al-Andalus that was later passed down from generation to generation.[5]

Ibn Sanāʾ al-Mulk refers at several points in his treatise to the *music* (*talḥīn*) of *muwashshaḥāt*, and in his other writings he refers to the performance of *muwashshaḥāt* as "singing," using terms that unambiguously refer to musical performance, such as the verbs *ghannā, shadā, tarannama,* etc.[6] This fact has far-reaching consequences, because the *muwashshaḥāt* included in Ibn Sanāʾ al-Mulk's collection are among the earliest known to us, and he understands them to be *songs*, not poems. The careful study of his collection, along with his other writings, proves beyond any reasonable doubt the truth of many of the arguments that James T. Monroe made nearly three decades ago about the musical nature of the *muwashshaḥ/zajal* form.[7] To give but one example, Ibn Sanāʾ al-Mulk discusses in one passage the use of nonce syllables (e.g. la la la) when singing *muwashshaḥāt*:

> *Muwashshaḥāt* are in one other respect divided into two groups: those in which the text fits the music and which require no assistance in this (*qismun yastiqillu al-talḥīnu bihi wa-lā yaftaqiru ilā mā yuʿīnuhu ʿalayhi*), and this group includes the majority of *muwashshaḥāt*; and those [of the second type] in which the text does not fit the music and

4. The earliest *muwashshaḥ* collections that have come down to us are *Dār al-ṭirāz*, by Ibn Sanāʾ al-Mulk, *Tawshīʿ al-tawshīḥ*, by Ṣalāḥ al-Dīn al-Ṣafadī (1297–1363 CE), *ʿUddat al-jalīs*, by ʿAlī ibn Bishrī (d. after 1375 CE), *Jaysh al-tawshīḥ*, by Lisān al-Dīn Ibn al-Khaṭīb (d. 1397 CE), and *ʿUqūd al-laʾāl*, by al-Nawājī (1386–1455 CE).

5. The misconception that most or all *muwashshaḥāt* were composed in al-Andalus has been proliferated by certain modern scholars, sometimes unintentionally, through their constant references to the genre's origins in al-Andalus. This idea is also found among some modern Arab musicians, who wish to assert the Andalusī origin of their repertory for a variety of motives, including claims to authenticity, nostalgia for an imagined lost "golden age," anticolonial sentiments, and other reasons. The truth, however, is that just as not all opera comes from Italy and not all jazz comes from the United States, not all "Andalusian" music comes from al-Andalus: the vast majority of extant *muwashshaḥāt* were composed outside of Iberia.

6. These terms stand in contrast to other common, but more ambiguous, words such as *qāla* (to say, compose, recite, sing) and *anshada* (to say, recite, sing). See Monroe 1987, 282–86, and Reynolds 2007, 223–24 for more details.

7. See Monroe 1987 and Reynolds 2007.

cannot be sung without being supported by syllables that have no meaning, as a prop for the melody and a crutch for the singer (*qismun lā yaḥtamiluhu al-talḥīn wa-lā yamshī bihi illā bi-ʾan yataʿākaʾa ʿalā lafẓatin lā maʿna lahā tukūn daʿāmatan li-l-talḥīni wa-ʿukkāzan li-l-mughannī*), such as in the following lyrics by Ibn Baqī:

Man ṭālib // thaʾr qatlā zabayāt al-hudūj // fattānāt al-ḥajīj

Who shall seek // vengeance for those slain by the gazelles in their litters // temptresses of pilgrims?[8]

The melody would not be correct (*al-talḥīnu lā yastaqīmu*) without saying "*lā lā*" between the two sections ending in [the letter] *jīm* [i.e. between the words *hudūj* and *fattānāt*].[9]

Several observations can be made based on the evidence of this passage. First of all, the "*lā lā*" cited by the Ibn Sanāʾ al-Mulk here are clearly meant to indicate the necessity of inserting nonce syllables (*lafẓatin lā maʿna lahā*) to fit the melody and are not the Arabic words "No! No!" as has been proposed by Emilio García Gómez.[10] The second, and more important, observation is that Ibn Sanāʾ al-Mulk divides *muwashshaḥāt* into two and only two categories: those where the lyrics fit the melody and those where they do not. He is a very meticulous writer and very careful in his categorizations (almost to the point of absurdity), and yet he makes no mention anywhere of a *muwashshaḥ* that is not sung. There is in fact no indication in *Dār al-ṭirāz* or in Ibn Sanāʾ al-Mulk's other writings that he ever encountered, or even conceived of, a *muwashshaḥ* that was not a song. Third, it is clear that he expects all of his readers to be familiar with the *music* and be able to hear it "in their minds," so that they can confirm his argument that one has to insert the two nonce syllables "*lā lā*" in the spot he indicates or the words will not fit the melody. If his readers cannot hear the melody "in their heads," his argument makes no sense. Thus, not only is this evidence that the author himself knows this song, but that his broader readership was assumed to know it as well and, in all probability, to be familiar with the tunes to all of the songs included in his work. This particular poem was included in several later compilations

8. Although some sources cite *qatlī* rather than *qatlā*, I agree with al-Rikābī's Arabic edition of the text, for it is surely the maidens who slay (male) pilgrims with their arrow-like glances and not the poet who has slain the maidens. An alternative, though more awkward, reading would have qatlī mean "their killing of me."

9. Dār al-ṭirāz, 50. My translation.

10. García Gómez may have been misled by another occurrence of "lā lā" in the third stanza of the poem, where the words do indeed mean "No, no!" See García Gómez 1962.

of *muwashshaḥāt* by other writers with no indication that it was sung, and modern scholars have therefore – mistakenly – assumed that it, as well as most other early *muwashshaḥāt*, was a poem and not a song. This misapprehension needs to be corrected.

Scholars, both Western and Arab, have treated the emergence of the *muwashshaḥ/zajal* song-form almost entirely as a literary phenomenon, that is, they have engaged in debates about poetic meters, rhyme schemes, and the linguistic register of the *kharja* (the final verses of a *muwashshaḥ*) with a very strong emphasis on the question of *origin(s)*, but have, for the most part, ignored the *musical* dimension of this new form.[11] The goal of the present essay is to argue that examining this tradition without considering its musical dimensions is to miss the point entirely, for this was – and remains – primarily a song tradition, and not merely a poetic form.

To comprehend the impact of this new song-form, however, we need first to understand the musical structure of the courtly tradition that preceded the emergence of the *muwashshaḥ/zajal* song-form, namely, the *ṣawt*. It should be noted here that the *muwashshaḥ/zajal* song-form did not immediately replace the *ṣawt*; the *ṣawt* continued to be the mainstay of the courtly tradition for several centuries, even while the new Andalusī genre was spreading throughout the Arabic-speaking Middle East. The newer song-form was perceived as lighter and more popular, and it is only in later centuries (perhaps beginning in the fifteenth century, though this shift is hard to pin down), that the *muwashshaḥ* began to be perceived as the primary genre of Andalusī music, eventually completely overshadowing the older *ṣawt* tradition that had been imported from the East. Today when Arabs speak of Andalusī or Andalusian music (*al-mūsīqā al-andalusiyya*), they are speaking almost exclusively of *muwashshaḥ* songs. It is important to remind ourselves, however, that in the medieval period, the *muwashshaḥ/zajal* song-form constituted only a portion of the music that was performed in al-Andalus, and that it is only in later centuries that it became virtually the *sole* song-form to be identified as Andalusī.

The Musical Structure of the Medieval Ṣawt[12]

The courtly music of Damascus, Baghdad, Medina, and Cordoba, including that of the famous singer Ziryāb and his followers, was based on a song-form

11. The body of writings on the *muwashshaḥ* and *zajal* is truly massive, as can be seen from the 2714 entries in an annotated bibliography published by Heijkoop and Zwartjes in 2004, *Muwaššaḥ, Zajal, Kharja*, and the corpus of publications has continued to grow rapidly in the years since the publication of that work.

12. The term *ṣawt* is still in use in some regions of the Arabian Peninsula, but this folk genre shares little other than its name with the medieval courtly tradition examined here.

that contemporary authors referred to simply as *ṣawt* (pl. *aṣwāt*), literally "voice" or "vocal," meaning a "song."[13] Since the very rudimentary forms of musical notation from this period were used almost exclusively in treatises on music theory and were not used in transmitting actual compositions, no notated examples of medieval *ṣawt* have come down to us.[14] But the process of creating a *ṣawt* and some sense of the structure and intricacy of the genre can be derived from various passages in *Kitāb al-Aghānī* (*The Book of Songs* = *KA*), compiled in the tenth century, but which drew on extensive earlier documentation, including biographical works and earlier songbooks.[15]

In the period extending roughly from the sixth to the fifteenth centuries, many professional singers (m.s. *mughannī*, pl. *mughannūn*, f.s. *mughaniyya*, f. pl. *mughanniyāt*), were not singer-composers, meaning that they memorized and performed the compositions of other musicians.[16] A large number of the female singers of this era were slaves (s. *jāriya*, pl. *jawārī*, or *qayna*, pl. *qiyān* or *qaynāt*), while among male singers, some were slaves, but most were freemen. The most prominent musical figures from this period, however, were singer-composers who not only memorized prodigious amounts of repertory from other musicians, but also created new *ṣawt*-compositions (and sometimes instrumental pieces), supplying their patrons with a steady flow of new material.[17] Somewhat confusingly, there was not a separate title for these figures – they were simply referred to as singers, but historical texts note the fact that they also composed (*laḥḥana*) songs and did not simply perform the songs of others. These figures were accorded a higher status than singers who did not compose, and many of them were the subjects

13. The heading *ṣawt* was also placed over song texts in written works, which conveniently differentiated the texts of poems from lyrics that were to be sung. The terms *ṣanʿa* and *ʿamal* were also used to refer to a composition, but the song-form itself was referred to primarily as a *ṣawt*.

14. There are passages, however, in Abū al-Faraj al-Iṣbahānī's *Kitāb al-Aghānī* (*The Book of Songs*, hereafter, *KA*) that appear to indicate that some highly-trained musicians were able to transmit songs via writing. See, for example, al-Iṣbahānī X:110, where Ibrāhīm al-Mawṣilī is able to send Ibrāhīm al-Mahdī a written version of a new composition that included "its rhythm (*īqāʿ*) and its 'measured section' (*basīṭ*),"and also al-Iṣbahānī X:106, where the written message includes, "its melodic mode (*majrāhu wa-iṣbaʿuhu*), the syllables of the texts and their placement on the notes (*tajziʾatuhu wa-aqsāmuhu*), the location of every note by string and fret (*makhārij al-nagham*), the placement of every phrase (*mawāḍiʿ maqāṭiʿihi*), the measure of its rhythmic cycles and its meters (*maqādīr adwārihi wa-awzānihi*)." For the technical meanings of these terms, see Sawa 2015, which has been of invaluable assistance in creating these translations and the translations of other passages from *KA* that appear in this essay.

15. The three most important studies of *KA* are Kilpatrick 2003; Neubauer 1965; and Sawa 2004.

16. The term *muṭrib* (f. *muṭriba*) was also occasionally in use.

17. For a detailed study of the concept of "composers" in medieval Islamic culture, see Neubauer 1997.

of biographies that were later compiled into large collections, such as al-Iṣbahānī's.[18] In general, there was no commonly recognized social role for a composer (*mulaḥḥin*) who was not also a performer, though in a handful of cases, musicians who were gifted composers but possessed only mediocre vocal skills preferred to teach their compositions to other singers and have them perform their works in public, rather than perform themselves. However, the *function* of the composer (*mulaḥḥin,* f. *mulaḥḥina*) was recognized, and when songs were compiled in written works, the information given about each song usually included the name of the poet (m. *shāʿir*, f. *shāʿira*) who composed the lyrics, as well as the name of the composer who set the words to music, along with the rhythm and the melodic mode of the song.

In composing a *ṣawt,* a singer-composer would typically select a small number of verses from an already existing poem, sometimes by a well-known poet, but quite often by rather obscure poets. A singer-composer's knowledge of the poetic tradition and her/his ability to select material from a vast body of memorized poetry was therefore an indispensable part of his/her craft. The text of a *ṣawt* was usually very short, typically two to six verses in length, though some were slightly longer. The singer-composer did not necessarily select verses that occurred in sequence in the original poem, so the four verses of a *ṣawt* might actually be verses 6, 7, 12, and 15, for example, from a much longer poem of two or three dozen verses. Thus, although the singer-composer was usually not the original poet of the verses, s/he was definitely a creative force in assembling the text for the song, since the verses could, and often were, given new meanings by being excerpted and rearranged in a new context.[19]

Only occasionally were singer-composers called upon to compose their own poetry and then set those verses to music, at which point they functioned as poet, composer, and singer for a particular song. The composition of poetry was, in any case, a common skill among educated people, and was expected of nearly all courtiers, whatever their profession or specialization might be. Many of the examples that have come down to us of songs where the singer-composer was also the poet consist of verses composed extemporaneously that successfully captured the ambience of a moment

18. There were also collections of biographies of famous instrumentalists, such as Jaḥẓa's *Kitāb al-ṭunbūriyyīn* (*Book of Ṭunbūr-players*); unfortunately, none of these works has survived.

19. No large-scale study of the relationship between *ṣawt* lyrics and their original poems has yet been undertaken; we therefore have very little sense of the intertextual connections between the lyrics and the original poem, and even whether, for example, the audience of the song performance was meant to compare and interpret the sung lyrics in relation to the poem at all. To the best of my knowledge, very few comments are found in *KA* or elsewhere that judge or critique the selection of the verses from the original poem.

or responded well to a particular situation, and the patron or companions then requested that the verses be set to music. However, singer-composers sometimes created songs based on their own poetry for special occasions, carefully crafting works that might take extended periods of time to compose and polish for a particular performance.

Once the text for the song had been selected, a singer had the choice of using the melody from another song (with or without changes), or composing a completely new melody, the latter being the more common practice.[20] Even some of the greatest composers occasionally "borrowed" a melody from an older composition, sometimes changing the rhythm or the mode, and sometimes leaving the tune unchanged.[21] The reverse was also possible – a singer-composer could take a text that had been selected by another musician and set it to a new tune, usually of her/his own composition. For this reason, many of the songs listed in large compilations, such as *KA*, include references to other songs with the same text, or other songs with the same melody, attributed to different singer-composers. There is no sense that this practice, called *contrafactum* composition, was looked down upon if the singer-composer acknowledged the source of the material.[22] There are also references to songs by one singer-composer that included "revision" or "emendation" (*tahdhīb*) by a later singer-composer, often with the comment that the latter version is the one that is commonly performed. To claim the music of another as one's own, however, was unacceptable (see below).

The rhythm selected for the melody was crucial, because there were strong associations between certain rhythms and particular emotions and styles. The slower rhythms were both considered and labeled "heavy" (*thaqīl*). In the terminology developed by Isḥāq al-Mawṣilī and still used a century or so later by al-Iṣbahānī, three rhythms bore this name: "the first heavy" (*al-thaqīl al-awwal*), also known simply as *al-thaqīl*; "the second heavy" (*al-thaqīl al-thānī*), which, before al-Mawṣilī's reclassification, had

20. There was a rich vocabulary used to describe taking the tune from an older song and setting new words to it, including, for example: *akhada laḥnan min ṣawtin* (he took a melody from a song), *allafa* (compose by "putting together"), *banā ʿalā* (built upon), *ʿamila ʿalā* (made upon), *sariqa* (stole), *mazaja* (mixed), etc. See Sawa 2015 for the precise meanings of these and other related terms.

21. The opening melody of Isḥāq al-Mawṣilī's famous song "Tashakkā al-Kumayt" (al-Kumayt complained), which was still being sung in the thirteenth century according to al-Tīfāshī, was apparently taken from an earlier song by al-Abjar called "Mā abkāka" (What has caused you to weep?), see al-Iṣbahānī I:235.

22. For a discussion of the role of *contrafactum* composition, see Reynolds 2012, 82–84; this is, in effect, the musical equivalent of the Arabic concept of poetic *muʿāraḍa*, in which poets would "borrow" the meter, rhyme, and even the themes, of another poem.

been known as *thaqīl al-thaqīl*; and "light heavy" (*khafīf thaqīl*).[23] These songs were usually solemn, and were the most intricate and the most difficult to perform. At the other end of the spectrum were "light" (*khafīf*) rhythms such as *hazaj* (a 6/8 rhythm), which was used for faster, lighter, and easier songs. "Heavy" songs were considered "better" or "more valuable" (*ajwad*) for both the composer and the singer, and they were considered to be the domain of only the most outstanding singers.[24] These associations to some extent still hold true today and many song sequences in North Africa and the Eastern Mediterranean in modern times are organized starting with slower, more serious pieces in "heavier" rhythms moving toward lighter, faster rhythms that are considered less serious.

Most *ṣawt* songs were composed in a single rhythm, but some included a change in rhythm within the song, and all were based in a single melodic mode, though there may well have been melodic modulations within the song returning to the main mode at the end.[25] Thus nearly all of the songs in *KA* and similar works are listed with a single rhythm and melodic mode, and only a small number are cited as having more than one rhythm or mode, usually with an indication as to where in the song it changed. One rather common shift within a song, however, was the movement from unmeasured (i.e. non-rhythmic) singing, which was termed *nashīd*, in which the singer rendered the words and the melody at whatever pace s/he desired, to a measured (i.e. rhythmic) melody, which was termed *basīṭ* (see below for an example). If the change took place at a certain point in the text, then this was often indicated, such as when the caliph al-Muntaṣir (r. 861–62) ordered the female slave-singer ʿArīb to sing a particular song rendering the first verse in *nashīd* and the last verse in *basīṭ* (*fa-amara al-Muntaṣir ʿArīb an tughannī nashīdan fī awwal al-abyāt wa-tajʿal al-basīṭ fī al-bayt al-akhīr*).[26] In other songs the point of change is not noted, which presumably meant that the entire text was performed first as *nashīd* and then as *basīṭ*.

One of the stages in the setting of a text to music that is attested many times in the *KA* is the process of fixing the syllables of the text to the rhythm of the song, referred to as *istiwāʾ* (to "even out" or "smooth out") or *tajziʾa* (to "set the parts in place"). A number of anecdotes recount how musicians

23. In *KA* there are several variations of each of these names; for example, *al-thaqīl al-awwal* could also be called *awwal thaqīl*, and so forth. See Sawa 2015, 40–49, for more details.

24. Liu and Monroe 1989, 37.

25. The most extensive study of rhythms from the time period of *KA* is by George Sawa (Sawa 2004, a reprint with an updated bibliography of the original published in 1989). The bibliography was again updated in 2007. The melodic modes are still a topic of discussion: see, Farmer 1955, Wright 2005, and Sawa 2004, 73–91, for varying interpretations.

26. al-Iṣbahānī VIII:304

would go over and over a new composition alone or with an accompanist or with another singer to fix the syllables of the text to the melody and rhythm. In one well-known example, Ibrāhīm ibn al-Mahdī once "stole" a song from his rival Ibrāhīm al-Mawṣilī because he happened to walk down an alleyway underneath the veranda where the great musician was repeating a new song that he had composed for the caliph Hārūn al-Rashīd over and over with two of his female slave-singers in order to "smooth out" the words to the rhythm. When al-Mawṣilī performed the piece the following day in court before the caliph and claimed it was a new composition, Ibn al-Mahdī accused him of passing off an older, well-known composition as his own, and to prove his point, he performed the new piece exactly as al-Mawṣilī had, to al-Mawṣilī's astonishment and Hārūn al-Rashīd's rage. Only when al-Mawṣilī was threatened with dire punishments for his "lie" did Ibn al-Mahdī step forward to explain what had really happened.[27]

Another anecdote, one which gives some sense of the complexity of a fine *ṣawt*, involves a new song composed by Isḥāq al-Mawṣilī, son of Ibrāhīm al-Mawṣilī (both of whom were considered the best musicians of their age). The song is in the rhythm "light heavy" (*khafīf thaqīl*),[28] and al-Iṣbahānī comments that "this song is one of Isḥāq's eternal and most extraordinary compositions" (*wa-hādhā al-ṣawt min awābid Isḥāq wa-badā'i'ih*).[29] After hearing the song for the first time, the Caliph al-Wāthiq remarked:

> The first verse of this song is but four words ["The traces and remains have been abandoned by the people" – *al-ṭulūlu wa-l-dawārisu fāraqathā al-awānisu*].[30] Look and see whether there is any technique in the art of singing that Isḥāq did not manage to put into these four words! He started [the song] out in *nashīd* and then followed that with *basīṭ*, in it he shouts and he coos, [in some places] he gives preponderance to the melody and [in others] he steals from it, and he did all of this in four words! Have you ever heard of anyone among the ancients or the moderns who has composed the like or is even capable of this?[31]

Giving preponderance to the melody may refer to the use of long melismatic phrases in which syllables are stretched out over several notes, while "stealing from the melody" appears to refer to the opposite technique,

27. al-Iṣbahānī V:172.
28. See Sawa 2015.
29. al-Iṣbahānī V:427
30. This is a common trope in classical Arabic poetry – the vestiges of an abandoned campsite in the desert evoke for the poet a Beloved who has departed and/or the ephemerality of human existence.
31. al-Iṣbahānī V:426–427.

perhaps a type of *recitativo* singing in which the text is sung almost in a monotone. Even if we cannot be certain of some of the details, this passage demonstrates that a very simple text of a mere four words was set to an extremely sophisticated musical composition.

Unfortunately, we cannot reconstruct this or other songs from this type of description, but the cumulative portrait of the *ṣawt* genre that emerges from dozens of such anecdotes is of a genre that is melodically highly complex and composed to be performed by skilled, professionally trained singers to very short texts. It is therefore clear that the *ṣawt* was a *melocentric* genre in which a relatively short text served as the vehicle for rather lengthy, sophisticated melodic compositions that were intricately ornamented and performable only by highly trained professionals. A *logocentric* form, in contrast, is one where the focus is on the text and the music is typically not highly ornamented, such as in a traditional English folk ballad. This is precisely one of the great changes that took place when the new *muwashshaḥ/zajal* song-form emerged: the *ṣawt*, a highly melocentric tradition with simple texts and complex melodies, which was almost always performed by professional solo singers, was suddenly faced with a rival, the *muwashshaḥ/zajal* song-form, that boasted poetically ornate, and comparatively lengthy texts that were performed to relatively simple melodies, which were far more accessible to the masses and could be performed by many singers singing together as a chorus.

A Musico-Poetic Revolution in al-Andalus

The poems from which singer-composers chose the texts for their *ṣawt* songs were exclusively *mono-endrhymed* – which means that each verse[32] ended in the same rhyme throughout the duration of the poem. The poetry was also composed in *quantitative meters*, that is, sequences of long and short syllables, with each verse consisting of two equal half-lines, or hemistichs, divided by a break, termed the medial caesura. The *muwashshaḥ/zajal* song-form, however, broke with virtually every convention of classical Arabic poetry. Instead of a single mono end-rhyme, it featured dazzling displays of multiple rhymes, both at the ends of verses and within verses. Instead of dividing each verse into two equal hemistichs, verses were divided into multiple units, often of unequal lengths, in a variety of different patterns.

32. The English word "verse" is unfortunately highly ambiguous, for it is used to refer to several completely different things. The meaning used here is "a single line of poetry," thus a sonnet can be referred to as a form that typically has fourteen verses (or lines). Another common usage, most often referring to songs, is not used in this essay, and indicates an entire stanza or a strophe, such as the second "verse" of "Yankee Doodle" or of a church hymn.

Although some *muwashshaḥāt* followed the accepted meters of older Arabic poetry, many others did not, and instead were molded directly onto their melody – such that use of the traditional meters became optional and was no longer obligatory.[33] Instead of intricate melodic compositions that were performable only by highly trained professional singers, the new *muwashshaḥ* songs were built on a simple, repetitive two-part melodic structure (see below) that even common folk were able to master, enabling people to sing along in performances. The new song-form was so different and so unusual that every medieval scholar who attempted to describe and analyze it had to come up with his own terminology for its key elements because up to this point Arabic possessed no terminology for "strophe" or "stanza," no term for a "partial verse" that was not a hemistich, and no terminology to describe rhymes that changed or alternated or were located within verses rather than at the end of verses. Each author was on his own when it came to creating the vocabulary for describing this new song-form and no two authors agreed on what terms to use in describing its structure.

Beyond these innovations, however, lay a radical new idea, which may, in fact, have helped generate these remarkable new patterns in rhyme and meter. The poetic structure of the *muwashshaḥ/zajal* is completely integrated into its musical structure: Both the poetry and the music consist of two alternating units with the rhymes and melodies alternating in sync with each other.

In the *muwashshaḥ/zajal* form, one unit retains the same end-rhyme every time it occurs, and it is always sung to the same melody. For example, if two verses at the beginning of the song have the same rhyme (A), they are sung to the same melody (X). Because this rhyme remains constant throughout the song, we can refer to it as the "common rhyme" section. Whenever the A-rhyme recurs, those lines are always sung to the first melody (melody X):

———— A	melody X
———— A	melody X

The second, contrasting, unit has a different rhyme and is sung to a second melody (Y). The verses are usually of a different length than the verses of the "common rhyme" section and there may also be a different number of verses, such as three in the example below. If the verses are longer, they might also have a medial caesura, though the line might also be divided into

33. This aspect of the *muwashshaḥ* was already observed by Ibn Sanāʾ al-Mulk in the twelfth century, in Dār al-ṭirāz.

smaller, even unequal, units. Because the rhyme in this section changes each time it returns, we can refer to it as the "changing rhyme" section:

———— ————B melody Y
———— ————B melody Y
———— ————B melody Y

Together the "common rhyme" and "changing rhyme" sections (AA BBB) are understood to constitute a single strophe or stanza:

————A melody X
————A melody X
———— ————B melody Y
———— ————B melody Y
———— ————B melody Y

This pattern is then repeated throughout the length of the song. At the beginning of the second stanza, the original rhyme and the first melody (X) return; this is not a "refrain," however, because the words are different, even though the original rhyme and the initial melody are repeated (a true refrain involves singing the same words again). And the "changing rhyme" section comes back, but with a different rhyme, though sung to the now familiar melody Y:

————A melody X
————A melody X
———— ————C melody Y
———— ————C melody Y
———— ————C melody Y

And together these verses (AA CCC) constitute the second strophe or stanza. Many medieval *muwashshaḥāt* included five or more strophes, each of which might consist of five to eight verses. The *muwashshaḥ*, then, often had upwards of twenty-five or even forty verses, far longer than the classical *ṣawt* with only two to six verses, and as a result, the two melodies of the *muwashshaḥ* song might be repeated twenty or more times in a single performance, making the songs easily accessible even to non-musicians. There is also evidence that, at least in the Jewish communities of the Arabic-speaking world, the first two verses of the poem were sometimes sung by all present as a refrain (Hebrew *pizmon*) in between the stanzas, which would double the number of times that that melody would be heard in a single performance of the song.[34] And in some modern performance practices, particularly in North Africa, the melody is sometimes repeated instrumentally after each verse is sung (a practice termed *jawāb* "response"). It is therefore not at all difficult to see that audiences would soon learn the tunes and be able to sing along with the refrain. They would even be able to sing along with the main song as soon as they learned the lyrics, and one characteristic of the insistent repetition of rhymes is that the texts were relatively easy to memorize. In addition, modern Arab scholars of the musical history of the *muwashshaḥ* further note that the tunes are usually straightforward and that large amounts of embellishment and ornamentation are frowned upon in this tradition.[35] In musical terms, the *muwashshaḥ* is inherently capable of being performed either in solo or choral renditions.

This alternation occurs over and over again, first one melody and then the second, and returning to the first melody. The A-rhyme returns over and over again, but in between, there are different rhymes (CCC, DDD, EEE, FFF, etc.) giving the poet much more freedom than in a traditional classical Arabic poem where every single verse had to end in the same rhyme. In the example posited above, there are two verses in the "common rhyme" section and three verses in the "changing rhyme" section, creating a stanza of five (i.e. 2 + 3) verses, commonly called a *khumsiyya*, from the number five (*khamsa*). But this arrangement was quite flexible and one might, for example, have only one verse in the "common-rhyme" section and three in the "changing rhyme" section, or three verses in the "common rhyme" section and five verses in the "changing rhyme" section, and many other combinations.[36] Thus, in its simplest form, the *muwashshaḥ* as a musico-poetic form is one in which two units alternate back and forth, over and over again: one unit (the "common-rhyme" section) keeps the same rhyme and the same melody all the way through the song, and the other unit (the "changing rhyme" section) maintains its own melody, but has a new rhyme every time it recurs.

The critical, one might even say defining, characteristic of the *muwashshaḥ* song-form is that the melody changes in lock-step with the rhyme at the end of each verse – whenever the rhyme stays the same, the same melody is used (for example for the first two AA verses) and *the melody*

34. See Monroe 1987, 297.

35. Ḥilw 1965, 89: "It is well established that unnatural intricacy and diversity in the melodies [of *muwashshaḥāt*] are disagreeable…." (*wa-min al-thābit anna al-taʿqīd wa-l-tanwīʿ ghayr al-ṭabīʿī fī l-alḥān makrūh …*). My translation.

36. Ibn Sanāʾ al-Mulk spends a great deal of time discussing all of the various arrangements he had encountered in the opening section of *Dār al-ṭirāz*.

changes when the rhyme changes.[37] When the A rhyme changes to B, the music moves from melody X to melody Y. When the B rhyme comes to an end, and the A rhyme returns, melody Y changes back to melody X. This basic bipartite melodic structure is already referred to in Ibn Sanāʾ al-Mulk's *Dār al-tirāz* in the twelfth century, and holds true for the vast majority of *muwashshaḥāt* whose melodies are known to us today.[38] This structure is so widespread and has endured for so long, that it must be considered a distinctive musical feature of the *muwashshaḥ/zajal* song-form. This observation is critical to any comparisons to the music of the Occitanian and Catalan troubadours, as well as to other repertories, such as the *Cantigas de Santa Maria,* the *Cantigas de Amigo,* as well as the *rondeau, dansa, virelai, villancico, laude,* and *ballata.*[39]

It should be stressed that what has been described above is the *most basic form* of the *muwashshaḥ*, for no sooner had the bonds of the mono-endrhyme rules of classical Arabic poetry been broken, than poets began to delight in creating ever more complex and more sensational displays of the art of rhyme. The musical structure, however, did not partake in these extravagant developments and instead underwent only a handful of later developments.[40] One as yet unexplained development is that in North Africa, *muwashshaḥāt* over the centuries were often reduced to a single strophe or a single strophe plus one verse from what would have been the second strophe. No scholar has offered a convincing explanation for the emergence of this truncated form of the *muwashshaḥ*, which happened at a time when songbooks from Egypt, the Eastern Mediterranean, and even the Ottoman Empire still featured *muwashshaḥāt* with multiple strophes. What was in medieval times a song genre with lengthy texts became in North Africa, already in the eighteenth century, a form with relatively short texts, typically of five to ten verses while in the East it was still common to have texts of forty or more verses.[41]

37. This applies only to the rhymes located at the end of verses, not to the additional ornamental rhymes that are sometimes added within verses.

38. For Ibn Sanāʾ al-Mulk's observation, see Reynolds 2007. In addition to the *muwashshaḥ* tunes that are currently known and performed in the Arab Middle East, there are also hundreds, perhaps thousands, of song-texts that have come down to us in written form in songbooks and poetic anthologies, for which the melodies have been lost.

39. See Reynolds 2013, 196–97.

40. The addition of the *silsila* (a third melodic section) in the Mashriq in the fifteenth century created a tripartite musical structure (though this is a relatively rare form), and in Yemen unique developments led to the creation of tripartite and even more complex musical structures in what is termed *humaynī* poetry. These latter forms, however, are not found in any other region.

41. See, for example, the mid-ninteenth century collection of Shihāb al-Dīn al-Miṣrī, *Safinat al-mulk.*

One final note of clarification: There are several descriptions of the musical structure of the *muwashshaḥ* in western scholarship that rather confusingly speak of *three* melodic units, and because this is a common misconception, it is worth clarifying at this point before concluding. One such description, published by Lois Ibsen Al Faruqi, states that there are three main melodic units to a *muwashshaḥ*: the first is termed in Arabic either the *dawr* (cycle) or the *badaniyya* (body): this corresponds to our "melody X" above. She then states that the second melodic unit is termed the *khāna* or the *silsila*: this corresponds to our "melody Y" above. She then refers to a "third section": "The third section is called *qaflah* ("key," "closing"), *rujūʿ* ("return"), or *ghiṭā*[ʾ] ("cover"). It presents new poetic material set to a repeat of the musical elements of the *dawr*."[42]

As her description states, this is actually a return to the original melody (our melody X above), and is not so much a "third" musical section as a return to the opening melody. This section is referred to with specific terms only because it is the final, closing section of the song, not because there is any new musical material. Thus what is structurally a very simple process of two alternating melodies is oddly obscured by the references to a "third" musical section, which would make it seem that there is a third melody involved, when there is not. The "third" melodic unit is a repeat of the first melody, not a new melody.[43]

Conclusion

Scholars have hitherto addressed the emergence of the *muwashshaḥ/zajal* form almost exclusively as a question of literary form. They have assiduously sought out precursors for the multiple rhymes of the new genre, argued about the troublesome issue of poetic meters (or the lack thereof), and debated the role of the *kharja* (the closing verses). By ignoring the musical dimensions of the *muwashshaḥ* song-form, however, they may have inadvertently excluded some of the most critical and distinctive features of the genre. The examination above of the shift from the older *ṣawt* tradition to the new Andalusī *muwashshaḥ/zajal* song-form reveals four key observations about the musical history of the genre:

42. al Faruqi 1975, 21.

43. The terminology cited by al Faruqi is that used by musicians in modern-day Egypt, Lebanon and Syria; part of the confusion here is that the terminology used by different regional traditions varies, and in several cases she has conflated terms that actually refer to distinct things. The terms *khāna* and *silsila*, according to Salīm al-Ḥilw, for example, are used for when the second melody either climbs to the upper tetrachord of the melodic mode (*khāna*), or the reverse, drops into the tetrachord below the original tonic center (*silsila*), see al-Ḥilw 1965, 88. They are not two alternate terms for the same thing.

1) The *muwashshaḥ/zajal* form is characterized by a bipartite musical structure, in which two melodic units alternate;
2) The melodic units alternate in lockstep with the changes in the verse-end rhymes;
3) The *muwashshaḥ/zajal* form is a relatively simple musical form, which allowed for the creation of highly ornate and lengthy poetic texts (in contrast to the earlier *ṣawt* tradition that consisted of musically complex compositions for quite short, unadorned texts); and,
4) Its rapid expansion throughout urban centers of the Arabic-speaking world probably had more to do with the fact that ordinary people could learn the melodies, sing them chorally, and participate in performances even as audience members, than with the themes (most of which were borrowed from earlier poetic genres) or the poetic form of the genre.

Bibliography

Compton, Lois Fish. 1976. *Andalusian Lyrical Poetry and Old Spanish Love Songs: The* Muwashshaḥ *and Its* Kharja. New York.

Farmer, Henry George. 1955. "The Song Captions in the *Kitāb al-Aghānī al-Kabīr*." *Transactions of the Glasgow University Oriental Society*. Vol. 15 (1953–54, publ. 1955), 1–10; publ. separately London, n.d. (1955).

Al Faruqi, Lois Ibsen. 1975. "Muwashshaḥ: A Vocal Form in Islamic Culture." *Ethnomusicology* 19:1–29.

García Gómez, Emilio. 1962. "Estudio del *Dār at-Tirāz*: Perceptiva egipcia de la *muwaššaḥa*." *Al-Andalus* 27:21–104.

Heijkoop, Henk and Otto Zwartjes. 2004. *Muwaššaḥ, Zajal, Kharja: Bibliography of Strophic Poetry and Music from al-Andalus and Their Influence in East and West*. Leiden.

Al-Ḥilw, Salīm. 1965. *Al-Muwashshaḥāt al-andalusiyya*. Beirut.

Ibn Sanāʾ al-Mulk. (12th c.) 1977. *Dār al-ṭirāz fī ʿamal al-muwashshaḥāt*. Edited by Jawdat al-Rikābī. 2nd ed. Damascus.

Al-Iṣbahānī, Abū l-Faraj. 1963–64. *Kitāb al-Aghānī*. 23 vols. in 15. Cairo.

Kilpatrick, Hilary. 2003. *The Making of the Great Book of Songs*. London.

Liu, Benjamin M. and James T. Monroe. 1989. *Ten Hispano-Arabic Strophic Songs in the Modern Oral Tradition*. Berkeley/Los Angeles.

Al-Miṣrī, Shihāb al-Dīn. (1864) 1891. *Safīnat al-mulk wa-nafīsat al-fulk*. Cairo.

Monroe, James T. 1987. "The Tune or the Words? Singing Hispano-Arabic Poetry." *Al-Qantara* 8:265–317.

——. 1988. "Maimonides on the Mozarabic Lyric (A Note on the *Muwaššaḥa*)." *La Corónica* 17 no. 2:18–32.

Neubauer, Eckhard. 1965. *Musiker am Hof der Frühen ʿAbbāsiden*. Frankfurt am Main.

——. 1997. "Zur Bedeutung der Bregriffe Komponist und Komponistin in der Musikgeschichte der islamischen Welt." *Zeitschrift für Geschichte der arabisch-islamischen Wissenschaften* Band 11:308–363.

Reynolds, Dwight F. 2007. "Musical Aspects of Ibn Sanāʾ al-Mulk's *Dār al-Tirāz*." In *Muwashshah: Proceedings of the Conference on Arabic and Hebrew Strophic Poetry and its Romance Parallels*, October 8–10, 2004. School of Oriental and Asian Studies, University of London, 211–227. London.

——. 2012. "Lost Virgins Found: The Arabic Songbook Genre and an Early North African Exemplar." *Quaderni di Studi Arabi*, N.S. 7:69–105.

——. 2013. "Arab Musical Influence on Medieval Europe: A Reassessment." In *A Sea of Languages: Literature and Culture in the Pre-modern Mediterranean*, edited by Suzanne Akbari and Karla Mallette, 182–98. Toronto.

Sawa, George. 2004. *Music Performance Practice in the Early ʿAbbasid Era: 132–320 AH / 750–932 AD*. 2nd ed., Ottawa.
——. 2009. *Rhythmic Theories and Practices in Arabic Writings to 339 AH/ 950 CE. Annotated Translations and Commentaries*. Ottawa.
——. 2015. *An Arabic Musical and Socio-Cultural Glossary of "Kitāb al-Aghānī."* Leiden.
Wright, Owen. 2005. "Die melodischen Modi bei Ibn Sina and die Entwicklung der Modalpraxis von Ibn al-Munaggim bis zu Safi al-Din al-Urmawi (The Melodic Modes According to Ibn Sina and the Evolution of Modal Practice from Ibn al-Munajjim to Safi al-Din al-Urmawi)." *Zeitschrift für Geschichte der arabisch-islamischen Wissenschaften* 16:224–308.

Some Andalusī *Muwashshaḥāt* and Their Eastern Imitations

Teresa Garulo
Universidad Complutense, Madrid

BORN IN AL-ANDALUS, the *muwahshaḥāt* experienced great success in the East as they entered the second stage of their development in the fifth century AH/eleventh century CE. Ibn Sanāʾ al-Mulk (b. circa 550- d. 608 AH/1155–1211 CE), sometimes credited as the first poet in the East to compose *muwashshaḥāt*, is the author of the first treatise (*Dār al-ṭirāz*) on the rules of this genre, and thereafter he is always quoted as the authority in this matter. Prior to Ibn Sanāʾ al-Mulk and his treatise on *muwashshaḥ* poetry,[1] some Eastern poets from Egypt and Syria knew this genre and composed *muwashshahāt*,[2] or even used its *awzān* (meter)[3] in order to compose their own poems.[4]

The success of this kind of strophic poetry, with a prosody that defied the rules of classical Arabic metrics, was probably due to the tune or melody that accompanied it,[5] a melody that no doubt helped to adapt its metrical peculiarities and to create new poems following its pattern. From the very

1. In this article I use the terms *muwashshaḥ* or *tawshīḥ* when speaking of the genre (e.g. Andalusī strophic poetry), and *muwashshaḥa* and its plural, *muwashshaḥāt*, when I want to refer to a concrete poem. I use italics to indicate the lines of the common rhymes (the prelude or Ar. *maṭlaʿ*, and the refrain or Ar. *qufl*, pl. *aqfāl*; Sp. *vuelta*). This research is part of the "Contextos locales y dinámicas globales: al-Andalus y el Magreb en el Oriente islámico" (FFI2016–78878-R), project, directed by Maribel Fierro (ILC-CCHS Madrid, CSIC) and Mayte Penelas (EEA-Granada, CSIC).

2. Raḥīm 1987, 132–142. One of these early Eastern *muwashshaḥāt* that has been completely preserved is that by Ẓāfir al-Ḥaddād al-Iskandarī, which al-Ṣafadī has transmitted in *Al-Wāfī bi-l-wafayāt*, 16:301–302. This *muwashshaḥa*, a veritable powerhouse of alliteration, has a prelude (*maṭlaʿ*) and five strophes, with the following rhyme scheme and number of syllables:

aa aa aa aa *mm mm*
36 36 36 36 *3636*

3. *Wazn*, pl. *awzān*, that is: "measures" (Armistead and Monroe 1985, 224–225), "rhythm, meter, foot." Ibn Bassām (*Dhakhīra*, I, 469–470) seems to use *awzān* consistently when speaking of the metrics of the *muwashshaḥāt*, and *aʿārīḍ* (pl. of *ʿarūḍ* 'foot') when he refers to the classical Arabic meters. But later this distinction was not so clear. For an earlier use of the *muwashshaḥ*'s rhythms to compose a monorhymic poem, see Garulo 2005.

4. Raḥīm 1987, 139.

5. See, for instance, Monroe 1987 and Reynolds in the present volume.

beginnings of Arabic poetry up until the twentieth century, the *muʿāraḍa* (pl. *muʿāraḍāt*), an imitation or emulation of a previous poem using the same rhyme and meter of the original, have had a remarkable role in the poet's formation and practice, as it is a creditable form of learning from, or of paying homage to a great poet, or of even surpassing his achievement. It can also be a method of competition between rival poets. So it is no novelty in al-Andalus, where Ibn Shuhayd (d. 426 AH/1035 CE) penned a treatise on literary criticism in the form of a fictionalized journey to the land of the *jinn*, the *Risālat al-tawābiʿ wa-l-zawābiʿ*, where he gives expression to his desire to measure himself against his more admired Eastern poets.[6]

The *muʿāraḍa* (imitation) was very popular among practitioners in the field of *muwashshaḥ* poetry,[7] at least from the sixth century AH/twelfth century CE in al-Andalus,[8] and it is common to find accounts relating how some poets would profit from the success of a *muwashshaḥa* (usually in the form of a love or a wine poem), by composing a kind of *contrafactum* composition that could include a change in the poetic genre, like composing a *mujūn* (obscene, burlesque)[9] poem or an ascetic and devotional poem based on the original one whose subject was love or wine.

So it was in the East that some of the works composed to teach the art of the *tawshīḥ* frequently included a section with the author's *muʿāraḍāt* of his favorite strophic poems. For example, Ṣalāḥ al-Dīn Khalīl b. Aybak al-Ṣafadī (696–764 AH/1297–1363 CE), composed his *Tawshīʿ al-tawshīḥ*, a work that will be a guide in this paper, in this manner. And Ibn Sanāʾ al-Mulk also includes his own *muwashshaḥāt* in his *Dār al-ṭirāz*, although not all of them are *muʿāraḍāt* (imitations) strictly speaking.

But in the migration of the *muwashshaḥ* to Syria and Egypt, the music was indeed necessary, more than in al-Andalus, where this kind of strophic poetry was created, and where everybody would have been familiar with its prosody. It is important to remember that the rhythm of the *muwashshaḥa*, as Ibn Bassām (d. 543 AH/1147 CE) described it, was based on a short song or poetic utterance (*markaz*) in colloquial Arabic or in Romance, quoted at the very end (*kharja*) of the poem, to which the metrics of the entire composi-

6. Ibn Shuhayd 1967 and 1971.

7. Schippers 2012. The more evident *muʿāraḍāt* are those that use the *kharja* of a previous *muwashshaḥa*, a case well attested to and studied in the *muwashshaḥāt* with Romance *kharjas*, but evident also in those with a colloquial or classical Arabic *kharjas*, no matter if the poem is composed in classical Arabic, Hebrew, or in colloquial Arabic (that is, a *zajal* with a *muwashshaḥa* structure). For instance, there are three examples that Elinson (2001) studies: a *muwashshaḥa* by Ibn Baqī, and two strophic poems emulating it – an anonymous *muwashshaḥ* in Hebrew (perhaps by Judah ha-Levi), and a *zajal* by Ibn Quzmān.

8. See Elinson 2001.

9. Garulo 2009, 18–22.

tion had to be adjusted. Classical Arabic quantitative metrics, as defined by the Khalīlian system, does not apply to these two languages (Romance and colloquial Arabic), which ignore syllabic quantity.[10] The poet therefore had to adjust his composition to this colloquial meter.[11] Consequently, the poet had to adopt non-classical meters, which were perceived as irregularities by ears accustomed only to classical Arabic metrics and thus as something alien to the Khalīlian system. In the East, as Ibn Sanāʾ al-Mulk confessed to be his experience,[12] these irregularities could only be disregarded or ignored in the musical performance of the poem, for it was the melody that facilitated the creation of an imitation or *contrafactum* of the *muwashshaḥa.*

But there were also *muwashshaḥāt* composed in the classical Arabic meters. Ibn Sanāʾ al-Mulk disapproves of the latter,[13] because they are, in his opinion, too similar to *mukhammasāt*, another kind of Arabic strophic poetry (*musammaṭ*), less popular and less appreciated than the *muwashshaḥ*, from which, according to some scholars, the Andalusī genre derives.[14] Ibn Sanāʾ al-Mulk in his *Dār al-ṭirāz* classified them as *muwashshaḥ shiʿrī* (his Andalusi *muwashshaḥāt* numbers 24–29),[15] but at the same time they also may be scanned according to the principles governing the stress-syllabic meters of the Hispano-Romance prosody. This adaptation of the prosody of the *muwashshaḥ* to the Arabic metrics is a later development, already accounted for by Ibn Sanāʾ al-Mulk, and it is easy to explain why Eastern poets preferred these kinds of poems for their *muʿāraḍāt* (imitations) of Hispano-Arabic *muwashshaḥāt.*

Al-Ṣafadī,[16] our guide in this account, is a philologist, literary critic, and poet from Ṣafad, who lived mostly in Damascus and Cairo. He is known mainly as the author of a massive biographical dictionary, *Al-Wāfī bi-l-wafayāt* (*The Ultimate Book on Illustrious Men's Necrologies*), that has remained an indispensable source of information for scholars. Al-Ṣafadī collected his own *muwashshaḥāt* in his *Tawshīʿ al-tawshīḥ*, accompanied by those poems that inspired him to make *contrafactum* compositions. The poets he pays homage to are ʿUbāda b. Māʾ al-Samāʾ (d. 421 AH/1030 CE), Ibn al-Labbāna (d. 507 AH/1113 CE), al-Aʿmā al-Tuṭīlī ('The Blind Man of Tudela') (d. 525 AH/1130 CE), Ibn al-Zaqqāq (d. 530 AH/1135 CE), Ibn Zuhr al-Ḥafīd (d. 595 AH/1198 CE),

10. Corriente 1976 and 1977, 3.1.1–3.1.12; 1992, 2.1.3.1–2.1.3.1.4; 1997, 108.

11. Armistead and Monroe 1985; and Monroe 1985–86.

12. Ibn Sanāʾ al-Mulk, *Dār al-ṭirāz*, 35, and 83 (*muwashshaḥa* no. 33).

13. Ibn Sanāʾ al-Mulk, *Dār al-ṭirāz*, 33.

14. For a recent update on the ongoing debate to which Andalusī strophic poetry gives rise, see Garulo 2012.

15. Ibn Sanāʾ al-Mulk, *Dār al-ṭirāz*, 72–79. For *shiʿrī* (from *shiʿr*, [Arabic] poetry), Ibn Sanāʾ al-Mulk means "composed in the classical Arabic meters."

16. Rosenthal 2012.

and Ibn Sahl al-Isrāʾīlī (d. 649 AH /1251 CE), all of whom are from al-Andalus. He also pays homage to ʿAlī b. ʿAbd al-Ganī al-Ḥuṣrī (d. 488 AH/1095 CE), who worked and lived for different periods of his life in al-Andalus. Al-Ṣafadī also emulates two *muwashshaḥāt* by unknown Maghribī/Andalusī poets. His poetic models from the East are: Ibn Sanāʾ al-Mulk, from whom al-Ṣafadī derives a technical précis on the art of *tawshīḥ* included at the very beginning of his book, Aḥmad b. Ḥasan al-Mawṣilī[17] (d. 683 AH/1284 CE), Shihāb al-Dīn al ʿAzāzī[18] (633–710 AH/1235–1310 CE), al-Sirāj al-Mahhār[19] (d. 711 AH/1312 CE), and Shams al-Dīn al-Dahhān[20] (d. 721 AH/1321 CE). From *muwashshaḥa* number 52 onwards, al-Ṣafadī's poems are not *muʿāraḍāt* – at least he says they are not – but in his fifty-sixth *muwashshaḥa* he uses an older Hispano-Arabic *kharja*, "used by many authors from al-Andalus and elsewhere."[21] It is indeed the *kharja* of a very well-known *muwashshaḥa* by Ibn Baqī[22] (d. 545 AH/1150 CE), although al-Ṣafadī does not mention him as the author.

In the present article I comment only on the Andalusī *muwashshaḥāt*, focusing specifically on the poems most appreciated by their imitators. This said, I need to add that I will not follow rigorously al-Ṣafadī's anthology, because I want to underscore the success of some poets and poems, and al-Ṣafadī is most interested in his own poems and sometimes in those of his contemporaries.

In *Tawshīʿ al-tawshīḥ* the most popular of Andalusī poets would seem to be Ibn Zuhr al-Ḥafīd as five of his *muwashshaḥāt* are included – numbers 10, 25, 28, 37, and 41. But his success seems to be linked only to the fact that al-Ṣafadī based eight *muʿāraḍāt* (imitation poems) on his poetry. After Ibn Zuhr, the next most appreciated poet is al-Aʿmā al-Tuṭīlī. The *muwashshaḥāt* of both men, as imitated by al-Ṣafadī and his contemporaries, will be the focus of this paper, although other authors and their poems will also be mentioned because of their success in Eastern lands.

Ibn Zuhr al-Ḥafīd was one of the most accomplished men of his time. He was a physician, as were several members of his family,[23] and he served as the personal physician of the Almohad caliph Yaʿqūb al-Manṣūr (r. 580–95

17. Al-Ṣafadī, *Al-Wāfī bi-l-wafayāt* (henceforth *Al-Wāfī*), 6:199–205; Ibn Taghrī Birdī, *Al-Manhal al-ṣāfī*, 1:266–277; al-Maqqarī (d. 1041 AH/ 1632 CE), *Nafḥ al-ṭīb*, 7:89–95.

18. Al-Ṣafadī, *Al-Wāfī*, 7:99–105; al-Ṣafadī, *Aʿyān al-ʿaṣr*, 1:269–75; Ibn Taghrī Birdī, *Al-Manhal al-ṣāfī*, 1:362–373; al-Maqqarī, 7:89–95.

19. Ibn Shākir al-Kutubī, *Fawāt al-wafayāt*, 3:146–154 (no. 380).

20. Al-Ṣafadī, *Al-Wāfī*, 4:148–150.

21. Al-Ṣafadī, *Tawshīʿ al-tawshīḥ* (henceforth *Tawshīʿ*), 174.

22. Ibn Baqī's *muwashshaḥa* can be found in Ibn Sanāʾ al-Mulk, *Dār al-ṭirāz*, no. 20; Ibn Bishrī (eighth century AH/fourteenth century CE), *ʿUddat al-jalīs*, no. 253; its *kharja*, in García Gómez 1962, no. 13 and no. 20. On Ibn Baqī, see Granja 2012a; Ṭuʿma 1979; Özkan 2017.

23. Arnaldez 2012.

AH/1184–99 CE). In addition, he was a poet, and his *muwashshaḥāt* were always highly appreciated,[24] and frequently became an object of *contrafactum*.[25] Ibn Abī Uṣaybiʿa (d. 668 AH/1270 CE), in his biographical dictionary on Arab medicine, *ʿUyūn al-anbāʾ fī ṭabaqāt al-aṭibbāʾ*, includes six of them.[26]

The first of his *muwashshaḥāt* included in al-Ṣafadī's anthology (*Tawshīʿ* no. 10),[27] an elegant love poem, has as a prelude and five strophes, with the following rhyme scheme: a a a *m n*.[28] The prelude reads:

> *bi-ʾabī man rāba-hā naẓarī*
> *fa-badā fī waŷhi-hā l-jaŷalu*
>
> *How dear is to me that girl whom my glances disquiet*
> *and her face shows her shyness.*

and the last strophe with the *kharja*:

> ʾayna min-nī l-ṣabru wa-l-jaladu
> ḍiqtu dharʿan bi-l-ladhī ʾajidu
> al-hawā wa-l-baththu wa-l-kamadu
> *man arād ʾan yadrī ʾesh khabarī*
> *ʿishqu hū ʾayyu qalb yaḥtamilū*.[29]
>
> How can I have patience and endurance;
> I can not suffer what I feel:
> love, sadness and grieving.
> *O thou who wants to know about me,*
> *which heart can endure her love?*

All of the lines of this *muwashshaḥa* can be scanned as *madīd* hemistichs

24. Ghāzī 1979, 2:65–122 (22 *muwashshaḥāt* and three fragments).
25. Garulo 2009.
26. Ibn Abī Uṣaybiʿa, *ʿUyūn al-anbāʾ*, 521–528.
27. Ghāzī 1979, 2:112–113.
28. In describing rhyme schemes, I follow García Gómez's practice, namely using the letters of the alphabet up to the letter *l* for the rhymes of the *ghuṣn*, pl. *aghṣān* (Ibn Bassām)/*bayt, pl. abyāt* (Ibn Sanāʾ al-Mulk) – that section of the strophe whose rhymes change in every strophe (Sp. *mudanza*) – and from letter *m* onwards for the rhymes of the *qufl*, pl. *aqfāl* (Ibn Sanāʾ al-Mulk), the last section of every strophe – the *kharja* is the *qufl* of the last strophe – whose rhymes are common to all the strophes, in this manner: *m n* (prelude), a a a *m n*, b b b *m n*, c c c *m n*, d d d *m n*, etc. (the common rhymes are shown in italics). Describing the rhyme structure of a particular *muwashshaḥa*, I usually quote only the first strophe, the rest of them being alike. I will only include the prelude and *kharja* of the *muwashshaḥāt* under discussion: the prelude, because it is the common practice in Arabic used to identify a poem; and the *kharja*, because of its relevance in *muwashshsaḥ* poetry. When a *muwashshaḥa* lacks a prelude, I quote its first strophe in its entirety.
29. Also in Corriente 1997, 207.

× ᴗ — — | × ᴗ — | ᴗ ᴗ —[30] and this renders the *contrafactum* very easy for Arabic poets to imitate, but the *kharja*, in colloquial Arabic, conveys a rhythm easily perceived by Romance ears accustomed to poetry, namely that of a decasyllabic verse with stress on the third, sixth and ninth syllables, like the well-known Spanish poem: "Del salón en el ángulo oscuro... etc." by G. A. Bécquer (d. 1870).[31]

Al-Ṣafadī made two *muʿāraḍāt* of this poem – *Tawshīʿ*, numbers 11 and 12. Both are graceful love poems. In them these metrical subtleties are naturally lost, as he only perceives the Arabic rhythm of a *madīd* meter. *Tawshīʿ* no. 12 has five strophes, like its model, but *Tawshīʿ* no. 11 has six stanzas. In both of these poems the *kharja*'s language is colloquial Arabic and, deviating from Ibn Zuhr's poem, they (the *kharjas*) are introduced by a verb in the third-person feminine, the voice of a girl who addresses her mother complaining of her situation. The prelude of *Tawshīʿ* no. 11 is:

> *bittu min wajdī ʿalā khaṭari*
> *bī jirāḥun laysa tandamilu*
>
> *Because of my love I spend every night in great affliction,*
> *I have wounds that cannot be healed.*

and its *kharja*:

> *yā mmī hādhā jāru-nā l-tatarī*
> *fataḥa Llāh bū wa-qad qafalū*
>
> *O mother, our neighbor the Tatar,*
> *may God inspire him, has come back.*

And the prelude of *Tawshīʿ* no. 12 is:

> *kāna lī fīmā maḍā muqalu*
> *faniyat bi-l-damʿi wa-l-sahari*
>
> *Once I had beautiful eyes,*
> *which tears and insomnia had made infirm.*

And its *kharja* is:

30. In describing the quantitative Arabic meters, a small *x* represents a syllable that can be either long or short without affecting the metrical identification. All vowels before the caesura or verse end are metrically long, even when they are not grammatically long; I will only mark as long those that are really morphologically or grammatically long.

31. And here is an old Spanish verse: *Zagaleja del ojo rasgado, / vente a mí que no soy toro bravo* (Narrow-eyed shepherdess, come to me, for I am not a wild bull); in Cejador 1921, 107 (no. 171).

yā mmī yaḥlā lī ʾidhā ʿamilū
taḥsabī-h sukkar wa-zanda ṭarī

O mother, I like everything he does,
anybody would think he is sugar and fresh rhubarb.[32]

As can be seen, in his second *muʿāraḍa* al-Ṣafadī has inverted the order of the rhyme of the *aqfāl* or common rhymes (instead of *–rī* followed by *-lū* as in *Tawshīʿ* no. 10 and no. 11, in *Tawshīʿ* no. 12 the final rhyme is *-lū* followed by *–rī*). As al-Ṣafadī notes, it is possible to make a *contrafactum* by changing the rhymes of the original poem.

What al-Ṣafadī does not say is that Ibn Zuhr's *muwashshaḥa* (the poem that inspired al-Ṣafadī's *muʿāraḍa*) seems to be a *muʿāraḍa* itself – a poetic imitation inspired by a poem of Ibn Baqī that begins:

mattiʿi l-ʾalḥāẓa bi-l-naẓari
wa-yaqī-ka Llāhu wa-l-ʾajalu

Look at him and enjoy the way he looks at you,
may God and fate protect you.

And whose *kharja*,

qul wa-zid yā ṭayyiba l-khabari
baʿdiya l-ʾaḥbābu mā faʿalū,[33]

Tell me, O bringer of good news,
after I left, what have my loved ones done?

can, in turn, be found in a Hebrew *muwashshaḥa* by Todros Abulafia (d. 1285 CE).[34] In addition, with a small change in the rhymes – *ṣanaʿū* (have done) instead of *faʿalū* (have done), a word having essentially the same meaning – this *kharja* can also be found in another *muwashshaḥa* by Ibn Zuhr.[35] We will see below other instances of Ibn Zuhr imitating Ibn Baqī's poems that are not identified by al-Ṣafadī.

The second *muwashshaḥa* by Ibn Zuhr imitated by al-Ṣafadī is *Tawshīʿ* no. 25.[36] This is an interesting type of a poem, a *muwashshaḥa* "with an echo."[37] It

32. *Zand* is "a certain thorny tree." Lane 1863, 1:1257c. *Zand* is also "the upper one of the two pieces of stick, or wood, with which fire is produced." Lane 1863, 1:1257b.

33. Ibn Bishrī, *ʿUddat al-jalīs*, no. 177.

34. Monroe and Swiatlo 1977, no. 18.

35. Ibn Bishrī, *ʿUddat al-jalīs*, no. 292.

36. Ghāzī 1979, 2:114–115.

37. In Spanish metrics, *eco* ('echo') consists of the repetition of the last one or two syllables of the previous rhyme, forming a word. So, in this first strophe, *ṣāḥi* (companion), *lāḥī* (censor,

has five strophes, but lacks a prelude and its rhyme scheme is: aa aa aa *mm*. Its first stanza reads:

qalbī mina l-ḥubbi ghayru ṣāḥi
ṣāḥi
wa-ʾin laḥā-nī ʿalā l-milāḥi
lāḥi
wa-ʾinnamā bughyatu qtirāḥī
rāḥī
wa-ʾin darā qiṣṣatī washā-nī
shāni

My heart overflows with love,
O my companion.
If a reviler blames my love
for the lovely ones,
the wine will be my only
inspiration,
although if an enemy knew my case
he would slander me.

Although al-Ṣafadī criticizes this poem because, in his opinion, its concepts are not arranged in an orderly manner, nor do its terms go well together (*ghayr murtabiṭ al-maʿānī wa-lā multaʾim al-alfāẓ*), he duly appreciated Ibn Zuhr's use of the metrical device, the "echo," and composed two *muʿāraḍāt* based on it. As for the alleged disarray of the poem, it is probably due to the version known by the anthologist, for it is clear that in the poem transmitted by al-Ṣafadī, the fourth strophe must be the last one, because its *qufl*, which is the voice of a girl speaking to her mother in colloquial Arabic, should be the *kharja*.

Again, this *muwashshaḥa*, if the two-syllable feet of the echo are removed, may be scanned as hemistichs of a type of *basīṭ* meter (*al-basīṭ al-mukhallaʿ*). Its ten syllables follow the scheme × — ᴗ — | — ᴗ — | ᴗ — —. But in this poem syllabic quantity is irrelevant, as can be seen in lines one and three of the third stanza:

yā ʾUmma Saʿdin bi-smi l-suʿūdi
ʿūdī

or reviler), *rāḥī* (my wine), are the echo of *ghayru ṣāḥi* (not sober), *milāḥi* (the beautiful ones), *qtirāḥī* (my invention or suggestion); and *shāni* (one who hates, hater, an enemy) is the echo of *washā-nī* (he would slander me). See also García Gómez 1961, 73–78, who comments on a *muwashshaḥa* with an "echo" by Abū l-Ḥasan Ibn Nizār from Guadix, sixth century AH/twelfth century CE, included in Ibn Saʿīd (d. 685 AH/1286 CE), *Mughrib*, 2:147.

O Umm Saᶜd, in the name of good fortune,
come back.

and

ᶜalā malīkin taḥta l-bunūdi
nūdī,

[and be generous]
with a powerful man who has been called
to the colors.

scanned as × — ⏑ — | — — — | ⏑ — —, that is to say, with a second foot that is not possible in the *basīṭ* meter, namely one lacking the central short syllable.[38] Especially in the *kharja*, which consists of only long syllables, it is most evident that syllabic quantity is irrelevant, because the succession of long/short syllables that makes possible a quantitative metrics has disappeared. So reads the *kharja*:

wāḥid hū yā ʾummī min jīrānī
rānī.[39]

O mother, one of my neighbors
has seen me.

The first of al-Ṣafadī's two poems (no. 26) has five strophes and no prelude, like his model. It begins:

yā fāḍiha l-badri fī l-kamāli
mālī

O thou that outshine the moon in its fullness,
why?

Its *kharja*, said by a woman, in colloquial Arabic, reads:

law kān ᶜuwayqil fī mahrajānī
jā-nī

If he were wise, even a little bit, he would come to me
in my celebration.

The second *muᶜāraḍa* by al-Ṣafadī (*Tawshīᶜ* no. 27) is more of a tour de

38. One can speak, of course, of metrical errors, as Raḥīm (1987, 345–347) does, but I think that poets usually know what they are doing.
39. Also in Corriente 1997, 236.

force. As he tells the reader, one of his friends suggested to him to add a *tawshīḥa*[40] to the previous *muwashshaḥa*. So he added another foot of four syllables after the echo.[41] It is exactly the same poem, but with this extra foot. This is the first section:

yā fāḍiha l-badri fī l-kamāli
mālī
bi-lā manām

O thou that outshine the moon in its fullness,
why
I can't sleep?

The rhyme of this addition (*-ām*) will be, after the first stanza, the common rhyme of the poem, whose rhyme scheme is now (from the second strophe onwards): ccd ccd ccd *mmn*; eef eef eef *mmn*; ggh ggh ggh *mmn*; iij iij iij *mmn* (the first strophe, which should be aab aab aab *mmn*, is really aa*n* aa*n* aa*n* *mmn*). And the *kharja* should be:

law kān ʿuwayqil fī mahrajānī
jā-nī
bi-lā ḥtishām[42]

If he were wise, even a little bit, he would come to me
in my celebration
without reticence.

The next *muwashshaḥa* by Ibn Zuhr that al-Ṣafadī imitated is *Tawshīʿ* no. 28.[43] It is a *muwashshaḥa* with a prelude and five strophes (a a a *m n*). It begins:

ḥayyi l-wujūha l-milāḥā
wa-ḥayyi sūda l-ʿuyūni

40. *Tawshīḥa*, a name derived of *tawshīḥ*, like *muwashshaḥ*, seems to mean in this passage a foot, or a section with rhyme. For *tawshīḥ*, as the second section of a Yemeni *muwashshaḥa*, see Dufour 2011, 119–121.

41. It is problable that al-Ṣafadī was inspired to add this kind of extra foot after the "echo" by a *muwashshaḥa* of Aydamur al-Muḥyawī (d. 674 AH/1275–6 CE) (see al-Ṣafadī, *Al-Wāfī*, 10:8–9), with the same structure, the only difference being the lack of the "echo" in the common rhymes.

42. Albert Muṭlaq, *Tawshīʿ al-tawshīḥ*'s editor, reads: *law kān ʿuwayqil jā-nī / fī mahrajānī / bi-lā ḥtishām* (and surely it is so in the ms., but that does not make sense, metrically speaking, as the meaning does not change).

43. It is a well-known *muwashshaḥa*, included also in Ibn Bishrī, *ʿUddat al-jalīs*, no. 236; in Ibn al-Khaṭīb (d. 776 AH/1375 CE), *Jaysh al-tawshīḥ*, 246–248; in Ibn Saʿīd, *Mughrib*, 1:273; and in Ibn Abī Uṣaybiʿa, *ʿUyūn al-anbāʾ*, 527. See Ghāzī 1979, 2:73–75.

Welcome the beautiful faces
and greet the black eyes.

It ends with a *kharja* in classical Arabic:

marrū wa-ʾakhfaw l-rawāḥā
ʿan-nī wa-mā waddaʿū-nī.[44]

They went away and kept secret their leaving;
so, they did not say farewell.

As for its metrics, we are dealing with a classic of Spanish poetry, the eight-syllable verse of the Spanish ballads (*romances*). In its adaptation to Arabic metrics it can be scanned, as here, as hemistichs of the *mujtathth* meter (× — ᴗ — | × ᴗ — —). Hemistichs of other Arabic meters, such as the dimeter *ramal*, the dimeter *khafīf*, or the dimeter *rajaz*,[45] all of them with eight syllables, may be similarly adapted to Romance meters, and all of them provide an easy form of metrical adaptation. Al-Ṣafadī also appreciated his model's facile transitions in theme, from love to wine to love topics, and his *muʿāraḍa* (*Tawshīʿ* no. 29) is also a fine poem, with six strophes, whose prelude reads:

saqā l-muḥibbīna rāḥā
ṭāfat bi-kaʾsi l-jufūni,

He poured the lovers wine
which overflows the cup of his eyes,

and its *kharja*, in colloquial Arabic, is a girl's complaint of her lover's estrangement:

yā bnī ʿalesh dhī l-waqāḥā
mā la-k kadhā mā tajī-nī

O son, why this impudence,
why don't you come to me?

Al-Ṣafadī collects another *muwashshaḥa* that Ibn Zuhr similarly composed in this Spanish octosyllabic meter (al-Ṣafadī, *Tawshīʿ* no. 41).[46] It is a *muwashshaḥa* with a prelude and five strophes composed with the simple rhyme scheme (a a a *m n*), reminiscent of *Tawshīʿ* no. 28, that begins

44. Also in Corriente 1997, 244.

45. Monroe 1979, 178–179.

46. Ibn Bishrī, *ʿUddat al-jalīs*, no. 289 (Ibn Ḥamdīn); al-Maqqarī, *Nafḥ al-ṭīb*, 2:251–252; Ghāzī 1979, 2:116–117.

sallimi l-ʾamra li-l-qaḍā
fa-hwa li-l-nafsi ʾanfaʿu

Trust in God's will,
that would be more salutary to the soul

and whose classical Arabic *kharja* reads:

nūru-hum dhā lladhī ʾaḍā
ʾam maʿa l-rakbi yūshaʿu

Is their brightness what sheds light,
or have they appeared among the travelers?

But this time the Arabic meter adopted is a dimeter *khafīf* (× ⏑ — — | × — ⏑ —). The poem begins urging the reader/listener to seize the day, and drink and love, and it ends with a melancholic note of separation mitigated by the beauty of the beloved. Naturally, al-Ṣafadī appreciated the poem and he composed two *muʿāraḍāt* based on it, moved by its rhythmic smoothness and grace. The first one, *Tawshīʿ* no. 42, with six strophes, begins

kullu man ʿānada l-qaḍā
biʾsa mā bāta yaṣnaʿu

For every man who fights with Destiny,
all his deeds will be unfortunate.

In its *kharja*, a girl states:

jarra sīdī wa-lā taḍā-
rib fa-li-l-suqfi bā-rfaʿū[47]

Easy, my lord, don't hit me
or I will climb up to the roof.

Al-Ṣafadī introduces his second *muʿāraḍa* (*Tawshīʿ* no. 43) speaking again of his enthusiasm for Ibn Zuhr's poem, but announces that he will make some changes; and, indeed, he has changed the common rhymes of the poem, perhaps because the letter *ḍād* is not an easy rhyme. In this case, though, he does maintain the original five strophes. In the prelude, there is a clear allusion to, and reversal of, another *kharja* by Ibn Zuhr – *Tawshīʿ* no. 28 – in which the poetic voice tells that the loved ones have left without saying goodbye:

47. This is a tentative transcription and translation. I am not sure of how to read this: it could be either *lā taḍārab* or the colloquial *tuḍārib* and with the caesura in the middle.

nazalū fī ṭuwayliʿi
ḥīna sārū wa-waddaʿū

As dawn broke they halted,
then they left and said farewell.

Here the loved ones do say farewell. Further, the *kharja* of al-Ṣafadī's *muʿāraḍa* is in colloquial Arabic, and again put into the mouth of a girl, who tries to console her white-haired lover with a date:

lī ṣugayyar wa-mā yaʿī
qum maʿī tātafazzaʿū

I have a little one that is aware of nothing,
come with me, or you will frighten him.

The most renowned *muwashshaḥa* by Ibn Zuhr among those imitated by al-Ṣafadī is *Tawshīʿ* no. 37,[48] a *muwashshaḥa* with a prelude and five strophes (a a a *m n*). It begins with this prelude:

ʾayyuhā l-sāqī ʾilay-ka l-mushtakā
qad daʿawnā-ka wa-ʾin lam tasmaʿī

O cupbearer, our complaints are addressed to you;
we have called upon you though you do not listen!

and its classical Arabic *kharja* reads:

qad namā ḥubbī bi-qalbī wa-zakā
lā takhal fī l-ḥubbi ʾannī muddaʿī

My love for you has grown and increased.
Do not proclaim in matters of love: "I am a claimant!"[49]

Ibn Sanāʾ al-Mulk quotes this poem in *Dār al-ṭirāz* as an example of *muwashshaḥ shiʿrī* (adapted to the Arabic meters). In fact, it can be scanned as a *ramal* meter (× ◡ — — | × ◡ — — | × ◡ —)[50] and, although he has criticized *muwashshaḥāt* composed in Arabic prosody, he justified those that have different rhymes in the two parts of the *aqfāl*, like this one, because in doing so they differ from the common rhymes of the *mukhammasāt*.[51] Per-

48. Ibn Abī Uṣaybiʿa, *ʿUyūn al-anbāʾ*, 526; Ibn Bishrī, *ʿUddat al-jalīs*, no. 284; Ibn al-Khaṭīb, *Jaysh al-tawshīḥ*, 248–249; Ghāzī 1979, 2:76–78; Monroe 1974, 288–291.

49. Both translations by Monroe 1974, 288, 290.

50. One might also scan it, of course, as an eleven-syllable verse in Romance metrics, another classic of this prosody.

51. Ibn Sanāʾ al-Mulk, *Dār al-ṭirāz*, 33 and 73–74 (no. 25); García Gómez 1962, 50, 91–92.

haps, this meter, being specially linked to the music,[52] may be credited with its success.

Tawshīʿ no. 38 is al-Ṣafadī's *muʿāraḍa* of this *muwashshaḥa*, and he also informs his readers that its elegant manner of composition was imitated by many Andalusī poets. The poem opens with this prelude:

halaka l-ṣabbu l-muʿannā hal la-kā
fī talāfī-hi bi-waʿdin muṭmaʿi

The sorrowful lover is dying; why don't you
render justice to him as promised?

and again, its colloquial *kharja* is a girl's words:

kullu mā qālū ʿalimtū bi-l-dhakā
al-ḥadīth li-k wa-nti yā jāra smaʿī

I am familiar with the flavor of all that he said,
listen to his words, O girlfriend.

But Ibn Zuhr's *muwashshaḥa*, on which al-Ṣafadī based the above poem, was actually also a *muʿāraḍa*,[53] and his model was a poem of Ibn Baqī, one of the best *muwashshaḥ* authors of the Almoravid period. Ibn Baqī's *muwashshaḥa*, is also a love poem and begins:

galaba l-shawqu bi-qalbī fa-shtakā
ʾalama l-waŷdi fa-labbat ʾadmuʿī,

Desire has conquered my heart; and now
if it complains of the sufferings of love, my tears will respond.

and ends with this classical Arabic *kharja*:

lam ʾajid li-l-ṣabri ʿan-hu maslakā
fa-ntiṣārī bi-nsikābi l-ʾadmuʿi.[54]

I don't find a way to be patient,
my only victory is to let my tears flow.

Nevertheless, it is Ibn Zuhr's *muwashshaḥa*, not Ibn Baqī's, that is the model for later *muʿāraḍāt*, including the one by al-Ṣafadī. But the first imitation of this poem preserved is an ascetic poem by the *Ṣūfī* master Ibn ʿArabī (Murcia 560 AH/1165 CE- Damascus 638 AH/1240 CE),[55] whose prelude is

52. Stoetzer 2012; Stoetzer 1989, 61–73; Frolov 1999, chapter five.
53. García Gómez 1962, 92.
54. Al-Maqqarī, *Nafḥ al-ṭīb*, 4:237–238.
55. ʿInānī 1980, 66–67.

ʿindamā lāḥa li-ʿaynī l-muttakā
ḏubtu shawqan li-l-laḏī kāna maʿī

when the throne appeared to my eyes
I melted with desire for he who was with me.

Its *kharja* reads:

ʾayyu-hā l-sāqī ʾilay-ka l-mushtakā
ḍaʿati l-shakwā ʾiḏā lam yanfaʿi,

O cupbearer, our complaints are addressed to you;
the complaint is lost if it is of no use.

This *kharja* quotes the very beginning of Ibn Zuhr's poem, identifying the latter as the model *muwashshaḥa's* author, a rule of sorts in this kind of poem.[56] In such a quotation in this section, the poet must show, as Ibn ʿArabī has done, his atonement and ask God's forgiveness for his predecessor.

In addition to the *muʿāraḍa* of Ibn ʿArabī, there were other *muʿāraḍāt* of "ʾAyyuhā l-sāqī ʾilay-ka l-mushtakā." One was composed by Aydamur al-Muḥyawī (d. 674 AH/1275–6 CE), an Egyptian poet. It is a panegyric poem, with six strophes; its prelude is:

ʿahida l-baynu ʾilā ʿaynī l-bukā
thumma ʾawṣā-hā bi-ʾan lā tahjaʿī[57]

Separation made my eyes cry,
then urged them to be calm.

and its *kharja:*

wa-hwa fī l-māli kathīru l-shurakā
wa-mina l-ḥamdi kathīru l-shiyaʿi

He helps many people with his wealth,
and there are many poets who want to praise him.

56. Ibn Sanāʾ al-Mulk, *Dār al-ṭirāz*, 38; García Gómez 1962, 62. Ibn Sanā`al-Mulk, in his instructions, says that the ascetic *muwashshaḥ* (*mukaffir*) has to be composed following the rhythm of a known *muwashshaḥa* and to follow the *aqfāl* rhymes of that *muwashshaḥa*, and the *kharja* of the *muwashshaḥa* being imitated must be put at the end; that is to say, it is always a *contrafactum*. Ibn ʿArabī quotes not the *kharja*, but its prelude (as noted by Monroe 1986, 14), as this is the easier way to identify a poem in Arabic poetry, namely, quoting its first line.

57. Raḥīm 1987, 162, quotes this prelude from *Mukhtār Dīwān ʿAlam al-Dīn Aydamur al-Muḥyawī*, 31. The date of Aydamur's death was provided by Raḥīm, but it is not found in Ibn Taghrī Birdī, *Al-Manhal al-ṣāfī*, 3:172–176, nor al-Ṣafadī, *Al-Wāfī bi-l-wafayāt*, 10:6–11. His *muwashshaḥa* can also be found in these biographical dictionaries.

The next poet to write a *muʿāraḍa* of Ibn Zuhr's poem is ʿIzz al-Dīn al-Mawṣilī (d. 689 AH/1290 CE),[58] and his *muwashshaḥa* begins:

qum fa-ʾinna l-kaʾsa ʾaḍḥā falakā
wa-ḥabābu l-rāḥi shuhbu ṭalaʿi

Get up; now the cup is the sky,
and the bubbles of wine are the rising stars.

The last *muʿāraḍāt* of "ʾAyyuhā l-sāqī ʾilay-ka l-mushtakā" known to me are two poems by Muḥammad Saʿīd al-Ḥabbūbī (1850–1915), an Iraqi neoclassical poet[59] and a Shīʿa leader (*mujtahid*), a fighter against the British occupation of Iraq, who died in the aftermath of the battle of Shuʿayba (1915).[60] Both are very long *muwashshaḥāt*, [61] much longer than the five to seven strophes, as described by Ibn Sanāʾ al-Mulk or Ibn Khaldūn (732–84 AH/ 1332–82 CE) as ideal for the *muwashshaḥa* form, though it is not very surprising, given that al-Ḥabbūbī is a modern poet. But, as these *muwashshaḥāt* do not reflect the common rhymes used in Ibn Zuhr's poem, only the editor's commentaries guide the reader to the fact that his model is Ibn Zuhr's *muwashshaḥa*. As for the metrics, all of al-Ḥabbūbī's *muwashshaḥāt* - which number only ten - are composed in the *ramal* meter.

Beside Ibn Zuhr, the most imitated Andalusī poet in *Tawshīʿ al-tawshīḥ* is al-Aʿmā al-Tuṭīlī (the Blind Man of Tudela), the best *muwashshaḥ* author, in addition to Ibn Baqī, of the Almoravid period. Three of his *muwashshaḥāt* have been imitated in al-Ṣafadī's anthology. But only two are actually quoted. *Tawshīʿ* no. 3, by Aḥmad b. Ḥasan al-Mawṣilī, is in fact a *muʿāraḍa* of the most famous of al-Aʿmā's strophic poems, which begins *Ḍāḥikun ʿan jumān* (Laughing out of pearls).[62] The odd thing is that al-Ṣafadī collects three *muʿāraḍāt* of the poem, composed by three different poets, one of them his own poem, although he does not identify al-Aʿmā's as their model. Ibn Sanāʾ al-Mulk quotes al-Aʿmā's poem as a sample of *muwashshaḥ tāmm* (with a prelude),

58. Raḥīm 1987, 162, who provides this date as his death's; but the only famous poet with the name of ʿIzz al-Dīn al-Mawṣilī that I was able to find died in 789 AH/1387 CE (Ibn Ḥajar al-ʿAsqalānī [773–852 AH/1372–1449 CE], *Al-Durar al-kāmina fī aʿyān al-miʾa al-thāmina*, 3:43). Raḥīm's source is *Al-Durr al-maknūn fī al-sabʿa funūn*, by Ibn Iyās al-Ḥanafī (d. 930 AH/1523–4 CE). I did not see the complete poem.

59. Moreh 1988, 32, n. 3.

60. Nakash 2006, chapter 1.

61. Al-Ḥabbūbī 1983, 145–155, and 229–236. The first of al-Ḥabbūbī's *muʿarāḍāt* begins: *yā maqīla l-sarbi fī ẓilli l-ʾarāk* (O resting place for the herd at the shadow of the arāk tree); the second one: *halhalat bi-l-bushri warqāʾu l-hanā* (the grey dove of celebration sings this happy news).

62. Al-Aʿmā al-Tuṭīlī, *Dīwān*, 253–254; Ghāzī 1979, 1:247–250; Monroe 1974, 252–255.

and Ibn Bishrī and Ibn al-Khaṭīb both include it in their anthologies, as does Ibn Saᶜīd al-Maghribī in *Kitāb al-muqtaṭaf* (quoted by Ibn Khaldūn and al-Maqqarī [b. circa 986-d. 1041 AH/ 1577–1632 CE]). [63] It has five strophes, and its rhyme scheme is ab ab ab *mn mn*. Its six syllables for each rhymed section render the Khalīlian metrics useless. Its prelude reads:

ḍāḥikun ᶜan jumān
sāfirun ᶜan badri
ḍāqa ᶜan-hu l-zamān
wa-ḥawā-hu ṣadrī

Laughing out of pearls,
A full moon appears
Surpassing all Time
Though held in my heart.

Its *kharja* is in a colloquial Arabic very close to classical Arabic, lacking only some vowels of *iᶜrāb*:

qad raʾaytak ᶜayyān
lays ᶜalayk sā-tadrī
sā-yaṭūlu l-zamān
wa-sa-tansā dhikrī.[64]

I see that you're pining;
I say, "What's with you, man?"
You know Time will pass
And you will forget me.[65]

Instead of quoting al-Aᶜmā's poem, al-Ṣafadī has included the *muwashshaḥa* of Aḥmad b. Ḥasan al-Mawṣilī,[66] a Syrian poet (*Tawshīᶜ* no. 3) emulating that of al-Aᶜmā. It is a panegyric poem in which this al-Mawṣilī eulogizes the Ayyūbī ruler of Ḥamā. The prelude of this poem is:

bāsimun ᶜan laʾāl
nāsimun ᶜan ᶜiṭri
nāfirun ka-l-ghazāl
sāfirun ka-l-badri

63. Ibn Sanāʾ al- Mulk, *Dār al-ṭirāz*, 25, and 43–4 (no. 1); García Gómez 1962, 33 (no. 6), 65–66. Ibn al-Bishrī, *ᶜUddat al-jalīs*, no. 97; Ibn al-Khaṭīb, *Jaysh al-tawshīḥ*, 19–21; Ibn Saᶜīd, *Mughrib*, 2:453. Ibn Saᶜīd, *Kitāb al-muqtaṭaf min azāhir al-ṭuraf*, 256; see also Al-Ahwānī 1948.

64. Also in Corriente 1997, 172.

65. Both translations by Monroe 1974, 252, 254.

66. Al-Ṣafadī, *Al-Wāfī*, 6:199–205; Ibn Taghrī Birdī, *Al-Manhal al-ṣāfī*, 1:266–277; Raḥīm 1987, 153–154.

Smiling out of pearls,
redolent of perfume,
shy as a gazelle,
bareface like the moon.

Here it is easy to see how a relatively simple and unadorned poem can be the basis for a more contrived one. In al-Aʿmā's poem the paradigm for the active participle *fāʿil* (*ḍāḥikun, sāfirun*, etc.) only appears twice, while al-Mawṣilī has found it easier to repeat this form, in order to follow the rhythm. He uses the *fāʿil* form four times in the prelude, but also in the common rhymes (*aqfāl*) of strophes one (twice) and two (four times). The *kharja*, in classical Arabic and without transition, states

farʿu-hu ka-l-layāl
farqu-hu ka-l-fajri
ḥirtu bayna l-ḍalāl
wa-l-hudā fī ʾamrī

His hair is like the night,
his front like the dawn;
and I am confused
between right and wrong.

The *qāḍī* Shihāb al-Dīn Aḥmad b. Faḍl Allāh asked al-Ṣafadī and Jamāl al-Dīn Yūsuf al-Ṣūfī al-Khaṭīb (d. 750 AH/1349 CE)[67] to imitate this poem.

Tawshīʿ no. 4 is the *muʿāraḍa* that Jamāl al-Dīn al-Ṣūfī composed in response to the *qāḍī*'s request. It consists of seven strophes – not five like its model. Its prelude, like that of al-Mawṣilī's poem, plays on the *fāʿil* paradigm:

zāʾirun bi-l-jayāl
zāʾilun ʿan qurbī
bāhirun bi-l-jamāl
māhirun bi-l-ʿujbi

He came to me in my dreams,
because he is not with me,
splendid in his beauty,
filling me with delight.

Its *kharja*, also in classical Arabic, does not have a transition but it is a short dialogue between poet and beloved:

67. Raḥīm 1987, 210–211.

ṣadda tīhan wa-qāl
wa-hwa yabghī ḥarbī
laḥẓu ʿaynī nibāl
qultu ʾāh wā-qalbī.

He turned away in pride, and said
seeking to fight with me:
"My glances are arrows."
I said: "Ah! my poor heart!"

On the other hand, Al-Ṣafadī's *muʿāraḍa, Tawshīʿ* no. 5, maintains the five-strophe format, and all the rhymes of its model, Aḥmad b. Ḥasan al-Mawṣilī's *muwashshaḥa* – even though such fidelity to form was not at all necessary in an imitation. Perhaps this is the reason why al-Ṣafadī boasts about his prowess.[68] But nevertheless his poem seems less contrived than the previous one by Jamāl al-Dīn because, save in the prelude, he does not repeat such a characteristic paradigm.

jāmiḥun fī l-dalāl
jāniḥun li-l-hajri
khāṭirun fī l-jamāl
ʿāṭirun fī l-nashri,

Defiant in his coquetry,
inclined to part company,
he walks dressed in his beauty,
fragrant with perfume

Its *kharja*, in classical Arabic and without transition, continues the beloved's description:

jafnu-hu ḥīna ṣāl
fī khabāyā ṣadrī
law kafā-nī l-nibāl
la-ktafā bi-l-siḥri

His eyes, when they assail,
pierce my heart;
their charm will be enough
if their arrows spared me.

In *Tawshīʿ* no. 30 we have almost the reverse. Al-Ṣafadī presents a new *muwashshaḥa* by al-Aʿmā al-Tuṭīlī, but only alludes to the existence of anoth-

68. Al-Ṣafadī, *Al-Wāfī*, 6:200.

er *muʿāraḍa* before presenting his own poem. Al-Aʿmā's *muwashshaḥa* is again a well- known poem,[69] especially interesting because of its Romance *kharja*.[70] It has a more complicated metrical scheme: its *aqfāl* (common rhymes) have three sections, the first and third with eleven syllables, and the second with four syllables, as can be seen in the prelude:

damʿun safūḥun wa-ḍulūʿun ḥarār
māʾun wa-nār
mā ŷtamaʿā ʾillā li-ʾamrin kubār,

Pouring eyes and passionate heart,
water and fire,
only come together when matters are serious,

However, in this poem the *aghṣān*, the lines whose rhymes change in every strophe, have four sections or lines, and all are hendecasyllabic. The rhyme scheme of the poem's five strophes is a a a a *m m m*, b b b b *m m m*, etc. The scansion of the long sections is: — — ᴗ — | — ᴗ ᴗ — | — ᴗ —, that is to say, a *sarīʿ* meter; and with its four occurrences (in every *ghuṣn*) it is really similar to an Arabic meter of a regular *qaṣīda*, the monorhymic poem of classical Arabic poetry, a long line with caesura. In fact, it is printed in al-Aʿmā's *Dīwān* in this classical format. Even the section of four syllables is a foot admitted in Arabic prosody, × — ᴗ —, the basic foot of *rajaz* and other meters of its family, like *sarīʿ* for instance. The poem's *kharja*, as read by García Gómez,[71] is

me-w l-ḥabīb enfermo ḏē mew ʾamār
¿ké no a d'eshtār?
¿non fés a mībe ke sh'a ḏe nō legār?

My beloved loves me to distraction.
How can he be any other way?
Don't you see that he cannot come to me?

Like al-Aʿmā's imitation, Al-Ṣafadī's, *Tawshīʿ* no. 31, which has six strophes, is a love poem and begins:

69. Al-Aʿmā al-Tuṭīlī, *Dīwān*, 261–2; Ibn Bishrī, *ʿUddat al-jalīs*, no. 124; Ibn al-Khaṭīb, *Jaysh al-tawshīḥ*, 26–28; Ghāzī 1979, 1:261–262.

70. García Gómez 1990, 139–143 (no. 8).

71. García Gómez's translation in modern Spanish is: «Mi amigo [está] enfermo de mi amor. / ¿Cómo no ha de estar[lo]? / ¿No ves que a mí no se ha de acercar?» (My beloved is lovesick / How could he not be? / Can't you see, he can not come near me?). García Gómez 1990, 142. Al-Ṣafadī seems more daring than Ibn Sanāʾ al-Mulk, who never quotes a *muwashshaḥa* with a Romance *kharja*.

sāla ʿalā l-khaddayni min-hu l-ʿidhār
wa-mā stadār
mā ʾaḥsana l-rayḥāna fī l-jullanār.

On his cheeks blooms the down
which overflows them.
How beautiful is the myrtle on the pomegranate blossom.

Its *kharja*, in colloquial Arabic, is put in the mouth of a woman who complains to her neighbors about the jealousy of her husband:

taʿā bṣurū mā ṣab-nī dhā l-nahār
qāl hū yaghār
wa-ṭūlu ʿumrū mithla tays mustaʿār.

Come and see what happened to me today:
he said that he will watch me closely,
and he is always like a billy goat!

Al-Ṣafadī's *muwashshaḥa* is not the first *muʿāraḍa* of al-Aʿmā's poem. As he himself points out (*Tawshīʿ*, 109), another Eastern poet, Shihāb al-Dīn al-ʿAzāzī (633–710 AH/1235–1310 CE),[72] had composed a poem emulating that of al-Aʿmā, with this prelude:

yā laylata l-waṣli wa-kaʾsa l-ʿuqār
dūna stitār
ʿallamtumā-nī kayfa khalʿu l-ʿiḏār.

O night of love, O glass of wine,
without being veiled,
both of you had taught to me to throw off all restraint.

Al-Ṣafadī does not quote the complete *muwashshaḥa* by al-ʿAzāzī in this anthology, but he does so in *Al-Wāfī bi-l-wafayāt*.[73] It is a love poem, like that of al-Aʿmā, also with five strophes, and its *kharja*, in classical Arabic and in the first person, says:

yā laylatan ʾanʿama fī-hā wa-zār
shamsu l-nahār
ḥuyyīti min bayni l-layālī l-qiṣār.

72. Al-ʿAzāzī, born in Syria but living as a merchant in Cairo, is a poet much appreciated by al-Ṣafadī, who included him in his two biographical dictionaries (*al-Wāfī bi-l-wafayāt* and *Aʿyān al-ʿaṣr*), and chose one of his *muwashshaḥāt* (*Tawshīʿ* no. 19) to emulate (*Tawshīʿ* no. 20).

73. Al-Ṣafadī, *Al-Wāfī*, 7:102–103; also in Ibn Taghrī Birdī, *Al-Manhal al-ṣāfī*, 1:365–367; and al-Maqqarī, *Nafḥ al-ṭīb*, 7:89–90.

O night, how fortunate you are. The morning sun
has come to you.
May God preserve you between so many short nights!

But this poem does not have the same structure as al-Aʿmā al-Tuṭīlī's *muwashshaḥa*, because its *aghṣān*, the sections whose rhymes change in every strophe, has only three lines, not the four of both al-Aʿmā's and al-Ṣafadī's poems. Therefore, it is likely that al-ʿAzāzī is imitating another poem with a very similar structure, but not identical with the other two. Al-Ṣafadī himself gives a clue, because in his biography of al-ʿAzāzī he comments that this *muwashshaḥa* is a *muʿāraḍa* of a poem by Aḥmad b. Ḥasan al-Mawṣilī, another favorite author of al-Ṣafadī already quoted in *Tawshīʿ al-tawshīḥ* as an imitator of al-Aʿmā al-Tuṭīlī (*Tawshīʿ* no. 3). And in fact, in *Al-Wāfī bi-l-wafayāt*, his biographical dictionary, al-Ṣafadī includes among Aḥmad al-Mawṣilī's poems[74] the one that elicited al-ʿAzāzī's imitation. It has only three lines in its *aghṣān*, as does al-ʿAzāzī's. It is also a love and wine poem of six strophes, whose prelude says,

bī ḥārisun fī khaddi-hi l-jullanār
ʿalā l-bahār
bi-narjisi l-ṭarfi wa-ʾāsi l-ʿidhār.

The narcissus of his eyes and the myrtle of his down
prevent me from picking
in his cheeks the pomegranate blossoms over the lilies.

Its *kharja*, in classical Arabic, is an extension of the cupbearer's description:

shabbahtu-hu lammā ʿalay-nā ʾadār
kaʾsa l-ʿuqār
badra l-dujā yasʿā bi-shamsi l-nahār.[75]

He is, when he moves around us
with the cup of wine,
like a full moon in the dark that holds the morning sun.

Both Eastern poets – al-Mawṣilī and his imitator al-ʿAzāzī – have chosen to compose the *kharjas* of their poems in classical Arabic, avoiding the problems that use of an unfamiliar language could create. Al-Ṣafadī, sticking to the rule of code-switching as proposed by Ibn Sanāʾ al-Mulk, even when he

74. Al-Ṣafadī, *Al-Wāfī*, 6:199–205.
75. Al-Ṣafadī, *Al-Wāfī*, 6:204–205.

knows that many of his contemporary colleagues do not follow it, did compose his in colloquial Arabic.[76]

And again, although al-Ṣafadī seems to ignore this, the poem by Aḥmad al-Mawṣilī imitates an Andalusī *muwashshaḥa* that probably was also the source for al-Aʿmā al-Tuṭīlī's poem, namely a poem by Ibn al-Labbāna (d. 507 AH/1113 CE), one of the poets of Seville's ruler al-Muʿtamid (d. 487 AH/1095 CE). Ibn al-Labbāna begins his *muwashshaḥa*, a praise poem celebrating al-Maʾmūn (r. 435–467 AH/1043–1075 CE), Toledo's ruler, with an encomium of his two pleasures, love and wine,[77]

> *hayyā, ʿadhūlī! Qad khalaʿtu l-ʿidhār*
> *bi-lā ʾiqṣār*
> *ʿan ẓibāʾi*[78] *l-insi wa-sharbi l-ʿuqār*
>
> *Come on, O my rebuker, I have thrown off all restraint*
> *and I don't stop*
> *from loving human gazelles and drinking wine.*

He then follows his eulogy of the Party-King (strophes 3 and 4), and in the fifth strophe suddenly he introduces a girl by the sea who cries in pain because of separation from her beloved. In the *kharja*,[79] a Romance one like that by al-Aʿmā, the girl says,

> *yā qoražōnī, ke kéresh bōn ʿamār!*
> *a liyorār*
> *laita[-nī ʾobiese] weliyosh de mār.*
>
> *O my heart who wants a good love;*
> *in order to cry,*
> *I wish my eyes had all the water of the sea.*

This same structure, but with different rhymes, can be found in at least two other Andalusī *muwashshaḥāt*. That is to say, every strophe has three lines in the *aghṣān* (a a a), all of them with eleven syllables, conforming to the *sarīʿ* meter of Arabic metrics; and, in the *aqfāl*, three lines of different length (11-4-11 syllables) and the same rhyme (*m m m*). Both of the poems

76. Al-Ṣafadī, *Tawshīʿ al-tawshīḥ*, 29.

77. Ibn al-Khaṭīb, *Jaysh al-tawshīḥ*, 1997, 78–79; Ghāzī 1979, 1:229–231; García Gómez 1990, 319–324 (no. 29); Hadjadji 1997, 106–109.

78. This is García Gómez's transliteration, based on the manuscripts of *Jaysh al-tawshīḥ* (*ẓibā*); Ghāzī reads *ẓabyati*, in accordance with the supposed *sarīʿ* meter of the poem.

79. I follow García Gómez's transliteration, 1990, 323; his Spanish translation is: «¡Ay, corazón mío, que quieres buen amar!/ ¡Para llorar / ojalá tuviese los ojos del mar!» (Oh, my love, who wants to love well! If only you had eyes [as deep as] the sea for crying!).

have five strophes. The most famous, because its author is one of the most successful poets of al-Andalus, is that by Ibn Sahl (d. 649 AH/1251 CE), whose prelude is:

bākir ʾilā l-ladhdhati wa-li-ṣṭibāḥ
bi-shurbi rāḥ
fa-mā ʿalā ʾahli l-hawā min junāḥ,[80]

Take the enjoyments and an early drink
of wine;
there shall be no sin for the lovers.

and its *kharja*, in classical Arabic, in the first person,

ʾamā tarā-nī qad ṭaraḥtu l-silāḥ
ʾayya ṭṭirāḥ
ʾaḥlā l-hawā mā kāna bi-l-iftiḍāḥ.

Don't you see that I have thrown off my weapons
without exception?
All the sweetness of love is in humility.

The second example that follows the structure of Ibn al-Labbāna's *muwashshsaḥa* is an anonymous *muwashshsaḥa* in Ibn Bishrī's anthology.[81] It is a love poem that begins:

yā ṭāʾira l-bānati kam dhā l-niyāḥ
ʾilfu-ka rāḥ
ʾam hazza ʿiṭfay-ka nasīmu l- ṣabāḥ,

O bird on the willow, what a sad cooing.
Has your lover parted,
or is the breeze of the morning moving your heart?

and ends with a *kharja*, in classical Arabic in the first person, claiming that wine and disgrace are licit in love:

yā sāqiya l-khamri ʾadir-hā ṣurāḥ
fa-l-iftiḍāḥ
fī wuddi man ʾahwā mubāḥun mubāḥ.

O cupbearer, serve a pure wine;
disgrace
in loving my beloved is absolutely right.

80. Ibn Sahl al-Isrāʾīlī, 1985, 437–438 (*muwashshaḥa* no. 7). Ibn Sahl de Sevilla 1996, no. 37.
81. Ibn Bishrī, *ʿUddat al-jalīs*, no. 55.

It seems probable that one of these poems with the same structure as Ibn al-Labbāna's was a *muʿāraḍa*, an imitation, of the other one, but it is difficult to say which one is the original poem.

There are also other poems with their common rhymes exactly like the *aqfāl* of these two. Al-Maqqarī, when dealing with Ibn al-Khaṭīb's strophic poems, quotes the prelude of a famous *muwashshaḥa* (known by its first verse) – so famous that he does not give its author's name:

banafsaju l-layli tadhakkā wa-fāḥ
bayna l-biṭāḥ
ka-ʾanna-hu yasqī bi-miskin wa-rāḥ.[82]

The violets of the night spread and difuse their fragance
in the valleys,
it is as if they were bathed with musk and wine.

Although al-Maqqarī does not provide the entire poem, one of its strophes has survived in *Kunnāsh al-Ḥāʾik* of Muḥammad al-Andalusī al-Tiṭwānī al-Ḥāʾik (twelfth AH/eighteenth century CE),[83] the great compilation of Andalusian Arab songs still preserved in Morocco. After that prelude, the only preserved stanza says,

wa-l-shuhbu yushbihna kuʾūsa l-mudīr
ʿalā ghadīr
laysa bi-dhī mawjin wa-lā hadīr
wa-lā kadīr
mustaʿriḍan bi-l-ufqi wa-mustadīr
ṣunʿa l-qadīr
tafattaḥat fī l-shaṭṭi min-hu ʾaqāḥ
dārat wishāḥ
ka-l-sawsani l-ghaḍḍi tamāma l-liqāḥ.

The stars are like the cups of wine
upon a pond
without waves, and without noise,
never turbid,
showing in the sky all around
the works of the Almighty.
The camomiles open their flowers on the bank
encircling the pond like a belt,
they seem like fresh lilies in bloom.

82. Al-Maqqarī, *Nafḥ al-ṭīb*, 7:86.
83. Al-Ḥāʾik 1999, 271–272 (no. 221).

This strophe shows a combination of eleven and four syllables, and it suggests a later elaboration of a pattern basically equal to that by Ibn Sahl or, even before, that by Ibn al-Labbāna: three members or sections in the *aghṣān*. But in this *muwashshaḥa*, the author added another foot of four syllables like in the *qufl*, with the same rhyme as the long segments, so that the structure is: aa aa aa *m m m* (11-4-11-4-11-4- *11-4-11*). [84]

According to al-Maqqarī this poem, "Banafsaju l-layl," had at least two imitations. One, by Ibn al-Khaṭīb, begins,

qad ḥarraka l-juljula bāzī l-ṣabāḥ
wa-l-fajru lāḥ
fa-yā ghurāba l-layli ḥuththa l-janāḥ.

The hawk of the morning stirred the little bell,
and the dawn broke;
O crow of the night, spread your wings now and go away.

Al-Maqqarī informs us that he thinks that Ibn al-Khaṭīb's *muwashshaḥa* is an excellent poem, but he cannot quote it in its entirety because he has left his books behind, in the Maghreb, before leaving for Egypt.[85] So it is not known how many segments of its *aghṣān* there were or what they or their rhymes were like. In other words, it is impossible to tell if the four-syllable foot has the same rhyme of the long segments, as in "Banafsaj al-layl."

The next *muwashshaḥa* quoted by al-Maqqarī, as an imitation of "Banafsaj al-layl," is that of Ibn Nubāta (Cairo 686–768 AH/1268–1366 CE),[86] a well-known writer of poetry and prose, and the author of a commentary of *Al-Risāla al-hazliyya* by Ibn Zaydūn (394–473 AH/1003–1070 CE), whose poems were frequently imitated in Arabic poetry until the twentieth century.[87]

84. There is another *muwashshsaḥa* with a similar structure (Ibn Bishrī, *ʿUddat al-jalīs*, no. 184), but its common rhymes are different. Its prelude is *ẓabyun nafūrun wa-muḥibbun dhalīl / ḥāra l-dalīl / ʿalay-ka yā qalbī bi-ṣabrin jamīl*) (Shy gazelle and submissive lover, / what a confusing affair! / O my sad heart, be more enduring). It rhymes in *-īl* instead of *-āḥ*. It has also an extra four-syllable foot in its *aghṣān* (which is only three lines), with the same rhyme as the long section (aa aa aa *m m m*).

85. Al-Maqqarī (b. Tlemcen, Algeria 986- d. Cairo 1041 AH /1577–1632 CE), composed his great history of al-Andalus and its literature, *Al-Nafḥ al-ṭīb*, in Egypt as a frame to his study of the life and works of Ibn al-Khaṭīb, the most brilliant author of the Nasrid Granada, the last Muslim kingdom of Spain.

86. Rikabi 2012.

87. Ghazāl (2004) has collected sixty-nine *muʿāraḍāt* of Ibn Zaydūn's poems, most of them emulating his *qaṣīda* rhyming in letter *nūn*, addressed to princess Wallāda. This most famous poem has been imitated by fifty-two authors, from the eleventh century onwards. At least two of them are formally *muwashshaḥāt*, one by the Egyptian Ibn Wakīl (665–716 AH/1266–1316 CE) (al-Maqqarī, *Naḥf al-ṭīb*, 1:632–634) (Ghazāl 2004, 251–252); and the other one by the Lebanese playwright Ibrāhīm al-Aḥdab (1826–1891 CE). Ghazāl 2004, 38–41.

Ibn Nubāta's poem begins,[88]

mā saḥḥa muḥmarru dumūʿī wa-sāḥ
ʿalā l-milāḥ
ʾillā wa-fī qalbī l-muʿannā jirāḥ.

The eyes don't overflow and run red tears
because of the beautiful beloved,
except when my worried heart is hurt.

Al-Maqqarī cites the complete *muwashshaḥa*, so it is possible to see its structure. Its *aghṣān*, with four sections – one more than "Banafsaj al-layl," which has only three – have this extra foot of four syllables, like "Banafsaj al-layl." However, unlike that poem, it has a different rhyme in the long segments, save in strophe 4. So, its structure is ab ab ab ab *m m m*. It has five strophes, and its *kharja*, in the mouth of the lover, uses colloquial Arabic. Its complete fifth strophe, with its *kharja* reads:

Wa-mughramin lā yakhtashī min raqīb
wa-lā ʿadhūl
muʿallaqi l-qalbi bi-shajwin ʿajīb
wa-lā wuṣūl
yaskaru lākin bi-ṣifāti l-ḥabīb
lā bi-l-shamūl
lammā ranā l-ẓabyu wa-māsa l-qaḍīb
ʾaḍhā yaqūl:
kam yantaḍī jafnak wa-ʿiṭfak ṣifāḥ
ʿalā rimāḥ
mā dhī maḥāsin dhī khazāyin silāḥ.

How many times a lover who doesn't fear a warden
or a censor,
whose heart is full of strange sorrows
cannot reach his love!
How many times has he been drunk with the beauty of his beloved,
not with cool wine!
When the gazelle gazed and the twig swung,
he began to say:
"*How often your eyes and your fine figure have unsheathed*
sword and spear!
What a beauty and what deadly weapons!"

As can be seen, al-Aʿmā's *muwashshaḥa* "Damʿun safūḥun wa-ḍulūʿun

88. Al-Maqqarī, *Nafḥ al-ṭīb*, 7:86–88.

ḥarār" (*Tawshīʿ* no. 30), the second poem by al-Aʿmā that al-Ṣafadī imitates in his anthology, is part of a family of very successful poems, despite its sophisticated structure. No less than nine other *muwashshaḥāt* are related to it.

The last of al-Aʿmā's *muwashshsaḥāt* in al-Ṣafadī's anthology is *Tawshīʿ* no. 35.[89] It has not survived in another Arabic source. It is a love poem with five strophes and a four-line *aghṣān* (a a a a m n). Its prelude, complaining of the beloved's absence, and playing with the topic of his image appearing in dreams, says:

yā nāziḥa l-dāri sal khayālak
yunbī-ka ʾan ṣirtu ka-l-khayāli

O thou away from home, ask your image in my dreams,
it will announce to you that I am now as disembodied as you are.

And its *kharja*, in the first person, is an amiable answer to the beloved's jealousy:

ʿAlī ḥabībī khaṭar bi-bālak
ʾannī bi-gayrak shagaltu bālī.[90]

ʿAlī, my beloved, what has pushed you to believe
that another love distracts me from you?

The poem, all of whose lines are decasyllabic, can also be scanned as a *basīṭ* meter (× — ⏑ — | — ⏑ — | ⏑ — —) (*al-basīṭ al-mukhallaʿ*); and this, in addition to its having four sections in the *aghṣān*, renders it a very easy poem to imitate, notwithstanding two metrical irregularities in lines 2 and 3 of the first strophe.

Tawshīʿ 36 is al-Ṣafadī's *muʿāraḍa*, also a love poem. It is longer – six strophes – and more abundant in rhetorical devices than his model, because, fascinated by the paronomasia (*tajnīs*) or pun of both the prelude and *kharja* in al-Aʿmā's *muwashshaḥa*, he has extended it to all the rhymes of the *aqfāl* (*ghāla-k/ ghālī, ghazāla-k/ ghazā lī, khāla-k/ khālī, bāla-k/ bālī*, and *ḥalā la-k/ ḥalālī*). He also used it in the rhymes of the prelude:

yā qāmata l-ghuṣni man ʾamālak
mā liya fī l-dhulli min ʾāmālī,

O tender bough, who makes you swing?
In the humility of love I have no hopes.

and the colloquial Arabic *kharja*:

89. Ghāzī 1979, 1:312–314.
90. See also Corriente 1997, 211.

hādhā nta ḥanayta l-yawma wā-lak
qaṭṭu l-maḥabbah kānat bi-wālī.

This is what you wished today, alas!
Love never has any power.

But again, Arabic quantitative metrics appears to be irrelevant in this case because al-Ṣafadī's poem exhibits more metrical irregularities – in strophes 1, 2, 4, and 6, and, of course its *kharja* – than in al-Aʿmā's *muwashshaḥa*. But while they do not affect a stress-syllabic metrics, they do affect the succession of long and short syllables of a quantitative metrics.[91]

It is interesting that *Tawshīʿ* no. 39, a *muwashshsaḥa* by Ibn al-Labbāna – and its *muʿāraḍā* by al-Ṣafadī (*Tawshīʿ* no. 40) – is also a poem in decasyllabic verses, but if scanned according to Arabic quantitative metrics, conforms to the *madīd* meter, not to the *al-basīṭ al-mukhallaʿ* meter like these two poems – al-Aʿmā's (*Tawshīʿ* no. 35) and al-Ṣafadī's (*Tawshīʿ* no. 36). That is to say, that in the same way that a Romance octosyllabic verse may be rendered by four Arabic meters – *mujtathth*,[92] dimeter *ramal*, dimeter *khafīf*,[93] or dimeter *rajaz*[94] – *a* decasyllabic line may be rendered in Arabic metrics by at least two meters: a *madīd*,[95] or a *basīṭ mukhallaʿ*;[96] and a line of eleven syllables may be rendered either by a *sarīʿ* meter[97] or a *ramal*.[98]

For al-Ṣafadī, no other Andalusī poets are as successful or as remarkable as Ibn Zuhr or al-Aʿmā al-Tuṭīlī. In highlighting their work, al-Ṣafadī provides his reader with a general view of the most brilliant period of the practice of *tawshīḥ* poetry in al-Andalus, the sixth century AH/twelfth century CE: al-Aʿmā al-Tuṭīlī, in the first half-century, and Ibn Zuhr, in the second. Although I have not emphasized them in this article, his other choices are by no means less meaningful. He further composes other *muʿāraḍāt*:1) in *Tawshīʿ* no. 32 he imitates a poem of ʿUbāda b. Māʾ al-Samāʾ (d. 421/1030),[99] the first poet whose *muwashshāt* had been preserved; 2) in *Tawshīʿ* no. 39 he

91. Ibn Mujbir from Murcia (d. 588 AH / 1192 CE), composed another imitation of al-Aʿmā's *muwashshaḥa*. It is included in ʿInānī 1991, but without the Arabic text.

92. See for instance, Ibn Zuhr (*Tawshīʿ* no. 28).

93. Ibn Zuhr (*Tawshīʿ* no. 41).

94. Ibn Sahl (*Tawshīʿ* no. 50).

95. As exemplified by Ibn Zuhr (*Tawshīʿ* no. 10); Ibn al-Labbāna (*Tawshīʿ* no. 39); and Ibn al-Zaqqāq/ Ibn Baqī (*Tawshīʿ* no. 46).

96. As exemplified by Ibn Zuhr (*Tawshīʿ* no. 25) and al-Aʿmā al-Tuṭīlī (*Tawshīʿ* no. 35).

97. As exemplified by al-Aʿmā al-Tuṭīlī (*Tawshīʿ* no. 30) (and Ibn al-Labbāna, and Ibn Sahl, Ibn al-Khaṭīb, and other Andalusi poems of this family); and Ibn Māʾ al-Samāʾ (*Tawshīʿ* no. 32).

98. As, for example, in Ibn Zuhr's *Tawshīʿ* no. 37 (and his model, Ibn Baqī; and his imitator Ibn ʿArabī).

99. Granja 2012b.

imitates Ibn al-Labbāna (d. 507 AH/1113 CE), a poet of the transition from the period of the Taifas to the Almoravid period (whose importance can be inferred from his being the model for some other poets, as seen in al-Ṣafadī's anthology; and 3) in *Tawshīʿ* no. 50 he imitates a poem by a late poet, Ibn Sahl al-Isrāʾīlī (d.649 AH/ 1251 CE), whose poetry announces the end of a golden age of the Arabic literature of al-Andalus. Al-Ṣafadī only quotes a single *muwashshaḥa* from each, but this is not in accordance with Ibn Sahl's success in general, nor with the diffusion of Ibn Māʾ al-Samāʾ's poem, a theme that can be elaborated another time.

Almost all Andalusī *muwashshaḥāt* considered in the present paper have in common the fact that their Romance prosody does not preclude them from also conforming to Arabic metrics. Their creators have leveled some irregularities, adjusting them to well-known Arabic meters, in a process already evident in the work of late Andalusī poets, like Ibn Sahl (seventh/thirteenth century). It is not a surprise that his *muwashshaḥa* "Hal darā ẓaby al-ḥimā" was so successful in Maghreb and Eastern lands:[100] it featured hendecasyllabic verses that could be scanned as *ramal* hemistichs, a meter identified with music; and strophes with an even number of lines, almost equal to the long Arabic verses with caesura! This ambiguity between Romance prosody and Arabic meter is already present in poets from the late eleventh to the twelfth centuries CE, who enjoyed playing with it. Ibn Sanāʾ al-Mulk, who only perceived the Arabic prosody, called them *muwashshaḥāt shiʿriyya* (adapted to the classical Arabic metrics). Some of these poems, open to both Romance and Arabic prosodies, were successfully imitated in Syria and Egypt, from the thirteenth to the fourteenth centuries CE and onwards. In al-Ṣafadī's anthology of *tawshīḥ* poetry, accompanied by his own *muwashshāḥāt*, *Tawshīʿ al-tawshīḥ*, the Andalusī poems are almost invariably composed in this kind of double prosody. Eastern poets can depend on it: to write a poem in a totally alien prosody would be a feat not always crowned with success. In this, music also was instrumental, as it was in the diffusion of *muwashshaḥ* poetry.

100. Būdhayna 1994.

Bibliography

al-Aʿmā al-Tuṭīlī. 1963. *Dīwān al-Aʿmā al-Tuṭīlī Abī Jaʿfar Aḥmad b. ʿAbd Allāh b. Abī Hurayra (t. 525h) wa-majmūʿa min muwashshaḥāti-hi*, edited by Iḥsān ʿAbbās. Beirut.

al-Ahwānī, ʿAbd al-ʿAzīz M. 1948. "El *Kitāb al-muqtaṭaf min azāhir al-ṭuraf* de Ibn Saʿīd." *Al-Andalus* 13:19–33.

Armistead, Samuel G. and James T. Monroe. 1985. "Beached Whales and Roaring Mice: Additional Remarks on Hispano-Arabic Strophic Poetry." *La Corónica* 13:206–242.

Arnaldez, R. 2012. "Ibn Zuhr." In *EI2*, edited by P. Bearman, Th. Bianquis, C. E. Bosworth, E. van Donzel, and W. P. Heinrichs, III:976a. Leiden. http://dx.doi.org.ezp1.lib.umn.edu/10.1163/1573-3912_islam_COM_0348.

Aydamur al- Muḥyawī. 1931. *Mukhtār Dīwān ʿAlam al-Dīn Aydamur al-Muḥyawī*. Cairo. http://www.kadl.sa/Browse.aspx?id=p4kerroubvyx6qfn9zi2i0xjpfzrtpnkqlgryivs88vrfw25jtvzwipxwl9t16&p.

Būdhayna, Muḥammad. 1994. *Muwashshaḥat Ibn Sahl al-Ishbīlī «Hal darā ẓaby l-ḥimā». Sharḥu-hā wa-muʿāraḍātu-hā*. Hammamet, Tunisia.

Cejador y Frauca, Julio. 1921. *La verdadera poesía castellana. Floresta de la antigua lírica popular*. Madrid.

Corriente, Federico. 1976. "Acento y cantidad en la fonología del hispano-árabe. Observaciones estadísticas en torno a la naturaleza del sistema métrico de la poesía popular andalusí." *Al-Andalus* 41:1–13.

——. 1977. *A Grammatical Sketch of the Spanish Arabic Dialect Bundle*. Madrid.

——. 1992. *Arabe andalusí y lenguas romances*. Madrid.

——. 1997. *Poesía dialectal árabe y romance en Alandalús. (Cejeles y xarajāt de muwaššaḥāt)*. Madrid.

Dufour, Julien. 2011. *Huit siècles de poésie chantée au Yemen. Langue, mètres et formes du ḥumaynī*. Strasbourg.

Elinson, Alexander. 2001. "Contrapuntal Composition in a *Muwashshah* Family, or Variations on a Panegyric Theme." *Medieval Encounters* 7, nos. 2/3:174–96.

Frolov, Dmitri. 1999. *Classical Arabic Verse. History and Theory of ʿArūḍ*. Leiden.

García Gómez, E. 1961. "Una *muwaššaḥa* andaluza 'con eco'." In *Studia Philologica. Homenaje a Dámaso Alonso*, 2 vols., 73–78. Madrid.

——. 1962. "Estudio del *Dār al-ṭirāz*, preceptiva egipcia de la *muwaššaḥa*." *Al-Andalus* 27:21–104.

——. 1990. *Las jarchas romances de la serie árabe en su marco*. Madrid.

Garulo, Teresa. 2005. "*Wa-huwa wazn lam yarid ʿan al-ʿarab*. Métrica no jalīliana en al-Andalus." *Al-Qanṭara* 26:263–267.

——. 2009. "La reutilización en la poesía estrófica de al-Andalus. El caso de Ibn Ḥazmūn." In *Remploi, citation, plagiat. Conduites et pratiques médiévales (X^e-XIIe siècle)*, edited by Pierre Toubert and Pierre Moret, 9–22. Madrid.
——. 2012. "Literaturas en contacto." In *711-1616: de árabes a moriscos. Una parte de la historia de España*, edited by M. I. Fierro, J. Martos, J. P. Monferrer, and M. J. Viguera, 133–159. Córdoba.
Ghazāl, ʿAdnān Muḥammad. 2004. *Muʿāraḍāt qaṣāʾid Ibn Zaydūn*. Kuwait.
Ghāzī, Sayyid. 1979. *Dīwān almuwashshaḥāt alandalusiyya*. 2 vols. Alexandria.
Granja, Fernando de la. 2012a. "Ibn Baḳī." In *EI2*, edited by P. Bearman, Th. Bianquis, C. E. Bosworth, E. van Donzel, and W. P. Heinrichs, III:729b. Leiden. http://dx.doi.org.ezp1.lib.umn.edu/10.1163/1573-3912_islam_SIM_3099.
——. 2012b. "Ibn Māʾ al-Samāʾ." In *EI2*, edited by P. Bearman, Th. Bianquis, C. E. Bosworth, E. van Donzel, and W. P. Heinrichs, III:855. Leiden. http://dx.doi.org.ezp1.lib.umn.edu/10.1163/1573-3912_islam_SIM_3274.
al-Ḥabbūbī, Muḥammad Saʿīd. 1983. *Dīwān al-Sayyid Muḥammad Saʿīd al-Ḥabbūbī*. Edited by ʿAbd al-Ghaffār al-Ḥabūbī. Baghdad.
Hadjadji, Hamdane. 1997. *Ibn al-Labbâna. Le poète d'al-Muʿtamid, Prince de Séville ou le symbole de l'amitié*. Paris.
al-Ḥāʾik al-Tiṭwānī. 1999. *Kunnāsh al-Ḥāʾik*. Edited by Mālik Bennūna. Introduction by ʿAbbās al-Jarārī. Rabat.
Ibn Abī Uṣaybiʿa. n.d. *ʿUyūn al-akhbār fī ṭabaqāt al-aṭibbāʾ*. Edited by Nizār Riḍā. Beirut.
Ibn Bassām. 1978. *Al-Dhakhīra fī maḥāsin ahl al-jazīra*. Edited by Iḥsān ʿAbbās. 8 vols. Beirut.
Ibn Bishrī, ʿAlī. 1992. *The ʿUddat al-jalīs. An Anthology of Andalusian Arabic Muwashshaḥāt*. Edited by A. Jones. Cambridge.
Ibn Furkūn. 1987. *Dīwān Ibn Furkūn*. Edited by Muḥammad Bencherifa. Casablanca.
Ibn Ḥajar al-ʿAsqalānī. 1974. *Al-Durar al-kāmina fī aʿyān al-miʾa al-thāmina*. 4 vols. Hayderabad.
Ibn Khallikān. 1978. *Wafayāt al-aʿyān*. Edited by Iḥsān ʿAbbās. 8 vols. Beirut.
Ibn al-Khaṭīb. 1997. *The* Jaysh al-tawshīḥ *of Lisān al-Dīn Ibn al-Khaṭīb. An Anthology of Andalusian Arabic* Muwashshaḥāt. Edited by Alan Jones. Cambridge.
Ibn Sahl al-Isrāʾīlī. 1985. *Dīwān*. Edited by Muḥammad Qūbaʿa. Tunis.
Ibn Sahl de Sevilla. 1996. (= Ben Sahl de Sevilla. 1996) *Poemas*. Edited and translated by Teresa Garulo. Madrid.
Ibn Saʿīd. n. d. *Al-Mughrib fī ḥulā al-Magrib*. Edited by Shawqī Ḍayf. 2 vols. Cairo.

Ibn Saʿīd al-Andalusī. 1983. *Kitāb al-muqtaṭaf min azāhir al-ṭuraf*. Edited by Sayyid Ḥanafī Ḥasanīn. Cairo.
Ibn Sanāʾ al-Mulk. 1949. *Dār al-ṭirāz*. Edited by Jawdat al-Rikābī. Damascus.
Ibn Shākir al-Kutubī. 1973. *Fawāt al-wafayāt*. Edited by Iḥsān ʿAbbās. 5 vols. Beirut.
Ibn Shuhayd. 1967. *Risālat al-tawābiʿ wa-l-zawābiʿ*. Edited by Buṭrus al-Bustānī, Beirut.
——. 1971. *Risālat attawābiʿ wazzawābiʿ. The Treatise of Familiar Spirits and Demons by Abū ʿĀmir ibn Shuhaid al-Ashjaʿī, al-Andalusī*. Introduction, translation and notes by James T. Monroe. Berkeley.
Ibn Taghri Birdī. 1963. *Al-Nujūm al-zāhira fī mulūk Miṣr wa-l-Qāhira*. 16 vols. Cairo.
——. 1984. *Al-Manhal al-ṣāfī*. Edited by Muḥammad Muḥammad Amīn. 13 vols. Cairo.
Al-ʿImād al-Iṣfahānī. 1951. *Kharīdat al-qaṣr. Qism Miṣr*. Aḥmad Amīn and Shawqī Ḍayf. 2 vols. Cairo.
ʿInānī, Muḥammad Zakariyyā. 1980. *Al-Muwashshaḥāt al-andalusiyya*. Kuwait.
——. 1991. "Ibn Muğbir de Murcia y su única *muwaššaḥa*." In *Poesía estrófica. Actas del Primer Congreso Internacional sobre Poesía Estrófica Árabe y Hebrea y sus Paralelos Romances (Madrid, diciembre de 1989)*, edited by F. Corriente and A. Sáenz-Badillos, 177–186. Madrid.
Lane, Edward William. 1863. *Arabic-English Lexicon*. 2 vols. London.
al-Maqqarī. 1968. *Nafḥ al-ṭīb*. Edited by Iḥsān ʿAbbās. 8 vols. Beirut.
Monroe, James T. 1974. *Hispano-Arabic Poetry. A Student Anthology*. Berkeley.
——. 1979. "Kharjas in Arabic and Romance: Popular Poetry in Muslim Spain?" In *Islam: Past Influence and Present Challenge*, edited by Alford T. Welch and Pierre Cachia, 168–187. Edinburgh.
——. 1985–86. "On Re-reading Ibn Bassām: 'Lírica románica' after the Arab Conquest." *Revista del Instituto Egipcio de Estudios Islámicos en Madrid* 23:121–147.
——. 1986. "Poetic Quotation in the *Muwaššaḥa* and Its Implications: Andalusian Strophic Poetry as Song." *La Corónica* 14:230–250.
——. 1987. "The Tune or the Words? (Singing Hispano-Arabic Strophic Poetry)." *Al-Qanṭara* 8:265–317.
Monroe, James T. and David Swiatlo. 1977. "Ninety-Three Arabic *Ḫarǧas* in Hebrew *Muwaššaḥs*: Their Hispano-Romance Prosody and Thematic Features." *Journal of the American Oriental Society* 97:141–163.
Moreh, Shmuel. 1988. *Studies in Modern Arabic Prose and Poetry*. Leiden.
Nakash, Yitzhak. 2006. *Reaching for Power: The Shīʿa in the Modern Arab World*. Princeton.

Özkan, Hahan. 2017. "Ibn Baqī." In *EI3*, edited by Kate Fleet, Gudrun Krämer, Denis Matringe, John Nawas, and Everett Rowson. Leiden. http://dx.doi.org.ezp1.lib.umn.edu/10.1163/1573-3912_ei3_COM_30732.
Raḥīm, Miqdād. 1987. *Al-Muwashshaḥāt fī bilād al-Shām*. Beirut.
Rikabi, J. 2012. "Ibn Nubāta." In *EI2*, edited by P. Bearman, Th. Bianquis, C. E. Bosworth, E. van Donzel, and W. P. Heinrichs, III:899b. http://dx.doi.org.ezp1.lib.umn.edu/10.1163/1573-3912_islam_SIM_3325.
Rosenthal, F. 2012. "Al-Ṣafadī." In *EI2*, edited by P. Bearman, Th. Bianquis, C. E. Bosworth, E. van Donzel, and W. P. Heinrichs, VIII:759–60. http://dx.doi.org.ezp1.lib.umn.edu/10.1163/1573-3912_islam_SIM_6437.
al-Ṣafadī. 1966. *Tawshīʿ al-tawṣīḥ*. Edited by Albert Ḥabīb Muṭlaq. Beirut.
——. 1998. *Aʿyān al-ʿaṣr*. Edited by ʿAlī Abū Zayd, Nabīl Abū ʿUmsha, Muḥammad Mawʿid and Maḥmūd Sālim Muḥammad. 6 vols. Damascus.
——. 2000. *Al-Wāfī bi-l-wafayāt*. Edited by Aḥmad al-Arnāʾūṭ and Turkī Muṣṭafā. 29 vols. Beirut.
Schippers, A. 2012. "*Muʿāraḍa*." In *EI2*, edited by P. Bearman, Th. Bianquis, C. E. Bosworth, E. van Donzel, and W. P. Heinrichs, VII:261. http://dx.doi.org.ezp1.lib.umn.edu/10.1163/1573-3912_islam_SIM_5276.
Stern, S. M. 1950. "Muhammad ibn ʿUbāda al-Qazzāz. Un andaluz autor de «muwaššaḥas»." *Al-Andalus* 15:79–108.
——. 1974. *Hispano-Arabic Strophic Poetry*. Edited by L. P. Harvey. Oxford.
Stoetzer, W. 1989. *Theory and Practice in Arabic Metrics*. Leiden.
——. 2012. "Ramal." In *EI2*, edited by P. Bearman, Th. Bianquis, C. E. Bosworth, E. van Donzel, and W. P. Heinrichs, VIII:421. http://dx.doi.org.ezp1.lib.umn.edu/10.1163/1573-3912_islam_COM_0908.
al-Ṭuʿma, ʿAdnān Muḥammad. 1979. *Muwaššaḥāt Ibn Baqī al-Ṭulayṭulī wa-jaṣāʾiṣu-hā al-fanniyya. Dirāsa wa-naṣṣ*. Bagdad.

Monroe's Methodology in Analyzing Andalusī Meters and Its Relevance to a Comparative Analysis of a Classical Persian Meter, the *mutaqārib*

Olga M. Davidson
Institute for the Study of Muslim Societies and Civilizations, Boston University

THE STARTING POINT OF THIS ESSAY is an article by James T. Monroe about two poetic forms known in classical Arabic as the *zajal* and the *muwashshaḥa*. The title of his article poses a question and already points to an answer: "Which Came First, the *zajal* or the *muwashshaḥa*? Some Evidence for the Oral Origins of Hispano-Arabic Strophic Poetry."[1] Why does it matter, which of these two poetic forms "came first"? It is because, as Monroe argues, the answer to this question helps clarify the "oral" origins of these two genres of classical Arabic poetry. Monroe's analysis breaks new ground in accounting for the diachronic relationship of the *zajal* and the *muwashshaḥa* with various forms of strophic songmaking in Romance-language traditions. Basically, he argues that the *muwashshaḥa* was derived from the *zajal*, and that both these forms, as Arabic genres, derived ultimately from corresponding vernacular forms originating from and interacting with various pre-existing Hispano-Romance oral traditions in al-Andalus. My project here switches from al-Andalus as a realm of western Islam to Persia as a realm of eastern Islam. In making this switch, I apply Monroe's methodology to a meter known in classical Arabic as the *mutaqārib*, which was the rhythmical framework for the basic verse-form of classical Persian epic. I will argue that the Persian *mutaqārib* originated not from the meter known by that name in classical Arabic poetry but rather from a pre-existing Iranian metrical form that eventually evolved into the form that we see attested in classical Persian epic. In terms of this argument, the *mutaqārib* meter of classical Arabic poetry originated from a pre-existing Persian meter. Such an argument, then, mirrors Monroe's project of showing that both the *zajal* and the *muwashshaḥa*, as used in classical Arabic poetry, originated from forms that were used in the strophic songmaking of Romance traditions.

In making my argument, I have been strongly influenced by a book on classical Persian meters by L. P. Elwell-Sutton, *The Persian Metres* (1976). The author of this book argues convincingly that the classical Persian form of

1. Monroe 1989.

the *mutaqārib* originated from earlier "Middle Persian" poetic traditions and not, as has generally been thought, from some Arabic prototype of the classical Arabic form of the *mutaqārib*. In making such an argument, Elwell-Sutton relies on a diachronic methodology, which is similar to Monroe's.

Before I proceed, I will offer some background about terminology and about the relevant poetic traditions, conventionally described as Andalusī and Persian. First, I will make an observation on terminology and then I will review some details about the relevant poetic traditions.

In using the term *diachronic*, which I contrast with *synchronic*, I follow the definitions of Ferdinand de Saussure, with reference to language as a structure. Saussure notes that the synchronic approach concerns a current state of a structure while the diachronic approach examines different phases in the evolution of that given structure.[2] My point here is that the methodology used by both Monroe and Elwell-Sutton can be described as diachronic, since both researchers are building models designed to explain how existing forms of poetry evolved from pre-existing forms.

Now I review some details about the relevant poetic traditions. I start with the basic facts about the Andalusī tradition, and from there I will move to comparable facts about the Persian tradition.

Here is Monroe's succinct summary of the basic facts about the *zajal* and the *muwashshaḥa*:

> From a linguistic point of view, the *zajal* is composed entirely in the vernacular Arabic dialect of Andalus, occasionally besprinkled with words or phrases in Hispano-Romance. In contrast, the *muwaššaḥa* is in Classical Arabic, with the exception of its final element, which is normally in vernacular diction, either Arabic, Romance, or a combination of both....
>
> The *zajal* proper always has an initial refrain (*maṭlaʿ*) of which a typically common form is a couplet rhymed AA, followed by an indefinite number of strophes ... followed by a final element that rhymes with the refrain (a) but reproduces exactly half of the refrain's rhymes. This [final] element is called *markaz*.
>
> The basic *muwaššaḥa* pattern is similar to that of the *zajal* except that its *markazes* reproduce the entire set of rhymes found in the refrain and are symmetrical with it: AA, bbbaa (AA), cccaa (AA), dddaa (AA), etc. Three further differences are:
>
> (1) About one-third of the extant Andalusian *muwaššaḥas* lack a refrain.

2. Saussure 1916, 117.

(2) The overwhelming number of *muwaššaḥa*s are only five strophes long, whereas *zajal*s are often considerably longer.

(3) The final *markaz* of the poem, technically called *ḫarja*, is usually in the vernacular [= either Arabic, Romance, or a combination of both]; it is introduced as a quotation and, in many cases, it can be shown that it is actually a quotation from another *zajal* or *muwaššaḥa*, normally a refrain, but sometimes a *ḫarja* from a previous poem.[3]

On the basis of these structural relationships between the *zajal* and the *muwashshaḥa*, Monroe argues that the *muwashshaḥa* originated from the *zajal*, and not the other way around. His argument, however, runs into two primary obstacles: (1) the terminus post quem for the formal attestation of the *zajal* is the poetry of Ibn Quzmān, whose death-date is 1160 CE, whereas we find attested references to the "invention" of the *muwashshaḥa* that can be dated as early as the ninth century CE, and (2) the non-*kharja* part of a typical *muwashshaḥa* composition is much closer to classical Arabic in form, especially with regard to its metrical structure.[4] Monroe removes the first of these two obstacles by adducing earlier attestations of the form that eventually became known as the *zajal* in the later era of Ibn Quzmān. As for the second obstacle, he shows how the various arguments for claiming that the *zajal* originated from the *muwashshaḥa* depend on two false premises:

(a) It is a mistake to assume that the *zajal* was a lower form of art that resulted from some kind of a debasement of the *muwashshaḥa* after this high form of literary art was supposedly absorbed into an oral tradition. As Monroe shows, the *zajal* became a high form of literary art in its own right, and it stemmed from an oral tradition that combined Andalusī Arabic and Romance elements.

(b) It is likewise a mistake to assume that the metrical structures that we see at work in the *muwashshaḥa* can be traced back to the quantitative meters of Arabic poetry. Although Monroe expresses some uncertainty about the original metrical structures, he argues convincingly that "the *muwaššaḥa* is a derivative of an early and truly popular *zajal* genre in vernacular Arabic and Romance, now lost, which existed orally."[5]

Having reviewed some relevant facts about the Andalusī *zajal* and *muwashshaḥa*, we now turn to the classical Persian *mutaqārib*. By contrast with the *zajal* and the *muwashshaḥa* of Andalusī poetry, where the basic

3. Monroe 1989, 38–39.

4. The bibliography for opinions about these two points that have been published by a variety of experts is vast: for a sampling, see the references collected by Monroe 1989, 41 n. 14.

5. Monroe 1989, 42, with further bibliography.

form of composition is strophic or stanzaic, the basic form of *mutaqārib* as the meter of classical Persian epic is stichic rather than strophic. What is meant by stichic is that the basic metrical unit of classical epic is a verse, not a stanza. Each verse is a *bayt* or "couplet" consisting of two rhythmically symmetrical and rhyming half-verses. The technical term for the verse is *bayt*, and the technical term for the half-verse or hemistich is the *misrā*ᶜ. The primary example of classical Persian epic is the *Shāhnāma* of Ferdowsi, completed around 1000 CE and consisting of around 50,000 verses in the Moscow edition.[6] The number of verses attested in the manuscripts is even more vast; for example, the Baysonghori manuscript features around 58,000 verses.

Here is where the book of Elwell-Sutton, cited at the beginning of my essay, becomes most relevant. As I already noted, Elwell-Sutton argues that the classical Persian form of the *mutaqārib* originated not from the classical Arabic meter known by that name but rather from earlier "Middle Persian" poetic traditions, so that the prototype of the Arabic *mutaqārib* was an Iranian meter. This argument, however, has been undervalued, devalued, or simply ignored in most publications dealing with Persian meters. Even an authority such as C. E. Bosworth, who together with Carole Hillenbrand edited a Festschrift in honor of Elwell-Sutton (1984), holds back from fully endorsing the work of Elwell-Sutton on Persian meters. For example, in his otherwise most appreciative retrospective survey of Elwell-Sutton's work on Persian literature in general, Bosworth stops short when he comes to *The Persian Metres*:

> Prosody and metrics were a special interest of his, marked by a chapter [Elwell-Sutton 1975] on the *robā*ᶜ*ī* [in *Cambridge History of Iran* IV (pp. 633–657)] and above all, by *The Persian Metres* (Cambridge, 1976), his most technical and closely-argued work. In this, he reacted – perhaps too strongly – against the notion that the meters of the New Persian are wholly derived from the quantitative Arabic ones and based his own analysis on the Persian meters summarized in his article "ᶜArūż" [Elwell-Sutton 1986] as they actually occur in New Persian literature. So far, few scholars would quarrel with this assessment, but Elwell-Sutton went further, asserting that the quantitative metres of Persian have nothing to do with the Arabic ones, but continue the patterns of pre-Islamic Middle Persian poetry; yet it seems probable that the latter was essentially a minstrel poetry based on syllables and stress, with no noticeably quantitative

6. Bertels 1960–1971.

elements (see F. de Blois [1992] p. 49, for a critique of this [= Elwell-Sutton's] view). *The Persian Metres* nevertheless remains a model of meticulous analysis.[7]

The undervaluing that we see here on the part of Bosworth helps explain why the work of Elwell-Sutton on the *mutaqārib* is mostly ignored. In my own work, I have defended the argument of Elwell-Sutton:

> L. P. Elwell-Sutton [1976] makes a strong case for quantitative meter as the basic principle of Middle Persian poetry, thereby directly linking it with the quantitative meter of New Persian poetry, like the *mutaqārib* lines of Ferdowsi's *Shāhnāma* [Elwell-Sutton 1976, especially pp. 180–183]. Moreover, Elwell-Sutton argues convincingly that Ferdowsi's *mutaqārib* meter, as well as other meters related to it, is not derived from the corresponding Arabic meter, one that is unattested in pre-Islamic Arabic poetry, extremely rare in the Umayyad period (661–750 CE), and relatively frequent only in ʿAbbāsid times (750–1258 CE); rather it is the Arabic *mutaqārib* that seems to be modeled on the Persian [Elwell-Sutton pp. 172–173]. In fact, the New Persian *mutaqārib* seems to be derived from Middle Persian forms [p. 172; see also Marr 1944]. The thrust, then, of Elwell-Sutton's findings is that the attested fragments of New Persian poetry before Daqiqi and Ferdowsi consistently reveal the formal characteristics of Middle Persian poetry [pp. 172–179]. I cite Elwell-Sutton's illuminating survey of these New Persian poetic fragments, such as the three surviving lines attributed to the Sasanian minstrel Barbad [quoted in Lazard 1975, 605]; part of a hymn recited by the Zoroastrian priests at the fire-temple of Karkoy [as in Lazard 1975, 605, 614]; and a two-line lament for the ruin of Samarqand [as in Lazard 1975, 605].[8]

What makes Elwell-Sutton's metrical analysis of these poetic fragments even more compelling, as we see from the interwoven references to the commentaries of Gilbert Lazard (1975) in the summary I have just quoted, is that the poetic content in these examples is evidently just as traditional as is the meter in which this content is framed. To illustrate the convergence of traditional form and content, I cite here a couplet memorialized by Dowlatshāh in his *Taẕkeratoš-šoʿarā* (1487 CE). It was composed by Abu Tāher Khātuni, a poet dated to the late eleventh century CE. This couplet was reportedly inscribed on the ruins of Qaṣr-e Širin. I quote the couplet here, along with the translation of Elwell-Sutton:

7. Bosworth 1998, 372.
8. Davidson 2013a, 22–23.

hežabrā be-geihān anušah be-zī
jahān-rā bedīdār-e tō šah be-zī

May the lion live prosperous on the earth.
May the world gain a king at the sight of you.[9]

Here is another illustration, featuring four lines composed by Ḥanżale of Bādqis, dated around 870 CE. These lines represent one of the very oldest examples of classical Persian verse. I quote the text along with the translation of Elwell-Sutton:

mehtarī gar be-kām-e šīr dar ast
šou khatar-kon ze kām-e šīr be-juy
yā bozorgīy o ʿezz o neʿmat o jāh
yā čo mardānt marg-e rūyārūy

Even if chieftainship be in the mouth of a lion,
Be reckless, seek it from the lion's mouth!
Either greatness, glory, wealth and pomp,
Or meeting death face to face like a man![10]

More needs to be said about the attempts to devalue the findings of Elwell-Sutton, as in the case of F. de Blois, the critic cited in the statement I quoted earlier from Bosworth. Such attempts, I argue, are based on the unsustainable notion that Iranian meters were originally based on accentual patterns. Here is my summary of such a notion:

> [De Blois 2004] thinks that the traditional Iranian meters, going all the way back to the Gāthās, "conform to a system of accentual metre" (p. 44). While he says at first that this claim of his is "a minority view" ([de Blois] p. 42) "to which the present author inclines" ([de Blois] p. 44), he says seven pages later: "In fact, as has already been mentioned, a very strong case for an accentual basis of Middle-Iranian poetry has been made by such experts as Henning and Boyce" ([de Blois] p. 49). This "strong case" is reported merely by way of a passing reference ([de Blois] p. 45) to the views of Henning (1942, 52–56; 1950) and Boyce (1954, esp. pp. 45–59). [In that passing reference, de Blois p. 45 says:] "The same accentual principle underlies, according to the penetrating analyses of Henning and Boyce, pre-Islamic Middle-Persian and Parthian poetry."[11]

9. Elwell-Sutton 1976, 173.
10. Elwell-Sutton 1976, 175.
11. Davidson 2013b, 2–3 n. 13.

By contrast, I follow Elwell-Sutton (1976) in resisting the idea of a proto-Iranian "system of accentual metre."[12] Elwell-Sutton says about Persian meter: "It is probable that the question of stress does not arise at all."[13] This probability, as formulated by Elwell-Sutton, seems to me far preferable to the formulation of Bosworth (citing de Blois) in claiming that Middle Persian poetry "was essentially a minstrel poetry based on syllables and stress."[14]

Working against such a refusal to consider quantity instead of stress as a basic principle in the metrical systems of Middle Persian poetics, Elwell-Sutton had adduced the decisive comparative evidence of Indo-European linguistics:

> This rugged refusal to consider quantity as a factor in these [Persian] metrical systems is all the more curious when it is remembered that the concept has never been questioned in the case of another major branch of Indo-European prosody, the Greek. If the Greeks understood this principle from the earliest times, why not the Iranians and, for that matter, the Indians?[15]

Some clarification is needed with reference to the second sentence as quoted here from Elwell-Sutton. What he says is not that there was any cultural contact between Greek and Indo-Iranian metrical traditions. Rather, his reasoning is based on the well-known fact that Greek and Indic meters are cognate, originating from a common Indo-European heritage,[16] and then he adds another fact, also well known: that Indic and Iranian poetry are closely related. On the basis of these two facts, he goes on to argue that Indo-Iranian meter must have been cognate with Greek meter. So, according to Elwell-Sutton, Iranian meter must have been originally quantitative, just as Indic and Greek meter were quantitative. This is not to say, however, that quantitative meter is incompatible with "syllables and stress" – to quote again from Bosworth's description of the "minstrel poetry" of Middle Persian traditions. In the case of ancient Greek meter, for example, the system of quantitative meter included the factor of stress.[17] So also in the case of

12. Elwell-Sutton 1976, 181–182, and with reference to Henning, 170.
13. Elwell-Sutton 1976, 75; Davidson 2013b, 2–3 n.13.
14. Bosworth 1998, 372.
15. Elwell-Sutton 1976, 181.
16. See Nagy 1974.
17. On "stress" in ancient Greek, which includes the phonological features of duration and intensity but not pitch, see in general Allen 1973. See also Nagy 1990, 34–35. For details, see Nagy 1974, 49–56; Allen 1973, 255–259 and 1987, 113–114. From the standpoint of general phonetics, stress may be a matter of duration, intensity, and pitch. Allen's main argument is that ancient Greek had a system of duration and intensity that was independent of its system

Middle Persian meter, as Gilbert Lazard has argued, the factor of quantity can be correlated with the factor of "syllables and stress."[18]

I should add that some quantitative patterns in Greek meters even match what we find still attested in Persian meters: for example, the interchangeability of ⏑ — ⏑ — with — ⏑ ⏑ — (where "⏑" and "—" stand for short and long syllables respectively) as found in Persian meters[19] is matched by a parallel interchangeability of the "iamb" (⏑ — ⏑ —) with the "choriamb" (— ⏑ ⏑ —) as found in Greek meters - an interchangeability that is occasionally attested even in the canonical meter known to Hellenists as the iambic trimeter.[20] Here we see just one of a variety of examples where, as Elwell-Sutton shows, the patterns of New Persian meters are older - far older - than the patterns of the Arabic meters from which they supposedly derive.

Reaching the end of my argument, I come back full circle to the work of Monroe on the meters of the Andalusī poetic forms known as the *zajal* and the *muwashshaḥa*. Both forms, as Monroe points out, "contain puzzling departures from the rules of classical Arabic metrics."[21] And the reason for such departures, as Monroe makes clear, is that these Andalusī genres are more basic - in fact, far older - than the corresponding classical Arabic genres. As Monroe also shows, "both genres originated in Andalus and not in the East."[22]

Such a thesis is parallel to the earlier thesis of Elwell-Sutton about the Persian/Arabic meter known as the *mutaqārib*, which was the building block of the New Persian epic tradition as exemplified by the *Shāhnāma* of Ferdowsi. Both this meter, and the genre that it represents, originated from Middle Persian poetic traditions and not, as has generally been thought, from some Arabic prototype of the classical Arabic form of the *mutaqārib*.

of pitch, though these two systems merged in Modern Greek, where the inherited patterns of pitch were correlated with both duration and intensity. See Allen 1973, 96–125, 258.

18. Lazard 1970, 1994.
19. Elwell-Sutton 1975, 125.
20. Nagy 1974, 40.
21. Monroe 1989, 38.
22. Monroe 1989, 38.

Bibliography

Allen, W. S. 1973. *Accent and Rhythm. Prosodic Features of Latin and Greek: A Study in Theory and Reconstruction*. Cambridge.

——. 1987. *Vox Graeca: The Pronunciation of Classical Greek*. 3rd ed. Cambridge.

Bertels, Y. E., et al., eds. 1960–1971. *Ferdowsi: Shāhnāma*. Moscow.

Blois, F. de. 1992. *Persian Literature. A Bio-Bibliographical Survey Begun by the Late C. A. Storey*. Vol. 5, part 1, *Poetry to ca. AD 1100*. London.

——. 2004. *Persian Literature. A Bio-Bibliographical Survey*. Vol. 5, *Poetry of the Pre-Mongol Period*. 2nd, rev. ed. London.

Bosworth, C. E. 1998. "Elwell-Sutton, Laurence Paul." In *EIr* VIII, fasc. 4, 372–73. http://www.iranicaonline.org/articles/elwell-sutton. Re-approved 2011.

Bosworth, C. E., and Hillenbrand, C., eds. 1992. *Qajar Iran, Political, Social and Cultural Change 1800–1925. Studies Presented to Professor L.P. Elwell-Sutton*. Edinburgh. Reprint, Costa Mesa, 1984.

Boyce, M. 1954. *The Manichaean Hymn-Cycles in Parthian*. London.

Davidson, O. M. 2013a. *Poet and Hero in the Persian Book of Kings*. 3rd ed. Cambridge MA. 1st ed., Ithaca 1994; 2nd ed., Costa Mesa 2006.

——. 2013b. *Comparative Literature and Classical Persian Poetry*, 2nd ed. Cambridge MA. 1st ed. Costa Mesa 2000.

Elwell-Sutton, L. P. 1975. "*Rubāʿī*." In *The Cambridge History of Iran*, edited by R. N. Frye. Vol. 4, *The Period from the Arab Invasion to the Saljuqs*, 633–657. Cambridge.

——. 1976. *The Persian Metres*. Cambridge.

——. 1986. "ʿArūż." In *EIr* II, fasc. 6–7, 670–679. http://www.iranicaonline.org/articles/aruz-the-metrical-system. Last updated 2011.

Henning, W. B. 1942. "The Disintegration of Avestic Studies." *Transactions of the Philological Society* 1942, 40–56.

Henning, W. B. 1950. "A Pahlavi Poem." *Bulletin of the School of Oriental and African Studies* 13:641–648.

Lazard, G. 1970. "*Ahu-ye kuhi*: le chamois d'Abu Hafs de Sogdiane et les origines du *robâi*." In *W. B. Henning Memorial Volume*, 238–244. London.

——. 1975. "The Rise of the New Persian Language." In *Cambridge History of Iran*, edited by R. N. Frye. Vol. 4, *The Period from the Arab Invasion to the Saljuqs*, 595–632. Cambridge.

——. 1994. "Le mètre épique baloutchi et les origines du *motaqâreb*." In *Arabic Prosody and its Applications in Muslim Poetry*, edited by L. Johanson and B. Utas, 81–90. Stockholm.

Marr, N. 1944. "Wazn-e šeʿr-e Šāh-nāma." In *Hazāra-ye Ferdowsī*, 188–197. Tehran.

Monroe, J. T. 1989. "Which Came First, the *zajal* or the *muwaššaḥa*? Some Evidence for the Oral Origins of Hispano-Arabic Strophic Poetry." *Oral Tradition* 4, no. 1/2:38–74.

Nagy, G. 1974. *Comparative Studies in Greek and Indic Meter.* Harvard Studies in Comparative Literature 33. Cambridge, MA. http://nrs.harvard.edu/urn-3:hul.ebook:CHS_Nagy.Comparative_Studies_in_Greek_and_Indic_Meter.1974

——. 1990. *Pindar's Homer: The Lyric Possession of an Epic Past.* Baltimore. http://nrs.harvard.edu/urn-3:hul.ebook:CHS_Nagy.Pindars_Homer.1990. The Appendix at pp. 439–464 supplements the argumentation in Nagy 1974.

Saussure, F. de. (1916) 1972. *Cours de linguistique générale*. Edited by T. de Mauro. Paris.

Seville, Where *Miḥrābs* Weep and Pulpits Lament: Al-Rundī's Elegy in the Classical Poetic Tradition

Raymond K. Farrin
American University of Kuwait

AL-RUNDĪ'S POEM on the fall of Seville (1248) during the Reconquista stands as the most famous work in the subgenre of "lament for cities" of the Arabic elegy. This chapter considers the poem in context, noting the critical historical moment for Arab-Islamic civilization in the Iberian Peninsula and identifying the poem as both a continuation of, and contribution to, the Arabic literary tradition. Examining the *qaṣīda* structurally and thematically, it furthermore shows how the work is arranged according to the principles of ring composition and how this structure serves to emphasize the poem's message about the need for help to save al-Andalus. As a result of the discussion, it is hoped that we may better appreciate the artistic construction of al-Rundī's elegy and more fully sense its poignancy: as a call from the heart that, due to tight political circumstances at the time in North Africa and the Near East, went unanswered.

The lament for cities is an ancient Near Eastern form, going back at least as far as the Sumerians of Mesopotamia, who mourned the destruction of Ur by the Elamites around 1840 BCE.[1] In Arabic culture this type of expression is latent in the early pre-Islamic poetry of Arabia, in such motifs as the weeping at abandoned campsites, the questioning of remains about the fate of those departed, and the incitement in some elegies for relatives to take revenge after the loss of a warrior.[2] However, as a distinct kind of expression, *rithāʾ al-mudun*, as the lament for cities is known in Arabic, emerges in the literature only during the Abbasid period, in the wake of the Islamic conquests and coinciding with society's urbanization. Below we will briefly consider a few first examples, before shifting our attention west and focusing on al-Rundī's elegy.

The initial poems of this type were composed following episodes of unrest in Iraq. The siege of Baghdad during the civil war between al-Amīn

1. As noted in Sperl 2013, 5–7.
2. Examples are discussed in Farrin 2011, 1–24, 46–91. For an overview of this subgenre, see Muḥammad 1983.

and al-Maʾmūn, which took place between 809–13 CE, prompted several responses, the most famous being the long *qaṣīda* by al-Khuraymī of 135 lines. Regarding al-Khuraymī's work, we find that it opens nostalgically, recalling the city's early days:

> They said, when Time had not yet toyed with Baghdad,
> nor laid for it its snares,
> When she was like a bride, whose inner secrets are alluring to the
> young man,
> as well as her outward appearance:
> "An eternal garden, an abode of bliss,
> a place unfamiliar with misfortunes."

Al-Khuraymī describes this paradise in detail, with its gardens, bridges, and palaces. Toward the middle of the poem, he attributes its loss to the moral weakening of the inhabitants:

> God granted the city a respite
> then punished it when it became enveloped in sin.

The extent of laxity even causes the poet to wonder if hope remains:

> How many acts of disobedience we have seen in Baghdad –
> will the One Full of Majesty forgive it?

Al-Khuraymī goes on to portray the devastation of Baghdad, including the use of siege engines, which launch projectiles on the populace, and the rampaging of horsemen. Many verses decry the tragic results. He closes his elegy by calling on al-Maʾmūn to step in and restore the city to its former glory, and also by referring to the fineness of his own poem, a composition which the messenger (whom he has dispatched to al-Maʾmūn's vizier) will repeat again and again out of admiration.[3]

Ibn al-Rūmī's lament for Basra, composed in 871, is similar in that it concerns a city's devastation and calls for strong action. In 871 the Zanj, or slaves from Africa, who were forced to work in the fields and marshes of southern Iraq, rebelled against caliphal authority. Among other cities in the region, they sacked Basra. In response, Ibn al-Rūmī penned this *qaṣīda* of eighty-six lines. At its opening, he registers his sadness and disbelief:

3. Al-Khuraymī (d. ca. 821), *Dīwān*, 27–37. This poem is discussed in Elinson 2009, 20–24, and Kennedy 2013, 160–164. By contrast to al- Khuraymī's expression, an anonymous poet in a contemporary lament attributes the downfall to the evil eye. See Kennedy 2013, 157.

Preoccupation with shedding tears
drove pleasing sleep from my eye.
How can I sleep, after what has befallen Basra
in the way of mighty disasters?

He asks God not to guide their *imam*, whom he calls a "cursed traitor." After describing the depredations by the rebels, he directs his two travel companions to halt at the ruins (a motif borrowed from pre-Islamic poetry, as in the famous opening of the *Muʿallaqa* by Imruʾ al-Qays, d. 542: "Halt, let us weep in memory of a beloved and an abode, / by the sand crest between al-Dakhūl and Ḥawmal.")[4] He urges his companions to ask the place and its congregational mosque, though mute, about the fate of this once bustling port, this noted center of Islamic learning. Indeed, as Stephan Sperl has shown in his impressive analysis of the poem, the *qaṣīda* highlights at its middle a terrible annihilation, skulls at its center. This poem is intended to stir anger, and, in the last twelve verses, which correspond symmetrically with the opening twelve (wherein the poet expresses his sadness and shock), the poet calls for revenge.[5]

More personal and philosophical are the few lines left about Samarra by Ibn al-Muʿtazz. The author was born in the new capital city located up the Tigris. It had been founded only twenty-five years earlier by his great-grandfather, al-Muʿtaṣim (r. 833–42). While Ibn al-Muʿtazz was a boy, between the ages of five and eight, his father ruled there as caliph. The great city did not endure as a capital, though: in 892, when Ibn al-Muʿtazz was thirty-one, his cousin al-Muʿtaḍid returned the seat of power to Baghdad, and Samarra was left to neglect – after being combed through for materials. Ibn al-Muʿtazz commented:

Samarra is desolate;
nothing is permanent.
Its columns have been carried away
like reeds from the thicket.
It died like an elephant dies
whose tusks are extracted.[6]

In these lines we discern another possible reaction to death, besides outrage and a call for action: in the attempt by al-Sumaysir to put the event

4. Cited in Farrin 2011, 4.

5. Ibn al-Rūmī (d. ca. 896), *Dīwān*, 6:2377–2382; Sperl 2013, 12–16.

6. Ibn al Muʿtazz (d. 908), *Dīwān*, 649–650. This author unfortunately came to a dark end, strangled on the day of his accession to the caliphate. See Nicholson 1956, 325.

in perspective. Samarra was taken apart prematurely, as is evident to the poet. But its ultimate decline was inevitable, since nothing is permanent.

Both responses to the city's destruction, deep disturbance and appealing for action, as in al-Khuraymī's and Ibn al-Rūmī's poems, and struggling to come to terms with it as in Ibn al-Muʿtazz's poem, exist in the pre-Islamic elegy, depending on the mortality of the lamented person (whether from fighting or from sickness or accident, for example). Both such reactions persist in the Andalusī *rithāʾ al-mudun*, to which we turn now.

Slightly to the northwest of Cordoba, pride and capital city of al-Andalus, on a spur overlooking the Guadalquivir valley, the Umayyads likewise built a new royal city. Its founder, ʿAbd al-Raḥmān III (r. 912–61), named it al-Zahrāʾ (The Bright-Faced) after a favorite concubine. He invested enormously there, and soon the place became the magnificent center of Umayyad power in al-Andalus, attracting delegations from across Europe and North Africa. Expansion and further improvement continued under his son, al-Ḥakam II (r. 961–76). But the vizier who gained control after him transferred operations to a new location east of Cordoba, and al-Zahrāʾ fell into disuse around 980, less than fifty years after its founding in 936. The final blow came in 1013 when Berber forces destroyed the city.

Thereafter, al-Zahrāʾ became a site of visitation and reflection on life's transience. The Cordoban notable Ibn Jahwar (d. 1043) passed by once and grew melancholy. As we read in *Nafḥ al-ṭīb min ghuṣn al-Andalus al-raṭīb* (*The Effusion of Fragrance from the Tender Branch of al-Andalus*) by al-Maqqarī (d. 1632), the source for much of the poetry below about al-Andalus, Ibn Jahwar related of his experience:

> One day, I asked the dwelling of a people who had vanished:
> "Where are your inhabitants so dear to us?"
> It replied: "They stayed for a while and then set out,
> to where I know not."

An anonymous poet offered this account:

> Abodes glitter in the midst of playgrounds,
> and no one living there – a wasteland.
> From every side doves coo plaintively,
> falling silent for a while and then giving utterance again.
> So I addressed a singing bird,
> with sorrow in its heart and taken with fright:
> "What gives you complaint?" I asked. "What are you mourning?"
> It replied, "A time that passed and will not return."

In the same vein are the lines of al-Sumaysir (d. 1087):

> I halted in al-Zahrāʾ in a contemplative mood,
> considering and shedding tears over scattered ruins.
> I exclaimed, "O Zahrāʾ, return to us!"
> It replied: "Does one who died ever return?"
> So I remained there, crying over it –
> but how impossible that my tears be of use!
> It was as if the monuments left behind
> were female wailers lamenting the dead.[7]

These sentiments clearly compare to those of Ibn al-Muʿtazz about Samarra in the attempt to put its destruction in perspective. More in line with al-Khuraymī and Ibn al-Rūmī, on the other hand, is the expression by Ibn Shuhayd during the chaotic last years (1008–31) of the Umayyad caliphate. He rues the deterioration of Cordoba and the changes that have occurred to its society following attacks and civil wars. Toward the beginning of his elegy, he states: "For the likes of Cordoba, the one who bursts into tears, reacts too mildly."[8] Occupying the center of the thirty-line elegy are recollections of the palaces and the good life enjoyed inside them, the new royal residence to the east, the beautiful pleasure boats, the crowded Great Mosque, and the busy markets. Unlike al-Khuraymī and Ibn al-Rūmī, though, and perhaps reflective of a recognition that the Umayyad dynasty in al-Andalus had entered its death throes, he does not call on anyone to save the city. Rather, he ends by reiterating his profound grief and affliction:

> For its leaders, its transmitters of knowledge,
> its honest men, its defenders, my sadness recurs.
> For its graces, its serenity,
> its elegance and splendor, my soul emits sighs.
> For its scholars, its composed minds,
> its literary lights, its refined and witty persons, my insides tear apart.[9]

Following Ibn Shuhayd's lament, and sharing in its general sentiment, is the great elegy by North African Ibn Rashīq (Ibn Rashīq's poem, in turn, would later influence our poet al-Rundī, as al-Rundī adopts the rhyme-letter, ends his poem with the last word of the first line, *īmān*, "belief," and

7. Al-Maqqarī, *Nafḥ al-ṭīb*, 1:523–528.

8. Judging from a subsequent reference to the Ḥammūdīs, who were of Berber origin, he probably composed his poem in the late 1010s or early 1020s; Monroe 1974, 160. For a history of the period and of al-Andalus generally, see Kennedy 1996.

9. Ibn Shuhayd (d. 1035), *Dīwān*, 64–67. This poem is analyzed in Elinson 2009, 38–49.

incorporates many of the motifs used by the North African poet). For Ibn Rashīq, the tragedy happened in Tunisia. In 1057, the inland capital of Qayrawan was overrun by Bedouin Arab tribes, having been left by the sultan Muʿizz ibn Bādīs for the coastal fortress of al-Mahdiyya. Qayrawan had been an important center of Islamic learning, with the Great Mosque its heart, but the metropolis had become isolated and difficult to defend against the growing power of the Banī Hilāl and Banī Dahmān.[10] This is how Ibn Rashīq remembers his city:

> How many noble princes resided therein,
> with shining faces and lofty belief!
> Working together for religion and piety,
> committed to God in public and private.
> And how many an upright man, abounding in virtues,
> bestowing his favor and safeguarding his honor.
> And *imams* who brought the sciences to bear,
> smoothing *hadith* and hard parts in the Qurʾan.
> And scholars who, when asked, exposed blindness
> through learning, eloquence, and clarity.
> Who, when matters became abstruse and their doors closed,
> and when adversaries contended,
> Unraveled the mysteries of every difficult matter
> with manifest evidence and irrefutable proof.
> They abandoned their beds in obedience to their Lord,
> seeking the best halting place and lodging.
> When the darkness spread, you would see them
> celibately devoting themselves to God like monks.
> Indeed, in the Garden of Paradise is the noblest abode
> amidst black-eyed beauties and youthful servants.
> For it, they exchanged the earthly paradise attainable by profits –
> how excellent a line of business: obeying the Merciful!
> They are the ones who feared God as He should be feared,
> who knew the wiles of Satan.

Toward the middle of this poem, he recalls the city's rank among urban centers. Yet its preeminence attracted harm – sin could not have ruined the place, evidently, with such scholars there. He says:

> On account of them, Qayrawan was considered,
> when counting the minbars, the flower of cities.
> It outshone Cairo – deservedly so, boasting of such men –

10. Brett 2008, 77–79.

and rose over Baghdad.
It gained in beauty. And when its fine looks reached completion,
and every eye ascended toward it,
And all virtues gathered therein,
and it became the location of security and faith,
Time looked at it askance,
as one brooding, harboring envy.
Until it was settled that the fates descend,
and the decree drew near for a period and term.
Then Time drove her to dark strife,
prodding her forward with wooden rods,
Assailing her with the calamities of Fādigh and Ashālib,
among those of Banī Dahmān.

He concludes his fifty-six-line poem wondering if Time will reverse its gloomy deed, making Qayrawan fair and lustrous again and reuniting its inhabitants.[11]

Turning back to al-Andalus, we see a major change occurring at the end of the eleventh century. The Almoravids (*al-murābiṭūn*, or those banding together; cf. Qur᾽an 3:200), a Berber movement originating in the deserts of southern Morocco and advocating a return to the roots of Islam, had been invited into the Peninsula by the Taifa or Party Kings (*mulūk al-ṭawā᾽if*). These various potentates had replaced Umayyad rule in al-Andalus, and now they faced a significant Christian threat to the north. The Almoravids succeeded in protecting al-Andalus, although at the expense of independence. In the 1090s, the petty kingdoms of the Party Kings were seized and Almoravid governors sent up from Morocco to rule. Al-Muᶜtamid, for instance, poet and much-loved king of Seville, suffered a dramatic change of fortune. He fought successfully alongside the Almoravids against Alfonso VI at Zallāqa in 1086, but five years later the Almoravids came for Seville. The king died in exile, at Aghmat near Marrakesh, in 1095.[12]

Andalusī court poets mourned the change, since Berber-speaking governments meant a loss of patronage for them, and we may add their laments to the body of works about the loss of cities – or, in this case, the loss of minor kingdoms–inherited later by al-Rundī. For example, Ibn al-Labbāna, court poet at Seville, said:

11. Ibn Rashīq (d. 1064) in al-Dabbāgh of Qayrawan (d. 1297), *Maᶜālim al-īmān*, 18–20. For more on this event and the poetry surrounding it, see Brett 2008, 77–89. The ruin of Qayrawan is also described in a *maqāma* by al-Saraqusṭī (d. 1143). This *maqāma* has been translated by Monroe (al-Saraqusṭī 2002, 302–306) and is discussed in Elinson 2009, 51–79.

12. Kennedy 1996, 162–164.

For everything there is an appointed time,
and wishes have their limits.
Fate is saturated with a chameleon's dye;
the colors of its garb are always changing.
And we, in this game of chess, are being manipulated:
perhaps, at an occurrence, the king boasts of taking a pawn.
So shake off the dust of this world and its inhabitants;
the earth has become barren and the people have died.
And say to this lower world about the realm above:
"Aghmat has taken its beloved and concealed it."[13]

Thus he begins his ode, before launching into a recollection of al-Muᶜtamid's merits and grieving the end of his family's rule at Seville. Comparable is the long lament (seventy-five lines; the *qaṣīda* by Ibn al-Labbāna contains forty-one) by Ibn ᶜAbdūn, court poet of al-Mutawakkil in Badajoz northwest of Seville. When al-Mutawakkil was dethroned in 1094, Ibn ᶜAbdūn lost his employment. Like Ibn al-Labbāna, Ibn ᶜAbdūn opens with observations about a larger force operating:

Fate afflicts us, first with the blow and then with its effect,
so why weep over dreams and idle fancies?
I warn you, I warn you, still I warn you
against dozing between the claws and fangs of the lion!

A few lines later, he adds further caution:

So do not be fooled by the "slumber" of this world –
its eyes have no business but to be vigilant.

This poem is remarkable for its many learned references, in lines 9–47, to vanished glory: among Greeks, Persians, and other peoples of antiquity. It may be mentioned here that the work was studied in al-Andalus; the poet Ibn Badrūn (d. 1211), for example, wrote a commentary on it.[14] Following these historical references, Ibn ᶜAbdūn turns to the subject of al-Mutawakkil's family dynasty, before concluding with three lines about the excellence of the poem itself. As he says, the work (due to its eloquence and message) shall "interrupt the vain chatter uselessly poured forth in the desert and in the towns."[15]

13. Cited in Muḥammad 1983, 169–170.
14. Ibn Badrūn, *Sharḥ qaṣīdat Ibn ᶜAbdūn*.
15. The poem is included in Monroe's anthology, 1974, 228–241; the translation of this last phrase is by Monroe. On the loss of patronage as a catalyst for literary creativity, in al-Andalus and elsewhere, see Monroe and Pettigrew 2003, 138–177.

This period also witnessed the beginning of a direr trend in al-Andalus. In 1085 Toledo, south of the Cordillera Central Range, was taken by Alfonso VI, and, despite an Almoravid attempt to recuperate the city in 1109, it never returned to Muslim hands. In response to Toledo's fall, an unknown poet composed a lament of seventy-two lines. He opens his elegy with a rhetorical question about the grievous event:

> On account of your loss, how can faces smile,
> when other faces have been taken captive?

In the middle of the ode, he mixes instigation, a call for *jihad* from fellow Muslims, with incredulity and reproach:

> Take revenge in religion's name – come to its aid –
> seeing that vultures have circled over the dead.
> Don't be weak; draw every sharp sword
> whose stiff blow necks dread.
> And die, all of you! Death is more fitting
> than to be wronged or to do wrong.
> Do you exhibit patience after a trial and a seizure of captives?
> In such times, the tranquil, forbearing heart is blamed.
> The bereaved mother has lost all her females,
> and the falcon mother has lost all her chicks.
> Verily, we low when struck with calamities –
> and there is nothing amazing about lowing cows –
> And we take fright instead of roaring. Yet if we took courage,
> not succumbing to cowardice, we would roar!

Further on he prods again, calling for action to replace the tears, and then poses, in the next line, a fundamental question:

> Enough of grief! People have asked,
> "Where to now? Which way do we go?"
> Do we leave our houses in flight,
> while beyond the sea we have no houses?

Through the remainder of the poem, he continues to evoke the plight of the affected people and to urge a strong response, wishing finally that God will grant them aid.[16]

It would be another century and a half before we find a new series of poems in the same spirit. The Almohads (*al-muwaḥḥidūn*, upholders of God's unity against prevalent anthropomorphist ideas of the time), another

16. Al-Maqqarī, *Nafḥ al-ṭīb*, 4:483–486.

movement of Berber origin, replaced the Almoravids in al-Andalus after the takeover of Marrakesh in 1147. For a while they brought the fight to the Christian enemy, such as during the Huete campaign east of Toledo in 1172. But they suffered a major defeat in 1212 at Las Navas de Tolosa, north of a number of Andalusī cities, and then withdrew from al-Andalus altogether in 1228.[17] Needless to say, they left the situation perilous. Sure enough, the years 1228–48, the twilight period for al-Andalus, witnessed a major Christian advance. First Cordoba fell in 1236, shocking the Andalusīs.[18] Meanwhile Valencia, located on the east of the Peninsula by the Mediterranean, faced grave danger. The poet Ibn al-Abbār departed to Yaḥyā ibn ʿAbd al-Wāḥid, Hafsid ruler of Tunis, to garner support (the Hafsids, installed in Tunisia by the Almohads in 1207, had gained in power and had come to rule independently). He opens his appeal thus:

> Reach with your steeds – the steeds of God – al-Andalus,
> for its path to salvation has disappeared.
> And bestow what it asks of your cherished support,
> for your great support remains what is sought.
> And give a breath of life to ease its suffering;
> long has it tasted affliction, both morning and night.
> O Peninsula, whose people have become slaughter-camels to events,
> whose luck has turned wretched,
> Every rising star portends approaching calamity,
> whose funeral gathering, to the enemy, is a wedding.
> And every setting star bodes near misfortune,
> at which security becomes apprehension and happiness misery.

At the middle of the poem, he points to the *qaṣīda* itself and speaks of its recipient:

> These are its messages calling from up close –
> and you are the best hope to one in despair.
> They have come running, wishing for success
> from the contented prince and sagacious lord.
> They braved the sea, whose waves took them high and low,

17. The scholar and poet Ibn al-Dabbāgh of Seville (d. 1259) said of this battle, known in Arabic as *al-ʿIqāb* (The Punishment):

> A woman said: "I see you absorbed in reflection,
> as if you are standing on the Day of Judgment."
> I said to her: "I am reflecting on what called for punishment,
> and led to the Battle of the Punishment."
> "In its aftermath, there is no place of residence in al-Andalus;
> tribulation has entered from every door." Al-Maqqarī, *Nafḥ al-ṭīb*, 4:464.

18. Al-Maqqarī, *Nafḥ al-ṭīb*, 4:453.

such that they suffered ferocity and abatement.
Perhaps they even swam, facing strong gales,
exerting themselves like whipped stallions –
Heading straight for Yaḥyā ibn ʿAbd al-Wāḥid ibn Abī Ḥafṣ,
and kissing the sanctified ground before him.

Finally, he calls again for support, ending his sixty-seven-line work on an optimistic note:

So fill – and may this give you enjoyment – its battlefield with aid:
short-haired chargers or racers on tracks.
And set an appointment for triumph, one al-Andalus can expect.
It may be that the enemy's day of tumult has come.[19]

The Hafsid ruler did send a small fleet to Valencia, but it was driven off. The inhabitants had to endure the siege alone, and in 1238 Valencia fell. Incidentally, following this outcome, a longer work of ninety lines by an anonymous poet was sent to the same ruler in Tunis. The poet begins this work with an even more desperate tone, after the seaside stronghold had been taken. He says:

Al-Andalus has called you, so answer its call,
redeem it from the devils of the Cross!
It cried to you with lofty appeal,
so grant from your mercy what will protect its soul.

Later, he tries to tempt the Hafsid with the prospect of attractive bounty:

Bare your swords to wipe clean the enemy's traces,
killing off their lions and capturing their gazelles.

Yet the ultimate reward, of course, will be heavenly. Moreover, his travel conditions to al-Andalus, according to the poet, promise to be favorable. In short, this is the Hafsid's golden opportunity to please God and acquit himself as a hero:

Embark on the waters and they will be a calm sea;
cross going towards it the desert.
May the one crying out be requited by God,
and may the inhabitants, desiring His reward, patiently endure.
This is the abode of *jihad*. So do not let a war zone elude you
whose martyrs now equal the living.

19. Al-Maqqarī, *Nafḥ al-ṭīb*, 4:457–460.

Lastly, after a section of considerable praise, the poet ends by offering apology for not giving the ruler and his kin proper due.[20]

Yet the subsequent years witnessed a succession of catastrophic losses. First Murcia fell (1243), then, to the west, Jaen fell (1246), then it was Jativa's turn (1247) back to the northeast, and finally, further down the Guadalquivir, Seville met its fate (1248). The heartland of al-Andalus was lost – leaving only the southern Nasrid kingdom of Granada (which, as events turned out, was to last until 1492).[21]

Seville's fall was especially devastating. Since the eleventh century, it had replaced Cordoba as al-Andalus' leading city. Though it had seen political vicissitudes, overall it had grown and prospered. We are told that a man who had visited Syria and Egypt was asked, "Which is more beautiful – one of those places, or Seville?" The man replied Seville, explaining his choice in reference to the other two: "Its elevated Sharaf region is a forest without lions, and its river is a Nile without crocodiles." The city was surrounded by olive trees. Figs, sugarcane and fish also were abundant. We may form an additional idea of the place from a contemporary description: "It is a thriving city on the banks of the waterway known as the River Cordoba, over which there is a bridge where boats are tied. It has standing markets and profitable commerce. Its inhabitants possess great wealth, most of which derives from the sale of olive oil." The olives, we are told, were stored in cellars for thirty years and then pressed.[22]

This brings us to our poet, and we may pause here briefly to recall his life before considering his poetic response. Unfortunately, only a bare outline of his life can be provided from the sources. Abū al-Baqāʾ al-Rundī hailed from the town of Ronda in the southern part of al-Andalus. He spent time in Malaga, along the coast, and also visited Granada numerous times petitioning kings. He was reportedly of religious disposition, a man of good deeds, and skilled in applying divine law. In literature, his talents were varied; he wrote poetry, prose, and *maqāmāt*. His death occurred in 1285.[23]

In terms of the *rithāʾ al-mudun* subgenre, it will be apparent how al-Rundī draws on the existing tradition. As a cultured and learned poet, he certainly was aware of these elegies, and he probably had more than a few memorized. At the same time, the terrible event of Seville's fall clearly af-

20. Al-Maqqarī, *Nafḥ al-ṭīb*, 4:479–483. On al-Andalus as an arena for *jihad* and martyrdom, resembling Jerusalem during the time of the Crusaders, see Stearns 2009, 363–366.

21. Kennedy 1996, 266–272.

22. Al-Maqqarī, *Nafḥ al-ṭīb*, 1:157–159, 208. Concerning the last detail, the olives reportedly yielded more oil that way than if pressed fresh. They were preserved most likely with salt.

23. See Ibn al-Khaṭīb (d. 1374), *al-Iḥāṭa*, 3:360–376; al-Maqqarī, *Nafḥ al-ṭīb*, 4:486–490. The text of his poem is found in *Nafḥ al-ṭīb*, 4:487–488.

fected and moved him. For in his elegy he reworks inherited motifs in a new way, contributing to the classical heritage a poem notably distinct and valuable.

Al-Rundī's elegy consists of two main elements: an introduction and a three-part body. Below we will discuss each section individually. Next, we will provide a structural summary, highlighting the use of ring composition in the work, and then offer a few concluding remarks.

Introduction: Ubi Sunt

1 Everything after completion goes into decline,
so let no person be fooled by life's good times.
2 Events are revolving, as you've seen them:
who is made happy for a time is saddened for longer.
3 This worldly abode does not preserve anyone,
nor do circumstances remain unchanged.
4 Inevitably, Time rends every coat of mail
if Yemeni swords and spearheads glance off.
5 And it unsheathes every sword for extinction,
even if the sword be Sayf ibn Dhī Yazan and the scabbard Ghumdān.[24]
6 Where are the crowned kings from Yemen –
where are their crowns and diadems?
7 And where is what Shaddād erected in Iram,
and where is Sāsān's kingdom among the Persians?[25]
8 And where are Qārūn's acquisitions of gold,
and where are ʿĀd, and Shaddād, and Qaḥṭān?[26]
9 An unstoppable event came upon them all,
and they passed into oblivion as if they had never existed.
10 What once was of royalty and of dominion,
became like recollections of the person roused from sleep.
11 Time turned on Darius and his slayer;
as for Kisrā, his Iwān afforded him no refuge.[27]
12 It is as if hardship never was softened by an occasion of joy,
as if Solomon never ruled the world.
13 Time's misfortunes are indeed varied and diverse;

24. Sayf ibn Dhī Yazan was a pre-Islamic king of Yemen, and Ghumdān was his castle.

25. Shaddād, son of ʿĀd, was the leader of a people who came after Noah. They were rich and mighty, and erected the city of "Iram of lofty pillars" (cf. Qurʾan 89:6) presumably near Oman.

26. Qārūn was a minister of Pharaoh who was proud of his enormous wealth (Qurʾan 28:76; 29:39; 40:24). For ʿĀd, see preceding note. Qaḥṭān was the progenitor of the South Arabians.

27. Darius' slayer was Alexander the Great. The vaulted palace of Kisrā was in Ctesiphon.

time brings both pleasures and sorrows.
14 Consolation then follows, making events easier to bear –
but there is no consolation for what has befallen Islam.

Al-Rundī opens his poem with a reflection about life's transience. Philosophical statements, it may be observed, are common at the beginning of elegies, such as in this statement by al-Mutanabbī (d. 965) in the poem he composed after hearing of his grandmother's death:

> To such as he was, the youth returns,
> going back to his original state, decreasing as he once increased.

Or, for example, in these words from his elegy for Sayf al-Dawla's mother at Aleppo:

> We sharpen the Mashrafiyya swords, and we ready the tall spears,
> and then Fate kills us without a fight.
> And we tie the fastest horses close by,
> but they do not save us from the galloping approach of Time.[28]

Such sentiments about the inevitability of death and the limited term of existence may be found in pre-Islamic elegies, and they occur, as we have noted, in the elegies to fallen cities or fallen kingdoms.[29] They manifest one of two possible reactions to the event of mortality, reflecting an attempt to come to terms with the loss.

In the middle of the introduction, we encounter the *ubi sunt* motif,[30] a motif also discernible in pre-Islamic poetry about abandoned campsites and common to the *rithāʾ al-mudun* pieces. Here the idea is expressed through numerous examples from history, including kings from Yemen, Darius and Alexander, and Kisrā of Ctesiphon. Psychologically, these instances represent a sustained attempt at acceptance and putting death in perspective. Impermanence marks human endeavors, it may be seen, and every great acquisition is lost. The repetition, moreover, bespeaks intensity of reaction and depth of emotion. Ibn Rashīq has noticed, with regard to this phenomenon, that repetition occurs in elegies more often than in other poetry, "being found where there is calamity and strongly felt pain." Moreover, repetition may well have a therapeutic purpose, to lead to a mental state of calm. As Alexander Elinson observes pertinently in *Looking Back at al-Andalus*, such repetition creates:

28. Al-Mutanabbī, *Dīwān*, 115, 172.

29. For instance, at the beginning of Ibn al-Labbāna's *qaṣīda* for al-Muʿtamid and the ʿAbbādids of Seville, cited above.

30. From the Latin *ubi sunt qui ante nos fuerunt*? (Where are those who were before us?).

> a rhythm and a continuity that allows for a certain comfort and expectation that can act as a counterbalance to the unpredictability and severe rupture that can occur with a traumatic loss. As well, this expectation can serve to shorten the distance between the poet and audience: after a rhythm is established, the audience comes to sense what comes next.[31]

The psychological intent of these examples, then, is to take away the surprise, to diminish the shock.

Yet the course of this introduction is what makes its ending all the more surprising. Ultimately, al-Rundī's attempt to put the loss in perspective – which should lead him and his audience to some form of consolation – fails. For, notwithstanding these earlier downfalls and disappearances from the world, the loss of al-Andalus is exceptional, as al-Rundī underscores in the next part of the poem (which I have designated as part *A* and given the title, "Tragedy of the Evil Eye").

A: Tragedy of the Evil Eye

15 An event has overtaken the Peninsula for which there can be no solace;
Mount Uḥud has collapsed, and Mount Thahlān has fallen.[32]
16 The evil eye has struck, bringing religious tribulation,
to the extent regions and lands are emptied of Islam.
17 Ask Valencia what happened to Murcia.
And where is Jativa? Where is Jaen?
18 Where is Cordoba, the abode of sciences,
in which many a scholar rose to prominence?
19 And where is Hims, with its abundant delights
and clear river running high?[33]
20 They were the foundations of the country.
So how can it endure, without its foundations?
21 Now monotheism weeps out of sorrow,
just as the passionate lover weeps for his beloved,
22 For abodes destitute of Islam,
while infidelity is thriving.
23 Where mosques have become churches –
nothing in them but bells and crosses.

31. Elinson 2008, 86. Ibn Rashīq's remark cited in Elinson 2008, 85.

32. Uḥud is located near Medina, and Thahlān is another mountain of the Hijaz. Thahlān is mentioned also in Ibn Rashīq's lament of Qayrawan, l. 44.

33. Seville was given the familiar name of Hims, after the Syrian city. The troops that settled in Seville upon the conquest of al-Andalus five centuries earlier came from Hims.

24 Even the prayer niches cry, though solid;
even the minbars lament, though wooden.

Having failed to lead his audience in the introduction, by means of historical reflection, to a state of tranquility and a certain acceptance of events, the poet undertakes now the expression of grief proper. Here, in the *qaṣīda* body's opening, the full shock is registered and the tears are shed. The first line above recalls pre-Islamic al-Khansāʾ upon hearing of her brother Ṣakhr's death. In one elegy, she says of herself in her tent:

> I got up, and my spirit, devastated at his demise,
> almost went after him.
> It was if, in mental soundness and physical capability,
> I was a drunkard: now rising, now falling down.[34]

Here, though, in al-Rundī's elegy, mountains in the Arabian Peninsula near Medina collapse. Thus we may comprehend the magnitude of the loss; the pre-Islamic motif of falling down has been reworked and expanded to express convulsive shock at the loss of cities.

Familiar too from pre-Islamic poetry is the theme of weeping. It will be recalled that in the *nasīb*, or nostalgic prelude of the desert ode, the poet cries over his lost beloved. According to the established pattern, the beloved belongs to another tribe, and though she and the poet have shared happy times during the verdant spring, when Bedouin tribes might pasture together, at the onset of the dry season she must return with her kin to their permanent water source. We might mention as well that intertribal marriage, as a rule, is forbidden, and that, in all probability, the poet will never see her again. Thus he weeps painfully. In this case, though, Islam is weeping for its lost beloved, al-Andalus.

We note also a difference here between al-Rundī and the earlier poets in the *rithāʾ al-mudun* tradition. All of those mentioned in this study speak of their own sadness or point to themselves crying as a result of the various tragedies. By contrast, al-Rundī does not figure as a character in this poem. He was said to have been modest, and perhaps for this reason he does not include himself. Or, perhaps he felt that the magnitude of the tragedy dictated something altogether more emotive and forceful than a personal expression of sadness. Whatever the reason, the poet absents himself and personifies Islam. At this tragedy, indeed, mountains in the Arabian heartland collapse, the religion itself weeps, and its symbols lament.

Structurally, we notice the architecture of the *qaṣīda* in the form of a

34. Cited in Farrin 2011, 75–76.

center-periphery connection.[35] That is to say, we find rhetorical questions, the *ubi sunt* theme, in the center of the previous section. And here we find rhetorical questions, directed at cities, in the periphery or first part of the body. Thematically, the questioning in this place reflects the development of a pre-Islamic motif from the *nasīb*: the interrogation of encampment remains about the whereabouts of a former sweetheart (cf. Labīd: "I stopped to question them. Yet how does one question/ deaf, permanent, inarticulate stones?"[36]). But the placement of such rhetorical questions at the first part of the body, corresponding to rhetorical questions earlier at the center of the introduction, also reflects careful design.

We proceed now to the core of the poem, designated as *B*: "Ringing of Alarm and Cry for Help." According to the logic of ring composition, this part has special significance.

B: Ringing of Alarm and Cry for Help

25 O heedless one, for whom Time carries a warning,
though you may be slumbering – Time is awake!
26 And who strolls cheerfully, diverted by his homeland –
can homelands beguile, after what happened to Hims?
27 That disaster obliviated what preceded it,
and never will it, in the length of time, be forgotten.
28 O riders of lean thoroughbreds,
like eagles on the racetrack,
29 Wielding sharpened, Indian swords,
like flames in the dark, dust cloud of battle;
30 And those enjoying a pleasant life, beyond the sea,
possessed of might and authority in their lands:
31 Do you have news of the people of al-Andalus?
For riders have set off by night with word of what happened.
32 How much the weak and helpless call out to us for aid,
dying or falling captive, yet not a person stirs.
33 What disunity is this in Islam, between you –
are not you, O worshipers of God, brothers?
34 Are there no proud souls filled with resolution and ardor,
are there no helpers and supporters of good?

35. Note Lund's Fourth Law from *Chiasmus in the New Testament*: "There are also many instances of ideas, occurring at the centre of one system and recurring in the extremes of a corresponding system, the second system evidently having been constructed to match the first." Lund 1942, 41. This type of composition is also very common in the Qurʾan.

36. Cited in Farrin 2011, 48.

In the center of the *qaṣīda* body, al-Rundī expresses his essential message. It is twofold and directed at those living abroad in comfort, in North Africa and further east, such as in Egypt. The message includes a grave warning that the same destiny could be in store for them and an urgent summons for help. Relating to the first half of this message, we find another example of the center-periphery connection we identified in the last section. For here, in the center of the body of the poem, we find a connection to the beginning of the introduction. This would be in the figure of the heedless person, strolling cheerfully and diverted by his homeland – does he not realize that the good times pass? Amused and carefree he might be, but he should remember that circumstances change. Thus we observe a reinforced, or double, connection between the body and introduction: previously, between the first section of the body and the center of the introduction (in the questioning of Andalusī cities and the earlier *ubi sunt* questions); and here, between the center of the body and the first lines of the introduction (in the wakeup call to the slumberer, alerting him to the fleeting nature of security and happiness).[37]

We indicated above that the introduction represents a failed attempt to come to terms with the fall of Seville and other Andalusī cities. For the poet, notwithstanding the fact that civilizations come to an end and riches disappear, no consolation can be found for what has happened in al-Andalus. The body of the poem, then, expresses the other reaction to loss: not trying to come to terms, therefore, but rather deep distress and a call to action. Accordingly, following the tears, in this section (*B*) there is instigation (*taḥrīḍ*). Such a reaction obtains in the pre-Islamic elegy, in the prompting of listeners to take vengeance after a warrior has been slain, for example, and it occurs frequently in the *rithāʾ al-mudun* – in all those poems, indeed, composed after cities of al-Andalus were taken, as Toledo and Valencia. But unlike in the majority of *rithāʾ al-mudun* that aims to galvanize and motivate, the address in this case is general, not directed at a particular sultan or authority. This may be because two poems already had been sent to the Hafsid ruler of Tunis concerning the fate of Valencia. Or perhaps al-Rundī felt that all strong actors should be summoned, given the magnitude of the recent loss and the severity of the threat to Muslims.

Yet hope glimmers in this section: at its middle, in the form of wielded swords appearing like flames in the dust cloud of battle. This feature of the composition, the mention of light at the center, may well call to mind Abū Firās al-Ḥamdānī's (d. 967) famous elegy for his mother, composed while he

37. On a smaller level, the same type of connection exists between the middle of section *A*, and the beginning of *B*, in the repetition of the word Hims.

was in a Byzantine prison in Constantinople. He begins this elegy by asking God that gentle rain might fall on her gravesite in Syria, and ends it by consoling himself that, though separated from her at death, he will meet her soon in the afterlife. In the middle of the poem he recalls her attributes. She used to shelter the oppressed and help the poor, and she fasted patiently, even on hot days. In the central line (10), he mentions her nocturnal habit of rising for prayer, befitting a devout Muslim. Frequently she remained devotional until, after the passage of hours, bright dawn appeared (from the poem, the reader likely feels that Abū Firās' mother has gone to Heaven).[38] Al-Rundī makes use of a similar transition of night to day in two of his panegyrics, wherein the night, or his dark despair, gives way at the center to the brightness of his patron's face.[39] And we detect a related darkness-to-brightness transition in this elegy, from thick dust cover to a flash of swords. Perhaps military action can save al-Andalus after all; maybe, at the end of the tunnel, there is light. Next we come to the last section, which I have labeled as *A′* because of the similarities with section *A* above, as I discuss in detail below, and entitled "Parting Scenes":

A′: Parting Scenes

35 O who will come help a people humiliated after their standing tall,
whose state was changed by disbelief and oppression?
36 Yesterday they were kings in their stately domiciles,
while today they are slaves in infidelity's domain.
37 Were you to see them, guideless and confused,
arrayed in outfits of shame and lowliness;
38 Or see them weeping upon being sold,
the affair would appall you, and sorrows would transport you.
39 Oh, many a child has been separated from his mother,
just like the spirit is pulled from the body;
40 And many a young girl, as beautiful as the sun rising,
or like the ruby and pearl necklace –
41 Forcibly the barbarian leads her to a loathsome end,
her heart bewildered, her eye crying.
42 At such a sight the heart melts out of grief,
if that heart contains any faithfulness and Islam!

In this last section, al-Rundī repeats the urgent call for help and pulls seriously at the heartstrings. He evokes here scenes of the victims. Of course, the ideas of family separation and violation of women feature typically in

38. Abū Firās, *Dīwān*, 162–163.
39. Ibn al-Khaṭīb, *al-Iḥāṭa*, 3:362–363; al-Maqqarī, *Nafḥ al-ṭīb*, 4:489–490.

the lament for cities subgenre. Yet unlike his predecessors in this area, who, as a rule, depict these outrages in the plural, highlighting, besides the crimes themselves, the frightful toll of victims, al-Rundī, after calling to mind the slave market and alluding to the large numbers ("Many a ...") for general background, focuses like a movie director on individual persons. Here is a boy being torn from his mother, there a young beauty being dragged off by a brutish man. Such scenes, if any, should leave an impact!

Structurally, we notice a return in section *A′* to the themes of *A*, in accordance with the principles of ring composition. The poet comes back here, with variation, to separation and weeping. In *A*, Islam sheds tears at the loss of al-Andalus; now in *A′*, a young girl cries at being torn away. Also, after opening *A* with a statement about the impossibility of finding solace, al-Rundī closes the poem with a rhetorical statement about the effect of parting scenes. Thus the Muslim reader or hearer of the poem, having envisioned what has transpired, and providing that person's heart contains at least a trace of belief, cannot help but be moved and grief-stricken.

The diagram below further illustrates the *qaṣīda*'s plan and the use of ring composition in the work.

Structural Summary

Introduction

1–5 Decline is inevitable; brief happiness gives way to sadness; Time rends every coat of mail, and it unsheathes every sword for extinction.

6–10 Ubi Sunt: where are the kings and their kingdoms? Where are the storied acquisitions? Where are the leaders and their peoples? They passed like dreams.

11–14 Time turned on Darius, Alexander, and Kisrā; Time's misfortunes are diverse; consolation then follows, but there is no consolation for what has befallen Islam.

A

15–16 An extraordinary event has overtaken the Peninsula, causing mountains in Arabia to collapse; the evil eye has struck; regions and lands are emptied of Islam.

17–20 Ask about Murcia, Jativa, Jaen, Cordoba, and Hims [Seville]; how can the country endure without its foundations?

21–24 Monotheism weeps like the passionate lover, for abodes destitute of Islam; mosques have been converted to churches; prayer niches cry and minbars lament.

B

25–27 Time carries a warning for the heedless person; can homelands beguile, after what happened to Hims? Its disaster is unprecedented.

28–31 Do the horsemen wielding swords and the rulers living beyond the sea have news of the people al-Andalus? Riders have set off with word of what happened.

32–34 The weak and helpless call for aid, yet none responds; are not fellow Muslims their brothers? Is there no one who is proud and zealous, and who champions good?

A′

35–38 Who will help a people humiliated? Yesterday they were kings, while today they are slaves; if you saw them guideless and confused, or weeping upon being sold, you would be appalled and saddened.

39–41 Many a boy has been violently pulled from his mother; many a pretty girl has been dragged off, bewildered and crying.

42 At such scenes, the believer's heart melts.

Alas, al-Rundī's poem did not arrive at a propitious moment. In 1248, the year of its composition, the Almohad dynasty fell in Morocco. As mentioned above, already from Tunisia the Hafsids had sent help, to no avail. Looking east, the situation was no more encouraging. In Egypt, the Ayyubids were on the verge of collapse (their state would fail in 1250; it was replaced by a Mamluk one). Meanwhile, the Crusaders were still active in Palestine and Syria, and the Mongols were threatening Iraq (they would sack Baghdad in 1258). In short, other regions were beset with internal problems. Therefore, though this poem surely touched its listeners emotionally, it did not produce the desired effect.

We might estimate the contemporary response from a letter dating about a century later, from the Mamluk sultan al-Nāṣir Muḥammad to the Merinid sultan Abū al-Ḥasan (the Merinids were a Berber dynasty in Morocco, and Fes had replaced Marrakech as their capital). This Merinid sultan had fought the Christians in 1340 near Tarifa at the southern tip of al-Andalus, near Gibraltar, in coordination with Yūsuf I of Granada. The Muslims had suffered a major defeat. From the Tarifa area, Yūsuf I returned to Granada, and Abū al-Ḥasan went back to Fes. In fact, this was the last major effort by Berbers from Morocco to sustain al-Andalus, and no Muslim army would cross again into the Iberian Peninsula. After this failed campaign, Abū al-Ḥasan wrote to al-Nāṣir Muḥammad in Cairo soliciting *jihad*. The latter replied, expressing great sorrow for what had happened to the people of al-Andalus. But the letter, penned by his secretary, goes on to suggest difficulty and reservation:

> Were assistance truly possible, bridled horses carrying us would fly to you like eagles; the dried river beds there would fill and rush at your enemy with our curved bows and straight arrows; we would darken the stars' eyes with tips of lances, and rip through the dust cloud of battle with flashing swords; we would take their heads as decorative balls for the hilts of our weapons; we would fill war's narrow passes with repeated charges, bend our reins towards them, wade into streams of long blades, and tread on thorns of spears; we would split the very rocks with our cries, and make tears flow from the most dreadful of occurrences! Yet how removed the goal, how vast the distance! Does the hand, when it reaches up, touch Pleiades? All we can do, we and our subjects, is to supply you with an army of our prayers, and equip you with our sincere well wishes that accommodating angels know from our characters.[40]

The letter next expresses relief that the sultan and his men survived the blow, and reminds that war includes both setbacks and advances: perhaps today's defeat will be erased by tomorrow's victory. Indeed, the people of Egypt, as the letter indicates, are encouraged by the fact that Gibraltar remains secure, supposing its Rock would buttress the Andalusīs and enable them to vanquish the infidels. It thereafter assures the sultan that, when his delegations pass through on pilgrimage, they will be hosted grandly. The letter closes by asking God's protection for the sultan and his army, so that they might avenge the loss and grasp victory's ripe fruit, and by extending kind, scented greetings.[41]

In the area of poetry, however, the success of al-Rundī cannot be gainsaid. Working within the tradition, he deployed motifs innovatively to evoke the crisis of his time and place. His *qaṣīda* distinguished itself in a heritage already rich, and in turn, it served as a poetic model. When events in al-Andalus later, for example, went from bad to worse – or, rather, to dismal worst, since this time Granada fell – an anonymous poet clearly nods his head to al-Rundī (though he also adds a hundred lines for differentiation, making his work 142 instead of 42, and he attributes the loss to the Muslims' forgetting their obligations to God and their resulting weakness, not to their cities' attraction of envy).[42] Finally, we might recall in this connection what Tolstoy

40. Al-Maqqarī, *Nafḥ al-ṭīb*, 4:397.

41. Al-Maqqarī, *Nafḥ al-ṭīb*, 4:397–398.

42. Cited in Muḥammad 1983, 211–217 and analyzed in Hanna 2000, 51–56. Besides Granada, the poet laments Ronda, Malaga, and other urban centers as well.

proposed in *What Is Art?* He defined the artistic endeavor as "a human activity consisting in this, that one man consciously, by means of certain external signs, hands on to others feelings he has lived through, that others are infected by these feelings and also experience them."[43] The definition would seem perfectly applicable here. For in this work al-Rundī has employed, with great skill no doubt, his art to convey personal sentiments, leaving a poem that continues to resonate among audiences to this day.

43. Tolstoy 1960, 51.

Bibliography

Abū Firās al-Ḥamdānī. 1959. *Dīwān*. Beirut.

Brett, M. 2008. "The Poetry of Disaster: The Tragedy of Qayrawān, 1052–1057 CE." In *Continuity and Change in the Realms of Islam: Studies in Honour of Professor Urbain Vermeulen*, edited by K. D'Hulster and J. Van Steenbergen, 77–89. Leuven.

al-Dabbāgh, ʿA. R. 1968. *Maʿālim al-īmān fī maʿrifat ahl al-Qayrawān*. Edited by I. Shabbūḥ. Cairo.

Elinson, A. E. 2008. "Loss Written in Stone: Ibn Shuhayd's *Ritha'* for Cordoba and Its Place in the Arabic Elegiac Tradition." In *Transforming Loss into Beauty: Essays on Arabic Literature and Culture in Memory of Magda Al-Nowaihi*, edited by M. Hammond and Dana Sajdi, 79–114. Cairo.

——. 2009. *Looking Back at al-Andalus: The Poetics of Loss and Nostalgia in Medieval Arabic and Hebrew Literature*. Leiden.

Farrin, R. 2011. *Abundance from the Desert: Classical Arabic Poetry*. Syracuse.

Hanna, S. A. 2000. "An Anonymous Andalusian Elegy on the War of Granada." *Asian and African Studies* 9, no. 1:51–56.

Ibn Badrūn. 1846. *Sharḥ qaṣīdat Ibn ʿAbdūn: Commentaire historique de poème d'Ibn ʿAbdoun*. Edited by R. Dozy. Leiden.

Ibn al-Khaṭīb. 1975. *al-Iḥāṭa fī akhbār Gharnāṭa*. Edited by M. ʿA. ʿInān. 4 vols. Cairo.

Ibn al-Muʿtazz. 1995. *Dīwān*. Edited by Y. S. Farḥāt. Beirut.

Ibn Shuhayd. 1963. *Dīwān*. Edited by C. Pellat. Beirut.

Ibn al-Rūmī. 2003. *Dīwān*. Edited by Ḥ. Naṣṣār. 6 vols. Cairo.

Kennedy, H. 1996. *Muslim Spain and Portugal: A Political History of al-Andalus*. London.

——. 2013. "Pity and Defiance in the Poetry of the Siege of Baghdad (197/813)." In *Warfare and Poetry in the Middle East*, edited by H. Kennedy, 149–165. London.

al-Khuraymī. 1971. *Dīwān*. Edited by ʿA. J. al-Ṭāhir and M. J. al-Muʿaybad. Beirut.

Lund, N. W. 1942. *Chiasmus in the New Testament: A Study in Formgeschichte*. Chapel Hill.

al-Maqqarī. 1968. *Nafḥ al-ṭīb min ghuṣn al-Andalus al-raṭīb*. Edited by I. ʿAbbās. 8 vols. Beirut.

Monroe, J. T. 1974. *Hispano-Arabic Poetry: A Student Anthology*. Berkeley.

Monroe, J. T. and M. Pettigrew. 2003. "The Decline of Courtly Patronage and the Appearance of New Genres in Arabic Literature: The Case of the *Zajal*, the *Maqāma* , and the Shadow Play." *Journal of Arabic Literature* 34:138–177.

Muḥammad, ʿA. R. 1983. *Rithāʾ al-mudun wa-al-mamālik al-zāʾila fī al-shiʿr al-ʿarabī ḥattā suqūṭ Gharnāṭa*. Cairo.
al-Mutanabbī. 2005. *Dīwān*. Beirut.
Nicholson, R. A. 1956. *A Literary History of the Arabs*. Cambridge.
al-Saraqusṭī. 2002. *Al-Maqāmāt al-Luzūmīyah by Abū l-Ṭāhir Muḥammad ibn Yūsuf al-Tamīmī al-Saraqusṭī ibn al-Aštarkūwī (d. 538/1143)*. Edited and translated by J. T. Monroe. Leiden.
Sperl, S. 2013. "'O City Set Up Thy Lament': Poetic Responses to the Trauma of War." In *Warfare and Poetry in the Middle East*, edited by H. Kennedy, 1–37. London.
Stearns, J. 2009. "Representing and Remembering al-Andalus: Some Historical Considerations Regarding the End of Time and the Making of Nostalgia." *Medieval Encounters* 15:355–374.
Tolstoy, L. 1960. *What Is Art?* Translated by A. Maude. New York.

Astrology, Jinn, and Magical Healing in al-Saraquṣṭī's Forty-sixth *maqāma*

Michelle M. Hamilton
University of Minnesota, Twin Cities

JAMES T. MONROE has made available in English translation a series of important Andalusī works that reveal the great variety of original topics Andalusī authors introduced into Arabic literature – from reflections on Berber and Hispano-Christian customs to the adoption of indigenous poetic forms. These works show that Andalusī authors were deeply engaged and shaped by the larger literary and cultural traditions of the Arabic-speaking world, such as classical Arabic poetry or the Shu'ubbiya movement originating in Persia. These translations reveal the richness of the Andalusī literary corpus of the tenth-twelfth centuries. They include the poetry of some seventeen Andalusī poets (*Hispano-Arabic Poetry*), Ibn Quzmān's (d. 1160) *zajals* (*The Mischievous Muse*), Ibn Shuhayd's (d. 1035) treatise in which his familiar spirit meets the muses of the great poets of the Arabic tradition (*Risālat at-tawābi' wa z-zawābi'*), the Shu'ubbiya *risāla* of Ibn García (d. 1084) and five refutations (*The Shu'ubiyya in al-Andalus*), and the rhymed prose narratives of al-Saraquṣṭī ibn al-Ashtarqūwī (d. 1143) (the *Maqāmāt al-Luzūmīyah*). The latter twelfth-century collection of *maqāmāt*, modeled on the seminal collections of al-Hamadhanī (d. 1007) and al-Ḥarīrī (d. 1122) reflects an Iberian manifestation of this popular Eastern literary form. As a genre, the *maqāmāt* are defined as "short independent narratives written in ornamental rhymed prose (*saj'*) with verse insertions," whose plot involves the repeated interactions of two characters, the narrator and a picaresque anti-hero.[1]

The forty-sixth *maqāma* in al-Saraquṣṭī's collection, the "Maqāma al-Janiya" or "*Maqāma* of the Genie" is valuable in that it offers an early account of how popular healers used (or were thought to have used) what today would be considered magic or the supernatural as part of their medical healing in the medieval Arabic-speaking world. Their practice involved the use of astronomical tables to cast horoscopes and the treatment of *jinn* possession

1. Drory 2000, 190. Badī' al-Zamān al-Hamadhānī composed the first *maqāmāt* in tenth-century Nishapur. Al-Harīrī based his *maqāmāt* on those of al-Hamadhānī and the former's collection became the object of study and transmission among Andalusī scholars. Drory 2000, 193–195.

by exorcism, procedures whose use has been studied in the wider medieval Islamic world by Michael Dols and in the more modern Maghribi tradition by Vincent Crapanzano and Mohammed Maarouf.[2] In the Islamic tradition, the *jinn* are considered to be intelligent beings created, like men and angels, by God. They can be either good or bad in nature, the latter often famed in popular tradition for malevolently playing tricks on men, including turning them into animals and possessing them.[3]

This *maqāma* begins with the narrator, al-Sā'ib, who is suffering from some form of depression or illness, witnessing the trickster character, Abū Ḥabīb, exorcize, or at least appear to exorcise, a *jinnī* possessing a young man. This is followed by his divination or astrological prediction of a second young man's condition. Abū Ḥabīb performs both feats of magical healing in front of a crowd. The two victims, supposedly anonymous young men, are in all likelihood Abū Ḥabīb's two sons and part of the trickster's ruse. Unlike several other *maqāmāt* in which al-Sā'ib falls prey to Abū Ḥabīb's tricks without recognizing him, here he is suspicious of Abū Ḥabīb and his magical cures, and the *maqāma* ends with the former chastising the latter as an "incorrigible profligate whose bridle could not be turned away from sin."[4] Whether or not as readers we are meant to believe that Abū Ḥabīb has any skills in exorcizing *jinn* or in using astronomical tables and secret knowledge of the ancients to tell the future as he claims in this *maqāma*, al-Saraqusṭī's depiction of how such a faith healer and clairvoyant behaves is valuable as a testimony to such activities in al-Andalus.[5] Robert Irwin points out that while many medieval magical treatises of varying quality and authenticity have survived, very few testimonies survive about the ways such treatises

2. On the use of "*jinn* eviction" versus "exorcism," see Maarouf 2007. Maarouf argues that "*jinn* eviction" is preferable to differentiate the process (and contingent beliefs, such as *jinn*) from the Christian worldview associated with exorcism. "*Jinn* eviction (*ṣri'*) is addressed to both good and evil spirits" (Maarouf 2007, 2). In the current paper, I use "exorcism" because in both traditions this process is contingent on a series of beliefs regarding demons, the power of God over them, and humans' potential to harness that power to cause the spirit to leave their human victims.

3. D. B. Macdonald and H. Massé 2012. See also El-Zein 2009, 13–31.

4. Al-Saraqusṭī, *Maqāmāt*, 430; Monroe 2002, 460. All citations, unless otherwise noted, are to al-Warāglī's 1995 Arabic edition and James T. Monroe's 2002 English translation.

5. Michael Dols notes in his encyclopedic study on mental illness in the medieval Islamic world (Dols 1992, 11–12), "Unfortunately, historical descriptions of magical operations, especially exorcisms, are relatively rare, but the detailed studies by modern ethnographers and anthropologists of Islamic societies afford considerable data about the understanding of insanity and the patterns of healing, especially the exorcism of the *jinn* by magicians, that is largely impossible for the medieval period." While al-Saraqusṭī's account of *jinn* eviction or exorcism by a magician may be a fictional, skeptical if not satirical account, it nevertheless depends on the presumed medieval Arabic-speaking audience's familiarity or awareness of such practices.

and the knowledge they contain were actually used in medieval praxis.[6] One of the best-known medieval Arabic treatises in the Islamic magic and magical healing tradition, *Ghāyat al-Ḥakīm*, is attributed to the pseudo Maslama al-Majrīṭī (an Andalusī author), and was possibly contemporaneous with al-Saraquṣṭī's *maqāmāt*. It survives in the Latin translation of the mid-thirteenth century entitled the *Picatrix*. The latter translation is roughly contemporary with perhaps the best-known expert of Muslim magic, Aḥmad ibn ʿAlī al-Būnī (d. 1225), who was active in Egypt. The latter's treatises on medieval magic in the Muslim world postdate al-Saraquṣṭī's *maqāmāt* by some eighty years.[7] The allusions to astronomical tables, celestial observations and astrological horoscopes in al-Saraquṣṭī's *maqāmāt* does, however, like that of the *Ghāyat/Picatrix*, suggest that Andalusī scholars were deeply familiar with such thought.

The subject matter treated in these works – magic, medicine, and religious belief – shaped medieval attitudes toward mental illness and its potential cures. In the medieval Islamicate world there "were a number of possible responses by a devout Muslim to illness and to insanity particularly."[8] These responses included turning to God through prayer and asceticism, turning to a Galenic doctor, i.e. someone trained in the Greek-based science of medicine, or a third response: turning to "Prophetic medicine," which was a form of medicine based on the life and sayings of the Prophet Muhammad, but that also incorporated elements of Galenic medicine and other "indigenous practices and beliefs."[9] This seems to be the very scenario described in *Maqāma* 46, which opens with al-Sā'ib, the narrator, informing us that he is ill, emaciated and suffering from insomnia. "On that account I was referred to as 'the sick man.'"[10] Luckily, al-Sā'ib has a friend who tells him of the sudden appearance of a "skilled physician" to whom the friend has "described your complaint and expounded your ailment ... and he has promised a cure (*shifā'*) and an alleviation of the strange disease (*khafā'*) that afflicts you."[11] Al-Sā'ib's condition and the friend's description of the healer (who we find out later is none other than Abū Ḥabīb) clearly locate his mysterious condition as a medical problem.

When Abū Ḥabīb first appears in the narrative, al-Sā'ib notes that he attempts to establish credibility by mentioning the authorities and scholars with whom he is familiar and who define his training. He is "a man with a

6. Irwin, 2008, 104; See also Savage-Smith 2004, xiv-xv.

7. Sarton 1927, 668–669. Al-Bunī traced his intellectual genealogy and training in the occult sciences to Andalusī thinkers.

8. Dols 1992, 10.

9. Dols 1992, 9–11.

10. Al-Saraquṣṭī (d. 1143), *Maqāmāt*, 425; Monroe 2002, 452.

11. Al-Saraquṣṭī, *Maqāmāt*, 425; Monroe 2002, 452–453.

handsome appearance, yet a scowling countenance who, as he spoke, raised and lowered his voice, organizing his speech into paragraphs and sections, mentioning the ancient philosophers and learned scholars, providing information about their knowledge, and recognizing their contributions to it."[12] Abū Ḥabīb later tells the crowd: "I possess certain secrets, hidden knowledge, and indispensable information, all of which I obtained from scholars and gathered from the learned.... I possess exclusive and rare items of information; background and prior knowledge."[13] While few treatises on Prophetic medicine survive from the twelfth century, later ones have. The works of scholars such as Ibn Qayyim (d. 1292) and aṣ-Ṣayūṭī (d. 1505) that Michael Dols characterizes as works of Prophetic medicine (discussed above) combine the classical medical ideas of Galen and Hippocrates with ideas on medicine and healing culled from the Qur'an and *hadith*, based on the premise that the Prophet never called into doubt the effectiveness of empirical medicine.[14]

In this *maqāma* al-Sā'ib's illness and Abu Habib's latest disguise as a popular healer allow al-Saraqusṭī to present within the realm of fiction the medical ideas found in the works of Ibn Qayyim and aṣ-Ṣayūṭī. The ailing al-Sā'ib and his friend first come upon Abū Ḥabīb in the middle of treating another sick person,

> a youth dressed in rags, who was rolling in the dust like a donkey. Then he moaned, brayed, and his lungs became filled with air to the point of bursting ... until he stretched out languidly ... while one of his sides drooped, froth drooled from his mouth, his arm became contorted, he crossed his eyes, saliva clogged his mouth, and grief gave him its full meed.[15]

This youth seems to be suffering from what today we might suspect was an epileptic seizure. The latter condition was the subject of much debate among medieval Muslim thinkers. After witnessing Abū Ḥabīb's exorcism of the young man (discussed below) the narrator asks himself, "What is this?" – wondering about the young man's illness and using one of the terms, *lamam*, that Szombathy points out was used during the Middle Ages to refer to *jinn* possession, which resulted in "an epilepsy-like fit."[16] In the medieval Arabic-

12. Al-Saraqusṭī, *Maqāmāt*, 426; Monroe 2002, 453.
13. Al-Saraqusṭī, *Maqāmāt*, 427; Monroe 2002, 454.
14. Dols 1992, 244.
15. Al-Saraqusṭī, *Maqāmāt*, 426; Monroe 2002, 453.
16. Szombathy 2014. The young man's behavior may also be compared to that of the *kāhin* or soothsayer in the Arabic tradition, who could also be associated with forms of ecstatic divination and sorcery. See also Fahd 2012.

speaking world, epileptic-like disorders that involved fainting or seizures were treated as mental disorders that could or could not be caused by possession by *jinn* (who in turn could be either good or bad). Ibn Qayyim, in his treatise on Prophetic medicine, begins the chapter on epilepsy by citing the *hadith* that recounts how a woman came to Muhammad and asked for treatment. He told her she could be patient or he could intervene on her behalf with God.[17] According to Ibn Qayyim, epilepsy could be caused by a "humor imbalance" as well as by evil *jinn*.[18] In this *maqāma* Abū Ḥabīb offers cures that address both of these possible causes, telling the young man to seek God's help, as well as giving him medical treatments.

Al-Saraqusṭī makes it clear that the physician/Abū Ḥabīb believes (or wants the audience to believe) that the young man's apparently epileptic symptoms are caused by spirit possession. The old man lifts the young man and grabs "him by the hand and head."[19] Such physical manhandling of the possessed victim is a prescribed treatment. Ibn Qayyim relates having seen a similar treatment in which the beating of a possessed man caused the man's soul and the possessing *jinnī* to appeal to the healer, who invoked God's name to cause the spirit to leave the man's body.[20] In this *maqāma*, after grabbing the young man, the old man then "treats" the young man by telling him/the *jinnī* in him: "Seek refuge in God against these symptoms, and implore Him to lighten your complaints and maladies."[21] We are told that the old man uses incantations, while making the young man drink and giving him medicine, "through an instrument placed in the corner of the mouth."[22] The old man's treatments echo those used in the modern era in Morocco that involved "quasi-medical potions" considered to be "internal amulets."[23] Such remedies were also prescribed in medieval treatises. Aṣ-Ṣanawbarī al-Hindī's work on Prophetic medicine from 1412, *ar-Raḥma fi-ṭ-ṭibb wa l-ḥikma* (popular in North Africa according to the early twentieth-century scholar of magic and religion, Edmond Doutté) states that those suffering from epilepsy/melancholy, when caused by demonic possession, could be "aided by drinking a potion made of dill for three days."[24] Al-Sā'ib does not include details as to what exactly Abū Ḥabīb has the young man take, but it is sug-

17. Dols 1992, 251. This *hadith* is included in Ibn Qayyim, *aṭ-Ṭibb*, 135.
18. Ibn Qayyim, *aṭ-Ṭibb*, 63; Dols 1992, 251.
19. Al-Saraqusṭī, *Maqāmāt*, 426; Monroe 2002, 453.
20. Ibn Qayyim (d. 1292), *aṭ-Ṭibb*, 63.
21. Al-Saraqusṭī, *Maqāmāt*, 426; Monroe 2002, 453.
22. Al-Saraqusṭī, *Maqāmāt*, 426; Monroe 2002, 453.
23. Dols 1992, 284. On the importance of amulets and other talismanic objects in medieval magic, see Savage-Smith 2004, xxii-xxv. See also Caballero Navas 2004, 59–63.
24. Doutté 1909, 220. Dols 1992, 285.

gestive of a treatment like that described by aṣ-Ṣanawbarī, al-Hindī, and those used in modern Morocco.[25]

The next phase of the exorcism that al-Sā'ib witnesses in the *maqāma* involves the old man addressing the *jinnī* and commanding him to leave the young man's body:

> O refactory demon, your arrow pierces its prey; O rebellious spirit, what do you want? How tyrannical and rebellious you are! How far; how distant you are from good! Come out, O intruder, for you cause great concern! Begone, O deceiver, for you are a killer! "You shall not pass through except with authorization!" Keep away, you devil! Indeed, if you do not go peacefully, I will most certainly cause you to endure fatigue, return you to the black earth, and heap perfidy on your betrayal; I will most assuredly "rally troops against your horsemen and foot soldiers," pour the water out of your bucket and do away with your ancestors and your offspring; I will send against you troops of Qur'anic recitation, and ... Qur'anic memorization, that will scatter you in every direction, and destroy every *'ifrit* and vain suggestion of the devil.[26]

In the above description of how the healer Abū Ḥabīb exhorts the *jinnī* to leave the young man, we find a *jinnī* eviction/exorcism that reflects what later intellectuals such as Ibn Qayyim, Ibn Khaldūn (d. 1406) and Leo Africanus (d. 1554) would describe as the type they witnessed being used for possession.[27] Just as in the *jinn* exorcisms described in the treatises of Ibn Qayyim and aṣ-Ṣayūṭī, the old man in this tale uses Qur'anic verses and threats of violence to the possessing spirit as part of the public ceremony. The old man commands the spirit to leave ("Depart!") and then asserts that the *jinnī*'s possession of the youth is not authorized, and in so doing suggests that he, Abū Ḥabīb, has the authority to control it. This recalls Ibn Qayyim's description of an exorcism he witnessed in the thirteenth century in which the healer similarly commands the *jinnī* to leave the victim: "The shaykh says ... 'Depart! This is not lawful to you.'"[28] Szombathy further notes that in medieval "pietistic discourse, attempts to drive a spirit out of the body of the patient were sometimes understood as the removal of an unlawful occu-

25. Crapanzano relates seeing in Morocco a *faqīh* who prescribed placing some verses of the Qur'an (which he wrote out) in a bowl, with herbs, oil and garlic in order to cure a young girl. The girl's mother was told to rub the mixture on her as well as give her some to drink several times. Crapanzano 1973, 134. See also Dols 1992, 289, 292.

26. Al-Saraqusṭī, *Maqāmāt*, 426; Monroe 2002, 453–454.

27. Dols 1992, 283–284.

28. In Dols 1992, 252. Ibn Qayyim, *aṭ-Ṭibb*, 138–139.

pation," and could be effected by "commanding the spirit to leave, uttering curses against it as well as supplications to God for help" and the recitation of Qur'anic verses.[29] This reflects what the sheikh does in al-Saraquṣṭī's *maqāma* as described in the above passage, in which he commands the demon (*mārid*) supposedly possessing the young man. In addition to referring to this occupying spirit as a *mārid*, the active participle for rebellious one, used in Surah 37:7 to refer to rebellious demons, in this passage the old man further refers to the spirit as a satan (*shayṭan*) and *'ifrīt*. The *'ifrīt* is an even more powerful form of *jinn*.[30] Beyond commanding the rebellious spirit to leave the young man, Abū Ḥabīb utters a series of threats – claiming that should the spirit refuse to leave he will force him into the earth, not cease to fight him, and will go after his entire family – past and future.

The old man continues the exorcism with more threats, this time the threat of binding:

> "May your face be disfigured; your path and direction go astray! Depart, O intruder, as al-Hallaj departed! Free yourself from this body, otherwise I will bind you with a rope of palm-fiber and make you dwell at the bottom of the seas; I will enclose you, along with your nation, in deserts, and imprison you within dumb rocks, after I have restrained you with every kind of charm and fumigant." Then he recited passages from the Qur'an to him, mumbled (*zamzama*), contracted his body, shrank, opened his mouth, gaped, and attacked him, coming at him from all directions, like a wolf.[31]

Here after commanding the spirit to leave its victim, the old man "recites passages from the Qur'an." Ibn Qayyim notes that the healer he witnessed used the Throne verse (2:255), as well as the Surah al-Fajr (Dawn Surah 89) and The Surah an-Nas (Mankind Surah 114).[32] Here, the trickster uses Surah 55/The Beneficent (Ayah 33) and Surah 17/The Night Journey (Ayah 64)[33] – both relevant because the former is addressed directly to the "company of the *jinn* and men" and threatens both with suffering in hell, and in the latter Satan's tactics and false promises are discussed. Al-Saraquṣṭī further tells us that Abū Ḥabīb "mumbled" or whispered (*zamzama*) to the young man.

29. Szombathy 2014.

30. Chelhod 2015. According to Savage-Smith most medieval magic in the Muslim world was sought for protection against demons, and the use of Qur'anic surahs and invocations of God were considered the most effective safeguard against them. 2004, xvii, xxiii.

31. Al-Saraquṣṭī, *Maqāmāt*, 426–427; Monroe 2002, 453–454.

32. Ibn Qayyim, *aṭ-Ṭibb*, 169–171.

33. Qur'an 55:33. All citations from the Qur'an are from the Marmaducke Pickthall translation, available at "The Noble Qur'an." Quran.com 2016 https://quran.com.

Richard Bulliet notes that the verb *zamzama* was used in classical Arabic to refer to the "unintelligible whispering of magicians."[34] Ibn Isḥāq (d. 767) in the *al-Sīrat al-nabawiyya* further states that Walīd ibn al-Bulīgha (d. 622) describes the *kāhin* or soothsayers of Mecca as identifiable by their "unintelligent muttering" (*zamzama*), as well as their use of *saj'* or rhymed prose (the very form used by al-Saraqusṭī in the *maqāmāt*).[35] Should the reader think that Abū Ḥabīb was using only Prophetic healing, namely the use of Qur'anic recitation and talismans, al-Sā'ib's description of him as whispering as did magicians or *kāhins* hints that his healing calls upon other powers as well. The fact that in this passage Abū Ḥabīb threatens to bind the *jinnī* with a rope of palm fiber further echoes the association of Abū Ḥabīb's exorcistic practices to those of magical practitioners of the early Islamic period, such as the *kāhins*. Ibn Isḥaq further relates that al-Walīd ibn Bulīgha described the sorcerers (*sāḥir*) of Mecca as enacting their spells through "spitting" or "blowing" and "knots."[36] Using tied knots in exorcism is further documented by Dols in his discussion of *aṭ-ṭibb ar-rukka*, or old wives' medicine.[37]

Binding or tying the *jinn* to knots or other objects, as Abū Ḥabīb claims to want to do, could also prevent them from returning to their victims. In twentieth-century Egypt exorcists would use different strategies to keep the *jinn* from returning, including hurting, imprisoning, or killing them.[38] We also witness Abū Ḥabīb threatening to do this in this scene, when he threatens to torture the *jinnī* inhabiting the young man, and then to bind him in palm fiber and cast him away (to the bottom of the sea) and further threatening the entire race of *jinn*.

The punishment the old man imagines for the *jinnī* and his race recall the legends of King Solomon that circulated in the medieval Arabic-speaking world, according to which Solomon was the greatest of world rulers, endowed with "wonderful powers of magic and divination."[39] Dols notes that

34. Bulliet 2013, 68. See also Lane, who offers as possible definitions crying, uttering, making a confused and continued sound, and the making of unintelligible sounds that communicate while eating (done by Persians or Magians). Lane 1863, 1:1248. See also Ibn Manẓūr (d. 1311 CE) *Lisān al-Arab* (*z.m.m.*) in which various uses of *zamzama* are associated with magicians (al-magūs). Ibn Manẓūr 2017.

35. Zwettler 1978, 158–159. Ibn Isḥaq (d. 767), *al-Sīrat al-nabawiyya*, 121.

36. Ibn Isḥaq, *al-Sīrat al-nabawiyya*, 123; See also Qur'an 113:4, which mentions "the evil of the blowers in knots." Carmen Caballeros Navas notes that the magical procedure described in this passage, namely that of ligature, was commonly used "for amorous purposes" during the Middle Ages (Caballero Navas 2004, 61).

37. Dols 1992, 300–302.

38. Dols 1992, 307.

39. Walker and Fenton 2015.

Solomon is considered the founder of licit magic in the Islamic tradition.[40] According to Surahs 21:82 and 38:37 legions of satans were forced to work for him, and according to Surah 34:12 so were the *jinn*, who, if they refused were threatened with hell, much as Abū Ḥabīb threatens to punish the nation of *jinn* in this *maqāma*.[41]

After apparently having success in exorcizing the *jinnī* from the first young man, Abū Ḥabīb turns to the assembled crowd and asks anyone in need of his services to step forward. He offers a list of the types of conditions he can treat with his magical healing. The magical services he offers the crowd reflect the conditions addressed in works of Prophetic medicine such as that of Ibn Qayyim. He asks the assembled group if there are any others that have been possessed by *jinn*, anyone suffering from passion (*al-ashwāq*), epilepsy (*al-wasāwis*), insanity/hearing voices (*al-wasāwas*), a sore throat, or who has been enchanted (*saḥarahu sāḥirun*) or become a victim of the evil eye (*'aiyn*).[42] Such conditions were those addressed by medieval practitioners of Prophetic medicine. Ibn Qayyim includes treatments for these conditions, including chapters on treatments for the evil eye (including exorcism),[43] epilepsy (by exorcism), conjunctivitis, passion, those bewitched and other conditions such as ulcers and wounds in various places on the body, including the feet.[44] Like Ibn Qayyim, in the *maqāma* Abū Ḥabīb claims

40. Dols 1992, 266.

41. Abū Ḥabīb threatens the *jinnī* by means of a palm fiber, while Solomon wielded his magic powers via his famous talismanic signet ring that he used to control both the good and bad *jinn*. "The evil d̲jinn he imprisoned in vessels of lead (cf. Zech., v. 8). ʿAyd̲h̲āb, on the Red Sea, was assigned by him as a place of incarceration for the demons." Walker and Fenton 2015.

42. Al-Saraqusṭī, *Maqāmāt*, 427; Monroe 2002, 454–455. On the use of the term *waswas* used to designate epilepsy, see Szombathy 2012: "A further term related to *ṣar'* in some of its uses is *waswasa*, a Qur'ānic word designating the evil whisperings of Satan or malevolent spirits inhabiting a man. Because certain Qur'ānic passages and *ḥadīths* seem to suggest that the whispering entity is within the human body, the phenomenon of *waswasa* was often understood also as a kind of possession by malevolent spirits." See also Qur'an 114:5.

43. Ibn Qayyim begins his chapter on the evil eye by citing a *hadith* according to which the prophet stated that, "The evil eye is a reality. If there were a factor anterior to predestination it would be the evil eye." He further claims that "The wise persons of all nations – in spite of their different sects – do not refute the affliction of the evil eye, but they entertain different views as to its cause and impact." Ibn Qayyim 1994, 155–157. That said, Ibn Qayyim discusses some of the different explanations and underscores that envy is often a cause. According to Ibn Qayyim both *jinn* and humans can cause the evil eye. He includes a list of Prophetic incantations and amulets useful as prophylaxis against the evil eye. Exorcism is in Ibn Qayyim's opinion one of the "most beneficial" of treatments for both the evil eye and a venomous bite. Ibn Qayyim 1994, 165. "Sorcery, the evil eye, incantations, and the workings of the evil *jinn* were all considered to be causes of misfortune for mankind, resulting especially in disease and illness." Dols 1992, 255.

44. Ibn Qayyim, *aṭ-Ṭibb*, 61–65, 100–102, 155, 250–253, 121–122, 178, 47.

he can cure those suffering from love, ear and eye problems, and essentially any ailment: "my knowledge can cure all complaints."[45]

Despite his claims to cure all possible magic-induced ailments, people in the surrounding crowd do not immediately come forward to seek his healing: "the bystanders hesitated, and were on the point of rebuking him."[46] However, at that point another young man fortuitously appears:

> Suddenly, a youth appeared before them, displaying a touch of insanity and weakmindedness, trailing his mantle, and wearing a turban wrapped around his head. The old man hurried toward him, greeted him, and said:
>
> "I had detected the fragrance of his youth's scent some time ago."
>
> Then he consulted his astronomical tables, beginning with the proper position of the moon and the latter's deviation therefrom, saying:
>
> "I implore you by God, O hero in battles and penetrator of narrow mountain passes, would you kindly vouchsafe to these people that what I am about to report to you is as true as the information about you that I am now going to disclose to you"?[47]

Though the youth has just appeared, Abū Ḥabīb claims that he was aware of him some time ago because of his smell or scent, claiming, "I had detected the fragrance of his youth's scent some time ago." Odors and health were related in some medieval Arabic treatises of Prophetic medicine according to which one's scent correlated with the well being of one's soul. According to Ibn Qayyim in his chapter on perfume in *aṭ-Ṭibb*, cleanliness and smelling good is the duty of the Muslim. And while those who are spiritually in good order prefer good smells, "the wicked spirits like the stinking odor."[48] Seemingly Abū Ḥabīb was capable of smelling the young man's illness in this *maqāma*. In fact, according to Ibn Qayyim, smells or scents were not only symptoms of illness, but could also be used (in the form of aromatic herbs and perfumes) to treat spiritual ailments: "the redolent perfume is the soul's nutriment: the soul is the mount of forces that increase by perfume. In fact, perfume is profitable for the brain, the heart, and the rest of the internal organs."[49]

However, Abū Ḥabīb does not use perfumes to treat this young man. Instead, he uses his astronomical tables ("he consulted his astronomical tables,

45. Al-Saraquṣṭī *Maqāmāt*, 427; Monroe 2002, 455.
46. Al-Saraquṣṭī *Maqāmāt*, 427; Monroe 2002, 455.
47. Al-Saraqusṭī, *Maqāmāt*, 427; Monroe 2002, 455.
48. Ibn Qayyim, *aṭ-Ṭibb*, 262.
49. Ibn Qayyim, *aṭ-Ṭibb*, 261.

beginning with the proper position of the moon"). Contemporary scholars of the history of science focus on Andalusī advances in astronomy, including the refinement of the astronomical tables and the astrolabe, an instrument that uses the position of the stars and celestial phenomena to coordinate physical positions and that enabled such practical applications as maritime navigation and timekeeping. The medieval Andalusī scholar Maslamah ibn Aḥmad al-Majritī (d. 1007) translated Ptolomey's *Planispherium* and refined al-Khwārizmī's astronomical tables.[50] The Cordoban scholar al-Zarqālī (d. 1087) further built upon this knowledge to produce the famous Tables of Toledo (later the Alphonsine Tables). Al-Zarqālī also redesigned and improved the astrolabe.[51] Al-Saraqusṭī's *maqāma*, written a generation after these Andalusī scholars developed the astronomical knowledge and instruments that would lead to Atlantic exploration, reveals that this type of knowledge could be used for purposes other than timekeeping or navigation. In fact, the work of Andalusī scholars such as al-Majrītī and al-Zarqālī was used by their pupils and subsequent generations of scholars (contemporaries of al-Saraqusṭī) for the crafting of horoscopes, which is what al-Saraqusṭī depicts Abū Ḥabīb as doing in this *maqāma*.[52]

After finding the position of the moon and calculating where its orbit is supposed to be, Abū Ḥabīb prays to God. In his use of astronomical tables, Abū Ḥabīb conforms to a type of sorcerer that would later be described by Ibn Khaldūn. The latter classified three types of magicians, "those who exercised their power only by their minds or spirits over others in the natural world [and] those who used astrology and various techniques to make talismans."[53] In this *maqāma* Abū Ḥabīb consults his astronomical tables and intimates that based on the moon's position he has discovered a secret about the young man – a secret that is the cause of his affliction. This astrological prognostication is reinforced when the old man states: "Behold, I have calculated your ascendant, and identified the star of your rising good fortune, while my investigation informs me that you are a youth from whom great things are expected."[54] Abū Ḥabīb claims to use the position of the moon and stars and the astronomical tables to discern the moral character of the young man.

In his portrait of Abū Ḥabīb as popular astrologer who used the most advanced scientific knowledge of his time, al-Saraqusṭī draws upon the

50. Vernet 1999, 118, 170, 297. It was al-Majritī who revised the dates used in al-Qazwīnī's (d. 1283) tables, changing them from the Persian to the Arabic calendar.

51. Saliba 1999.

52. North 2008, 216–220; Savage-Smith 2004, xxxvi-xxxix.

53. Dols 1992, 268.

54. Al-Saraqusṭī, *Maqāmāt*, 427; Monroe 2002, 455.

Andalusī scientific tradition, but also on the Arabic literary tradition of the *maqāmāt*. In the twenty-ninth *maqāma* of perhaps the best known collection of *maqāmāt*, that of the Basran scholar, al-Harīrī (d. 1122), the trickster figure also assumes the role of popular astrologer/magician who uses an astrolabe to prognosticate the moral character of a young man and prove the latter's worthiness as a potential bridegroom.[55] Once the family of the bride has gathered, the trickster Abū Zayd begins using the astrolabe to comment upon the bridegroom's character: "[H]e busied himself in raising the astrolabe and lowering it, and in consulting the almanac and laying it aside, until the people became drowsy ... he cast a glance at the stars, and breaking loose from the tie of silence, he swore by [mount] Túr, and the written book."[56] He then praises God and the assembled crowd, then states that the bridegroom is the most worthy of son in laws, a free and noble man. This trickster – Abū Ḥabīb's predecessor – has, however, drugged the assembled crowd, who then pass out before he finishes praising the young man, who is, in fact, his associate. In al-Ḥarīrī's *maqāma*, the consultation of the stars and use of the astrolabe are clearly a ruse, suggesting that readers of al-Saraqusṭī's *maqāma* familiar with this well-known text would use it as a lens through which to judge the credibility of Abū Ḥabīb and his "victim," as well as his supposed scientific skills.

In al-Saraqusṭī's *maqāma* the crowd is not drugged, but rather witness as Abū Ḥabīb tells the young man's future:

> my investigation informs me that you are a youth from whom great things are expected, and that you will gain command and wield power, in all of which an angel and a demon will accompany you. One of the two will encourage knowledge and forbearance, while the other will promote injustice and oppression. Then terror after terror will pursue you, and possession after possession will escape your hand. After that your situation will increase ... proof of all this is that, at present, you possess a herd of one hundred camels, plus ten thousand *dirhams* ... and you own a singing-girl as rare as a gold nugget, who has large, bright eyes, who is a pleasure to behold, who is endowed with a voice that arouses desire.... She distracted your mind from your worries and made you forget your own paternal cousin.[57]

This wealthy young man has been distracted by his slave girl – possibly the victim of bewitchment and/or of passion – both considered common ail-

55. On the popularity and exemplary status of al-Ḥarīrī's *maqāmāt* as defining the genre, see Drory 2000, 194–195.

56. Al-Ḥarīrī (d. 1122), *Maqāmāt*, 303; Steingass 1898, 19.

57. Al-Saraqusṭī, *Maqāmāt*, 427–28; Monroe 2002, 455–56.

ments. Ibn Qayyim defines the bewitched as "a person who hurts himself as his heart is dependent on a thing to which he pays too much heed until this object of interest overrules his heart as he attaches to it great importance."[58] The young man's slave girl seems to have had this effect on him, distracting him to the point that he breaks his familial obligation to marry his cousin. The way that Abū Ḥabīb presents this information, as part of the psychological portrait of the young man, according to which he falls victim to the demon that accompanies him, further reflects Ibn Qayyim's depiction of the one afflicted by passion who is particularly susceptible to evil spirits:

> The malevolent spirits prevail over vulnerable spirits that tend to what fits this viciousness and that are devoid of divine force and disarmed. In that way, the vile spirits meet these disarmed souls that tend to degeneration and control them, influencing them by magic.[59]

Such a profile of the "disarmed soul" fits what we then learn of the young man. Although the only son of a noble and brave lord, he does not compare to his father in nobility or skill. Abū Ḥabīb tells him: "Fate made you fall short of his full range.... Vain desires sway you in every direction.... Such is the one who surrenders to his desires, obeys his passions."[60] The young man's future as foretold by Abū Ḥabīb underscores his moral failings. According to Prophetic medicine, someone's moral character could be the cause of illness. According to aṣ-Ṣayūṭī, "divine punishment in the form of ill-health is the result of moral infractions, such as drinking intoxicants and illicit sexual intercourse."[61]

In the *maqāma* the young man's relationship with his slave girl, underscored by the inclusion of the poem composed and sung by the young woman just the day before, in which she expresses her love and desire for him ("I have been overcome by an amorous rapture for you") reveals that their relationship is sexual in nature.[62] While having sex with a slave girl would not have been considered illicit, the inordinate desire the young man feels - a desire that keeps him from his other duties - would have been. Ibn Qayyim, in fact, notes that while passion is licit, it is also a disease that can have negative consequences for the victim: "he [the victim] should observe the corruptions that his desire engenders in this world and the interests it alters. Desire is a factor that sows corruption in this world and impedes

58. Ibn Qayyim, *aṭ-Ṭibb*, 122.
59. Ibn Qayyim, *aṭ-Ṭibb*, 122.
60. Al-Saraquṣṭī, *Maqāmāt*, 429; Monroe 2002, 457.
61. Dols 1992, 245.
62. Al-Saraqusti, *Maqāmāt*, 428: Monroe 2002, 456.

interests."[63] Abū Ḥabīb's recounting of the young man's love of his slave girl and the problems it has created in his family not only reveals to the reader how in this particular case passion is wreaking havoc in this man's life, but also seemingly makes the case visible to the young man himself.

The young man responds by stating that Abū Ḥabīb has revealed his secrets and cleared away the "rubble," so that both he and the surrounding crowd can identify the problem, namely his relationship with the slave girl:

> May your inspiring demon perish, and may your ties to life be saved! Indeed, you have put an end to my secrets, and bared the torrent-bed by sweeping away the rubble covering it; you have revealed what was veiled, and aroused one who has been wronged by the mother of a blood-relative, but to whom vengeance so far has been denied. It is as if you had personally witnessed my situation and felt disgust over what is inaccurate. You have spoken with the tongue of truthfulness ... indeed I am of the opinion that you are a soothsayer (*kāhin*), and believe that you fraternize with, and can outwit the *jinn*.[64]

The youth testifies to the effectiveness of Abū Ḥabīb's cure – his making the situation clear to the young man – but also verifies his powers of divination and ability to see both the future as well as the experiences of others. He further reiterates what we as readers have supposedly already witnessed, namely Abū Ḥabīb's ability to control or "outwit the *jinn*."

The narrator, though, clearly thinks that Abū Ḥabīb is a charlatan, for after the latter collects money from the crowd and administers to those who seek cures, al-Sā'ib follows him as he leaves, stating that he does so because of his doubts: "I followed him, for I felt contempt for his opinions."[65] He then has an exchange with Abū Ḥabīb in which he tells him directly, "You have devoted all your efforts to cunning, and exceeded all bounds in ascribing to yourself knowledge of others; you have misrepresented matters to the very *jinn* themselves, making an unwarranted claim upon every genus and species of knowledge.... How foul is treachery!"[66] He goes on to accuse him of being greedy and wicked. Abū Ḥabīb replies in verse with a justification familiar from the preceding *maqāmāt* in the collection, namely that the tumultuous times in which he is living require him to act in this way: "And yet, this age of ours is a torrent, whose sons are the rubble it sweeps away.... I have sharpened my spearhead in every valley when dust is stirred up by

63. Ibn Qayyim, *aṭ-Ṭibb*, 257.
64. Al-Saraqusṭī, *Maqāmāt*, 428: Monroe 2002, 457.
65. Al-Saraqusṭī, *Maqāmāt*, 429: Monroe 2002, 458.
66. Al-Saraqusṭī, *Maqāmāt*, 429: Monroe 2002, 459.

war."[67] Here Abū Ḥabīb's cynical advice delivered in poetic form echoes the ending of the typical *maqāma* repeated many times in the collection.[68] In this case, al-Sā'ib interprets his response as proof of his moral failings: "Then I realized that he was an incorrigible profligate whose bridle could not be turned away from sin ... an eloquent speaker with whose message and verbal skill none could compete."[69] It is not clear that al-Sā'ib is here discrediting the magical/Prophetic medicine that Abū Ḥabīb claims to use in his healing (although it may seem implied), but definitely does disparage Abū Ḥabīb's authority to practice it.

In this *maqāma* al-Saraquṣṭī contextualizes the encounter of Abū Ḥabīb and al-Sā'ib, narrator and dupe, within contemporary medieval beliefs of *jinn* possession and astrological prognostication current in the Arabic-speaking world. In this *maqāma* al-Sā'ib may be ill, but he is not seduced by Abū Ḥabīb's rhetoric and his promises of healing, but gives voice to his doubt and accuses the old man of being a fake at the end. While he may not be convinced by Abū Ḥabīb's performance and magic, al-Sā'ib, and presumably the reader along with him, is not so fast to dismiss the conditions that he witnesses the two young men suffering. During the *jinn* exorcism al-Sā'ib asks himself what could be the cause of the young man's ailments. The possibilities he entertains for the young man's possession whether feigned or not – epileptic-like fainting spells or insanity – were entertained as real by al-Sā'ib. Similarly, al-Sā'ib does not express doubt about the second young man's unhealthy relationship with his slave girl, or that astrological prognostication might be effective in revealing such secrets.

While al-Sā'ib's attitude toward the conditions and treatments that are the subject of this *maqāma* does not seem overly skeptical, his opinion that Abū Ḥabīb is not qualified to either diagnose them or practice such medicine is explicit. Abū Ḥabīb is again revealed as a charlatan or imposter, but the *maqāma* lacks a definitive answer with regard to the author's or even the characters' attitude toward medieval magic and its medical applications. It does, however, offer an early account of how the practitioners of such magic and medicine plied their trade, and in so doing is a valuable secondary testimony to the treatises and grimoires studied by such scholars as Dols and Cyril Elgood. As such this *maqāma* becomes one further example of the utility and importance of James Monroe's translations, editions, and studies of Andalusī works as unique sources on the history of medieval beliefs and material culture.

67. Al-Saraquṣṭī, *Maqāmāt*, 430: Monroe 2002, 459–460.
68. See Monroe's discussion of this in the introduction to the *Maqāmāt* (2002), 8.
69. Al-Saraquṣṭī, *Maqāmāt*, 460.

Bibliography

Bulliet, Richard. 2013. *Hunters, Herders, and Hamburgers: The Past and Future of Human-Animal Relationships*. New York.

Būnī, Aḥmad ibn ʿAlī Al-. 1840. *Kitāb al-Kashf fī 'ilm al-ḥarf*. MS Arab 229 Houghton Library. Harvard University. https://iiif-lib-harvard-edu.ezp3.lib.umn.edu/manifests/view/drs:11808010$6i.

Caballero Navas, Carmen. 2004. Introduction to *The Book of Women's Love and Jewish Medieval Medical Literature on Women*, edited and translated by Carmen Caballero Navas, 7–98. London.

Chelhod, J. 2015. "ʿIfrīt." In *EI2*, edited by P. Bearman, Th. Bianquis, C. E. Bosworth, E. van Donzel, and W. P. Heinrichs. Leiden. http://dx.doi.org.ezp3.lib.umn.edu/10.1163/1573-3912_islam_SIM_3502

Crapanzano, Vincent. 1973. *The Hamadsha: A Study in Moroccan Ethnopsychiatry*. Berkeley.

Dols, Michael. 1992. *Majnun: The Madman in Medieval Islamic Society*. Edited by Diana E. Immisch. Oxford.

Doutté, Edmond. 1909. *Magie et Religion dans l'Afrique du Nord*. Algiers.

Drory, Rina. 2000. "The Maqama." In *The Literature of al-Andalus*, edited by María Rosa Menocal, Raymond Scheindlin, and Michael Sells, 190–210. Cambridge.

Elgood, Cyril. 1951. *A Medical History of Persia and the Eastern Caliphate, from the Earliest Times until the Year A. D. 1932*. Cambridge.

—— 1962. "Tibb-ul-Nabbi or Medicine of the Prophet." *Osiris* 14:33–192.

Fahd, T. 2012. "Kāhin." In *EI2,* online edition, edited by P. Bearman, Th. Bianquis, C. E. Bosworth, E. van Donzel, and W. P. Heinrichs. Leiden. http://dx.doi.org.ezp3.lib.umn.edu/10.1163/1573-3912_islam_SIM_3784

Hamès, Constant. 2011. "al-Būnī." In *EI3*, online edition, edited by Kate Fleet, Gudrun Krämer, Denis Matringe, John Nawas, and Everett Rowson. Leiden. http://dx.doi.org.ezp3.lib.umn.edu/10.1163/1573-3912_ei3_COM_23727

al-Ḥarīrī, Abū Muhammad al-Qāsim ibn Alī ibn Muhammad ibn Uthmān. 1929. *Kitāb Maqāmāt al-Ḥarīrī*. Cairo. https://archive.org/details/rad-ibn-khashab.

Ibn Isḥaq. 1955. *Al-Sīrat al-nabawiyya. The Life of Muhammad*. Translated by Alfred Guillaume. Oxford.

Ibn Manẓur, Muḥammad ibn Mukarram. 2017. "Z.m.m." In *Lisaan.net: Classical Arabic Linguistic References*. http://lisaan.net/.

Ibn Qayyim al-Jawziyya, Muhammad ibn Abi Bakr. 1994. *The Prophetic Medicine. Aṭ-Ṭibb al-nabwī*. Translated by S. Y. Abou Azar. Beirut.

Ibn Shuhaid Abū ʻAmir al-Ashjaʻī al-Andalusī. 1971. *Risālat at-Tawābiʻ wa z-zawābiʻ The Treatise of Familiar Spirits and Demons.* Edited and translated by James T. Monroe. Berkeley.

Irwin, Robert. 2008. Review of *Magic and Divination in Early Islam*, edited by Emilie Savage-Smith. *Magic, Ritual, and Witchcraft*.3, no. 1:.104–109.

Lane, Edward William. 1863. *Arabic-English Lexicon.* London. http://www.tyndalearchive.com/tabs/lane/

Maarouf, Mohammed. 2007. *Jinn Eviction as a Discourse of Power: A Multidisciplinary Approach to Moroccan Magical Beliefs and Practices Islam in Africa.* Leiden.

MacDonald, D. B. and H. Massé. 2015. "D̲jinn." In *EI2,* edited by P. Bearman, Th. Bianquis, C. E. Bosworth, E. van Donzel, and W. P. Heinrichs. Leiden. http://dx.doi.org.ezp1.lib.umn.edu/10.1163/1573-3912_islam_COM_0191

Monroe, James T. 2002. Introduction and translation of *Maqamat al-Luzumiyah* by al-Saraqusṭī ibn al-Aštarkūwī, 1–110. Leiden.

——, ed. 1974. *Hispano-Arabic Poetry: A Student Anthology*. Berkeley.

——, ed. 2016. *The Mischievous Muse: Extant Poetry and Prose by Ibn Quzmān of Córdoba.* 2 vols. Leiden.

——, ed. 1971. *Risālat At-tawābiʻ wa z-zawābiʻ* by Ibn Shuhaid. Berkeley.

——, ed. 1970. *The Shuʻubiyya in al-Andalus: The* risāla *of Ibn García and five refutations*. Berkeley.

North, John David. 2008. *Cosmos: An Illustrated History of Astronomy and Cosmology*. Chicago.

Saliba, George. 1999. *Rethinking the Roots of Modern Science: Arabic Scientific Manuscripts in European Libraries.* Occasional Papers, Center for Contemporary Arabic Studies. Georgetown University.

al-Saraqusṭī, Abū l-Ṭāhir Muḥammad ibn Yūsuf al-Tamīmī ibn al-Aštarkūwī. 2002. *The Maqāmāt al-Luzūmīyah.* Edited and translated by James T. Monroe. Leiden.

Sarton, George. 1927. *Introduction to the History of Science.* Vol. 1 (part 2). Carnegie Institution of Washington.

Savage-Smith, Emilie. 2004. Introduction to *Magic and Divination in Early Islam*, xiii-liii. Trowbridge.

Steingass, F., tr. 1898. *Maqāmāt. The Assemblies of al-Hariri.* London. https://archive.org/details/assembliesofalha015555mbp.

Szombathy, Zoltan. 2012. "Exorcism." In *EI3*, online edition, edited by Kate Fleet, Gudrun Krämer, Denis Matringe, John Nawas, and Everett Rowson. Leiden. http://dx.doi.org.ezp3.lib.umn.edu/10.1163/1573-3912_ei3_COM_26268

Vernet, Juan. 1999. *Lo que Europa debe al Islam de España*. Barcelona.
Walker, J. and Fenton, P. 2015. "Sulaymān b. Dāwūd." In *EI2*, edited by P. Bearman, Th. Bianquis, C. E. Bosworth, E. van Donzel, and W. P. Heinrichs. Leiden. http://dx.doi.org.ezp3.lib.umn.edu/10.1163/1573-3912_islam_SIM_7158
al-Warāglī, Ḥasan, ed. 1995. *Al-Maqāmāt al-Luzūmīyah: Ta'lif Abū l-Ṭāhir Muḥammad ibn Yūsuf al-Tamīmī al- Saraqusṭī*. Rabat.
El-Zein, Amira. 2009. *Islam, Arabs, and the Intelligent World of the Jinn*. Syracuse.
Zwettler, Michael. 1978. *The Oral Tradition of Classical Arabic Poetry: Its Character and Implications*. Columbus, OH.

"The Threefold Cord": On Hebrew and Arabic in the Work and Identity of Judah al-Ḥarīzī

Shamma Boyarin
University of Victoria

ONE OF JAMES T. MONROE'S GREAT CONTRIBUTIONS to our understanding of the Arabic *maqāmāt* is his observation that the didactic message embedded in these stories is never straightforward, and that one must pay attention to inconsistencies, such as contradictions between the narrator's claims and what the readers see happening, or statements that seem to contradict the tenets of the author's cultural system.[1] Monroe writes: "The text [of the *maqāma*] is riddled with contradictions in logic deliberately designed to permit the perceptive reader to conclude that the anti-hero's arguments are basically flawed and, thus, to reject them."[2] According to Monroe, this is a literary response to a world where "appearances are an illusion" behind which lies "a disappointing reality."[3] In this essay, I will argue that this mode of suspicious reading is useful for understanding Judah al-Ḥarīzī's Hebrew book of *maqāmāt, Sefer Taḥkemoni.*[4] I argue that this approach will serve to provide a better understanding of al-Ḥarīzī's attitude towards Hebrew and Arabic, and will align better with what we know about him as an author, particularly in regard to his attitudes toward Arabic literature.

Although Judah al-Ḥarīzī wrote both in Hebrew and Arabic, many scholars view him as having a preference for Hebrew over Arabic, and discount his Arabic compositions. For example, Jefim Schirmann states:

> There is no doubt that the Hebrew tongue was al-Ḥarīzī's sole desire, and to her he gave his life and vigor. His love for the Hebrew language shows a pure idealistic side in him, which ought to be emphasized in

1. For example, Monroe 1983, chapter 4, where he analyzes the theme of begging in the *maqāmāt* of al-Hamadhānī and discusses its relationship to debates over issues such as free will.

2. Monroe 2002, 3.

3. Monroe 1983, 22–23.

4. On this see also Wacks 2007, 184–185.

> order to truly value his colorful character. His excellent control of the depths of the Arab tongue did not cause him to lose his mind.[5]

Ezra Fleischer adds to this: "Judah al-Ḥarīzī is the first among the Hebrew writers who feels the upcoming calamity. With the sharp intuition of a true poet ... al-Ḥarīzī cries 'corruption!' over the Jews' betrayal of the Hebrew language."[6]

Further, Fleischer, who is more aware than Schirmann of the extent of al-Ḥarīzī's Arabic writings, treats them as an indication that at this time the status of Hebrew as the language of poetry had become weak, implying that otherwise al-Ḥarīzī would have written in Arabic much less, or not at all.[7] Rina Drory also believes that the decline of Hebrew poetry motivated al-Ḥarīzī, and notes: "[Al-Ḥarīzī] wished to redirect the Eastern Jewish public back to their forsaken language by proving that Hebrew was no less suitable for literary and eloquent writing than Arabic and, perhaps, was even more suitable."[8]

That is, she too sees al-Ḥarīzī as a champion of Hebrew over Arabic. Matti Huss has compared the differences between al-Ḥarīzī's approach to translation and that of the Ibn Tibbon family of translators. While the latter, according to Huss, viewed Arabic as superior to Hebrew, and translated accordingly, al-Ḥarīzī's translation method was informed by his view of the "Hebrew language as dominant, and Arabic as inferior."[9] To support this, Huss cites statements that al-Ḥarīzī makes in the *Taḥkemoni*, which, he argues, reflect al-Ḥarīzī's attitude towards Hebrew. Indeed, these passages in the *Taḥkemoni* are the only, or nearly the only, evidence that these scholars have to support their claim that al-Ḥarīzī preferred Hebrew over Arabic, and this claim depends on the assumption that these statements accurately reflect the author's own opinions. The only scholar to significantly depart from this view is Joseph Sadan, not so much because he offers a different reading of the *Taḥkemoni*, but rather based on the testimony of a Muslim biography of al-Ḥarīzī, which suggests that things might be more complicated.[10] In this paper, I will show how my reading of the *Taḥkemoni* both supports and is supported by Sadan's arguments. I will also explore Drory's position further; although I disagree with some elements of it, there are also some key points of agreement between us.

5. Schirmann and Fleischer 1997, 188.
6. Schirmann and Fleischer 1997, 214.
7. Schirmann and Fleischer 1997, 174.
8. Drory 2000, 224.
9. Huss 1995, 171.
10. See for example Sadan 1996, 32 point 9.

There are three different dedications to the *Taḥkemoni*, because al-Ḥarīzī, through his travels, searched for a patron who would support him financially; each of the three dedications is addressed to a different candidate.[11] In addition, there are two prefaces to the work: one in Judeo-Arabic rhymed prose, and one in Hebrew. Both prefaces present the work as a response to the crises of Hebrew. For example, in the Arabic one he writes: "Lo, I have seen that most members of the Israelite tribe who are in these Eastern lands are empty of the Hebrew language and are naked, not clothed in her fancy garments."[12] He goes on to describe this as one of the greatest calamities to have befallen the Jews in the diaspora, and therefore has decided to compose this book, the *Taḥkemoni*, with its fifty Hebrew *maqāmāt*, which will entice the readers to learn Hebrew by engaging with its text. It is important to note that in this preface, he paints the loss of Hebrew as being particular to the Jews of the East.

This is slightly different from how he presents the problem in the much more flowery Hebrew preface, where the speaker, the authorial voice of Judah al-Ḥarīzī, tells us that his intellect is rebuking him for metaphorically sleeping while Hebrew is in a state of crisis. His intellect tells him:

וְאַתָּה תֶאְזוֹר מָתְנֶיךָ
וּלְבַשׁ קְנָאוֹת / לֵאלֹהֵי צְבָאוֹת / וְלִלְשׁוֹן הַנְּבוּאוֹת / הַיּוֹרֶדֶת פְּלָאוֹת
וְהָסֵר תִּלְבּוֹשֶׁת הַבֹּשֶׁת מֵעָלֶיהָ

> Now you, gird your loins, and dress yourself with zealousness for the Lord of Hosts and for the language of prophecy, which has been astoundingly debased; and remove the garb of shame from her.[13]

Here he presents the debasement of Hebrew as a universal problem, unlike in the Arabic introduction, where he calls it specifically the problem of the Jews of the East. Moreover, the speaker presents it here as a problem that he is called upon to fix.[14]

In the first *maqāma*, al-Ḥarīzī again refers to the idea that Hebrew, as the language of prophecy, is superior to all other languages, including Arabic.[15]

11. This phenomenon is discussed by Joseph Yahalom and Naoya Katsumata (2010, xlvi–lii).

12. al-Ḥarīzī, *Taḥkemoni*, 55.

13. al-Ḥarīzī, *Taḥkemoni*, 70, lines 161–3.

14. In this argument Judah al-Ḥarīzī is following in the footsteps of a well developed line established by Hebrew poets in al-Andalus. For more on this see, for example, Brann 1991, 23–24 and Wacks 2015, 37–45. Finally, see Pearce 2014, for an important discussion of the complex relationship between Arabic and Hebrew.

15. Of course, this argument mirrors the well-known Muslim argument that God has cho-

Heman the Ezraḥite, the narrator of the *maqāmāt* in the *Taḥkemoni*, states that the "author of the book" has told him the reason for its composition, by telling Heman the following story: One day, while the author is in Kiriath-Jearim, a biblical city near Jerusalem, he finds himself in the company of Hebrew youths, who are all extremely bright and accomplished poets. One of them stands out as being even brighter than the rest, and an even better poet; he turns to the rest, addressing them in rhymed Hebrew (the basic language and form of the *maqāma*), and praises the Arabic *maqāmāt* of al-Ḥarīrī as being sublime and matchless. He then continues:

וְאִלּוּ כַּסֵּפֶר הַזֶּה יְחוּבַּר בְּלָשׁוֹן אַחֶרֶת חוּץ מִלְּשׁוֹן עֲרָב / נָפַל מִמֶּנּוּ רָב...
/ כִּי לְשׁוֹן עֲרָב אֵין בְּכָל הַלְּשׁוֹנוֹת כָּמוֹהָ צַחָה נְקִיָּה

> If the like of this book had been composed in any language other than Arabic, much would be lost ... for there is no language like Arabic, with its pure clarity.[16]

The speaker goes on to praise Arabic's linguistic qualities at length, to the point that the author becomes enraged and must intervene. The author agrees with the speaker that Arabic is superior to all other languages, and that in comparison to it, the latter are all lacking and strange – except for the "Holy Tongue," that is, Hebrew. For God spoke Hebrew to his prophets, used this language to sanctify His people with it at Mount Sinai, and provided his teachings in it. Thus, the author says:

וְחָלִילָה לָאֵל בּוֹרֵא כָל הַלְּשׁוֹנוֹת לִבְחוֹר מֵהֶם לְעַמּוֹ הַשָּׂפָה הַחֲסֵרָה

> Far be it from God, creator of all languages, to choose from them a deficient one for His people![17]

He then goes on to give the young man an historical explanation for the decline of Hebrew from its glory days during "our kingdom" until today, and extensively extols the virtues of the Hebrew language. When the youth hears this, he challenges the author to back up his claims by composing a book in Hebrew that will rival what exists in Arabic. The author accepts the challenge, and tells us that this book, the *Taḥkemoni*, is the result. In short, the first *maqāma* seems to provide clear evidence that Schirmann and the

---

sen Arabic to be the language of the Qur'an because it is the perfect medium for expressing his message. It is beyond the scope of this article to fully explore how this idea, in both Islam and Judaism, becomes a useful trope for literary expression. For more background on this move among Jewish poets of al-Andalus see Brann, 1991, 23.

16. al-Ḥarīzī, *Taḥkemoni*, 83.
17. al-Ḥarīzī, *Taḥkemoni*, 84.

other scholars are right, for it portrays a situation where the author of the book, that is, al-Ḥarīzī, encounters a Hebrew scholar who declares his great admiration of al-Ḥarīrī's writings, and who praises the Arabic language above all – and the author sets out to prove him wrong.

I have spent some time paraphrasing and quoting these sections of the first *maqāma* because they show why there is almost unanimous agreement among scholars that al-Ḥarīzī's goal was to defend the honor of Hebrew. Drory, Huss, and others cite the statements of "the author of this book" in this story to make the case that al-Ḥarīzī is an embattled defender of Hebrew. Yet if we start with these quotations to observe the "contradictions in logic" that Monroe states are endemic to the *maqāma* genre, we will see that they hint that the situation is far more complex. Although there is a tendency to view elements of the *Taḥkemoni* as reflecting historical moments from al-Ḥarīzī's life,[18] it is clear that the events portrayed in the first *maqāma* must be viewed as fictional. There is no way that the real author of the *Taḥkemoni* told Heman the Ezraḥite, a character in the *Taḥkemoni*, how the composition of the *Taḥkemoni* came about. Moreover, the exceptional youth, whose praise of al-Ḥarīrī and Arabic goads "the author of this book" to create the *Taḥkemoni*, turns out to be none other than Ḥever the Qenite – the rogue antihero appearing in each of the remaining *maqāmāt* in the *Taḥkemoni*. So, just as Heman and Ḥever are literary characters, so too must we view "the author of this book" as a literary character, dwelling in the fictional setting of the *maqāmāt*. As David Wacks has already observed, al-Ḥarīzī breaks the "fourth wall" and "inverts the mimetic relationship between narrator and author" and in doing so "announces the work's fictionality."[19] In fact, at one point the line is blurred between the characters of the "author of this book" and the narrator, when the "author" is referred to as *ha-maggid*, "the narrator," a term that al-Ḥarīzī commonly uses in the *Taḥkemoni* to refer to Heman, the narrator of the *maqāmāt*. Indeed, after the opening section, when the narrator, Heman, tells the reader that he is relating a story told to him by the "author," Heman does not reappear in this *maqāma*.[20] Rather, his function is replaced by that of "the author," who, just like Heman and

18. For example, Schirmann and Fleisher (1997, 151–161) who reconstruct stages of al-Ḥarīzī's trip based on the *Taḥkemoni*, despite the fact that part of the convention of the genre is that each *maqāma* begins at a different place. For a discussion of geography in the genre, see Monroe 2002, 8.

19. Wacks 2007, 185

20. As Huss (1995, 137) notes, the use of "the Narrator" here to describe a character other than Heman, the normal fixed narrator of the *maqāmāt* in the *Taḥkemoni*, follows from the fact that there are two nested levels of narration in this particular *maqāma*, and the "author" is the narrator of the interior, more important, level of narration.

Ḥever, is a literary character in the *Taḥkemoni*, and, more importantly, becomes the first-person narrator of this *maqāma.* As Monroe notes, the use of first-person narration in *maqāma* literature "has an important function, insofar as it allows the protagonist to tell his tale, while simultaneously allowing the reader to judge its veracity."[21] In the case of the *Taḥkemoni*, this makes us suspect that al-Ḥarīzī's claim that he was inspired to write the work in reaction to a Hebrew scholar who admired Arabic too much is not necessarily historical truth.

Another signal that things are more complicated then they might seem is that when the youth, Ḥever, declares the superiority of the Arabic language, he does so in perfectly stylized Hebrew, effectively undercutting the content of his words through his Hebrew rhetorical and linguistic skill. Thus, there is a contradiction between what Ḥever says, that Arabic is the only language suitable for a *maqāma*, and what the reader experiences and learns from his words, that Hebrew can fulfil the stylistic needs of the genre. Not only are his words presented in rhymed prose, the basic stylistic component of the genre, but they also contain the various elements prized in both the classical Arabic and the Hispano-Hebrew literary traditions. One example epitomizes this effect: when speaking about the Arabic language, he says: וְהִיא מִכָּל לָשׁוֹן עֲרֵבָה *ve-hi mi-kol lashon 'areva* (She is more pleasant than any tongue).[22] The word for "pleasant," *'areva*, is similar in sound to the word for Arabia, *'arav*, a word that appears several times in Ḥever's speech here, as part of the expression *leshon 'arav*, "Arabian Tongue"; although that expression is not found directly in this line, nonetheless the word *'areva* still creates an echo of sound play, a kind of paronomasia that is one of the elements of poetics in both the Arabic and Hebrew traditions. As Monroe notes, the highly embellished rhetoric in *maqāma* literature functions as a means of "obfuscation," creating a chasm between appearance and reality.[23] In this case, the chasm is between the claim that Arabic is the only language in which these rhetorical embellishments can be accomplished, and the reality that the speaker is accomplishing them in Hebrew while saying this. Thus, neither of the arguments in the *maqāma* – Ḥever's arguments in favor of Arabic, or the "author's" arguments in favor of Hebrew – can be taken at face value as reflecting al-Ḥarīzī's true position.

I argue that Judah al-Ḥarīzī's blurring of the boundaries between himself, the real author of the *Taḥkemoni*, on the one hand, and the character of "the author of this book," on the other, extends also to the introductory

21. Monroe 2002, 6.
22. al-Ḥarīzī, *Taḥkemoni*, 83.
23. Monroe 2002, 6.

material. As we have noted, there are a number of dedications found in the manuscript tradition, prefacing different versions of the *Taḥkemoni*, indicating that al-Ḥarīzī went around dedicating the same work to different people, probably for the purpose of receiving their patronage. In this behavior, he is acting very similar to a stock character found in his own work, as well as in prominent Arabic *maqāmāt*, which influenced him. Abdul Rahman Maree traces the development of this theme in the works of four authors, and notes that the literary character of the beggar combines characteristics found in poor folk from the margins, on the one hand, with a high degree of literary education, on the other.[24] Further, Maree notes, "The embedding of the theme of begging in the *maqāma* was influenced directly and indirectly from the court culture and from the dependence of authors on benefactors. The poets used to praise kings and leaders, and due to their poetry they gathered riches and wealth and lived honorably."[25]

Thus, we see that there is a direct correlation between the literary figure of the roguish beggar, who uses his intelligence and ability as a poet to swindle others out of their money, and al-Ḥarīzī's attempt to do so with his multiple dedications to his work. Further, we learn from an Arab biographer, who knew al-Ḥarīzī when he was in Syria, that he was known for composing poems of praise and derision, in Hebrew and Arabic, which were the source of the poet's income.[26] As Yahalom and Katsumata put it, al-Ḥarīzī "became the archetype of the wandering adventurer, not very different from the protagonist of his own *maqāma*s, possessing the character of the hero in the *Taḥkemoni*."[27] Just as we cannot take the hero's words in the *maqāma* at face value, so too must we take a suspicious view of al-Ḥarīzī's other writings, especially those dedications and prefaces to the *Taḥkemoni* which are part of his mode of making money.

Here is another example where one must read behind the apparent meaning of al-Ḥarīzī's words to see what is actually happening. He states in one of the Hebrew prefaces to the *Taḥkemoni*:

וּבְכָל הַדְּבָרִים אֲשֶׁר בַּסֵּפֶר הַזֶּה זָכַרְתִּי
דָּבָר מִדִּבְרֵי סֵפֶר הַיִּשְׁמְעֵלִים לֹא לָקַחְתִּי / לְבַד אִם שָׁכַחְתִּי
אוֹ נִפְלְאָה מִלָּה אוֹ שְׁתַּיִם בְּמִקְרֶא וְאָנֹכִי לֹא יָדַעְתִּי

24. Maree 2000, 26.

25. Maree 2000, 28.

26. For writing poems of praise, the author receives a reward; whereas the poems of derision serve the patron as either a warning or a punishment for not paying the poet.

27. Yahalom and Katsumata 2010, lii.

רַק כָּל עִנְיָנֵי הַסֵּפֶר הַזֶּה מִלְּבָבִי נִבְרָאוּ / חֲדָשִׁים מִקָּרוֹב בָּאוּ
וּמִמֵּי יְהוּדָה יָצָאוּ

> And in all the things that I have mentioned in this book, I have not taken a thing from the words of the book of the Arabs, unless if I have forgotten, or if by chance I did not notice a word or two, and I did not know. All the topics of this book were created in my mind; they are newcomers, flowing from the waters of Judah.[28]

This statement encapsulates two apparent concerns of the author: that his Hebrew work be viewed as having no Arabic influence, and that he himself be viewed as an original author, the sole source of the ideas found in the book.[29] He contrasts this with his previous accomplishment, translating al-Ḥarīrī's *maqāmāt* from Arabic to Hebrew, which he claims was a mistake:

רָאִיתִי כִּי הִסְכַּלְתִּי עֲשׂוֹ / וְגָדַל עֲוֹנִי מִנְּשֹׂא
בְּעָזְבִי לְחַבֵּר סֵפֶר מִמְּלִיצוֹת תּוֹרָתֵנוּ
וְהָלַכְתִּי לְהַעְתִּיק דִּבְרֵי זוּלָתֵנוּ

> I realized that I acted foolishly, and that my sin is too great to bear, for I abstained from writing a book using the rhetorical devices of our Torah, and went to translate the words of others.[30]

If we take these two paragraphs at face value, they seem to continue the theme we have already explored: al-Ḥarīzī, in his jealousy for Hebrew, wants to compose a text that has no influence from Arabic whatsoever, unlike his earlier work, which was a translation of al-Ḥarīrī. This statement is misleading, for even if we set aside the impossibility of completely avoiding all Arabic influence, there are clear examples of such influence in the *Taḥkemoni*: it is based on an Arabic literary genre, and many of its elements come from the conventions of that Arabic genre, including the number of chapters, the use of rhymed prose and poetry, and even the use of a fixed narrator and fixed anti-hero. Eight out of the fifty *maqāmāt* of the *Taḥkemoni* are based on *maqāmāt* written by the man credited with creating the genre, Badīʿ az-Zamān al-Hamadhānī.[31] Though scholars have long noted the in-

28. al-Ḥarīzī, *Taḥkemoni*, 77.
29. These two components – his personal status as an author, and his fight for the status of Hebrew – are frequently intertwined in complicated ways.
30. al-Ḥarīzī, *Taḥkemoni*, 78.
31. For detailed analysis of the relationship between al-Ḥarīzī's eight *maqāmāt* and their source in the *maqāmāt* of al-Hamadāni, see Dishon 2012, chapter 12.

fluence of al-Hamadhānī, they have assumed that there is no influence from al-Ḥarīrī, perhaps because they trust al-Ḥarīzī's statements that the *Taḥkemoni* represents a departure from the Arabic literary influence that dominated his earlier work. However, Abdul Rahmen Maree, after a detailed study of the influence of al-Ḥarīrī's *maqāmāt* on the *Taḥkemoni*, concludes: "[A]fter checking the five sources that were used as raw material for twenty-nine of the *maqāmāt* of the *Taḥkemoni*, it becomes evident that a decisive influence on these *maqāmāt* was from the *maqāmāt* of al-Ḥarīrī. Fourteen out of these twenty-nine, that is, half of them, are influenced by al-Ḥarīrī."[32] Maree lists three main ways this influence manifests (with multiple subtypes for each kind): a. structural influences, b. reworked stories, and c. motifs and artistic devices.[33] Thus, the evidence suggests that although al-Ḥarīzī claims that the *Taḥkemoni* is free from Arabic influence, particularly that of al-Ḥarīrī, in fact it is quite the opposite: "Al-Ḥarīrī's book of *maqāmāt* formed an exemplar and prototype for the *Taḥkemoni* of Judah al-Ḥarīzī."[34] As Maree and others have noted, this relationship would not have been considered problematic, for this kind of creative adaption of sources was not only viewed as acceptable, but in fact was praiseworthy: one demonstrated one's skill by showing that one could write the same poem as one's predecessor, using different rhymes, metaphors, and other rhetorical devices.[35]

If imitation of earlier models was esteemed in his culture, why does al-Ḥarīzī feel the need to claim that "all the topics of this book were created in my mind; they are newcomers, flowing from the waters of Judah," and that he did not take a thing from the book of the Arab, or the books of the Arabs? I believe it is in fact to draw attention to the fact that it is the opposite – that in fact, the *Taḥkemoni* owes as much to Arab sources as does *Maḥberot Iti'el*, the author's acknowledged translation of al-Ḥarīrī. Indeed al-Ḥarīzī's treatment of al-Ḥarīrī's *maqāmāt* in the *Taḥkemoni* follows his process in *Maḥberot Iti'el*, as Maree notes, following Avraham Lavi's study of *Maḥberot Iti'el*.[36] In short, not only is it false that al-Ḥarīzī has taken nothing "from the book of the Arab," but it is also misleading that he claims that there is a sharp distinction between his method in the *Maḥbarot Iti'el* and the *Taḥkemoni*.

Once again, al-Ḥarīzī has presented us with logical contradictions which,

32. Maree 1995, 283.

33. Maree 1995, 284–289.

34. Maree 1995, 283.

35. On the *Taḥkemoni* specifically, see Maree 1995, 283. For a discussion of this in the context of al-Ḥarīzī's Arabic poetry, see Sadan 1996, 42–46. For a discussion of the phenomenon in general in the context of Arabic poetics (particularly the *muwaššaḥ*) see Rosen 2000, 172–174.

36. Maree 1995, 284. For a full comparison of *Maḥbarot Iti'el* and their source see Lavi 1979.

as Monroe argues, are not only markers of this genre, but specific signposts for us to notice in order to decode the didactic lesson that the author wishes to impart. What, then do all these contradictions in the beginning of the *Taḥekmoni* suggest? They all point to a much more complicated attitude towards Hebrew and Arabic in al-Ḥarīzī's thought than most scholars would accept. Al-Ḥarīzī did, indeed, see himself as responding to a crisis; but this crisis was not merely the decline of Hebrew, but rather the dissolution of the complex literary and linguistic culture of the intellectual elite of Muslim Spain, which incorporated both Hebrew and Arabic. Framing the crisis in this way allows us to better understand not only the internal contradictions that we have seen in the *Taḥkemoni*, but also other elements of al-Ḥarīzī's life and work.

To be a part of the literary tradition that had been created by the elite, so-called "courtier-rabbis" of al-Andalus, one needed not only a deep knowledge of Hebrew, but also familiarity with Arabic and Arabic poetry and poetics.[37] The participants in this tradition were well aware of this, as we can demonstrate from several examples. Thus, Samuel ibn Nagrela (known as Samuel Ha-Nagid), one of the greatest of the poets in this tradition, and a military leader, encouraged his son, Joseph, to study Arabic poetry. Joseph prepared the collection of his father's poems (his *diwān*); in this collection, the son often provided short headings, explaining the context in which given poems had been composed. In regard to one particular poem, the son tells us a specific incident regarding his father's emphasis on Arabic education:

> וכתב בכתב ידו שירים ערביים נבחרים ושלחם לי ממחנהו היוצא לפשוט
> בניסן משנת תת"ו וגזר עלי וצוני לקראם למען ארגיל בהם לדבר ולרוץ
> בלשון הערבי וכתב לי עמם זה.

> He [my father] copied, in his own hand, some choice Arab poems, and sent them to me from his camp, where he was headed for an attack, in the month of Nisan [4]806 [March/April 1046 CE], and he decreed and commanded me to read them, so that I would become accustomed to them, and would develop the ability to speak fluently and easily in Arabic. Along with them [the Arab poems] he sent me this [Hebrew poem].[38]

The Hebrew poem that follows this heading contains instructions to the son to read the Arabic poems, and in general to study Arabic. Moreover,

37. For more on this see Brann 2000, 435–454.
38. Shemuel Ha-Nagid (d. 1055 or 1056), *Diwan*, 67.

in the Hebrew poem, the father stresses the mortal danger he is facing as he is about to go into battle, and thus indicates the importance that he attaches to Arabic education, for he is encouraging it in what may be his last action and communication with his son. Even if this is hyperbole, and Samuel ibn Nagrela did not really spend the night before battle copying Arabic poetry and sending it to his son, this rhetoric shows the importance that Arabic poetry had for him.

We see similar emphasis on Arabic education in the instructions of Judah ibn Tibbon, another father, to his son, in a family closely contemporaneous to Judah al-Ḥarīzī's period and circumstances. Judah ibn Tibbon had left Islamic Granada at the age of thirty and relocated in Southern France. In his ethical will, he instructs his son to read Arabic books regularly, and to read the weekly Torah portion in Arabic because it will help him maintain his Arabic vocabulary.[39] While Judah ibn Tibbon does not single out Arabic poetry specifically, he clearly values poetry, for he gives his son detailed instructions about composing poetry and quotes quite a bit of Hebrew poetry in the ethical will. It is clear that he, too, saw a deep connection between being learned in all aspects of Arabic literature and being a learned Jew.

While we do not know exactly where Judah al-Ḥarīzī was born, it was likely Toledo and it is clear from the sources that he was a product of that city, which although under Christian rule, was still very much culturally Arabic – especially in terms of written practice. In other words, he and his contemporaries in Toledo can best be understood as products of the culture of Islamic Spain. Yet Toledo was changing; though Arabic was still a language of prestige, it was no longer the language of power. Therefore, it is reasonable to suppose that al-Ḥarīzī sensed that the kind of cultural mix that had created and sustained his literary tradition was in danger. It is against this background that he first translated the *maqāmāt* of al-Ḥarīrī into Hebrew, and then moved to the East, where Islam was still dominant, and where he hoped to re-create the multilingual literary world of al-Andalus. Like Judah ibn Tibbon, who tried to recreate this ideal cultural environment in a new location, albeit just with his son, al-Ḥarīzī also moved, and tried to export the hybrid of Hebrew and Arabic learning along with him.

The most sustained argument that was made for the preservation of this cultural moment is found in *Kitāb al-Muḥāḍara wal-Mudhākara*, by Moses ibn Ezra (d. after 1135), a book about the Hebrew poetics of the Jews of Muslim Spain written in Judeo-Arabic, with extensive quotes from Arabic writers. Rina Drory argues that the book itself, written in the early twelfth century

39. Judah ibn Tibbon, (d. c. 1190), *Igeret HaMusar*, 43. For an extended study of Judah ibn Tibbon, see Pearce, 2017.

at what is considered the end of the Golden Age of Arabic influence on Hebrew authors in Spain, is Moses ibn Ezra's argument for the interconnected Hebrew-Arabic literary legacy of al-Andalus, and his attempt to present it for a new audience. For example, he has a whole section on why the Arabs are best in poetry, and then explains that because of the diaspora, the Jews have lost their knowledge of Hebrew, yet regained it in al-Andalus, through their contact with Arabic. Drory writes: "[Ibn Ezra] wrote this book out of a conviction that the Andalusī Jewish culture was in danger of oblivion in the foreign regions of Edom [Christian Spain], and that he must do his best to preserve it."[40] Much like Judah ibn Tibbon, who tried to transmit the mixed Hebraeo-Arabic culture of al-Andalus to his son in Christian Provence, Moses ibn Ezra tries to do the same, albeit on a larger scale, and in Christian Spain.

Drory argues that Moses ibn Ezra's audience must not have been as Arabized as he and his peers were, for otherwise the examples he gives and the argument he makes would be self-evident; yet at the same time, they must have had some ability to appreciate Arabic culture, for the book is written in Judeo-Arabic, and the examples that he gives require at least some Arabic literacy to understand. She notes that his book was never translated into Hebrew in the Middle Ages; indeed, it could not have been. While Drory recognizes that this is the same fear that prompted al-Ḥarīzī to write the *Taḥkemoni*, and to move to the Middle East, she nonetheless takes al-Ḥarīzī's statements at face value, that his goal is to prove that Hebrew is as suitable for literary use, or even more so, than Arabic. Although Drory correctly argues for the importance of both Arabic and Hebrew in al-Ḥarīzī's world, she errs in taking his statements in the *Taḥkemoni* at face value, and she does not allow for the possibility that he could value both languages.

As I noted earlier, the only scholar who has suggested that the issue might be more complicated is Joseph Sadan, who bases his conclusion on testimony about al-Ḥarīzī found in an Arabic biography, written by a Muslim who knew al-Ḥarīzī in Syria close to the end of his life. Based on this biographer's testimony that al-Ḥarīzī wrote poetry in Arabic for Muslim consumption, which was appreciated by Muslims, Sadan writes:

> We must explain how it happened that the uncrowned king of Hebraitas and Hispanitas, the man of Christian Spain, turned to the heart of the territory of Arabic culture, and pretended, seemingly, to be an Arabic poet. There is room to explain that this contradiction is not a contradiction, but rather one facet of a rich figure, [who

40. Drory 2000, 213.

> lived during] a diverse period, and that his Hebraitas and even the Christiano-Hispanitas do not contradict the presence of a base of "Arabitas" of one kind or another.[41]

Al-Ḥarīzī expressed this complex linguistic identity, or at least components of it, in his poetry. As his Muslim biographer tells us:

كان يعمل قصائد، انصاف ابياتها الأول بالعبري، والانصاف الاواخر بالعربي

> He would make poems where the first half of their lines was in Hebrew, and the last half was in Arabic.[42]

While part of the motivation for this was certainly to demonstrate his skill, it is also a clear expression of who he was as a poet: one who wrote both in Hebrew and Arabic. Al-Ḥarīzī performs this complex relationship between Hebraitas and Arabitas in the dialogue between Ḥever the Qenite and the "author of this book" in the first *maqāma*, as we have discussed earlier. Each of the two sides expresses elements of al-Ḥarīzī: one side truly admires Arabic, Arabic literature, and particularly al-Ḥarīrī; while at the same time he has a side that wants to show off the literary qualities of Hebrew. Rather than viewing the "author of this book" as representing al-Ḥarīzī's true opinions, and Ḥever as the kind of Arabized Jew against whom he was arguing, we should view each as representing one side of his own personality. Indeed, much of the Hebrew poetry found later in the *Taḥkemoni* is presented as being composed by Ḥever. While the episodic nature of the *maqāma* genre makes it difficult to know how much we are to make connections between a character's behavior in one *maqāma* and their actions in another, the fact that Ḥever is presented as a Hebrew poet nonetheless supports a reading of this character as also serving as literary representative of al-Ḥarīzī.

This feat of multilingual poetry comes up in a story in the *Taḥkemoni*, as well. In the twentieth *maqāma*, the narrator is in the Land of Israel, searching for wondrous sayings, well-crafted verses, and riddles, when suddenly, in an unnamed city, he sees people running and gathering into a group. He asks them why they are running, and he is told that a wise man, unmatched in crafting poetry, has arrived, and is visiting the city. The narrator rushes to the place where this wise poet has set up camp, and finds an old man, who is boasting of his literary ability. The locals decide to test the poet, challenging him to compose a poem constructed out of three languages. The poet

41. Sadan 1996, 32. Several such poems by al-Ḥarīzī have been published. See Yahalom and Blau 2002, 245, 247–251, 268.

42. Ibn al-Sha'ar al-Mawṣilī, cited in Sadan 1996, 52.

does so, and recites his poem, in which each line has three sections: the first section in Hebrew, the second in Arabic, and the third is in Aramaic. The first and second sections in each line rhyme with each other, whereas the third section, the Aramaic portion, has a rhyme that runs through the whole poem. Of this poem he says:

הִנֵּה שִׁירָה קְשׁוּרָה בְּחֶבֶל שָׁלֹשׁ לְשׁוֹנוֹת בַּל יֵרָתֵק
וְהַחוּט הַמְשֻׁלָּשׁ לֹא בִמְהֵרָה יִנָּתֵק

> Here is poetry bound in the rope of three tongues that cannot be severed, / and a threefold cord is not quickly broken.[43]

The onlookers are amazed by the poem, and then go on to challenge him to two more tests: first to compose an epistle in which every word has the letter *resh*, and then an epistle in which that very same letter does not appear at all. When he passes these two further tests, the people are amazed at his skill, and he reveals himself, in a poem, as none other than Ḥever the Qenite, the anti-hero of the *Taḥkemoni.*

I argue here that the attitude towards Hebrew and Arabic expressed in this *maqāma* better reflects Judah al-Ḫarizi's position than the attitudes discussed earlier. However, in keeping with the method outlined earlier, we cannot simply take the events of this *maqāma* at face value, but must be suspicious; only after we have problematized our suggested interpretation can we try to tease out hints that nonetheless provide support for this interpretation.

What problematizes this interpretation of the trilingual poem as reflecting al-Ḥarīzī's ideal Andalusī culture is the fact the poem uses Hebrew, Arabic, and Aramaic; whereas in our discussion of Andalusī Jewish literary culture, and al-Ḥarīzī in particular, we have seen only Hebrew and Arabic. How can we nonetheless resolve this? First of all, we must note that Aramaic had status as a national Jewish language, because it had served in conjunction with Hebrew as a written (and spoken) language in the formative period of Rabbinic Judaism. In the period when Jewish communities outside the Arabian Peninsula first came into contact with Arabic, Hebrew and Aramaic were their two written languages; Arabic gradually took over the functions of Aramaic, but never displaced it entirely. Thus, it makes sense that though al-Ḥarīzī himself focused on Arabic and Hebrew, he still believed that the ideal system included Aramaic as well. The poem's structure may, perhaps, be indicative of al-Ḥarīzī's primary interest in Hebrew and Arabic, for, as

43. al-Ḥarīzī, *Taḥkemoni*, 294.

we have noted, he makes the Hebrew and Arabic sections rhyme with each other, whereas the Aramaic section of each line only rhymes with the other Aramaic sections.

Now let us look for hints that al-Ḥarīzī intends us to take the multilingual virtuosity in this *maqāma* as a serious reflection of his own values. First of all, he praises the poem using a quotation from scripture: *and a threefold cord is not quickly broken* (Ecclesiastes 4:12). This is the first hint that perhaps we need take the statement made here more seriously, for the ideal expressed is supported by a quotation from scripture. Although the use of quotations from scripture is one of the rhetorical devices valued in this literary canon, and they can be found throughout the *Taḥkemoni*, a true poet knows how to make use of these rhetorical elements for multiple effects.[44] Moreover, although the crowd challenges Ḥever to compose two more poems, and the rhetorical feats that he accomplishes in them would be prized by the contemporary Jewish Andalusī literary system and its Arabic model, those poems are not as complex, nor do they contain as many poetic devices, as the one composed from three languages. Furthermore, the poems differ in content: each of the later two poems praises an anonymous earthly patron, but the trilingual poem is in praise of God. No topic can be more sublime than that; so the use of all three languages in this poem shows what sublimity can be achieved by using the full linguistic system. Moreover, a list of *maqāma* titles found in one early manuscript of the *Taḫkemoni* identifies this *maqāma* in Judeo-Arabic with a title that specifically emphasizes the trilingual poem as the center of the *maqāma*:

מקאמה וצף שער מתלת ג״אמע אלבלאגאת / כל בית מנה מולף מן תלת לגאת

> The *maqāma* of the tripled poem that includes poetic devices, in which each verse is comprised from three languages.[45]

This title thus emphasizes this specific poem as primary, not the other two poems in the *maqāma*. Finally, at the end of this *maqāma*, in the poem where he reveals himself, Ḥever alludes to this poem, and makes no mention of the other poems at all. He states:

44. For discussions of the use of this poetic device, known as *shibbutz*, see Rosen 1997, 45–47, Elizur 2004, 347–412, Schirmann and Fleischer 1997, 47–54, and Cole 2007, 542–543.

45. al-Ḥarīzī, *Taḥkemoni*, 56. Note that in this Judeo-Arabic list, the order of the *maqāmāt* is different from that in the manuscript used for the Yahalom-Katsumata edition. In the Judeo-Arabic list, it is the eleventh *maqāma*, not the twentieth.

אַחְבִּיר לְשׁוֹן עֵבֶר וְקֵדָר וַאֲרָם
כִּי לִי שְׁלָשְׁתָּן בֶּאֱמֶת תִּכְרַעְנָה

I combine the tongues of 'Ever (Hebrew), Qedar (Arabic), and Aram (Aramaic), for to me all three of them truly bow![46]

Thus, he points to the trilingual poem as his true accomplishment in this *maqāma*, and lists his ability in all three languages as part of his characteristics. This is in keeping with al-Ḥarīzī's practice, as noted above; once again, it supports a reading of Ḥever as an avatar for the author.

Unpacking Ḥever's character is significant to understanding his role in the didactic message of the *Taḥkemoni*. His name, Ḥever the Qenite, taken from that of a very minor, yet well-known, figure in the Bible, the husband of Jael, who kills the enemy of the Israelites when he comes to hide in her tents. Though al-Ḥarīzī never directly mentions the biblical character, al-Ḥarīzī's Ḥever mentions in the first *maqāma* that he dwells in Elon-Beẓa'anannim, the city where his biblical namesake dwells. At the same time, the three letters of his name – *ḥet, bet, resh* – can be, and are, used for wordplay. On the one hand, the name is from the same root as the word *ḥaver* 'companion', and related words connected to the concept of friendship. On the other hand, the same root is also seen in the word *meḥabber* 'author', and other related words. Thus, for example, when Ḥever says "I combine the [three] tongues" in the quote above, he uses the word *meḥabber*. The same root is at the center of the word that al-Ḥarīzī uses as the Hebrew equivalent of *maqāma*, namely *maḥberet*. So, through paronomasia, Ḥever's name is associated with central aspects of his function in the *Taḥkemoni*: he is the anti-hero "companion," who shows up in every *maqāma* of the collection; and he is the "author," who is frequently portrayed as composing the poetry that is one of the core components of the work.

Finally, the character of Ḥever is an important link between al-Ḥarīzī's translation of the *maqāmāt* of al-Ḥarīrī, *Maḥberet Iti'el*, and the *Taḥkemoni*. Despite the author's claim that the *Taḥkemoni* will be entirely different from his earlier major work, he uses the same name, Ḥever the Qenite, for the anti-hero of both works. This shows us, once again, that although, on the one hand, al-Ḥarīzī wants to draw a clear distinction between these two works, on the other hand there is also a deep connection between them. Indeed, al-Ḥarīzī's investment in the Hebrew-Arabic literary culture of al-Andalus is evident in both of these works: for he writes both of them in Hebrew, and

46. al-Ḥarīzī, *Taḥkemoni*, 300.

shows in both that his Hebrew writings contain the contributions of Arabic literature, and transmit them even to audiences that cannot read Arabic.

Coda: A dot extra

James T. Monroe once told me during a conversation that there is a theory that al-Ḥarīzī added the "al" to his name to make it resemble the surname of his role model al-Ḥarīrī. Indeed, in Arabic script the two names are different only in the presence of a single dot: al-Ḥariri is الحريري, whereas al-Ḥarīzī is الحريزي. In fact, there are references to a Solomon Ḥarizi in various texts close to the period, and the poet's father's name was Solomon; if these are the same person, then the poet's original surname was, indeed, merely Ḥarīzī, rather than al-Ḥarīzī. Moreover, in one of the prefaces to the *Taḥkemoni*, the poet lists his name as *Yehuda ben Shelomo Ha-sefaraddi ben Ḥarizi*, "Judah son of Solomon the Sephardi son of Ḥarizi" – without the "al."

Further the poet's biographer writes:

وحدثني ان اسمه بالعبرية يهوذا وانه نقله الا العربية

> He told me that his name in Hebrew was Judah, and that he had shifted it into Arabic.[47]

Here al-Ḥarīzī has done something interesting, for even though it was quite common for Jews in Arab countries to go by the Arabic forms of their name, such as Mūsā for Moshe, al-Ḥarīzī did not use the Arabic form of Judah, Yahūdhā, but rather used the name Yaḥyā, the Arabic form of John. While according to Sadan this was a common move for Jews in Arabic-speaking countries,[48] it has a specific twist in this case. Because it is common in Arabic tradition to include one's son's name when giving one's full name, we know that al-Ḥarīzī has a son named Zechariah, because the Arabic biographer lists his name as *Yaḥyā abu Zakarīyā*.[49] Thus, in Arabic he would be John the father of Zechariah, which alludes to John the Baptist, who was John son of Zechariah. While it might not seem surprising to find Jews to have name pairs that made reference to family relationships in the Hebrew Bible, this one, which alludes to the New Testament, is unique among Jews, as far as I know – though it occurs in Arab circles. Indeed Sadan notes that this part of the name, the *kunyah,* may not actually reflect that he has a son named *Zakarīyā* but rather is sometimes used as way of creating a "topical

47. Sadan 1996, 53.
48. Sadan 1996, 28 fn. 28.
49. Sadan 1996, 52.

connection."[50] Though Sadan doubts that al-Ḥarīzī would have consciously intended his choice of *kunyah* to sound more Arabic, given everything else about his persona it seems likely he did.[51] It seems that Judah al-Ḥarīzī went to great lengths to fashion himself an Arabized identity, one which, in some ways, paid homage to his literary hero, al-Ḥarīrī. Nonetheless, as we have seen in this paper, this identity was not meant to erase or take away from his Hebrew identity, but rather to complement and add to it.

50. Sadan, 1996, 29 fn. 31.
51. Ibid.

Bibliography

Brann, Ross. 1991. *The Compunctious Poet: Cultural Ambiguity and Hebrew Poetry in Muslim Spain*. Baltimore and London.

Brann, Ross. 2000. "The Arabized Jews." In *The Literature of Al-Andalus*, edited by María Rosa Menocal et al. The Cambridge History of Arabic Literature, 435–454. Cambridge.

Cole, Peter. 2007. *The Dream of the Poem: Hebrew Poetry from Muslim and Christian Spain 950–1492*. Oxford.

Dishon, Judith. 2012. *A Necklace of Wisdom: Delight, Moral and Wisdom in the Book of Tahkemoni by Judah Alharizi*. (Hebrew). Lod.

Drory, Rina. 2000. *Models and Contacts: Arabic Literature and Its Impact on Medieval Jewish Culture*. Leiden.

Elizur, Shulamit. 2004. *Hebrew Poetry in Spain in the Middle Ages*. (Hebrew). Vol. 3. Tel Aviv.

al-Ḥarīzī, Judah. 2010. *Taḥkemoni*. Edited by Joseph Yahalom and Naoya Katsumata. Jerusalem.

Huss, Matti. 1995. "The '*Maggid*' in the Classical *Maqama*." (Hebrew) *Tarbiẓ* 65:129–172.

Ibn al-Sha'ār al-Mawṣilī, al-Mubārak ibn Aḥmad. 1990. *Qalā'id al-ghumān fī farā'id shu'arā' al-zamān = Book on the Poets of the Age*. Edited and translated by Fuat Sezgin. Frankfurt am Main

Ibn Ezra, Moshe. 1975. *Kitāb al-Muḥāḍara wal-Mudhākara*. Edited and translated by Abraham Solomon Halkin. Jerusalem.

Ibn Tibbon, Yehudah. 2010. *Igeret HaMusar* (Hebrew). Edited by Pinhas Korakh, Makhon Mareh.

Lavi, Abraham. 1979. *A Comparative Study of al-Hariri's Maqamat and their Hebrew Translation by al-Ḥarīzī*. PhD diss., University of Michigan.

Maree, Abdul Rahman. 1995. *The Influence of Al-Hariri's maqāmāt on Tahkemoni's Mahbaroth*. (Hebrew). PhD diss., Bar-Ilan.

——. 2000. "The Theme of Begging in the *Maqāmah*; Studies in the Relationship Between Judah al-Ḥarīzī and the Arab Author of the *maqāmāt*." (Hebrew). *Pe'amim* 88:21–52.

Monroe, James T. 1983. *The Art of Badī' az-Zamān al-Hamadhānī as Picaresque Narrative*. Beirut.

——. 2002. Introduction to *Al-Maqāmāt al-luzūmīyah*, by Abū l-Ṭāhir Muḥammad ibn Yūsuf al-Tamīmī al-Saraqustī ibn al-Aštarkūwī, 1–108. Leiden.

Ha-Nagid, Shemuel. 1934. *Diwan*. (Hebrew). Edited by David Solomon Sassoon. Oxford.

Pearce, Sarah J. 2014. "In a Better and Older Language: The Redemptive Potential of Arabic and Its Translated Fictions." *La Corónica* 43, no. 1:179–199.

——. 2017. *The Andalusi Literary and Intellectual Tradition: The Role of Arabic in Judah ibn Tibbon's Ethical Will.* Bloomington and Indianapolis.

Rosen, Tova. 1997. *Secular Hebrew Poetry in the Middle Ages.* (Hebrew). Tel Aviv.

——. 2000. "The *muwashshah.*" In *The Literature of Al-Andalus*, edited by María Rosa Menocal et al. The Cambridge History of Arabic Literature, 163–189. Cambridge.

Sadan, Joseph. 1996. "Judah Alharizi as a Cultural Junction: an Arabic Biography of a Jewish Writer as Perceived by an Orientalist." (Hebrew). *Pe'amim* 68:16–67.

Schirmann, Jefim and Ezra Fleischer. 1997. *The History of Hebrew Poetry in Christian Spain and Southern France.* (Hebrew). Jerusalem.

Yahalom, Joseph and Blau, Joshua. 2002. *The Wanderings of AlHarizi: Five Accounts of His Travels.* (Hebrew). Jerusalem.

Yahalom, Joseph and Naoya Katsumta. 2010. Introduction to *Taḥkemoni*, by Judah al-Ḥarīzī, 11–80. Jerusalem.

Wacks, David. 2007. *Framing Iberia: Maqāmāt and Frametale Narratives in Medieval Spain.* Leiden.

——. 2015. *Double Diaspora in Sephardic Literature: Jewish Cultural Production Before and After 1492.* Bloomington and Indianapolis.

Drama and Multiculturalism in Crisis: Ibn Dāniyāl's Shadow Play

Samuel England
University of Wisconsin-Madison

IN A MOVE not meant to be academic in nature, British Prime Minister David Cameron declared multiculturalism a lost cause in 2011. The ideal may have been worthwhile, he said, but it had allowed ethnic and religious ghettoes to proliferate throughout Europe, where Muslims in particular drifted dangerously away from mainstream society. Cameron's proposal was for governments to encourage "a clear sense of shared national identity" that would overcome any tendency toward social isolationism and the appeal of terror organizations. While hardly an original sociopolitical argument among leaders – German Chancellor Angela Merkel had said much the same to a national audience in late 2010 – Cameron attempted to push the rhetorical campaign beyond the boundaries of individual states and make it continentally European.[1] He couched in his motivational language a telling insight into the resurgent, sometimes violent national sloganeering that we have since witnessed in his country and throughout the North Atlantic. The spectacular rise and fall of multiculturalism in the decades following the Cold War, and the battles that scholars have fought over it during the same period, suggest that the twenty-first century is a uniquely charged moment of debate on cultural difference. The more ambitious theorists see it as a controversy over how to define human communities through history, but few of us in the academy seem to have produced research to explain our own explosive historical moment, in which the mix of cultures is directly implicated.[2]

1. Cameron 2010. Context on Merkel and Cameron's respective comments, and how they have been received in Western research and teaching institutions, is provided in Race 2015, 127–133.

2. In Western academies of the past two decades, the theory of multiculturalism that has spurred the most responses on the topic is probably Kymlicka 1995. One of the most compelling critiques of multiculturalists' tendency to misappropriate Enlightenment universals is Brown 2008; see page 150 for her invocation of Islam in history, and pages 201–202 for explicit engagement with Kymlicka. Somewhat more sympathetic to Kymlicka's philosophical paradigm is Phillips 2009.

Multiculturalism as a policy keyword has fallen out of favor with presidents and prime ministers, and since the late twentieth century, ascendant far-right factions have specifically cited it as a phenomenon destroying North America and Europe. At the same time, historians seemingly far removed from that discourse have gradually set it aside. As an academic shorthand for describing historical trends, it clearly has peaked from its late-Cold-War heyday.[3] But if we consider James Monroe's emergence in the fields of Middle East and European studies during the 1960s, key parallels become clear between then and now. Furthermore, Monroe and his contemporaries provide us with important cautions about the polemical forces at work in the nationalist-versus-multiculturalist debates. Those forces are most powerful in imaginative literature of the kind I will address, the shadow dramas of Muḥammad ibn Dāniyāl (646–710 AH/1248–1311 CE), texts bearing all the marks of rich cosmopolitan art. The extant scholarly literature on his plays generally characterizes them as sophisticated carnivalesques, according to Mikhail Bakhtin's definition of carnival, and indeed Ibn Dāniyāl confirms many of the basic principles of "a boundless world of humorous forms and manifestations" valorized by Bakhtin.[4] The problem is that such a reading is so capacious that it has bled into our understanding of cultural difference. When we universalize the shadow play as a carnival, we tend to see it as more ambassadorial, even transcendent, than its text indicates. Ibn Dāniyāl offers a literature of festivals, humorously adapting the traditions that intermingled in medieval Egypt: ancient Greek, Persian, and Iraqi rituals, along with Eastern Orthodox ecclesiastical rites. In the mix, he positions a diverse group of Middle Eastern and Saharan African puppet characters, grotesque in their names, shapes, and behavior. Many Arabists have praised Ibn Dāniyāl for mixing cultures in a discrete theatrical space and for providing his audience with a delightfully warped mirror of medieval Egypt.[5] I wish

3. For critical perspectives on the temporary nature of multicultural discourse among medievalists and modernists alike, see Rosser-Owen 2012, 3–4; and Soifer 2009, 19–20. New theories on the Mediterranean seem to hold the most promise for building upon twentieth-century multiculturalist thought while staking out new conceptual territory. See especially the reading of that region as "a space of hermeneutic indeterminacy" in medieval Italian literature, maintaining a critical balance between, on one hand, "cross-confessional and inter-confessional violence" and, on the other, the "practical expediency" of fictional characters for whom their sea-borne trade is more important than the Crusader xenophobia they are supposed to believe in during the late Middle Ages. Kinoshita and Jacobs 2007, 186.

4. Bakhtin 1984, 4.

5. For multicultural interpretations of Ibn Dāniyāl that tend to valorize him, see Corrao 1996, 98–100; Jamāl al-Dīn 1989, 9–10; Khūrshīd (blending the concepts of culture and social class to an extent to which they are difficult to discern from each other) 1991, 182–185; Molan 1988, 10; and Suleman 2013, 31. Buturović 2003 places the multicultural reading in formal and

to revise that premise, not because it is inaccurate in finding diversity, but because it portrays the playwright-poet as taking an ethical stance on culture that he does not seem to have actually espoused in any of his writing.

Although Ibn Dāniyāl's works stand out for their rich cultural palette and their sophisticated awareness of class tension, they betray a deep, surprisingly mainstream courtly ideology. It is critical to explore that quality of the poetic drama while acknowledging how attractive the multicultural approach has proven vis-à-vis the shadow play genre, for which the author is famous. Ibn Dāniyāl was a proudly cosmopolitan Iraqi, working in Mamluk Egypt just as Cairo was reaching its apex as a medieval power center and destination – a biographical fact that links the Abbasid Empire in Mesopotamia with the geographic center of multiculturalist scholarship, the Mediterranean. Bearing in mind the extraordinary achievements of multicultural pioneers such as Shmuel Goitein, María Rosa Lida de Malkiel, Américo Castro, Mahmud Ali Makki, and Monroe, and the importance of building upon their work in Mediterranean studies, it is equally important to recognize the inherent cultural chauvinism of literary fields during the Middle Ages – even bawdy Arabic shadow drama.[6] In our era of waning multiculturalist voices and strident national ones, we should look back upon our premodern curriculum and ask how modern readings have politicized it, because the political trends to come will no doubt seek to do the same thing all over again.

Monroe's statements on the debate still echo many years after he first wrote them (that is, during the final years of Spanish fascism), and they also shed light on much of what we now call "Mediterranean studies." He tells us that the suggestion that Spain was not an inherently Christian idea, and was shaped in large part by the many Muslim-majority kingdoms that had thrived in Iberia,

> has for many centuries elicited a widely varying response among Spanish scholars, ranging from outright hostility on the one hand, to gullible and uncritical acceptance of the most extravagant hypotheses concerning Arab "influences" on the other. The topic, furthermore,

---

sociological context; see especially 167. Mathews 2012 offers a broader appraisal of Mamluk court society as a pluralist enterprise, drawing mainly from material culture.

6. Antoon 2014 anticipates this move in his study of Arabic poetry predating Ibn Dāniyāl by 300 years. For Antoon, the most wildly grotesque classical Arabic literature, featuring outrageous words associated with the lower classes, could serve as a means by which courtly elites observed the habits of those classes – or at least they convinced themselves that they had a window on the commoners. Using late-Abbasid examples, Antoon argues that scatological poetry, in many ways very similar to Ibn Dāniyāl's, was a playful sort of sociological tool, an instrument of power (131–32).

> shows no sign of losing its capacity for arousing nationalistic passions.[7]

To be sure, the conflict pushes forward through the twenty-first century, albeit with a community of Hispanists considerably more ecumenical and attentive to Arabness than prior generations were. What also continues is the potential for exaggeration, and that is the problem that the present study seeks to address. In a case such as the early shadow play, scholars' admirable attempt to work against the legacy of ethnic nationalism has had the unintended effect of promoting a new limiting ideology, a language of long historical continuums and cultural universals. As necessary as it is to combat xenophobia by mapping out plural cultures, that work can also lead us to overlook key nuances in our sources of study. I ask us to reconsider Ibn Dāniyāl and the cultural politics of his writing. Unquestionably eclectic and innovative, he has gained a reputation for transcending the hierarchical categories of classical Arabic literary culture. In fact he confirms that hierarchy, even while ostensibly criticizing it.

Poetic Staging: Praise, Patronage, and Dramatic Composition

Arabists, theatre experts, and numerous medievalists benefit from two modern theses on the beginnings of Arabic drama. One thesis is historical: artistic patronage varied widely during the Mamluks' reign in Egypt and Syria. The other is formal: the shadow play (*khayāl al-ẓill*) sampled from nearly every major field of medieval Arabic literary production. The researcher adhering to these two arguments generally uses them to explain why Ibn Dāniyāl composed works seemingly so irreverent of courtly culture. Mark Pettigrew's opinion that "Arabic poets had limited opportunities at court" during the Mamluk apex of power, when Ibn Dāniyāl plied his craft, reflects the playwright's early career more than his more mature prime.[8] Li Guo appends a key point to this, showing how Ibn Dāniyāl improved upon his modest debut by producing an impressive number of panegyrics for the younger generation of Mamluk royals, who knew and appreciated Arabic much more deeply than their parents had. For an oculist of no great medical repute, treating patients in a working-class district of Cairo, Ibn Dāniyāl made a very respectable living for himself as a poet, especially given the less-than-ideal condition of the literary market. Although he did not enjoy the honor of praising the king himself at court – instead working for princ-

7. Monroe 1976, 69.
8. Monroe and Pettigrew 2003, 166.

es, second-level sultans, and viziers – he improved his lot little by little.[9] Therefore, when we read his puppetmaster character assuming the guise of a proud auteur, presenting *Ṭayf al-Khayāl* (The Shadow Figure), the masterwork of his three extant plays, his artistic claim is comprehensive rather than truly hyperbolic:

> البديع الماجن الخليع ... تذكر أن خيال الظل كتبت إلي أيها الاستاد (*sic*)
> قد ضجته الأسماع ونبت عنه لتكراره الطباع، وسألتني أن أصنف لك من
> هذا النمط ما يكون بديعا ... فجلت في ميدان خلاعتي وأجبت سؤالك لساعتي
> وصنفت من بابات المجون، والأدب العالي لا الدون

> My great mentor, depraved jester, you wrote to me ... to tell me that shadow plays were losing their audience ... and you asked me to come up with a truly exceptional one for you. ... So I jostled through my own depraved mind, and got right back to you on your request. I've composed a number of plays, from dirty slapstick to the literature of refined knowledge, nothing left out![10]

The complaint from the "great mentor" in shadow dramaturgy is a familiar one in classical Arabic: both the persona of the author and his teacher claim that their artistic form has decayed, a function of society's larger moral regression. To cure that ill, the puppetmaster searches through his encyclopedic knowledge of literary and dramatic techniques. His facility with *mujūn*, a literary term for lighthearted humor (which I translate above as "dirty slapstick"), identifies him as a member of the courts' well-educated pranksters, who helped define a broad field of Egyptian *adab* during the Mamluk era. This preamble to the script is full of praise – for the patron, the playwright, the frame character Ṭayf al-Khayāl with his hunched back, and ultimately for Ibn Dāniyāl's home city of Mosul.[11] He makes a telling gesture

9. Guo 2012, ix, 47.

10. Ibn Dāniyāl 1992, 1. This edition, by Kahle, of Ibn Dāniyāl's plays includes the Arabic texts and a section of explanatory writings in English, the two sections of the book numbered independent of one another. All citations here will be to the Arabic section, and all translations are mine unless otherwise noted. Ibn Dāniyāl's putative mentor here is one ʿAlī ibn Mawlāhum, on whom we know almost nothing but who seems to have not only taught the budding litterateur, but also may have supported him financially. ʿAlī appears at discrete moments in Ibn Dāniyāl's plays. See Guo 2012, 94.

11. Ibn Dāniyāl 1992, 2–3. The script's praise of Mosul stems from the Arabic root consonants ḥ-d-b, which produce a variety of terms for hunching and humps. A common epithet for Mosul was al-Ḥadbāʾ, "the Hunchback," for its famous leaning minaret. Scholars have noted Ibn Dāniyāl's synecdochic techniques for connecting the character of Ṭayf al-Khayāl to Mosul, Guo exploring them in the greatest detail (2012, 5). The classical Arabic term *adab* also requires explanation here. It has been widely translated as "belles-lettres" in recent decades,

toward the hierarchy of literary modes with his "*wa-lā dūn*," assuring in its tone but, consistent with the satirical logic throughout his work, deeply ambivalent. *Wa-lā dūn* denotes both "nothing less," as in nothing is left out in Ibn Dāniyāl's capacious project; and "nothing inferior." As the audience absorbs both meanings, they consider the boast as well as the claim to courtly language: no matter how much *mujūn* they might find in the script, they will recognize it as proper literary Arabic, a product of a proudly libertine segment of high society. Ibn Dāniyāl writes insistently about the vertical order of culture, rather than the more horizontal axis on which we modern readers try to imagine distinct medieval cultures identifiable by ethnicity, language, and religion. To be sure, *khayāl al-ẓill* illustrates cultural dispersion, but Ibn Dāniyāl is so dedicated a subscriber to the ideals of classical *adab* that he uses them, in a hierarchical way, as the organizing principle of his drama.

ʿAjīb wa-Gharīb, the other great shadow play in which Ibn Dāniyāl juxtaposes literary ideals with frowned-upon social behavior, echoes this self-promotional language.[12] Despite their hideous appearance and moral depravity, the two eponymous main characters ʿAjīb and Gharīb (the former name means "Wonder Worker" in context, the latter is "Strange Man") flaunt their confidence before the text's imagined spectators. So long as both buffoons master the courtly arts, their deviations from mainstream norms become fascinating quirks rather than horrors, or lasting stigmas, or grounds for arrest. This is the signature achievement of the Banū Sāsān, a nebulous societal group in the Middle East and Central Asia to whom they claim affiliation. Having appeared in classical Arabic poetry at least 250 years before Ibn Dāniyāl's career, the literature of the Banū Sāsān alternately delighted and vexed Islamic courts.[13] Our understanding of them remains partial and, I would argue, will benefit greatly from further analysis of *ʿAjīb wa-Gharīb*. A blanket term used to describe professional beggars in the Mid-

---

but Samer Ali revises the term, yielding the more accurate definition "humanistic knowledge" (2010, 14). On the prominence of *mujūn* in Mamluk literature, see Irwin 1998, 503. The very apt observation that Irwin makes – i.e that authors in Mamluk Egypt and Syria gravitated toward both conservative Islamic literature and risqué humor – suffers slightly in that he chooses the term "pornography" to describe *mujūn*. For an important critical review of Arabists' hasty application of the pornography label in a classical context, see Antoon 2014, 21–24.

12. Ibn Dāniyāl authored three well-known shadow plays. The third, *Al-Mutayyam wa-l-Yutayyim* (title translated as "The Charmed and the Charmer" in Guo 2012, 14), is significant for its treatment of love and sexuality themes, but it is not as overtly interested in the status of Arabic and Arabness as are the other two parts of the dramatic trilogy. For a revealing study of *Al-Mutayyam wa-l-Yutayyim* and its intervention in the tradition of love-themed literature, see Rowson 1997.

13. Bosworth 1976, 1:30–47, 1:72–79; al-Munajjid n.d., 7–9, 101–105.

dle East, Banū Sāsān marked its own poetic subgenre in the latter centuries of the Abbasid Empire.[14] Poets and Buyid patrons popularized it as a creative format through which beggar personas could speak about their craft. The Banū Sāsān argot seems to have been a highly developed code. Its basic appeal to beggars and enterprising travelers hardly disappeared with the Banū Sāsān themselves – coding one's speech for an illicit trade, of course, seems transhistorical. For modern attestations, we might look to itinerant Americans traversing the continent by freight train from the nineteenth to the twentieth century, scrawling graffiti code words and pictures around train yards.[15] Medieval and modern alike, the argots conjoined members of fugitive networks, allowing vagabonds to avoid detection by legal authorities, property owners, and other unsympathetic citizens of the general populace. What also seems to run through the history of such codes is that they have occasionally fascinated a few prominent elites. That is why we have a *sāsānī* manuscript record from Abbasid courts, texts to which Ibn Dāniyāl may have had access. While we do not know precisely which literary pieces he read, it is clear that the Banū Sāsān were well known in his home region of Mosul and in Mamluk territory.[16]

The concern the puppetmasters voice in *Ṭayf al-Khayāl*, that they have

14. *Banū sāsān* literally means "Sasanians," leading some scholars to conclude that the Abbasid Arabs who pioneered so-called *sāsānī* literature had believed ancient professional beggars originated in Iran. Bosworth notes the scarcity of reliable sources to confirm such a theory. He goes on to define the archetypal piece of creative literature on the Banū Sāsān as "long poems written substantially in the beggars' jargon ... in which many of their tricks and scabrous practices are delineated." Bosworth 2012. Such poems clearly inform the composition of *ʿAjīb wa-Gharīb*. Whatever the ethnic and geographic origins of professional beggars in the Abbasid Empire, they seem to have traveled throughout Islamic territories as early as the first/eighth century. Experienced mendicants would teach their techniques to interested parties, and the enterprise began to fascinate the late-era Abbasid courts with its special jargon, even while the Banū Sāsān proved to be an enduring legal conundrum for imperial governments. Bosworth 1976, 4–5, 15–18.

15. Researchers apply the term "hobo graffiti" to icons, words, and phrases found in and around train yards in North America, its heyday generally thought to be the first three decades of the twentieth century. Clandestine passengers on freight trains would announce their presence; tell jokes; and give useful information about the area for their peers, e.g., when police patrolled the yards, where food and sex were easily available, etc. For an introduction, see Ross 2016, 27–35.

16. For a Banū Sāsān-themed short narrative widely known throughout Islamic empires, describing professional beggars in western Syria, see Badīʿ al-Zamān al-Hamadhānī (358–95 AH/968–1008 CE), *Maqāmāt*, 100. There is little concrete evidence of the Banū Sāsān's physical presence in Egypt, although if they were as widespread as poetry and creative prose would have us believe, they populated all manner of Islamic cities and especially Hajj routes. That would certainly place them in Cairo and perhaps other major stops across northern Egypt and the Sinai.

been "losing their audience," conveys the sense of opportunity that the Banū Sāsān exploit, as petty criminals and self-fashioned intellectuals. ʿAjīb, Gharīb, and their coworkers mourn the passing of a better age only briefly before they contrive a way to profit from it. The degraded moral state of the narrative present – the key historical idea of this literature – ultimately benefits these professional beggars, who take advantage of the populace's desire for good news. Even as Cairo's taverns and brothels are officially being shut down by the government of the Mamluk king al-Ẓāhir Baybars (620–76 AH/1223–77 CE), the Banū Sāsān can take refuge in their own ethos. Heartened, they offer the people around them more-than-compensatory cheer, whether by feigning religious devotion, indulging people's superstitions, or appealing to their repressed generosity. If those techniques do not succeed, the Banū Sāsān can simply scare their audience into some form of payment. They also purport to have mastered all sorts of courtly talents. Addressing the play's puppetmaster, Gharīb recounts his own past, making the connection between fellow would-be courtiers:

وكم أمسيت ...
وأكل الفار والأمزار دأبي مع المهتار عنتر أو بلال
...
ولكني رأيت العلم زينا فعدت إلى المدارس والجدال
وتبت فصرت في الفقهاء أقصى وأفتي في الحرام وفي الحلال
ونظم الشعر صرت به فريدا وطلت به على السبع الطوال
وقطعت العروض بفاعلاتن بأوتاد وأسباب ثقال
وعلم النحو فيه النصب فني على ما كان ذا جاهٍ ومال

Many evenings I spent ...
Eating rats, drinking beer all the time with that idiot ʿAntara, or with Bilāl.
...
But then I saw the beauty in knowledge! I went back to school, learned how to craft a sound argument.
I repented, became the ultimate jurisprudent, started issuing fatwas on what's allowed and forbidden.
And I began composing poetry, making it something truly special, something that'd measure up to the Seven Great Ones.
I could scan any kind of meter, every simple or long syllable.
I knew grammar, a real expert on the accusative case – and I could case the joint for high-class people to rip off, too![17]

17. Ibn Dāniyāl, 59–60.

Ibn Dāniyāl fixates upon the arrival of Islam, constantly oscillating between the period just before it and the first generation of Muslim cultural life. As multiculturalist readers have noted, the prose and poetry of his shadow play scripts encompasses many eras, including the ancient Near East and the Hellenic world, but his most forceful moments of satire gravitate toward pagan Arabia and the eventual revelation-moment of the Qur'an.

Gharīb conducts his drunken life with an elite group of poets who enthrall audiences but also spur ethnic controversies. ʿAntara ibn Shaddād (525–615? CE) and Bilāl ibn Rabāḥ (580–640 CE) are two towering figures of Arab history, both known as East Africans. Ibn Dāniyāl uses them to play upon two uncomfortable binaries: paganism/monotheism and Arabness/blackness.[18] The poet warrior ʿAntara is of a generation ignorant of Islam; Bilāl offers one of the great Muslim conversion stories, having been tortured by his slave owners for his monotheism, later joining the Prophet's Companions in Medina and earning great respect as a loyal early believer. Impishly tossing out their names as generic signifiers of Black Africa, Gharīb reproduces two pieces of classical Arabic received wisdom. First, Sub-Saharan Africans are predisposed to crude joviality.[19] Second, nomads (ʿAntara was said to be half African, half Arab, and lived as a Bedouin) eat a variety of animals that urban Arabs disdain, including rats. When Gharīb sees his way out of consorting with fellow drunkards and uncouth pagans, he appreciates how he might use religiosity to gain control of his social domain. His desire for status in a fixed, institutional setting leads him to the official education system, where he develops respectable professional abilities while maintaining his base motives. By conjuring up a picture of intellectual reform here, he divides the question of morals from that of education level. While this kind of satire might seem to denounce the Islamic *madrasa* itself, instead it advertises the versatility of the successful student's credential. Gharīb studies not just to be a religious authority but also in order to challenge "the Seven Great Ones," the composers of the pre-Islamic *muʿallaqāt* (sing. *muʿallaqa*), the legendary poems of their age which, chronicles report, were adjudged by intertribal Arabian authorities to be the finest works in Arabic, an appraisal reinforced two centuries later by the Abbasids.[20] ʿAntara himself is known as a *muʿallaqa*

18. ʿAntara may be more legendary than historical as a figure. His identity is complicated by his dual reputation, namely, as a knight-poet and as the subject of lengthy folk epics. Dates for both ʿAntara and Bilāl are given only in CE because their lifespans do not fit the AH calendar, which begins in 622 CE.

19. Ibn Khaldūn (732–808 AH/1332–1406 CE), *Muqaddimat Ibn Khaldûn* 1:155.

20. For prominent examples of Abbasid discourse on anthologizing, understanding, and in some cases ranking pre-Islamic poems, see al-Mufaḍḍal al-Ḍabbī (dates unknown: born in the Umayyad era, died in the Abbasid era), *Dīwān al-Mufaḍḍaliyyāt* and Ḥusayn ibn Aḥmad al-Zawzānī (date of birth unknown: died 486 AH/1093 CE), *Sharḥ al-Muʿallaqāt al-Sabʿ*.

author, so Gharīb has now come full circle. Poet, rhetorician, and theologian, he derives the most impressive qualities of his old friends, insisting that they are useless if not fully Arabized, the key step in winning the confidence (and money) of the populace. He exaggerates, but maintains the logic of, the would-be courtier's aspirational ideal in a triumphalist Islamic empire.

From Abbasid to Ayyubid to Mamluk: Exploiting Political and Poetic History

By making those playful statements of ideology, the text ensures that its satire will make sense to multiple audiences. The series of jokes that comprises the shadow play aims to appeal to both courtly people and the urban mercantile classes. We know from prior scholarship that Ibn Dāniyāl indicts Egyptian politics and the humbled, secondary role of long-form poetry in the royal estate, but what are the cultural complaints on which he builds his irreverent fiction? I contend that much of the question remains unanswered, and that Bakhtinian theory applied too broadly misunderstands the plural society that Ibn Dāniyāl addresses in his works. The archetypal carnivalesque is supposed to overflow beyond the bounds of official ceremony, to destabilize any organized form of supervision over the people's aesthetic existence. Ibn Dāniyāl's carnivalesque, though, constantly affirms that it fits *within* the cultural hierarchy in effect, and furthermore recruits its wide variety of dramatis personae to pledge their fealty. Rather than transcending official culture (that is, the classical Arabic court overseen by Mamluks), he seeks to preserve it from potential dilution.

The Mamluk character al-Amīr Wiṣāl ("Prince Love Connection"), whose sex life and prospective marriage provide the central story of *Ṭayf al-Khayāl*, exchanges poems with his subjects in a highly functional – if obscenely humorous – court. In one, the prince describes his insatiable sexual-cultural appetite:

كم مرام فهمته حين وافى لي رسول ببقجة وسداب
فبعثت الجواب سرا وواعدت على أن أزور بعد جوابي
تقنعت كالنسا وتأزرت وأخفيت لحيتي بنقاب
ثم وافيتها عشاء...
ولقد كان يعتريني إنعاظ فأغشا الأتان بين الدواب

...
وغشيت المناخ ليلاً وثورت جمال الأعجام والأعراب
وتدليت خلفها وتعلقت بكفي في عرى الأقتاب
ولعمري لو لم يغب أسد الغاب لهونت نيك أسد الغاب

Oh, I knew what it meant, the many times a messenger would
bring me a bundle of ladies' clothes and some aphrodisiac
herbs.
I'd send back a discreet reply, saying that I'd come visit soon.
I'd dress myself up like a woman, putting on a wrap and hiding
my beard under a niqab,
Then I'd go visit her at nightfall....
I was so horny, I even picked – out of all animals – she-asses to get
it on with!
...
Under cover of darkness, I'd raid the Arabian and Persian stables,
getting their camels all stirred up.
I'd squirm behind them, my hands jiggling their humps, riding
their backs bare.
I promise, if lions hadn't forsaken our forests, I'd have screwed
more than my share![21]

Nostalgia is the main mood in which al-Amīr Wiṣāl creates a sense of lost Arab ideals. His lengthy ekphrasis tempts the audience into imagining their powerful sultan, Baybars, desperately seducing low-life Egyptians and animals. Through the extremes of his sexual imagery, the prince perverts the traditional Arab ethnic boasts while he tells a story of literary culture gone bad. Despite the fact that he reigns over Egypt, he longs to tap the essence of his ethnically diverse subjects, and produce meaningful classical

21. Ibn Dāniyāl 1992, 37–38. Editors and translators have missed a few elements of this poetic performance in the play. Mahfouz and Carlson translate the first line I have cited as "I used to understand every cuckold's hint at / Offering me a whore while he was carrying a bundle of clothes": see Ibn Dāniyāl 2013, 57. The suggestion of "whore" seems mistaken in context here, although certainly al-Amīr Wiṣāl speaks at length about the sex trade. Guo correctly identifies *sadāb* as a Persian-derived word for the herb rue (*ruta* in Latin), but it requires explanation not given in any studies of Ibn Dāniyāl that I have found. In Persian, *sadāb* can refer to a distinct plant, called wild rue (*peganum harmala*). It was considered an aphrodisiac in premodern Iran (Flattery and Schwartz 1989, 149), from which it was exported and the wisdom on its medicinal properties was probably adopted among Egyptian pharmacists. This seemingly minor lexicographical point is crucial to understanding the passage, because *ruta* plants were used by medieval doctors to dampen sexual desire, not increase it, and that would contradict the intent of the poetry here. Wild rue is therefore the only logical possibility. See Nasrallah 2007, 669–670. Yet another multivalent term, *asad/usd al-ghāb*, analyzed at length in this essay, could in theory refer to the Syrian plain of al-Ghāb, a highly contested site throughout the Crusades. That possibility seems more remote than those I have included in the main text, given the lack of available evidence that al-Ghāb was of special interest to Ibn Dāniyāl and Mamluk-era Cairene audiences. Future research may suggest a connection; the Mamluk archive remains under-studied. Sincere thanks are due to Adam Talib for corresponding with me about the peculiar metrics and double-entendres embedded in this poem.

Arabic from his exploits. He cross-dresses as an updated version of ʿUmar ibn Abī Rabīʿa (ca. 23–93 AH/644–711 CE), the Umayyad poet who depicted himself seducing the beloved Nuʿm, a rival tribe's unmarried woman. In that legendary poem, ʿUmar's heroic poetic persona must depart Nuʿm's camp after their night together. She and her sisters aid him by sandwiching his body between the group of young women, that is, hiding him in their long robes.[22]

Al-Amīr Wiṣāl turns ʿUmar's poetry of rule-breaking and sexual achievement into a poetry of emasculation. When not trysting with his correspondent – and wearing her clothes – the prince services donkeys and camels. The poem's reference to the stables as Persian and Bedouin Arabian (the camels belonging to *al-aʿjām wa-l-aʿrāb*) illustrates a sexual deviant so desperate for satisfaction that he harasses not only the pride of old Arabia, its dromedary steed, but also the Bactrian camel from Central Asia, which Arab traditionalists considered inferior in warm desert climes such as Egypt's.[23] By raiding remote Persian stables, he also recalls the Banū Sāsān's rallying cry: in *sāsānī* literature, the proud swindlers extol their travels far and wide in search of sustenance. Likewise, the grotesque heroes of both *Ṭayf al-Khayāl* and *ʿAjīb wa-Gharīb* gesture toward the ability of travel to teach the traveler useful lessons on trade and psychology, a benefit that scoundrels derive from following their ambitions across empires. For the Banū Sāsān, gaining new knowledge – intellectual and carnal – makes them more perfectly shaped members of the literary underclass. Al-Amīr Wiṣāl therefore develops a creative travesty out of both the heroic ʿUmar and the anti-heroic Banū Sāsān. Much as he moves between gender roles, he also bridges eras of literary production. He spectacularly, satirically fails every masculine ideal of the court, except that of attaining high education in classical *adab*. That criterion he masters, filling out the perverse figure of the anti-hero while educating the dramatic audience.

Al-Amīr Wiṣāl's most pointed statement on Arab Muslim identity is his oath on *asad al-ghāba*, the Lion of the Forest (shortened to *asad al-ghāb* in the poem, punned upon with the verb for being absent: *ghāba*, the lion "is gone"). Baybars used the lion as his emblem and decorated his royal buildings with the animal throughout Cairo, sharpening the literary cliché into a

22. ʿUmar ibn Abī Rabīʿa (d. 711 CE), *Dīwān*, 127. Historical and literary figures known chiefly by their first names, such as ʿUmar, are cited by first name in this study.

23. The camel binary is of course playful and not reflective of the actual history of these regional camel breeds. Despite the cultural pride attached to particular camel breeds among Middle Eastern peoples, the historical record suggests that only in antiquity were these genetic lines preserved. Camels were interbred from the early years of Muslim expansion outside of Arabia, on which see Bulliet 1975, 157; and Hill 1963, 70–73.

political barb. In the classical poetic tradition, the grammatically masculine lion is a gender-ambiguous metaphor for the beloved. Amorous poems addressing women and submissive boys speak alternately of a lion or gazelle that destroys its smitten, lonely suitor. Even with the scato-sexual language of al-Amīr Wiṣāl's poem, *Ṭayf al-Khayāl* offers constant reminders of the rhetorical knowledge framing its humor. In poetry, *asad al-ghāba* spurs the loving rhapsodist to dwell upon the pains of desire, functioning as a sort of heuristic prompt to the voice of chaste love. He embodies an exterior, visual world on which the lover fixates while contemplating his own interior emotions, all of which is anticipated by al-Amīr Wiṣāl's own prose in the dialogue, such as his statement that

والافكار جمر يتوقد ... يفوح بما يلقى فيه، فإذا كان طيّبا فيا طِيبَ قوافيه

> Deep thought is a glowing coal that ... fills the air with the scent of whatever is tossed on it. (Sprinkle on it) something pleasant, and oh how sweet the rhymes waft![24]

Observing the interior/exterior duality of the love tradition, and of the *jidd/hazl* (seriousness/joking) that he maps here, Ibn Dāniyāl invests much more into the lion than is immediately apparent to a late-modern readership such as ours. His audiences would have recognized the wordplay, though. With its martial, honorific flavor, the singular *asad al-ghāba* was a favorite of the Prophet's companions in their self-descriptions. Historians of Islam adopted the nomenclature during the era just preceding Ibn Dāniyāl's. *Usd al-Ghāba fī Maʿrifat al-Ṣaḥāba* (Lions of the Forest in the Prophet's Inner Circle, abbreviated hereafter to *Usd al-Ghāba*) was among the most important Islamic reference texts of Ibn Dāniyāl's age. Its author-compiler, ʿAlī ibn al-Athīr (555–630 AH/1160–1233 CE), is now famous almost exclusively for his Crusade chronicles, but in that moment less than a century after his death, his primary reputation as a scholar of early Islam was much fresher in his readers' minds than in ours. *Usd al-Ghāba* made up part of the courtly curriculum in Egypt and the Levant, from Ibn al-Athīr's own Ayyubid period onward.[25] Al-Amīr Wiṣāl's poetic expression, *usda l-ghābī*, ending the line, confirms that he has been using the lion image to allude to the Prophet's Companions, not merely to the stock persona of the beloved. Al-Amīr Wiṣāl sounds two nostalgic notes at once, using a single animal metaphor as a means by which to recall the vanished figure of chaste love poetry (which

24. Ibn Dāniyāl, *Ṭayf al-Khayāl*, 22.
25. Muḥammad al-Dhahabī (673–748 AH/1274–1348 CE), *Tadhkirat al-Ḥuffāẓ*, 4:86; Hillenbrand 2000, 432, 505n8; Robinson 2003, 99.

came into its own before Islamic revelation) and the long-dead first Muslim generation.

Ibn Dāniyāl was much more than a formal innovator, middling panegyrist, and master of *mujūn*. *Ṭayf al-Khayāl* proves this, with its willingness to touch upon the Prophet's own social circle, snidely calling them passive sodomites. Beneath the shameless surface, though, al-Amīr Wiṣāl's poem inquires into the artistic tradition from which it comes. Religious discourse on Islamic history tends to be just as nostalgic as amorous literature, although it contains a much more complex discussion of time's passage than the love poetry itself. Medieval and early-modern Islamic scholars generally agreed that "the age of the Prophet and his companions represented the Golden Age of Islam and that the farther Muslims were from this age the worse the state of degeneration be."[26] Therefore, when al-Amīr Wiṣāl remarks in passing that the lion no longer inhabits the forest, he is gazing back upon historical periods of moral righteousness, political legitimacy, and unconsummated poetic love that he promises to consummate in spectacular fashion.

Given the famously strict legal zone of Mamluk Cairo during Ibn Dāniyāl's prime years as a dramatist, we must ask why he would be allowed to flirt with heretical statements. Not only that, al-Amīr Wiṣāl is the figure who satirically stands for the sultan, Baybars, whose harsh policies of closing down Cairo's taverns and brothels were supposed to aggressively promote piety. Even the less serious matter of "[l]ove of handsome young *mamluk*s does not seem to have been characteristic of the first few Mamluk sultans and certainly not of the stern Baybars."[27] How would public authorities countenance this spectacle of their Mamluk king, fantasizing about sodomy with Islam's original core believers? One hypothesis is that Ibn Dāniyāl's scandal-filled dramas never reached magistrates or their close contacts, but such a notion is unconvincing. All available evidence suggests that even semi-colloquial shadow plays were not limited to the working classes: a broad swath of Arab intellectuals wrote about them, and at least a few well-known written anecdotes describe politicians reacting to performances, including those in Egyptian public spaces.[28]

What seems most probable instead is that Ibn Dāniyāl took refuge in the Abbasid literary tradition. Even were he not an Iraqi himself, he worked in Egypt's deeply Abbasid idioms of panegyric; short occasion-based poems;

26. Hallaq 1986, 138.

27. Rowson 2008, 217. The quotation's lower-case "mamluk" refers to the generic term *mamlūk*, here meaning "slave." When used as a proper noun in English, "Mamluk" refers to the warrior-slaves who rose to power in Egypt and Syria.

28. Moreh 1987, 47–50.

and the prose *maqāmāt*, the rogue misadventures so essential to the shadow play. While Ibn al-Athīr produced *Usd al-Ghāba*, Ayyubid theologians and litterateurs adopted a variety of Abbasid conventions in their written work. And, because much of this adoption process was initiated by the kings ruling over them, Abbasid style in general carried with it an unspoken kind of royal authorization.[29] The effects in the Mamluk centuries were profound. Late-medieval Arabic courts from Central Asia to al-Andalus engaged and internalized Abbasid literature, but the Ayyubids distinguished themselves for their stated fealty to the tradition – when the Mamluks took over, their new courts relied upon the manuscripts and courtly practices of the Ayyubid-Abbasid interface.[30] For Ibn Dāniyāl, identifying as an artist of *mujūn* gained him more than just a reputation and a financial supplement to his work as an oculist and composer of serious panegyrics; it gave him a versatile excuse for all kinds of scandalous language. Abbasid anthologies offered Mamluks diverse stories of *mujūn* poets' exculpating themselves for religious infractions, and indeed some cases in which their deep knowledge of the tradition gave them the upper hand on their political superiors. The more closely Ibn Dāniyāl hewed to the concept of the all-important Abbasid legacy in Mamluk imperial culture, the more shelter he could take from royal anger or legal interdiction.[31]

Conclusion

In a book building on the work of another paradigmatic thinker, Terry Eagleton slips in a brief and revelatory emendation of Bakhtin: "the necessary political criticism is almost too obvious to make. Carnival, after all, is a *licensed* affair in every sense, a permissible rupture of hegemony."[32] We scholars of Arabic, Mediterranean cultures, and the Middle Ages would do well to meaningfully respond to Eagleton's warning. The enthusiasm to apply the carnival model to compositions such as the shadow play is logical, but risks misreading Ibn Dāniyāl's remarkable project. He was more interested in the license, to use Eagleton's term, than in the carnival itself as a cultural tableau. He spent a considerable part of his career trying to gain ac-

29. On the Ayyubids' official uses for Abbasid textual models, see Hermes 2012, 160–161; and Ibn al-Athīr, *Al-Kāmil* 10:33–35.

30. Ehrenkreutz 1972, 205; Pfeiffer 2014, 132.

31. One anecdote about *mujūn*-as-excuse during the height of Abbasid power is related by al-Khaṭīb al-Baghdādī (392–463 AH/1002–71 CE), *Taʾrīkh Baghdād*, 7:441–42. Another story, in which an Abbasid vizier uses his precise knowledge of *mujūn* to coerce his sovereign into begging him to attend the royal court, is in Abū Manṣūr al-Thaʿālibī (350–429 AH/961–1038 CE), *Yatīmat al-Dahr*, 3:237.

32. Eagleton 1981, 148. Italics original.

cess to, and a reward in, the royal courts, all the while keenly aware of their varying legitimacy in the eyes of educated Egyptians and Syrians. When he composed drama, full of pseudo-courtly scenes and ostentatious poetic performances, he recognized the ambiguity of his position.

In short, Ibn Dāniyāl was satirizing the very institution from which he sought sustenance, never seriously cleaving from the court. That is why, I argue, his repeated dramatic gestures to poetic, overblown, self-conscious Arabness do not indict the elitist notion of *adab*, as critics have argued, but instead promote *Ṭayf al-Khayāl* and *ʿAjīb wa-Gharīb* as their own subset of high literature. We see evidence of that in the Mamluk-era literary production that succeeded Ibn Dāniyāl's work. As the Baḥrī Dynasty of Mamluks came to a close in the fourteenth century, poets and anthologists such as the prolific Ṣafī al-Dīn al-Ḥillī (675–750 AH/1276–1349 CE) deepened the exploration of heteroglossia and humor vis-à-vis the diverse Levantine cultural mix. In so doing, he expanded his group of patrons well beyond that which Ibn Dāniyāl had enjoyed.[33] The prose writers Khalīl ibn Aybak al-Ṣafadī (696–764 AH/1297–1363 CE) and ʿAlī ibn Sūdūn al-Bashbughawī (810–68 AH/1407–64 CE) demonstrated the enduring market for satiric, grotesque pieces of literature by compiling noteworthy examples of them for politically powerful individuals and salons in the Mamluk Levant. As professional authors, all of these individuals' fortunes varied, but the patronage system thrived until the advent of modernity. It will be a very long time before we understand in detail the full scope of Mamluk literary production, and the lengths to which its authors went in maintaining the symbolic power of classical Arabic – even when they did so in self-ironizing fashion. From a modern reader's perspective, the cyclical structure of Ibn Dāniyāl's carnivalesque comes to rest by affirming the long-term strength of the court.

Watching the sanctioned irreverence end with the conclusions of *Ṭayf al-Khayāl* and *ʿAjīb wa-Gharīb*, we might imagine the shadow play's audiences returning to their customary positions in the Mamluk-ruled system, and Ibn Dāniyāl resuming work as a middling eye doctor. The modern academic movement promoting multiculturalism, too, seems to have ebbed away, poised to be replaced by another critical language on Mediterranean history. Whether or not that process will soon reach completion, it is salutary to reflect upon multiculturalists' achievements and the resistance that they have confronted. Perhaps there is no truly opportune time to make the kind of intervention that Monroe and like-minded medievalists achieved. His mentor Américo Castro's exile from Spain has become a cautionary tale about *franquismo*, the military regime against which multicultural Hispan-

33. Bosworth 1976, 1:119.

ists aligned themselves, some of them risking imprisonment and torture. The twenty-first century now seems marked with other strains of nationalism around the Atlantic and Mediterranean. We see new dictators taking power and, just as troubling, large groups of citizens expressing nostalgia for the strongmen of the mid-twentieth century. Torture and anti-immigration policies enjoy a moment, perhaps even an extended period, of vogue. Having advocated immigrants' adoption of "a clear sense of shared national identity," David Cameron might be alarmed at the racial identity arguments that subsequently entered the mainstream in his country, and throughout Europe, and certainly the United States as well.

But if Merkel and Cameron's speeches presage a period of growing isolation, Monroe's words, too, offer signs of future developments. Ibn Dāniyāl, he and Pettigrew tell us, innovated with the shadow play as a result of a "crisis in courtly patronage," a set of harsh material circumstances affecting authors at particular moments, from al-Andalus to Central Asia.[34] Adopting the term *crisis* here, I point to its sense of emergency but, more importantly, its original denotation, of a crossing-point. We scholars of the Middle East and the Mediterranean are currently at such a point, asking what follows multiculturalism. While I cannot pretend to answer the question, I see ample cause for optimism in precisely the national sloganeering that echoes around us. Monroe is not only the pupil of an escapee of fascism, he also watched from afar as his own childhood home of Chile fell under dictatorship. We can and should draw energy from the dogmatic nationalism around us as we chart theories beyond the multicultural.

34. Monroe and Pettigrew 2003, 139.

Bibliography

Ali, S. 2010. *Arabic Literary Salons in the Islamic Middle Ages: Poetry, Public Performance, and the Presentation of the Past*. Notre Dame.

Antoon, S. 2014. *The Poetics of the Obscene in Premodern Arabic Poetry: Ibn al-Ḥajjāj and Sukhf*. New York.

Bakhtin, M. 1984. *Rabelais and his World*. Bloomington.

Bosworth, C. 1976. *The Mediaeval Islamic Underworld: The Banū Sāsān in Arabic Society and Literature*. 2 vols. Leiden.

———. 2012. "Sāsān." *EI2*, edited by P. Bearman, Th. Bianquis, C. E. Bosworth, E. van Donzel, and W. P. Heinrichs. Leiden. http://dx.doi.org.ezp3.lib.umn.edu/10.1163/1573-3912_islam_SIM_6660.

Brown, W. 2008. *Regulating Aversion: Tolerance in the Age of Identity and Empire*, Princeton.

Bulliet, R. 1975. *The Camel and the Wheel*. Cambridge, MA.

Buturović, A. 2003. "The Shadow Play in Mamluk Egypt: The Genre and Its Cultural Implications." *Mamluk Studies Review* 7:149–176.

Cameron, David. 2011. "PM's Speech at Munich Security Conference." February 5, 2011. U.K. Government National Archives. http://webarchive.nationalarchives.gov.uk/20130109092234/http://number10.gov.uk/news/pms-speech-at-munich-security-conference/.

Corrao, F. 1996. *Il riso, il comico e la festa al Cairo nel XIII secolo: Il teatro delle ombre di Ibn Dāniyāl*. Rome.

al-Dhahabī, Muḥammad. 1998. *Tadhkirat al-Ḥuffāẓ*. Edited by Z. ʿUmayrāt. 5 vols. Beirut.

Eagleton, T. 1981. *Walter Benjamin: Towards a Revolutionary Criticism*. London.

Ehrenkreutz, A. 1972. *Saladin*. Albany.

Flattery, D. and M. Schwartz. 1989. *Haoma and Harmaline*. Berkeley.

Guo, L. 2012. *The Performing Arts in Medieval Islam: Shadow Play and Popular Poetry in Ibn Dāniyāl's Mamluk Cairo*. Leiden.

Hallaq, W. 1986. "On the Origins of the Controversy about the Existence of *Mujtahids* and the Gate of *Ijtihād*." *Studia Islamica* 63:129–141.

al-Hamadhānī, Badīʿ al-Zamān. 1923. *Maqāmāt*. Edited by M. ʿAbd al-Ḥamīd. Cairo.

Hermes, N. 2012. *The [European] Other in Medieval Arabic Literature and Culture*. New York.

Hill, D. 1963. *The Mobility of the Arab Armies in the Early Conquests*. Durham, UK.

Hillenbrand, C. 2000. *The Crusades: Islamic Perspectives*. New York.

Ibn al-Athīr, ʿAlī. 1964–67. *Al-Kāmil fī l-Taʾrīkh*. Edited by C. Tornberg. 12 vols. Beirut.

Ibn Dāniyāl, Muḥammad. 1992. *Three Shadow Plays by Muḥammad Ibn Dāniyāl*. Edited by P. Kahle. Cambridge, UK.

——. 2013. *Theatre from Medieval Cairo: The Ibn Dāniyāl Trilogy*. Edited and translated by S. Mahfouz and Marvin Carlson. New York.

Ibn Khaldūn, ʿAbd al-Raḥmān. 1858. *Muqaddimat Ibn Khaldûn: Prolégomènes d'Ebn-Khaldoun*. Edited by É. Quatremère. 3 vols. Paris.

Irwin, R. 1998. "Mamlūks." In *Encyclopedia of Arabic Literature* (vol. 2), edited by J. S. Meisami and P. Starkey, 501–503. London.

Jamāl al-Dīn, ʿUthmān. 1989. *Khayāl al-Ẓill li-bn Dāniyāl: Dirāsa fī Tamthīliyyat Ṭayf al-Khayāl fī ʿAṣr al-Mamālīk bi-Miṣr*. Khartoum.

Kahle, P. 1945. *Bonn University in Pre-Nazi and Nazi Times (1923–1939): Experiences of a German Professor*. London.

al-Khaṭīb al-Baghdādī. 1966. *Taʾrīkh Baghdād*. Edited by Muḥammad Saʿīd ʿUrfī, 14 vols. Beirut.

Khūrshīd, F. 1991. *Al-Judhūr al-Shaʿbiyya li-l-Masraḥ al-ʿArabī*. Cairo.

Kinoshita, S. and J. Jacobs. 2007. "Ports of Call: Boccaccio's Alatiel in the Medieval Mediterranean." *Journal of Medieval and Early Modern Studies* 37:163–195.

Kymlicka, W. 1995. *Multicultural Citizenship: A Liberal Theory of Minority Rights*. Oxford.

Mathews, K. 2012. "Mamluks and Crusaders: Architectural Appropriation and Cultural Encounter in Mamluk Monuments." In *Languages of Love and Hate: Conflict, Communication, and Identity in the Medieval Mediterranean*, edited by S. Lambert and H. Nicholson. Turnhout.

Molan, P. 1988. "*Charivari* in a Medieval Arabic Shadow Play." *Al-Masāq* 1:5–24.

Monroe, J. 1976. "The Hispano-Arabic World." In *Américo Castro and the Meaning of Spanish Civilization*, edited by J. Rubia Barcia and S. Margaretten, 69–90. Berkeley.

Monroe, J. and M. Pettigrew. 2003. "The Decline of Courtly Patronage and the Appearance of New Genres in Arabic Literature." *Journal of Arabic Literature* 34:138–177.

Moreh, S. 1987. "The Shadow Play ('*Khayāl al-Ẓill*') in the Light of Arabic Literature." *Journal of Arabic Literature* 18:46–61.

al-Mufaḍḍal al-Ḍabbī. 1921. *Dīwān al-Mufaḍḍaliyyāt*. Edited by C. Lyall. Oxford, UK.

al-Munajjid, Ṣ. n.d. *Al-Ẓurafāʾ wa-l-Shaḥḥādhūn fī Baghdād wa-Bārīs*. Cairo.

Nasrallah, N. 2007. *Annals of the Caliphs' Kitchens: Ibn Sayyār al-Warrāq's Tenth-Century Baghdadi Cookbook*. Leiden.

Pfeiffer, J. 2014. "Confessional Ambiguity vs. Confessional Polarization." In *Politics, Patronage and the Transmission of Knowledge in 13th-15th Century Tabriz*, edited by J. Pfeiffer. Leiden.
Phillips, A. 2009. *Multiculturalism without Culture*. Princeton.
Race, R. 2015. *Multiculturalism and Education*. London.
Robinson, C. 2003. *Islamic Historiography*. Cambridge, UK.
Ross, J. 2016. *Routledge Handbook of Graffiti and Street Art*. New York.
Rosser-Owen, M. 2012. "Mediterraneanism: How to Incorporate Islamic Art into an Emerging Field." *Journal of Art Historiography* 6:1–33.
Rowson, E. 1997. "Two Homoerotic Narratives from Mamluk Literature: al-Ṣafadī's *Lawʿat al-shākī* and Ibn Dāniyāl's *al-Mutayyam*." In *Homoeroticism in Classical Arabic Literature*, edited by J. Wright and E. Rowson, 158–191. New York.
———. 2008. "Homoerotic Liaisons among the Mamluk Elite in Late Medieval Egypt and Syria." In *Islamicate Sexualities: Translations across Temporal Geographies of Desire*, edited by K. Babayan and A. Najmabadi, 204–238. Cambridge, MA.
Soifer, M. 2009. "Beyond *convivencia*: Critical Reflections on the Historiography of Interfaith Relations in Christian Spain." *Journal of Medieval Iberian Studies* 1, no. 1:19–35.
Suleman, F. 2013. "Making Love not War: The Iconography of the Cockfight in Medieval Egypt." In *Eros and Sexuality in Islamic Art*, edited by F. Leoni and M. Natif, 19–42. Surrey.
al-Thaʿālibī, Abū Manṣūr ʿAbd al-Malik. 1983. *Yatīmat al-Dahr*. Edited by M. M. Qumayḥa, 5 vols. Beirut.
ʿUmar ibn Abī Rabīʿa. 1966. *Dīwān*. Beirut.
al-Zawzānī, Abū ʿAbd Allāh. 1860. *Sharḥ al-Muʿallaqāt al-Sabʿ*, n.p.

Heraclius in al-Andalus*

Maribel Fierro
Institute of the Languages and
Cultures of the Mediterranean, CCHS-CSIC

Legitimizing and Serving the Former Enemy

THE FAMOUS JEWISH WRITER Josephus (d. ca. 100 CE) fought against the Romans at the head of Jewish forces in Galilee until he surrendered in the year 67 to Vespasian and was taken captive. Convinced that God had chosen him "to announce the things that are to come," Josephus claimed that the Jewish prophecies about the Messianic king who shall come from Judea referred to the Roman victor and predicted that he would become emperor of Rome. Vespasian kept him as slave and interpreter. Shortly after, in the year 69, Vespasian did become emperor and freed Josephus, who became a Roman citizen. Josephus's collaboration with his former enemies included accompanying Vespasian's son, Titus, in the siege of Jerusalem, thus witnessing the destruction of the Second Temple. Among the works he wrote – and that were later translated into Latin – is the *Bellum Judaicum*, which dealt with the Jewish-Roman war in which he had taken part, while his *Antiquitates Iudaicae* started with the creation of humankind and continued with the remaining history of the Jews.[1]

Collaboration on the part of the vanquished with the former enemy, including exalting and magnifying him, as well as a commitment to memorialize past history in order to serve present needs, was a path taken by other scholars before and after Josephus, and examples of this can be found in diverse geographical and politico-religious contexts. The period of Almohad rule in al-Andalus triggered two cases.

Regarding the first case, the Almohads considered those Muslims who did not follow their belief, the Almohad *tawḥīd*, not only as enemies but also

*I wish to thank Patrick Henriet, Luis Molina, Linda Northrup, and Hélène Sirantoine for their valuable help, as well as all the colleagues who have generously answered my bibliographical queries (J. Albarrán, C. Ayala, F. Bauden, St. Borgehammar, S. Brentjes, G. Martin, Th. Martin, I. Pérez Martín, E. Ramírez Vaquero, R. Salicrú, M. Vallejo).

1. Hollander (2014, 68–138) offers a discussion about the historicity of Josephus's narrative of his captivity.

as infidels, so that those who "converted" were interested in firmly certifying their adhesion to Almohad belief.[2] Muḥammad b. ʿAbd al-Raḥmān b. Aḥmad b. ʿAbd al-Raḥmān b. Ṭāhir al-Qaysī (d. 574 AH/1178 CE) was one such "convert." He belonged to an important family in Murcia that had ruled the town during the Taifa period. He himself ruled for some months in the year 540 AH/1145 CE, at the time when several Andalusī towns were trying to get rid of Almoravid rule. In the year 542 AH/1147 CE, Murcia came under the control of Ibn Mardanīsh (d. 567 AH/1172 CE), a man of the sword who carved a reign for himself in the region during the period of the disintegration of the Almoravid Empire. Ibn Ṭāhir continued to live in the town under Ibn Mardanīsh's rule. When the Almohads conquered Murcia in 567 AH/1172 CE, after Ibn Mardanīsh's death, Ibn Ṭāhir eventually joined them and was named its governor, dying in Marrakech in the year 574 AH/1178 CE.[3] He felt the need to explain why he had joined the Almohads and he did so by writing a short tract in which he discussed the proofs that certified that Ibn Tūmart--the founder of the Almohad movement--had been the Mahdī, that is, the rightly guided one or Messiah.[4] In his work, Ibn Ṭāhir compares the previous political and religious situation in al-Andalus with the "perfect city" brought by the Almohads, that is, he applied to the Almohad polity the philosophical category of *al-madīna al-fāḍila* developed by al-Fārābī (d. 339 AH/950 CE).[5] Ibn Ṭāhir explains that before he had felt a "stranger" (*gharīb*) among his contemporaries, but when he was informed of what the Prince of the Believers ʿAbd al-Muʾmin – the first Almohad caliph – stood for, then he realized that the end had come for the cities of ignorance thanks to the Mahdī and his successors, the Muʾminid caliphs, who illuminated the lawful path in this life and also the path to the afterlife.[6]

The other case, in which Heraclius makes finally his appearance, refers to the times of the conquest of al-Andalus by the Almohads and to a region that long resisted them. The protagonist is Ibn Ḥubaysh (504–584 AH/1111–1188 CE), a scholar who was in the citadel (*qalʿa*) of Almería when the town was captured by the Christians in the year 542 AH/1147 CE profiting from Almoravid weakness caused by Almohad military activity and the anti-Almoravid rebellion of the Andalusī towns.[7] Ibn Ḥubaysh himself nar-

2. Fierro 2014b.

3. Puig Montada 2000, 181–186; Martín Castellanos and Forcada 2007, 461–463.

4. The short tract is referred to as *Maqāla ʿilmiyya yuqarrir fīhā ṣiḥḥat amr al-mahdī al-qāʾim bi-amr Allāh* or *al-Kāfiya fī barāhīn al-imām al-mahdī*. It has been preserved in Ibn al-Qaṭṭān (ca. 580 AH/1184CE-d. after 650 AH/1252 CE), *Naẓm*, 101–122.

5. Walzer 1985.

6. On the ghurabāʾ (sing. *gharīb*), see Fierro 2000, 230–260.

7. The Muslims recovered Almería ten years later. On this episode see Rodríguez Figueroa, 1999–2000, 10:11–55.

rated that, having been made prisoner by the Christians, he told Alfonso VII of León and II of Castile (r. 1126–1157 CE) – the conqueror of Almería – that he knew the King's genealogy back to Heraclius (*innī aḥfaẓu nasabaka minka ilā Hirqal*), the emperor of Constantinople.[8] Having pleased his captor with the information, the king granted freedom to Ibn Ḥubaysh, to his family and to those who were with him, and they were not required to pay any ransom (*anta wa-ahluka wa-man maʿaka ṭulaqāʾ bi-lā shayʾ*) (you and your family and those who are with you are freed without having to pay anything). A Christian source, however, says that those in the citadel had to pay 30.000 *maravedíes* (Almoravid dinars) to be freed.[9] Ibn Ḥubaysh's autobiographical report is found in a late source, al-Maqqarī's (d. 1041 AH/1632 CE) *Nafḥ al-ṭīb*,[10] a voluminous compilatory work written by a Maghrebi scholar for a Syrian Muslim audience interested in the history of al-Andalus and the achievements of its inhabitants once the former Muslim territory in the Iberian Peninsula had been lost to the Christians.[11]

Once he was back in Muslim territory, having settled in the area of Murcia, and after that area was conquered by the Almohads, Ibn Ḥubaysh wrote a voluminous *Kitāb al-maghāzī* on the orders of the second Muʾminid caliph, Abū Yaʿqūb Yūsuf (r. 558–580 AH/1163–1184 CE). With it, he served the ruler's policy of self-legitimization through jihad against the Christians, as the Muʾminid Caliphs were compared in their military campaigns with the first and rightly guided caliphs of Islam. Ibn Ḥubaysh thus enhanced the Almohad caliphs' religious credentials and helped to strengthen their legitimacy.

Ibn Ḥubaysh: Life and Scholarship

Although his impact in both his and later times cannot be compared to that achieved by Josephus, who like him was made prisoner and through his exal-

8. In the text, Ibn Ḥubaysh refers to Alfonso VII as *zaʿīm al-rūm al-sulayṭīn wa-huwa ibn bint al-Adhfūnsh* [leader of the Christians, the "little" sultan, who is the son of Alfonso's daughter], i.e. the grandson of Alfonso VI. Indeed, Alfonso VII was the son of Alfonso VI's daughter Urraca I of León, a succession that was striking for Muslims given their strict patrilinear political culture. Alfonso VII is also referred to as *ibn bint al-Adhfūnsh*, "the son of the daughter of Alfonso," by a contemporary of Ibn Ḥubaysh, the scholar al-Suhaylī, who also had something to say about Heraclius, as we shall see. See notes 67 and 70 below.

9. Found in the fragments of the *Annales Ianuenses* in Caffaro 1973, 28 and 29, cited in Rodríguez Figueroa 1999–2000, 15.

10. Al-Maqqarī (d. 1041 AH/1632 CE), *Nafḥ al-ṭīb min ghuṣn al-Andalus al-raṭīb*, 4:463. Al-Maqqarī does not indicate where he found this autobiographical report; perhaps he found it in Ibn Ḥubaysh's bibliographical repertory, where he recorded his transmissions (*barnāmaj*). The story was translated by Gayangos 1840, 2:312.

11. Fierro and Molina 2009, 273–283.

tation of the enemy managed to transform his plight into a gain, Ibn Ḥubaysh did become a prominent figure in al-Andalus during troubled times.[12]

Abū l-Qāsim ʿAbd al-Raḥmān b. Muḥammad b. ʿAbd Allāh b. Yūsuf b. Abī ʿĪsā b. Ḥubaysh al-Anṣārī al-Mariyyī al-Mursī was born in Almería in 504 AH/1111 CE and died in Murcia in 584 AH/1188 CE, thus witnessing the rule of both the Almoravids and the Almohads, and also that of Ibn Mardanīsh, the Andalusī man of the sword who ruled independently in the Levantine region (with his capital in Murcia) between the Almoravid and the Almohad periods. The *nisba* al-Anṣārī indicates that Ibn Ḥubaysh was most probably a convert of non-Muslim origins.[13] His ethnic background cannot be determined without further information, although given the demography of conversion the possibilities are high that he was the descendant of a local convert, i.e. a Christian or a Jew.

Ibn Ḥubaysh's grandfather had been born in the Levant of al-Andalus, in Jérica (today in the province of Castellón), but he moved to Almería. There Ibn Ḥubaysh spent the first years of his life studying Qurʾanic readings with local teachers, among them Abū l-Aṣbagh ʿĪsā b. Ḥazm b. ʿAbd Allāh Ibn al-Yasaʿ (d. after 525 AH/1130 CE).[14] When he was 26 years old, in 530 AH/1136 CE, Ibn Ḥubaysh travelled to Cordoba where he stayed for three years studying with important scholars such as Abū Bakr b. al-ʿArabī (d. 543 AH/1148 CE), Yūnus b. Muḥammad b. Mughīth (d. 532 AH/1138 CE) and the judge Muḥammad b. Aṣbagh Ibn al-Munāṣif (d. 536 AH/1141 CE).[15] Ibn

12. The Arabic sources recording Ibn Ḥubaysh's biography are al-Ḍabbī (d. 599 AH/1203 CE), *Kitāb bughyat al-multamis*, no. 988; Ibn al-Abbār (d. 658 AH/1260 CE), *al-Takmila*, no. 1617; Ibn al-Zubayr (d. 708 AH/1308 CE), *Ṣilat al-Ṣila*, 195–197 no. 338; al-Dhahabī (d. 748 AH/1348 CE), *Siyar aʿlām al-nubalāʾ*, 21:118–121, no. 59, and *Tadhkirāt al-ḥuffāẓ*, 4:98–100, no. 1101; al-Ṣafadī (d. 764 AH/1362 CE), *al-Wāfī bi-l-wafayāt*, 18:258, no. 311; Ibn al-Jazarī (d. 833 AH/1429 CE), *Ghāyat al-nihāya*, 1:378, no. 1611; al-Suyūṭī (d. 911 AH/1505 CE), *Bughyat al-wuʿāt*, 2:85, no. 1503; al-Timbuktī (d. 1036 AH/1627 CE), *Kitāb nayl al-ibtihāj* (in the margins of Ibn Farḥūn's *Kitāb al-dībaj al-mudhhab*), 162vi; al-Maqqarī, *Nafḥ al-ṭīb*, 2:605 and 4:463; Makhlūf (d. 1340 AH/1921 CE), *Shajarat al-nūr al-zakiyya* 1:157, no. 482; Cheneb 1907, 210, no. 182; Kaḥḥāla, 1957–1961, 5:182–183; al-Ziriklī, 1980, 3:327–328. Apart from the Arabic sources, studies in Western languages include: Pons Boigues, 1898, 253, no. 205; Dunlop 2012 and 1941, 359–362; Rodríguez Figueroa 2004, 472–476, no. 619.

13. Fierro 2006, 232–247.

14. Al-Ḍabbī, *Kitāb bughyat al-multamis*, no. 1142; Ibn al-Abbār, *al-Takmila*, no. 1925; al-Marrākushī (d. 702 AH/1302 CE), *al-Dhayl wa-l-Takmila*, 5/2, 493, no. 899; Ibn al-Zubayr, *Ṣilat al-Ṣila*, 51, no. 85; Ibn al-Jazarī, *Ghāyat al-nihāya*, I, 608, no. 2486. He is the father of al-Yasaʿ b. Ḥazm (d. 575 AH/1179 CE or 595 AH/1199 CE), who wrote a book for Saladin on the history of the Maghrib that was denounced as including false reports. Fierro 1995, 15–38. I will return to al-Yasaʿ b. Ḥazm at the end of this paper.

15. On these well-known Andalusī scholars see *Historia de los Autores y Transmisores de al-Andalus* at http://kohepocu.cchs.csic.es/.

Ḥubaysh also traveled to other unspecified Andalusī towns, studying with many other teachers either directly or through *ijāza* (a certificate allowing him the transmission of certain works that could be granted without the student having met the teacher), among them ʿAbd Allāh b. ʿAlī al-Rushāṭī (466–542 AH/1074–1147 CE) who died during the conquest of Almería by the Christians,[16] and ʿIyāḍ b. Mūsā al-Sabtī (d. 544 AH/1149 CE).[17] Qāḍī ʿIyāḍ was the author of a seminal work on the Prophet Muḥammad in which reference is made to the famous *ḥadīth Hirqal*, that tells of how Heraclius, while he was in Jerusalem, met Abū Sufyān b. Ḥarb b. Umayya, who had traveled there as trader. The emperor asked him about the Prophet of the Arabs, realizing through Abū Sufyān's answers that Muḥammad was a true prophet.[18] Also, reference is made to the seventh-century Byzantine emperor, Heraclius (*Hirqal ṣāḥib Rūma ʿālim al-naṣārā wa-raʾīsuhum*), as being among those who would have acknowledged the Prophet's mission and one of the recipients of the letters that the Prophet sent to different rulers.[19]

With Ibn Mughīth in Cordoba, Ibn Ḥubaysh learned al-Bukhārī's *Ṣaḥīḥ* - which includes the *ḥadīth Hirqal*[20] - and al-Nasāʾī's *Sunan*. Ibn Ḥubaysh also studied the *ḥadīth*s transmitted by the (alleged) Companion of the Prophet Jaʿfar b. Nasṭūr al-Rūmī, *al-Aḥādīth al-nusṭūriyya*, which he learned from Abū Umayya Ibrāhīm b. Munabbih (d. after 555 AH/1160 CE), a scholar also from Almería who had traveled to Mecca and there had studied these traditions, which were in fact a forgery.[21] Ibn Ḥubaysh was also known for his transmission of Ibn Abī Khaythama's *Taʾrīkh*, of which a partial edition has recently appeared.[22]

In 533 AH/1138 CE, Ibn Ḥubaysh returned to Almería, where he devoted himself to teaching, excelling because of his knowledge of *ḥadīth* and gaining many pupils. He was there when the town was conquered by the allied Christian troops of Castile, León, Navarra, Catalonia, Genoa, and Pisa. After having been granted pardon, his family and those who were with him did not have to pay ransom - or so he said - in reward for the imperial genealogy going back to Heraclius that he produced for Alfonso VII of León. Ibn Ḥubaysh left Almería, first settling in Murcia under Ibn Mardanīsh, and then

16. Lirola Delgado and Navarro i Ortiz 2012, 215–221, no. 1671.

17. Serrano Ruano, 2009, 404–434, no. 1479.

18. The *ḥadīth Hirqal* is found in one of the canonical compilations of *ḥadīth*, al-Bukhārī's *Ṣaḥīḥ*, in the *Kitāb badʾ al-waḥy*. An English translation is available at: http://sunnah.com/bukhari/1/7 (consulted on 24/08/2016). See Pouzet 1992, 59–65.

19. Qāḍī ʿIyāḍ 1984, 190, 460. On the relevance of the letters, see below.

20. See note 18 above.

21. I will deal in another study with this forgery that circulated in al-Andalus during the sixth/twelfth century.

22. Ibn Abī Khaythama (185–279 AH/801–892 CE), *Akhbār al-makkiyyīn*.

shortly afterwards in Alcira, where he lived for twelve years. This transfer from Christian Almería to Muslim Murcia seems to be related to the fact that Ibn Mardanīsh is said to have administered Almería in the name of Alfonso VII from the time of its conquest in 542 AH/1147 CE until it was regained by the Almohads ten years later. Ibn Ḥubaysh was thus moving within an area controlled by the same Muslim ruler, Ibn Mardanīsh, who acted as vassal of the King of León and Castile in his fight against the Almohads in order to preserve the independence of his kingdom.[23]

In Alcira, Ibn Ḥubaysh was put in charge of the direction of prayer and the Friday sermon and also given some judicial duties. In 556 AH/1161 CE he settled in Murcia, where he continued performing as Friday preacher with some of his sermons being recorded in writing. In 575 AH/1179 CE, when Murcia had passed into the hands of the Almohads after Ibn Mardanīsh's death and after his sons acknowledged the Almohad *tawḥīd*, Ibn Ḥubaysh was named judge, a position he occupied until he died. He wrote his *Dhikr al-ghazawāt al-ḍāmina al-kāfila wa-l-futūḥ al-jāmiʿa al-ḥāfila al-kāʾina fī ayyām al-khulafāʾ al-ūlā al-thalātha* for the Almohads. The Almohad caliph Abū Yaʿqūb Yūsuf (r. 558–580 AH/1163–1184 CE) commissioned its composition with the intention of drawing parallels between the three first caliphs and the Almohad caliphs.[24] Ibn Ḥubaysh's work contains many references to Heraclius.[25]

In connection with the figure of the Byzantine Emperor, Ibn Ḥubaysh may have heard of the famous prediction made by the Sevillan scholar and *bāṭinī* (esoteric) thinker Ibn Barrajān (d. 536 AH/1141 CE) regarding the date for the Muslim conquest of Jerusalem from the Crusaders. The prediction was linked to Ibn Barrajān's interpretation of the famous Qurʾanic verses 30:2–5.[26] Although Heraclius is not mentioned by name, these Qurʾanic verses refer to the war between Byzantines and Persians at the time when the Byzantine Emperor Heraclius managed to defeat his enemy, the Sassanian monarch, who had taken Jerusalem:

> The Greeks [*rūm*] have been vanquished in the nearer part of the land; and, after their vanquishing, they shall be the victors in a few years.

23. Bosch-Vilá 2012. See also Rodríguez Figueroa 1999–2000, 20, 26, discussing Jesús Zanón's findings on a trend among many Andalusī scholars of the times to avoid the lands conquered by the Almohads while showing preference for the Levantine region where there was a longer resistance to the Almohads.

24. On the relation between the writing of this type of works and the legitimization needs of the Almohads see Urvoy 1993, 45 and 1990, 106; Albarrán 2016.

25. There are two editions: the edition of Ghunaym, 1983–1987, and the edition of Zakkār, 1992. The one consulted for this article is the Ghunaym edition and the references to Heraclius are found in vol. 2:33–37, 41, 66, 103–105; vol. 3:13, 17, 18, 23, 24, 26, 28, 41, 79, 80, 84–86, 89–95, 184, 185, 187, 195, 196, 198, 212–215; vol. 4:31, 66, 91.

26. See the detailed study in Bellver 2014, 252–286.

> To God belongs the Command before and after and, on that day, the believers shall rejoice in God's help; God helps whomsoever He will; and He is the All-mighty, the All-compassionate.[27]

Ibn Barrajān read those verses in such a way that they could be interpreted as referring not to a future victory of the *rūm* (a term that involves both the Byzantines in particular and the Christians in general),[28] but to their future defeat at the hands of the Muslims. That future Muslim victory could be applied – and it was – to Saladin's conquest of Jerusalem in 583 AH/1187 CE, but more generally it conveyed the hope that Christian victories and conquests will eventually be stopped, thus giving comfort to those who, like the Muslims of the Iberian Peninsula, felt increasingly threatened by Christian military power.[29]

Heraclius in the Muslim *imaginaire*

The figure of Heraclius as represented in the Arabic sources was also "comforting" for the Muslims. Heraclius (ca. 575–641 CE) is the only Roman Emperor to whom sustained attention is paid in Islamic literature, because of the Qurʾanic verses quoted above, and mainly because he is mentioned in *ḥadīth* and the biography of the Prophet (*sīra*) as having shown interest in the Muslims, their religion, and Muḥammad (ca. 570–632 CE), of whom Heraclius was a contemporary. As noted, Heraclius would have met the Prophet's relative Abū Sufyān who traveled to Jerusalem because of trade and who answered the emperor's questions regarding the new religion of the Arabs, answers that convinced Heraclius that a true prophet had appeared.[30] Heraclius also had contact with Muḥammad by way of the Prophet's Companion Diḥya al-Kalbī, who brought him a letter in which Muḥammad invited the Byzantine Emperor to convert to Islam.[31] The Prophet Muḥammad is in fact alleged to have written letters to the most important rulers of his times, including the Persian king Kisra Parwiz (r. 591–628 CE), the Negus of Abyssinia,[32]

27. Tr. A. J. Arberry.

28. On the use of the term *rūm* to refer to the Christians in general, see Lapiedra 1997.

29. Christians figure prominently in Muslim eschatological and apocalyptic literature, with a special role given to Constantinople and its conquest. For a work written in al-Andalus containing this kind of materials, see Abū ʿAmr al-Dānī (d. 444 AH/1053 CE), *al-Sunan al-wārida fī l-fitan*, especially 3:1113–1130 (with mention of Constantinople as *madīnat Hirqal* in numbers 612 and 619).

30. On this meeting see El Cheikh 1999; Conrad 2002; note 18 above and note 35 below.

31. Bashear (1997, 64–91) offers a critical analysis of the traditions reporting this mission and its different variants and interpretations.

32. Hamidullah 1969; 1985; 1965, 57–69. Hamidullah accepts the historicity of these letters, while most modern scholars do not.

and also the Byzantine emperor.[33] In those letters he urged them to convert to Islam, a precedent to the precept listed in some Islamic legal texts that during the war against the infidels (*jihad*), Muslims should invite their enemies to convert and if they refuse, then it is legitimate to fight them.[34] Here is the translation of one of the versions of such a letter to Heraclius:

> In the name of God, the Merciful, the Compassionate. From Muhammad the servant of God and his messenger to Heraclius the great leader of the Rūm. Peace on whoever follows the right path. I invite you to Islam. Become Muslim and you shall be safe, become a Muslim and God shall bestow upon you a double recompense. If you turn away, the sins of the *arīsiyyīn* will fall upon you. O People of the Book, come towards an utterance which is the same for both of us: that we worship only God and do not associate anything with him, and no one among us takes as lords (*arbāb*) any others outside of God. If they turn away you will say: witness that we are Muslims.[35]

While the Persian king would have torn the letter he received to pieces – and thus lost his empire – Heraclius kept his letter and even tried to convince his people to convert to Islam, and the Byzantine Empire continued to exist for many centuries.[36] Muslim historians also claim that Heraclius answered Muḥammad in the following way:

> To Aḥmad, the Messenger of God, announced by Jesus. From Caesar, king of the Rūm. I have received your letter with your ambassador and I testify that you are the messenger of God found in our New Testament. Jesus, son of Mary, announced you. I did ask the Rūm to believe in you but they refused. Had they obeyed, it would have been better for them. I wish I were with you to serve you and wash your feet.[37]

According to a number of sources, having converted to Islam, Heraclius also tried to convert the ruling class of the Empire, but they resisted

33. Hamidullah 1955, 97–110.

34. As recorded for example in al-Bukhārī's *Ṣaḥīḥ, kitāb al-jihād*, in the chapter on "the invitation to Islam before combat (*al-daʿwa qabla l-qitāl*)." For the possible influence of this precept in a similar practice recorded in Iberia, see Lemistre 1970.

35. El Cheikh 1999, 11. This is the translation of one of the many versions that exist with only small variations; the term *arīsiyyīn* has been interpreted in different ways; the most convincing explanation is that given by Conrad 2002, 129–130. The reference to a "common word," a phrase taken from the Qurʾān, was used in 2007 in a letter directed by Muslim religious leaders to the Christians, summoning them to an interfaith dialogue: http://www.acommonword.com/the-acw-document/

36. Bowen Savant 2013, 228–235.

37. El Cheikh 1999, 12.

so strongly that he reversed his course and claimed that he was just testing their faith in Christianity.[38]

This Muslim representation of Heraclius explains why he was seen in positive terms in the Islamic historical and religious tradition, and why a historian like Ibn Kathīr (d. 774 AH/1373 CE) said of him: "Heraclius was one of the wisest men and among the most resolute, shrewd, deep and opinionated of kings. He ruled the Romans with great leadership and splendor."[39] In the Arabic sources, Heraclius is portrayed as pious (he walked barefoot from Ḥimṣ to Jerusalem when he brought back the Holy Cross that had been stolen by the Persians),[40] concerned for his subjects, an upright ruler inclined to compassion and justice, an admirer of the virtues of the early Muslims, and a censor of the bad ways of his own people; in sum, he has "all the attributes of an ideal ruler. His almost perfect character and flawless use of authority, his piety and sense of justice, his wisdom, intelligence, magnanimity and courage all proclaim him as an outstanding ruler whose opinions and pronouncements approach infallibility."[41]

The positive image of Heraclius in the Muslim sources responds fundamentally to the need for narratives in which non-Muslims upheld the Islamic *kerygma* or message. In other words, the Heraclius narratives aimed at legitimizing Muḥammad's status as a prophet also provided legitimacy for the new state, and to be effective, the fact that Heraclius was a Christian was decisive. Thus, when discussing the proofs of Muḥammad's prophethood in his *Muqaddima*, the Maghrebi historian Ibn Khaldūn (d. 809 AH/1406 CE) quotes the letter sent by the Prophet to Heraclius and the interview between him and Abū Sufyān.[42] If a powerful Christian ruler such as Heraclius acknowledged the truth of Muḥammad's prophethood, this validates conversion to Islam: it was the right thing to do. Heraclius can be seen as the paramount example within the Islamic tradition of those who legitimize

38. On these reactions see Bashear 1997, 79, 83, 86. Among the sources quoted by Bashear on Heraclius, there are two Andalusī works: Ibn ʿAbd al-Barr (d. 463 AH/1071 CE), *Kitāb al-istīʿāb fī asmāʾ al-ṣaḥāba*, and al-Suhaylī (d. 581 AH/1185 CE), *Kitāb al-rawḍ al-unuf.* I will return to al-Suhaylī's work below.

39. El Cheikh 1999, 7, quoting volume 6 p. 417 of Ibn Kathīr's *Tafsīr*, published in Cairo in 1347. See Conrad (2002, 130–131), who alerts readers to the varied and complex nature of the early materials regarding Heraclius that do not allow one to deduce a single view on him, and who explores (2002, 155) the reasons for the positive Muslim portrayal of Heraclius.

40. This humility on the part of Heraclius was taken from Christian sources. Maranci 2009.

41. El Cheikh 1999, 9.

42. Ibn Khaldūn, *Muqaddima*, index. The Fatimid caliph al-Muʿizz also resorted to the example of Heraclius to prove his own legitimacy. El Cheikh 1999, 14–15.

their enemy, and thus he comes close to the figures of Josephus, Ibn Ṭāhir, and Ibn Ḥubaysh.

When telling Alfonso VII of León that he could give the king a genealogy back to Heraclius, Ibn Ḥubaysh did not have in mind the Heraclius as he was represented among the Western Christians, a representation to be dealt with in the next section. What he had in mind was the Heraclius who – according to Islamic tradition – had been the recipient of a letter sent by the Prophet Muḥammad and who had been receptive to it to the extent that he even acknowledged the truth of Islam, although he had to recant his conversion because of the opposition of those who surrounded him. Ibn Ḥubaysh's story is directed to a Muslim audience with several possible meanings – not necessarily mutually exclusive, as we shall see.

It mostly served to prove that Ibn Ḥubaysh had been freed from his enslavement in Almería without contributing to the payment of the huge sum of thirty thousand *maravedíes* that the Muslims in the citadel gave to the Christians to obtain their freedom, a freedom that was probably restricted to the notables while not affecting the common people.[43] The genealogy Ibn Ḥubaysh said he had provided does not seem to have been important enough to be preserved. What this silence suggests is that the genealogy offered by Ibn Ḥubaysh was a forgery told to the Christian to gain something. If so, the story would also suggest that the Christians were ignorant and also vain, and that when their vanity was stirred by the acumen of their Muslim adversaries, their behavior could be turned to the Muslims' advantage. And it also conveyed the message that the Christian king who had conquered Almería, being the descendant of a just and pious emperor, could act towards the subject Muslim population according to the virtues his grandfather had, and thus Ibn Ḥubaysh contributed to legitimize Ibn Mardanīsh's policies of collaboration with the Christians. In other words, Ibn Ḥubaysh was conveying a message more to his co-religionists than to the conqueror of Almería, a message along these lines: "Those in command are now not Muslims, but their king is a descendant of Heraclius and therefore we may expect that he will be a just ruler and treat us well. We should accommodate ourselves to the new circumstances, that is, to be ruled by a Christian king and even to collaborate with him." Thus, Ibn Ḥubaysh may have conceived of the story once he left Almería and settled in Ibn Mardanīsh's territories: the story proved how clever he was, how he had not profited as others had done from their elevated economic status to save themselves, abandoning those without

43. This meant that those with means were freed while many of those who were poor remained enslaved: Rodríguez Figueroa 1999–2000, 22.

means to do the same, and how collaboration with the Christian conqueror of Almería was acceptable.

Heraclius in the Christian *imaginaire*

But was Ibn Ḥubaysh aware that a Byzantine genealogy could be relevant for Alfonso VII? If so, how was it relevant? Could Ibn Ḥubaysh have said what he claimed to have said having in mind a Christian audience? Is there any evidence that Alfonso VII attempted to connect himself with the Byzantine Emperors?

Alfonso VII is one among the Iberian Christian kings who claimed the title of emperor. Before him, Alfonso I el Batallador, King of Aragón (r. 1104–1134 CE) had used the imperial title between the years 1109–1127 CE. In addition, King Alfonso VI (r. as king of León between 1065–1072 CE and 1072–1109 CE and of Castile between 1072–1109 CE) used the title from 1077 CE on, and his daughter and successor Queen Urraca (r. 1109–1126 CE) used it for a brief period between 1109 and 1114 CE.[44] For his part, Alfonso VII was crowned *Imperator totius Hispaniae* on May 26th, 1135 CE, in the Cathedral of León. Alfonso VII's decision to claim the imperial title has been given different explanations.[45] Church representatives, French noblemen and also the Muslim king Sayf al-Dawla (Zafadola), a descendant of the Hudids – the former Taifa kings of Zaragoza – who was a close ally and collaborator of Alfonso VII as was Ibn Mardanīsh, the Muslim ruler of Murcia, were present at his coronation. In the year 541 AH/1146 CE, when the Almohad caliph ʿAbd al-Muʾmin disembarked in Algeciras, Alfonso VII made a pact with the Almoravid emir Ibn Ghāniya in order to stop the Almohad advance. Together with Ramón Berenguer IV, García Ramírez of Navarra, the Genoese fleet and French crusaders, Almería was conquered in October 542/1147. Ten years later, the Almohads took control of the town. Alfonso VII failed in reconquering it, dying while returning to León. He was succeeded by his son Fernando in León and by his other son, Sancho III, in Castile.

Alfonso García-Gallo proposed that the ceremonial protocol followed in the coronation of Alfonso VII in 1135 CE had Byzantine precedents (among other influences),[46] while it has also been proposed that some variants in his imperial titles may have a Byzantine origin and that his representation in seals may reveal Byzantine influences.[47] Facing the opposition of the King of

44. For a general overview see Sirantoine 2013.

45. Reilly 1998; Recuero Astray 2003. See also Pérez González 1997. Sirantoine discusses these and other previous views in her study.

46. García Gallo 1945, 199–228.

47. On these possibilities see Sirantoine 2013, 314–315 (ceremonial), 321–322 (titles), 327

Aragón–whose predecessor, Alfonso I el Batallador, also had imperial claims –and having to fight the Muslims now led by a man, the Almohad caliph, who had proclaimed himself to be Prince of the Believers and who claimed a genealogical link with the Prophet Muḥammad,[48] did Alfonso VII look for a genealogical link with the Byzantine emperors? There does not seem to be any evidence in support of this.[49] Could Alfonso VII have been pleased to be given one by a Muslim?

To be connected to Heraclius was certainly not something a Christian ruler would be displeased with, given how the Byzantine emperor was generally represented in the Christian sources.[50] Heraclius (ca. 575-February 11, 641 CE) was Emperor of Constantinople from 610 to 641 CE. His reign was marked by the war against the Sassanians (602–628 CE) whose troops reached the Bosphorus, but were unsuccessful in conquering Constantinople. Heraclius obliged the Persians to leave Asia Minor, defeating them at the battle of Nineveh in 627 CE. The Persian king Khosrau II was overthrown and executed by his son Kavadh II, who signed a peace treaty with the Byzantine emperor, returning to him the Cross on which Christ had died and which the Persians had taken after conquering Jerusalem in 614 CE. Soon afterward the Sassanian Empire fell to the Muslims, who also conquered Syria, followed by Mesopotamia, Armenia, and Egypt. Heraclius died in 641 CE after having witnessed the loss of such territories. Heraclius adopted the ancient Persian title of *King of kings* after his victory over Persia, and later he also adopted that of *basileus*, the Greek word for "sovereign," a title that remained in use by the Byzantine emperors. Heraclius was responsible for introducing Greek as the official language of the empire, while he unsuccessfully tried to reunite the different religious groups that divided the Church.[51]

As for Heraclius's fame in the Western Church, he was remembered favorably for having retaken Jerusalem from the Persians and for his recovery of the Cross. After touring the empire with the Holy Cross, Heraclius returned

---

(seal). On the use of the title *basileus* in previous times by the king of León Ramiro III (year 974), see Sirantoine 2013, 102 and 118–119.

48. Fierro 2003, 77–108.

49. Such kinship is only attested with Alfonso X the Wise (r. 1252–1284 CE): his father Fernando III (r. 1217–1252 CE) married Beatriz of Swabia who descended from two emperors, the emperor of the Holy Roman Empire, Federico I, and the emperor of Constantinople, Isaac Commeno. See Estepa 1989, 205–216; Rodríguez López 1997, 613–630.

50. There were, however, some divergent views on Heraclius among the Christians, especially in the early period. Thus, in the chronicle by Fredegar (written ca. 660), Heraclius is accused of incest and heresy. There is no monographic study as to how Heraclius was portrayed in early medieval Iberian Latin sources, such as the so-called Arabic-Byzantine chronicle of 741 and the Mozarabic chronicle of 754 or *Continuatio Hispana a. 754*.

51. For detailed studied of his reign, see Kaegi 2003; Reinink and Stolte 2002.

it to Jerusalem on March 21, 629 or 630 CE.[52] Heraclius's achievement was something to be imitated: for Christians of the Western Medieval Europe, Heraclius became the "first crusader." The chronicler Fulcher of Chartres (ca. 1059–1127 CE) related that King Baldwin II (ca. 1058–1131 CE), while he was in Antioch, sent the True Cross to Jerusalem: the men of the procession conducting the relic "entered the Holy City rejoicing, on the day when they celebrated the festival of its exaltation, as the Emperor Heraclius had done when he brought it back [the Cross] from Persia."[53] Thus,

> For medieval writers he was a paladin, one of the heroes of Christianity along with Roland, Charlemagne, Godfrey of Bouillon and Richard Coeur de Lion. [...] None of the paladins of chivalry contributed quite so much to the movement as Heraclius: he reconquered the Holy Land and returned the True Cross of Jesus to Jerusalem – thereby adding the Feast of the Holy Cross to the Christian calendar on 14 September.
>
> Furthermore, Heraclius personified at that time the "eschatological emperor" who won the battle against the *Antichrist* Chosroes. This myth also entertains a parallel symbolism in the messianic figure of the "Last World Emperor" who battles the *Antichrist* and puts the True Cross back in its proper place.[54]

The iconography of Heraclius first appeared in western Christendom in the sanctuary at Mount Saint-Michel (ca. 1060 CE) and became popular especially in France, the Italian Peninsula, and the Holy Roman Empire. The story of the recovery of the Cross was included in Jacobus de Voragine's *Legenda Aurea*, a famous compendium of Christian hagiography compiled around the year 1260 CE. It found its way into the frescoes painted by Piero della Francesca (d. 1492 CE) in the Basilica of San Francesco in Arezzo, in which the battle between Heraclius and Khusraw has a place alongside Constantine's dream and Saint Helen's finding of the Cross in Jerusalem. The iconography was mainly based on the sermon known as *Reversio Sanctae Crucis* (BHL 4178), which was written by an anonymous author from the Italian Peninsula between the end of the seventh century and the year 750 CE, and

52. For Zuckerman (2013, 197–218), the wood contained in the reliquary brought to Jerusalem in 629 was not the real Holy Cross but a fake. Heraclius was aware of it, but he used it for political purposes.

53. Fulcher of Chartres 1973, 230. See also Kühnel 2004, 64–75.

54. Queiroz de Souza 2015, 28; Alexander 1978, 1–15; Regan 2003; Baert 2008, 3–20. See also Frolow 1953, 88–105 and Baert 2004. Note that the references to Heraclius and the Cross in Iberian iconography are few and late, the earliest being to the *Tapiz de la Creación* in the Cathedral of Girona, and this is debated (see note 58 below). For later figurative representations see Vallejo Girvés 2010, 2–9.

based on some Greek or Eastern sources from the 630s. In it, "Heraclius was portrayed as a valiant emperor who by courage, faith and, above all, humility was able to retrieve the Cross of Christ from the haughty Persian king Chosroes and restore it to its rightful place in Jerusalem."[55] More than 200 copies of the *Reversio Sanctae Crucis* exist.[56] There is a hypothesis that the partially lost lower portion of the famous *Tapiz de la Creación* (ca. 1100 CE) of the Girona Cathedral (Catalonia) presented an image of Heraclius, but this is still the subject of debate among specialists.[57] In any case, the historical Heraclius was, naturally, not unknown in Hispania,[58] but there seems to have been no Iberian development of his figure as "first crusader," an image that came from outside the Peninsula. In any case, by the time of the conquest of Almería in 1147 CE, Heraclius's religious fame in Western Christendom was well established, especially in France. However, Christian sources do not offer any evidence that Alfonso VII attempted to use to his favor Heraclius's positive image, and in fact the only suggestion that he may have done so comes from a Muslim source.

Was Ibn Ḥubaysh aware that Alfonso VII had proclaimed himself emperor? The fact that Sayf al-Dawla Ibn Hūd had been present at the coronation must have helped spread the news among the Muslims.[59] Did this knowledge trigger in Ibn Ḥubaysh the connection with Byzantium? Did Ibn Ḥubaysh think that as a Christian emperor Alfonso VII would be flattered to be connected with Heraclius? As mentioned above, in my opinion there is no way to know if Ibn Ḥubaysh ever said to Alfonso VII what he claimed to have said. But even if he had, what he would have had in mind was the Heraclius of the Muslim sources, the Christian emperor who had acknowledged Muḥammad's prophethood and almost converted to Islam. In those sources, Heraclius is remembered – as among the Christians – as the restorer of the Holy Cross to Jerusalem,[60] but Ibn Ḥubaysh – of course – would never have hailed him as "the first crusader."

55. Borgehammar 2009, 145. For more on the links between Christian and Muslim sources regarding Heraclius, see Conrad 2002, 144–152.

56. Borgehammar 2009 does not mention any Iberian copy, as he did not have access to catalogues including information on the Iberian Peninsula. I have been unable to find information on the circulation of this work in the Iberian Peninsula.

57. Baert 1999, 115–127. See also Castiñeiras 2011.

58. Mention of Heraclius is made by Isidore of Seville and in the *Continuatio Hispana a. 754*. See Vallejo Girvés 2006, 43–72; 1999, 489–499. See more generally Vallejo Girvés 2012.

59. Alfonso VII was referred to in the Arabic sources by the nickname of *al-sulayṭīn*, "the little sultan." Was the nickname a way of ridiculing the imperial claims of the King of Castile and León? In Ibn al-Kardabus's chronicle Alfonso VII is referred to as "imbiratur." Sirantoine 2013, 364–365.

60. El Cheikh 1999, 7.

To conclude, given the scarce evidence for any "Byzantine" agenda on the part of Alfonso VII, Ibn Ḥubaysh's story should be seen as a narrative told by a Muslim to a Muslim audience.

The Letter of the Prophet to Heraclius in the Iberian Peninsula

Ibn Ḥubaysh's story was not the only one circulating among Muslims in al-Andalus that had Heraclius as protagonist. After the fall of the Almohads, the Maghrebi historian Ibn Abī Zarᶜ (d. 726 AH/1326 CE) reported in his *Rawḍ al-qirṭās* that the letter that the Prophet had sent to Heraclius was in fact in the Iberian Peninsula in the possession of the King of Navarra.[61] According to this narrative – which is worth recording in full – the fourth Almohad caliph al-Nāṣir (r. 595–610 AH/1199–1213 CE) traveled with a powerful army from Marrakech to Seville, where he arrived in June 607 AH/1211 CE, this being the campaign that led to his defeat at Las Navas de Tolosa. The Christian kings became terrified when they heard of the caliph's arrival, abandoning the territories they had conquered from the Muslims and retreating to their fortresses. Most of them wrote to the Prince of the Believers (the caliph al-Nāṣir) asking for pardon. One of them, the King of Pamplona[62] – that is, Sancho VII el Fuerte of Navarra (r. 1194–1234 CE) – even decided to travel to meet the caliph in person, to humble himself and ask for peace and pardon. When he heard that the caliph had reached Seville, he looked for a way to save himself and his country, sending him an ambassador and asking for an interview. This was granted and the caliph wrote to all the towns of al-Andalus through which the King of Navarra had to pass telling them to host him for three days. Then, at the moment of his departure from each of those towns, the king had to leave behind one thousand of his horsemen. This was done: whenever the Christian king entered a Muslim town, he was received by the military commander with his soldiers and the notables, treated splendidly and when he left one thousand of his horsemen stayed behind. By the time the king reached Carmona, he had only one thousand horsemen left. When the time came to leave Carmona, he was told that those one thousand horsemen had also to stay behind. When he complained that then he would be left without any soldiers to escort him, he was told that he was now under the protection of the Prince of the Believers. The Christian king left Carmona with his relatives, his wife, his servants and the presents he had brought for al-Nāṣir. Among those presents there was the

61. Ibn Abī Zarᶜ, *Rawḍ al-qirṭās*, 235–6; Spanish translation by Huici Miranda 1964, 2:457–460. On the author see Manzano Rodríguez 2012, 761–766, no. 252.

62. In the text the term Bayūna (Bayona) appears, but it is considered a defective reading for Banbalūna (Pamplona) in Navarra.

letter that the Prophet had sent to Heraclius, the king of the Greeks (*malik al-rūm*). The reason the king of Navarra included such a valuable letter among the presents was to obtain intercession through it and to show that in the same way that he had inherited his throne from his ancestors (*kābiran ʿan kābir*), he also had inherited from them that letter which, covered by a green cloth, was preserved in a golden box (*ṣundūq*) full of musk as a sign of respect and exaltation for its true nature (*li-ḥaqqihi*). Al-Nāṣir ordered soldiers to line the route from the Gate of Carmona to that of Seville and to have the horsemen and the foot soldiers displayed in two lines, to the left and to the right, outfitted with the most wonderful clothes and weapons. The king of Navarra thus reached Seville. The caliph had his red tent erected outside the town, on the road to Carmona, and three seats put in it. Al-Nāṣir asked who among his military commanders knew the language of the Christian king, and a man called Abū l-Juyūsh ʿAsākir was identified for this task. The caliph called him in and told him:

> This infidel (*al-kāfir*) has come to visit me and I need to honor him. But if I rise when he enters the tent taking into account that I have given him my protection (*dhimma*), I will act against the *sunna* (tradition of the Prophet) by standing for a man who is an infidel. And if I stay seated, I will not be acting according to what he deserves because he is a great king whom I am hosting. Thus, you will sit in the seat which is in the middle of the royal tent (*al-qubba*) and when the infidel (*al-ʿilj*) enters into the tent I will enter from the entrance situated in front of his. Then, you will rise and taking me by the hand you will seat me on your right and you will do the same with him, seating him on your left. After that you will act as an interpreter.[63]

Abū l-Juyūsh did just this. Once they were seated, he introduced the caliph to the king of Navarra saying: "He is the Prince of the Believers." The king then greeted the caliph and started talking for a while, after which the caliph rode with the king behind him, followed by the Almohads and the army. People came out to witness the event and celebrations took place. Having entered Seville, the caliph hosted the king inside the town, gave him many presents, and a treaty (*ṣulḥ*) was signed negotiating conditions that remained in effect after Sancho and al-Nāṣir's deaths. Then the king returned to his kingdom.

The narrative, as many others found in the *Rawḍ al-qirṭās*, is a creative distortion of a real historical event. Sancho VII el Fuerte did travel to Almohad territory, where he seems to have stayed for a certain period of time,

63. Ibn Abī Zarʿ, *Rawḍ al-qirṭās*, 235–236.

but that had happened some twelve years before, when he was in need of aid against the king of Castile, Alfonso VIII (r. 1158–1214 CE), who had invaded Álava and besieged Vitoria in 1199 CE. Sancho VII was then seeking Almohad help against the king of Castile, hoping that they would attack his enemy and thus Castilian military pressure on his kingdom would diminish. He did not succeed, and after a considerable territorial loss, in 1207 CE Sancho VII signed a peace treaty for five years with Castile.[64] This event seems to have been conflated with another in which al-Nāṣir was in fact one of the protagonists and the other was not the king of Navarra, but the king of León Alfonso IX (r. 1188–1230 CE) whose visit to the Almohad caliph gave rise to discussions in the Almohad court about the adequate protocol to follow.[65] Problems of protocol had also arisen many centuries before when the caliph Abū Bakr (r. 11–13 AH/632–634 CE) sent another letter to Heraclius inviting him to convert.[66]

The trustworthiness of Ibn Abī Zarᶜ as a historian is not considered to be high. But even if the narrative summarized above is full of legendary material and mistakes, Ibn Abī Zarᶜ did not invent the presence of the letter to Heraclius in the Iberian Peninsula. Before him, a contemporary of Ibn Ḥubaysh and a much respected specialist in the study of the Prophet's biography and traditions, the Andalusī al-Suhaylī (d. 581 AH/1185 CE),[67] in his *Kitāb al-rawḍ al-unuf wa-l-mashraᶜ al-riwā fī tafsīr mā shtamala ᶜalayhi ḥadīth Sīrat rasūl Allāh li-bn Hishām wa-ḥtawà*[68] - completed in *jumādā* I 569 AH/December 1173 CE and written for the Almohad caliph Abū Yaᶜqūb Yūsuf - had already claimed that the letter had found its way to the Christian king Alfonso VI of León and Castile (ca. 1037–1109 CE). This information appears in the section in which al-Suhaylī deals with the expedition of Tabūk, when the Prophet decided to send his letter to Heraclius with Diḥya b. Khalīfa

64. On these events see Lino Munárriz y Velasco 1912, 5–39; Huici Miranda 1956, 220–223; Barbour 1967, 9–21; Fortún 1986, 165–174; Miranda García 2012, 325–349. There is another narrative regarding the King of Navarra's stay in Almohad territory, recorded by the English historian Roger of Hoveden (fl. 1174–1201), according to which the daughter of the Almohad caliph fell in love with Sancho VII – whose high stature and corpulence had made him famous – without having seen him and asked his father to facilitate her marriage to him, stating that she was willing to convert to Christianity in order to make the marriage possible. On how this story – one among others dealing with interfaith love affairs in Iberia – came into being see Barton 2015, 130–133, who suggests that it was "part of a concerted Navarrese diplomatic effort to "spin" King Sancho's otherwise inglorious sojourn in Muslim territory in the very best possible light."

65. Ghouirgate 2015. On other Christians visiting the Almohad caliphs see Shoval 2016.

66. El Cheikh 1999, 18–19.

67. Arias Torres 2012, 378–382, no. 1740.

68. The work is a commentary of the most famous biography of the Prophet, that of Ibn Isḥāq (d. 151/758) completed by Ibn Hishām (d. 213 AH/829 CE).

al-Kalbī, and Heraclius first announced his conversion to Islam and then recanted it, fearing for his life when he saw the opposition of his army and his entourage. Heraclius answered the Prophet with another letter, in which he confessed to be a Muslim although he could not reveal his conversion due to the hostility of his people. The emperor also sent a present. When the Prophet received the letter, he commented that Heraclius was lying and that he was not really a Muslim. Al-Suhaylī then includes a discussion regarding the Prophet's behavior with the presents sent to him by infidels, and at the end of it he states:

> Heraclius kept this letter from the Prophet in a golden box (*qaṣaba*) as a way to honor him. They [i.e. the Christian rulers] did not cease inheriting it in succession (*kābiran ʿan kābir*), treating it with great respect and having it in high esteem until it reached Adhfūnsh [Alfonso VI], the conqueror of Toledo and other regions of al-Andalus. Then it passed to his grandson [lit. the son of his daughter] (*ibn bintihi*) known by the name of al-Sulayṭīn [Alfonso VII]. One of my companions told me that he asked one of the military commanders who had seen it, a man known as ʿAbd al-Malik b. Saʿīd, about it.[69] He answered: "The box was shown to me and I cried; then I wanted to kiss it [the letter] and take it in my hand, but I was not allowed to do it out of respect for the letter. I was envied because of all this."[70]

Al-Suhaylī and Ibn Abī Zarʿ were not the only ones to refer to the letter from the Prophet to Heraclius as having ended up in the Iberian Peninsula. In Mamluk times, the Syro-Egyptian historian and traditionist al-ʿAynī (d. 855 AH/1451 CE) quoted al-Suhaylī's passage in his commentary on al-Bukhārī's *Ṣaḥīḥ* and added that the Mamluk sultan of Egypt Qalāwūn sent his ambassador[71] to the king of *al-Gharb* with a present. The king of *al-Gharb* sent

69. Abū Marwān ʿAbd al-Malik b. Saʿīd (d. 560 AH/1164 CE or 562 AH/1166 CE) was an Andalusī military commander who played a relevant role in the end of Almoravid rule in the Iberian Peninsula, establishing himself as an independent ruler in the family fortress of Alcalá la Real (Jaén) by making an alliance with the King of León and Castile Alfonso VII (this contact would have made it plausible that he could have seen the box and the letter). He eventually submitted to the Almohads and was imprisoned for a while, afterwards entering the Almohad army. He took part in the Almohad conquest of Almería in 552 AH/1157 CE and was among the Andalusī notables who welcomed ʿAbd al-Muʾmin when he crossed the Straits in 555 AH/1160 CE. Some of his relatives, including a son, sided with Ibn Mardanīsh when the latter conquered Granada and suffered punishment because of this, although ʿAbd al-Malik b. Saʿīd was eventually pardoned by Abū Yūsuf Yaʿqūb. Cano Ávila 2007, 168–170, no. 1069.

70. *Kitāb al-rawḍ*, 7:365 (in the margins of Ibn Hishām's Sīra). My translation diverges from that of Hamidullah 1955, 107.

71. The name given is Sayf al-dīn Qilīj al-Manṣūrī, but the second element appears in other forms in later sources. One of the emirs of the Mamluk sultan Baybars (r. 658–676 AH/1260–

the ambassador to the king of the Ifranj (*malik al-ifranj*) who showed him the golden box (*ṣundūq*) with the letter. The ambassador noticed that the writing in it had faded. The king told the ambassador that this was the letter that the Prophet Muḥammad had sent to his ancestor Qayṣar (Cesar) and that had been inherited by his successors who held the conviction that their rule would last as long as the letter was with them, this being the reason they treated it with so much respect.[72] While the king of *al-Gharb* remains anonymous,[73] the Christian king is to be identified with the king of Aragón, as *al-ifranj* is used in the Arabic sources to refer to the inhabitants of Catalonia and Aragón.[74] Sayf al-dīn Qalāwūn (r. 678–689 AH/1279–1290 CE) had diplomatic exchanges with King Alfonso III of Aragón (r. 1265–1291 CE), with whom a treaty was signed in the year 689 AH/1290 CE in connection with the Crown of Aragón's involvement in Sicily and Southern Italy.[75]

Ibn Faḍl Allāh al-ʿUmarī (d. 749 AH/1349 CE) – another Egyptian scholar who worked in the chancery of Qalāwūn's son, the Mamluk sultan Nāṣir al-dīn Muḥammad b. Qalāwūn (r. 693 AH/1293–1294 CE, 698–708 AH/1299–1309 CE, 709–741 AH/1310–1341 CE) – said that an ambassador[76] from "*al-Adhfūnsh*" had told him about the letter and that it was still in possession of his king, who was a descendant of Heraclius.[77] Diplomatic relations between Mamluk Egypt and the Crown of Aragón were intense during Nāṣir al-dīn Muḥammad b. Qalāwūn's reign, especially with Jaume II (r. 1291–1327 CE), who was succeeded by his son Alfonso IV (r. 1327–1336 CE).[78] Ibn Faḍl Allāh al-ʿUmarī's reference may thus be to this King Alfonso of Aragón, but it may also be to the king of Castile, as the latter was generically referred to as *Adhfūnsh* in the Arabic historical sources. Thus, the person referred to in the letter could be identified with Fernando IV (r. 1295–1312 CE), or more specifically with

1277 CE) was called Sayf al-dīn Qilīj al-Baghdādī (Lev 1997, 293), and perhaps they are the same person.

72. Al-ʿAynī (d. 1309–1310 AH.), *ʿUmdat al-qāriʾ*, 1:116; the same text is quoted by Ibn Ḥajar 1988, 1:38, and by al-Qasṭallānī 2004, 2:140.

73. The contact may have been established with the Ḥafṣid or the Marinid rulers of North Africa.

74. Hamidullah dated this embassy to 1283 and identified the Christian king with the king of Castile Alfonso X the Wise. 1955, 108.

75. Northrup 1998, 155; Holt 1995. Behrens-Abouseif 2014 makes no reference to Heraclius's letter in the section devoted to the Maghrib.

76. The name of the ambassador is not given, only the name of the person who acted as translator, one Ṣalāḥ al-dīn al-Tarŷumān al-Nāṣirī. See Martínez Montávez 1963, 519–520.

77. Hamidullah 1955, 109, quoting Ibn Faḍl Allāh al-ʿUmarī's *al-Taʿrīf bi-l-muṣṭalaḥ al-sharīf*, reproduced in al-Qalqashandī 1913–1919, 8:34. On later references to the presence of the letter in Iberia, see Hamidullah 1955, 109–110.

78. Capmany 1786; Atiya 1938; Masiá de Ros 1951; Mercé Viladrich 1996–1997, 501–510; Holt 1990, 23–29; Al-Nashshār 1997.

Alfonso XI (r. 1313–1350 CE).[79] Again, information about the letter of the Prophet to Heraclius is only found in the Arabic sources, with no Christian source–to my knowledge–making any reference to it. As the text of al-ʿAynī (d. 855 AH/1451 CE) proves, Mamluk scholars had learned from al-Suhaylī that such a letter had ended up in the Iberian Peninsula and thus, when ambassadors started to be exchanged with the Iberian kingdoms, questions were asked about it. Expectations regarding the letter may have led the Muslim ambassadors to invent tales of having seen it, or perhaps, being told about such expectations, the Christian kings produced the letter: the faded writing mentioned by al-ʿAynī would have made its reading difficult while at the same time proving its antiquity.

It is worth noting that the Mamluk scholars who recorded the letter's presence in the Iberian Peninsula – while aware of al-Suhaylī's text – completely ignored the narrative of Ibn Abī Zarʿ, in which the letter ends up in the hands of the Almohad caliph thanks to the visit paid to Seville by another Iberian Christian king, Sancho VII el Fuerte of Navarra.

Hamidullah, the modern Muslim scholar who has devoted a number of studies to Heraclius's letter, also ignored the narrative of Ibn Abī Zarʿ. Dealing with the other texts, Hamidullah expressed his hope that Byzantinists and Hispanists could shed light on the way in which Heraclius's letter reached the Iberian Peninsula. He also states that during the Spanish Protectorate in Morocco (1912–1956 CE) the Spaniards were questioned about the presence of the letter in the Iberian Peninsula, having to acknowledge that it could not be located in the Spanish archives.[80] Today the letter is said to be in the possession of the king of Jordan, as King Hussein announced its acquisition in 1977 CE.[81]

Returning to the earliest reference to the presence of the letter from the Prophet to Heraclius in the Iberian Peninsula, al-Suhaylī's work, one might ask, how did it come into being? In his report, the letter is said to have been first in the possession of Alfonso VI, the conqueror of Toledo and one of the Iberian kings who claimed the title of emperor. This claim, made also by his grandson, Alfonso VII, may have led the Muslims to connect both Alfonsos with the Byzantine emperor Heraclius. Alfonso VI did not only claim

79. Martínez Montávez 1963, 505–523 and 1962, 343–376.

80. Hamidullah 1955, 109n3.

81. El Cheikh 1999n23. The alleged letters sent by the Prophet to the rulers of his times can be seen at: "In Pictures: Prophet Muhammad's letters that were sent to rulers," Al-Arabiya English, May 14, 2017, http://english.alarabiya.net/en/features/2017/05/14/In-Pictures-Prophet-Mohammed-s-letters-to-heads-of-states.html. I owe this information to Virginia Vázquez.

the title, he also had in his possession the *arca sancta* (the Holy Ark),[82] still preserved today in the cathedral of the town of Oviedo, which allegedly contained relics of Jesus and Mary that had been safeguarded when the Persians conquered Jerusalem in 614 CE, thus avoiding the fate of the Holy Cross, which Heraclius had to rescue from Persian hands. That ark was brought to the Iberian Peninsula and ended up in the hands of Alfonso VI, who ordered it to be opened – an event narrated in a document dated 14 March 1075 CE that is generally considered to be a forgery and in which Jerusalem is not mentioned. Later, Bishop Pelagius of Oviedo (d. 1153 CE) in his *Liber testamentorum* (composed 1109–1112 CE) included the story of how the ark from Jerusalem reached the Iberian Peninsula. This was part of his efforts toward elevating the status of the bishopric of Oviedo and its cathedral.[83] If the Muslims had heard of this *arca sancta* that in the first half of the twelfth century helped transform Oviedo into a new Jerusalem, could it have ignited the idea that it may also have contained a copy of the letter sent to Heraclius by the Prophet Muḥammad?

Conclusions

The Sevillian Ibn Barrajān used the Qur'anic verses 30:2–5 in order to predict the Muslim conquest of Jerusalem by Saladin in the year 583 AH/1187 CE. Those verses were generally interpreted as referring first to Heraclius's defeat at the hands of the Persians and to his eventual victory over them. Read as Ibn Barrajān did, the verses were understood as referring first to Heraclius's victory and second to the eventual defeat of the Christians at the hands of Saladin.[84] Both al-Suhaylī and Ibn Ḥubaysh may have met Ibn Barrajān during their studies in al-Andalus, but even if they did not meet him, his prediction must have reached them, as it addressed one of the concerns of the times: Christian military success and how to counteract it.[85] Perhaps the prediction helped strengthen the memory of Heraclius among the Muslims of al-Andalus, but the figure of the emperor who had been a contemporary of the Prophet also served other functions, among them the legitimization of Muḥammad's prophethood, duly highlighted by Qāḍī ʿIyāḍ (d. 544 AH/1149 CE) in his famous work on the prerogatives and merits of the Prophet Muḥammad, which was written with the aim of counteracting

82. Gómez Moreno 1954, 125–136; Alonso Álvarez 2007–2008, 17–29; Bango Torviso 2011, 11–67.

83. Henriet 2006, 235–248. On Pelagius's historical work see Jerez 2008, 47–87, and Alonso Álvarez 2012.

84. El Cheikh (2004), 21–39 and see also Bellver 2014.

85. Fierro 1997, 155–178.

the appeal of the messianic founder of the Almohad movement.[86] Even if the letter could be used against Almohad messianism, the Almohads could also profit from the Muslim Heraclius and especially from spreading the idea that the letter was in the possession of the Iberian kings. The historian al-Yaᶜqūbī (d. after 292 AH/905 CE) had recorded that the Prophet's reaction to the response of Heraclius to his letter was: "their kingdom remains as long as my letter remains with them"; in other words, Byzantine – but more generally Christian – survival depended on their continued possession of the Prophet's letter.[87]

That possession could be used to serve different needs. It could serve to legitimize collaboration with the Christians and acceptance of their rule, for it could be argued that they would behave as honorably and according to justice as Heraclius had done, which is what Ibn Ḥubaysh seems to have done not by mentioning the letter, but by stating a direct kinship relationship between Alfonso VII and the Byzantine emperor. It could also serve to incite *jihad* against the Christians, as the Almohad caliphs started to increasingly use *jihad* in order to legitimize their rule,[88] while playing with the idea that recovering that letter would signal the end of Christian power. The story about the king of Navarre giving the letter as a present to the Almohad caliph may have served the purpose of propagating the idea that Christian defeat was ensured – writing under the Marinids, Ibn Abī Zarᶜ chose the caliph al-Nāṣir as the recipient, not ignoring that during his reign the Muslim defeat at Las Navas de Tolosa had taken place, but perhaps suggesting that the Marinids, as successors of the Almohads, were now in possession of the letter.

Be that as it may, the figure of Heraclius acquired new vitality among the Muslims of the Islamic West after the fall of Toledo into Christian hands (478 AH/1085 CE) and especially during the sixth/twelfth century, a century especially productive in forging the past. It was not only that al-Suhaylī located Heraclius's letter among the Iberian Christian kings and that Ibn Ḥubaysh coined a Byzantine genealogy for the king of Castile and León. Two of their contemporaries also put their imagination to work: al-Yasaᶜ b. Ḥazm

86. See note 19 above; Fierro 2011, 19–34; Albarrán 2015.

87. Al-Yaᶜqūbī 1980, 2:78; El Cheikh 1999, 15. Conrad 2002, 142 notes that in al-Azdī's *Futūḥ al-Shām* Heraclius predicts that in the future his empire will suffer the same fate as that of his army defeated by the Muslims at Yarmuk, and alerts to the fact that it contradicts the rest of the Heraclius materials that assume that Byzantium will survive. See also Cook 1992, 3–24. Al-Azdī's *Futūḥ al-Shām* depicts Heraclius in a very positive light. El Cheikh 1999, 9 and especially Conrad 2002, 132–144. *Futūḥ al-Shām* circulated widely in al-Andalus. Landau Tasseron 2000, 361–380; Mourad 2000, 577–593.

88. See note 24 above and Fierro 2014a, 53–77.

recreated the history of the Maghrib to convince Saladin to intervene in the Iberian Peninsula against the Christians,[89] while another Andalusī, Ibn Diḥya al-Kalbī (d. 633 AH/1235 CE), also an emigrant who had to carve out a position for himself outside al-Andalus, claimed descent from the Companion of the Prophet Diḥya al-Kalbī, who had played a crucial role in the envoys sent by the Prophet to Heraclius.[90] Ibn Diḥya al-Kalbī thus connected himself with a narrative that reminded Muslims of Christian defeat and of Christian acknowledgment of Muslim truth. Heraclius and the letter he received from the Prophet made its appearance in the Iberian Peninsula during the sixth/twelfth century in fulfilment of different Muslim needs against a threatening Christendom.

89. See note 14 above.
90. Gallega Ortega 2004, 63–69, no. 435. Ibn Diḥya was a student of al-Suhaylī.

Bibliography

Albarrán, Javier. 2016. "Ruptura, memoria y guerra santa: una lectura del *ŷihād* almohade." In *Órdenes militares y construcción de la sociedad occidental: cultura, religiosidad y desarrollo social de los espacios de frontera (ss. XII-XV)*, 287–313. Castilla-La Mancha.

———. 2015. *El Profeta: veneración y polémica. Muhammad en el cadí 'Iyāḍ (s. XII)*. Madrid.

Alexander, Paul J. 1978. "The Medieval Legend of the Last Roman Emperor and its Messianic Origin." *Journal of the Warburg and Courtauld Institutes* 41:1–15.

Alonso Álvarez, Raquel. 2012. "La obra histórica del obispo Pelayo de Oviedo (1089–1153) y su relación con la *Historia legionensis* (llamada *silensis*)." *e-Spania* 14. https://e-spania.revues.org/21586#quotation

———. 2007–2008. "*Patria uallata asperitate moncium*. Pelayo de Oviedo, el arca de las reliquias y la creación de una topografía regia." *Locvs Amoenvs* 9:17–29.

Arberry, A. J., trans. 1982. *The Koran*. Oxford.

Arias Torres, J. P. 2012. "al-Suhaylī, Abū l-Qāsim." In *De al-Qabrīrī a Zumurrud*, edited by Jorge Lirola Delgado, Biblioteca de al-Andalus 7, Almería.

Atiya, Aziz S. 1938. *Egypt and Aragon: Embassies and Diplomatic Correspondence between 1300 and 1330 AD*. Leipzig.

al-ʿAynī, Maḥmūd bin Aḥmad. 1309–1310. *ʿUmdat al-qāriʾ fī sharḥ al-Bukhārī*. 11 vols. Constantinople.

Baert, Barbara. 1999. "New Observations on the Genesis of Girona (1050–1100). The Iconography of the Legend of the True Cross." *Gesta* 38, no. 2:115–127.

———. 2004. *A Heritage of Holy Wood: The Legend of the True Cross in Text and Image*. Leiden.

———. 2008. "Héraclius, l'Exaltation de la Croix et le Mont-Saint-Michel au XIe siècle: une lecture attentive du ms. 641 de la Pierpont Morgan Library à New York." *Cahiers de Civilisation médiévale* 51:3–20.

Bango Torviso, Isidro G. 2011. "La renovación del tesoro sagrado a partir del Concilio de Coyanza y el taller real de orfebrería de León. El Arca Santa de Oviedo (1072)." *Anales de Historia del Arte*, Extra 2 (dedicado a Alfonso VI y el arte de su época), 11–67.

Barbour, Nevill. 1967. "The Relations of King Sancho VII of Navarre with the Almohads." *Revue de l'Occident musulman et de la Méditerranée* 4:9–21.

Barton, Simon. 2015. *Conquerors, Brides and Concubines. Interfaith Relations and Social Power in Medieval Iberia*. Philadelphia.

Bashear, Suliman. 1997. "The Mission of Diḥya al-Kalbī and the Situation in Syria." *Der Islam* 74:64–91.

Behrens-Abouseif, Doris. 2014. *Practising Diplomacy in the Mamluk Sultanate: Gifts and Material Culture in the Medieval Islamic World.* New York.

Bellver, José. 2014. "Ibn Barraǧān and Ibn ʿArabī on the Prediction of the Capture of Jerusalem in 583/1187 by Saladin." *Arabica* 61:252–286.

Borgehammar, Stephan. 2009. "Heraclius Learns Humility: Two Early Latin Accounts Composed for the Celebration of *Exaltatio Crucis*." *Millennium* 6:145–201.

Bosch-Vilá, J. 2012. "Ibn Mardanīsh." In *EI2,* edited by P. Bearman, Th. Bianquis, C. E. Bosworth, E. van Donzel, and W. P. Heinrichs. Leiden. http://dx.doi.org.ezp1.lib.umn.edu/10.1163/1573-3912_islam_SIM_3285.

Bowen Savant, Sarah. 2013. *The New Muslims of Post-conquest Iran: Tradition, Memory and Conversion.* New York.

Caffaro. 1973. *De captione Almerie et Tortuose.* Edited by A. Ubieto Arteta. Valencia.

Capmany, A. de. (1786) 1974. *Antiguos tratados de paces y alianzas entre algunos reyes de Aragón y dirigentes principales infieles de Asia y África, desde el siglo XIII hasta el XV.* Madrid. Facsimile Valencia.

Cano Ávila, P. 2007. "Ibn Saʿīd al-ʿAnsī, Abū Marwān." In *De Ibn Saʿāda a Ibn Wuhayb,* edited by Jorge Lirola Delgado, Biblioteca de al-Andalus 5, 168–170, no. 1069. Almería.

Castiñeiras, Manuel. 2011. *El Tapiz de la Creación. Catedral de Girona.* Girona.

Cheneb, M. Ben. 1907. *Étude sur les personnages mentionnés dans l'Idjāza du Cheikh ʿAbd al-Qādir al-Fāsy.* Paris.

Conrad, Lawrence I. 2002. "Heraclius in Early Islamic Kerygma." In *The Reign of Heraclius (610–641): Crisis and Confrontation,* edited by Gerrit J. Reinink and Bernard H. Stolte, 113–156. Leuven.

Cook, Michael. 1992. "The Heraclian Dynasty in Muslim Eschatology." *Al-Qanṭara* 13, no. 1:3–24.

al-Ḍabbī, Aḥmad ibn ʻAmīrah. 1885. *Kitāb bughyat al-multamis fī tárīkh rijāl ahl al-Andalus.* Edited by F. Codera and J. Ribera. Madrid.

al-Dānī, Abū ʿAmr. 1995. *Al-Sunan al-wārida fī l-fitan.* Edited by Riḍā Allāh b. Muḥammad Idrīs al-Mubarakfūrī. 6 vols. Riyad.

al-Dhahabī, Abū ʻAbd Allah Shams al-Dīn. 1968–70. *Tadhkirāt al-ḥuffāẓ.* Edited by ʿAbd al-Raḥmān Yaḥyà al-Muʿallimī. 4 vols. Hyderabad.

———. 1985. *Siyar aʿlām al-nubalāʾ.* 23 vols. Beirut.

Dunlop, D. M. 1941. "The Spanish Historian Ibn Ḥubaysh." *Journal of the Royal Asiatic Society* 73.4:359–362.

———. 2012. "Ibn Ḥubaysh." In *EI2,* edited by P. Bearman, Th. Bianquis, C. E. Bosworth, E. van Donzel, and W. P. Heinrichs. Leiden. III:826–827.

El Cheikh, Nadia. 1999. "Muhammad and Heraclius: a Study in Legitimacy." *Studia Islamica* 89:5–21.

——. 2004. *Byzantium Viewed by the Arabs*. Cambridge, MA.

Estepa, Carlos. 1989. "La política imperial de Alfonso X: Esbozo de una posible ideología política Alfonsina." In *La Historia en el contexto de las Ciencias Humanas y Sociales. Homenaje a Marcelo Vigil Pascual*, edited by M. J. Hidalgo de la Vega, 205–216. Salamanca.

Fierro, Maribel. 1995. "La falsificación de la historia: al-Yasaᶜ b. Ḥazm y su *Kitāb al-mugrib*." *Al-Qanṭara* 16:15–38.

——. 1997. "Christian Success and Muslim Fear in Andalusī Writings During the Almoravid and Almohad Periods." *Israel Oriental Studies* 17:155–178.

——. 2000. "Spiritual Alienation and Political Activism: the *ghurabāʾ* in al-Andalus during the Sixth/Twelfth Century." *Arabica* 47:230–260.

——. 2003. "Las genealogías de ᶜAbd al-Muʾmin, primer califa almohade." *Al-Qanṭara* 24:77–108.

——. 2006. "The Anṣārīs, Nāṣir al-dīn, and the Naṣrids in al-Andalus." *Jerusalem Studies in Arabic and Islam* 32:232–247.

——. 2011. "El tratado sobre el Profeta del cadí ᶜIyāḍ y el contexto almohade." In *Legendaria Medievalia en honor de Concepción Castillo Castillo*, 19–34. Córdoba.

——. 2014a. "La espada y la palabra: posturas frente al 'otro' durante la época almohade." In *La Península Ibérica en tiempos de las Navas de Tolosa*, edited by C. Estepa Díaz and M. A. Carmona Ruiz. Monografías de la Sociedad Española de Estudios Arabes 5, 53–77. Madrid.

——. 2014b. "The Religious Policy of the Almohads." In *The Oxford Handbook of Islamic Theology*, edited by Sabine Schmidtke. Oxford. http://www.oxfordhandbooks.com/browse?jumpTo=f&page=8&pageSize=50&sort=authorsort&t1=ORR%3AAHU03020

Fierro, Maribel and Luis Molina. 2009. "Al-Maqqarī." In *Essays in Arabic Literary Biography, 1350–1850*, edited by Joseph Lowry and Devin J. Stewart. Wiesbaden.

Fortún, Luis Javier. 1986. *Sancho VII el Fuerte (1194–1234)*. Iruña.

Frolow, Anatole. 1953. "La Vraie Croix et les expéditions d'Héraclius en Perse." *Revue des études byzantines* 11 no. 1:88–105.

Fulcher of Chartres. 1973. *A History of the Expedition to Jerusalem, 1095–1127*. Translated by Frances Rita Ryan. Edited by Harold S. Fink. New York.

Gallega Ortega, T. 2004. "Ibn Diḥya, Abū l-Jaṭṭāb." In *De Ibn al-Dabbāg a Ibn Kurz*, edited by Jorge Lirola Delgado and José Miguel Puerta Vílchez, 63–69, no. 435. Biblioteca de al-Andalus 3. Almería.

García Gallo, Alfonso. 1945. "El imperio medieval español." *Arbor* 4:199–228.

Gayangos, Pascual de. 1840. *The History of the Mohammedan Dynasties in Spain*. 2 vols. London.

Ghouirgate, Mehdi. 2015. "Comment se comporter avec un roi chrétien: l'ouvrage perdu d'Abū l-Ḥasan ʿAlī Ibn al-Qaṭṭān et les enjeux du cérémonial almohade." *Revue des Mondes Musulmans et de la Méditerranée* 138. https://remmm.revues.org/8587.

Gómez Moreno, M. 1954. "El Arca Santa de Oviedo documentada." *Archivo español de arte y arqueología* 69:125–136.

Hamidullah, Muhammad. 1955. "La lettre du Prophète à Héraclius et le sort de l'original." *Arabica* 2, no. 1:97–110.

——. 1965. "Original de la lettre du Prophète à Kisrà." *Rivista degli Studi Orientali* 40:57–69.

——. 1969. *Majmūʿat al-wathāʾiq al-siyāsiyya li-l-ʿahd al-nabawī wa-l-khilāfa al-rashida*. Beirut.

——. 1985. *Six originaux des lettres du Prophète de l'islam: étude paléographique et historique des lettres du Prophète*. Paris.

Henriet, Patrick. 2006. "Oviedo, Jérusalem hispanique au XIIe siècle. Le récit de la translation de l'*arca sancta* selon l'évêque Pélage d'Oviedo." In *Pèlerinages et lieux saints dans l'Antiquité et le Moyen Âge. Mélanges offerts à Pierre Maraval*, edited by B. Caseau, J.-Cl. Cheynet and V. Déroche. Centre de Recherche d'Histoire et Civilisation de Byzance 23, 235–248. Paris.

Hollander, William den. 2014. *Josephus, the Emperors, and the City of Rome: From Hostage to Historian*. Boston.

Holt, P. M. 1995. *Early Mamluk Diplomacy, 1260–1290: Treaties of Baybars and Qalāwūn with Christian Rulers*. Leiden.

——. 1990. "Al-Nāṣir Muḥammad's letter to a Spanish ruler in 699/1300." *Al-Masāq* 3:23–29.

Huici Miranda, Ambrosio. 1956. *Las grandes batallas de la Reconquista*. Madrid.

——trans. 1964. *Rawḍ al-qirṭās* by Ibn Abī Zarʿ. 2 vols. Valencia.

Ibn al-Abbār. 1887–9. *Al-Takmila*, edited by F. Codera. 2 vols. Madrid.

Ibn Abī Khaythama. 1997. *Akhbār al-makkiyyīn min Kitāb al-taʾrīkh al-kabīr*. Edited by Ismāʿīl Ḥasan Ḥusayn. Riyadh.

Ibn Abī Zarʿ. 1972. *Rawḍ al-qirṭās*. Rabat.

Ibn Ḥajar. 1988. *Fatḥ al-bāriʾ*. 14 vols. Beirut.

Ibn Ḥubaysh, Abū l-Qāsim ʿAbd al-Raḥmān. 1983–1987. *Dhikr al-ghazawāt al-ḍāmina al-kāfila wa-l-futūḥ al-jāmiʿa al-ḥāfila al-kāʾina fī ayyām al-khulafāʾ al-ūlā al-thalātha*. Edited by Aḥmad Ghunaym. 4 vols. Cairo.

Ibn al-Jazarī. 1932–33. *Ghāyat al-nihāya fī ṭabaqāt al-qurrāʾ*. Edited by G. Bergstraesser. 2 vols. Cairo.

Ibn Khaldūn. 1978. *Muqaddima*. Translated by Franz Rosenthal. London.
Ibn al-Qaṭṭān. 1990. *Naẓm al-jumān fī akhbār al-zamān*. Edited by Maḥmūd ʿAlī Makkī. Beirut.
Ibn al-Zubayr. 1993. *Ṣilat al-Ṣila (al-qism al-thālith)*. Edited by ʿAbd al-Salām al-Harrās and S. Aʿrāb. Rabat.
Jerez, Enrique. 2008. "Arte compilatoria pelagiana. La formación del *Liber cronicorum*." In *Poétique de la chronique. L'écriture des textes historiographiques au Moyen Âge (péninsule Ibérique et France)*, edited by Amaia Arizaleta, 47–87. Toulouse.
Kaḥḥāla, ʿUmar R. 1957–61. *Muʿjam al-muʾallifīn*. 15 vols. Damascus.
Kaegi, Walter Emil. 2003. *Heraclius, Emperor of Byzantium*. Cambridge.
Kühnel, Gustav. 2004. "Heracles and the Crusaders: Tracing the Path of a Royal Motif." In *France and the Holy Land: Frankish Culture at the End of the Crusades*, edited by Daniel H. Weiss and Lisa J. Mahoney, 64–75. Baltimore.
Landau Tasseron, Ella. 2000. "New Data on an Old Manuscript: An Andalusīan Version of the Work Entiled *Futūḥ al-Shām*." *Al-Qanṭara* 21:361–380
Lapiedra, Eva. 1997. *Cómo los musulmanes llamaban a los cristianos hispánicos*. Alicante.
Lemistre, Annie. 1970. "Les Origines du Requerimiento." *Mélanges de la Casa de Velázquez* 6:161–209.
Lev, Yaacov, ed. 1997. *War and Society in the Eastern Mediterranean, 7th-15th Centuries*. Leiden.
Lino Munárriz y Velasco, Pedro. 1912. "Viaje del rey don Sancho al África." *Boletín de la Comisión de monumentos históricos y artísticos de Navarra*, segunda época, año 3:5–39.
Lirola Delgado, J. and E. Navarro i Ortiz. 2012. "Al-Rušāṭī, Abū Muḥammad." In *De al-Qabrīrī a Zumurrud*, edited by Jorge Lirola Delgado. Biblioteca de al-Andalus 7, Almería.
Makhlūf. 1950–52. *Shajarat al-nūr al-zakiyya fī ṭabaqāt al-mālikiyya*. Cairo.
Manzano Rodríguez, M. Á. 2012. "Ibn Abī Zarʿ, Abū l-Ḥasan." In *De al-ʿAbbādīya a Ibn Abyaḍ*, edited by Jorge Lirola Delgado and José Miguel Puerta Vílchez, 761–66. Biblioteca de al-Andalus 1, Almería.
al-Maqqarī. 1968. *Nafḥ al-ṭīb min ghuṣn al-Andalus al-raṭīb*. Edited by Iḥsān ʿAbbās. 8 vols. Beirut.
Maranci, Christina. 2009. "The Humble Heraclius: Revisiting the North Portal at Mren." *Revue des Études Arméniennes* 31:359–372.
al-Marrākushī. 1984. *Al-Dhayl wa-l-Takmila li-kitabay al-Mawṣūl wa-l-Ṣila*. 8 vols. Rabat.

Martín Castellanos, A. J. and M. Forcada. 2007. "Ibn Ṭāhir al-Qaysī, Abū ʿAbd al-Raḥmān (nieto)." In *De Ibn Saʿāda a Ibn Wuhayb*, edited by Jorge Lirola Delgado, 461–463, no. 1235. Biblioteca de al-Andalus 5, Almería.

Martínez Montávez, Pedro. 1963. "Relaciones castellano-mamelucas: 1283–1382." *Hispania* 92:505–523.

——. 1962. "Relaciones de Alfonso X de Castilla con el sultán mameluco Baybars y sus sucesores." *Al-Andalus* 27, no. 2:343–376.

Masiá de Ros, Á. 1951. *La Corona de Aragón y los estados del norte de África. Política de Jaime II y Alfonso IV en Egipto, Ifriquía y Tremecén*. Barcelona.

Mercé Viladrich, María. 1996–97. "Noves dades sobre les relacions entre el soldà del Caire al-Nāṣir Muhammad ibn Sayf al-dīn Qalāwūn i el rei Jaume II." *Anales de la Universidad de Alicante. Historia Medieval* 11:501–510.

Miranda García, Fermín. 2012. "Intereses cruzados de la monarquía navarra en el siglo XIII." In *Fernando III: tiempo de cruzada*, edited by Carlos de Ayala and Martín Ríos Saloma, 325–349. México-Madrid.

Mourad, Suleiman. 2000. "On Early Islamic Historiography: Abū Ismāʿīl al-Azdī and his *Futūḥ al-Shām*." *Journal of the American Oriental Society* 120, no. 4:577–593.

al-Nashshār, Muḥammad Maḥmūd Aḥmad. 1997. *ʿAlāqat mamlakatay Qashtāla wa-Arājūn bi-salṭanat al-Mamālīk, 1260–1341 M/658–741 H*. al-Haram [Giza].

Northrup, Linda S. 1998. *From Slave to Sultan: the Career of al-Manṣūr Qalāwūn and the Consolidation of Mamluk Rule in Egypt and Syria (678–689 A.H./1279–1290 A.D.)*. Stuttgart.

Pérez González, Maurilio. 1997. *Crónica del Emperador Alfonso VII*. León.

Pons Boigues, F. 1898. *Ensayo bio-bibliográfico sobre los historiadores y geógrafos arábigo-españoles*. Madrid.

Pouzet, Louis. 1992. "Le Hadith d'Heraclius: une caution byzantine a la prophétie de Muhammad." In *La Syrie de Byzance a l'Islam VIe-VIIe siècles*, edited by P. Canivet and J.-P. Rey-Coquais, 59–65. Damascus.

Puig Montada, Josep. 2000. "Abū ʿAbd al-Raḥmān Ibn Ṭāhir. Addenda a 'Averroes, vida y persecución de un filósofo.'" *Revista Española de Filosofía Medieval* 7:181–186.

al-Qasṭallānī. 2004. *Al-Mawāhib al-laduniyya bi-l-minaḥ al-muḥammadiyya*. Edited by Ṣāliḥ Aḥmad al-Šāmī. 2 vols. Beirut.

Qāḍī ʿIyāḍ. 1984. *Al-Shifāʾ bi-taʿrīf ḥuqūq al-Muṣṭafā*. Edited by ʿAlī Muḥammad al-Bijāwī. 2 vols. Beirut.

al-Qalqashandī. 1913–1919. *Ṣubḥ al-aʿshā*. 14 vols. Cairo.

Queiroz de Souza, Guilherme. 2015. "Heraclius, emperor of Byzantium." *Revista Digital de Iconografía Medieval* 7, no. 14:27–38.

Regan, Geoffrey. 2003. *First Crusader. Byzantium's Holy Wars*. New York.
Recuero Astray, Manuel. 2003. *Alfonso VII, (1126–1157)*. Burgos.
Reilly, Bernard F. 1998. *The Kingdom of León-Castilla Under King Alfonso VII, 1126–1157*. Philadelphia.
Reinink, Gerrit J. and Bernard H. Stolte, eds. 2002. *The Reign of Heraclius (610–641): Crisis and Confrontation*. Leuven.
Rodríguez Figueroa, Antonio. 1999–2000. "Un ejemplo de exilio forzado: la conquista cristiana de Almería en 1147." In *Estudios onomástico-biográficos de al-Andalus. IX-X. Biografías almohades*, edited by Maribel Fierro and María Luisa Ávila. 2 vols. Madrid.
——. 2004. "Ibn Ḥubayš, Abū l-Qāsim." In *De Ibn al-Dabbāg a Ibn Kurz*, edited by Jorge Lirola Delgado and José Miguel Puerta Vílchez. Biblioteca de al-Andalus 3. Almería.
Rodríguez López, Ana. 1997. "El reino de Castilla y el Imperio germánico en la primera mitad del siglo XIII. Fernando III y Federico II." In *Homenaje al Profesor Abilio Barbero*, edited by María Isabel Loring, 613–630. Madrid.
Al-Ṣafadī. 1962–2013. *Al-Wāfī bi-l-wafayāt*. 32 vols. Stuttgart.
Serrano Ruano, D. 2009. "ʿIyāḍ, Abū l-Faḍl,." In *De Ibn al-Ŷabbāb a Nubḏat al-ʿaṣr*, edited by Jorge Lirola Delgado, 404–434. Biblioteca de al-Andalus 6, Almería.
Shoval, Ilan. 2016. *King John's Delegation to the Almohad Court (1212): Medieval Interreligious Interactions and Modern Historiography*. Turnhout.
Sirantoine, Hélène. 2013. *Imperator Hispaniae. Les idéologies impériales dans le royaume de León (IXe-XIIe siècles)*. Madrid.
al-Suhaylī. 1967–70. *Kitāb al-rawḍ al-unuf wa-l-mashraʿ al-riwā fī tafsīr mā shtamala ʿalayhi ḥadīth Sīrat rasūl Allāh li-bn Hishām wa-ḥtawà*. Edited by ʿAbd al-Raḥmān al-Wakīl. 7 vols. Cairo.
al-Suyūṭī. 1964–5. *Bughyat al-wuʿāt fī ṭabaqāt al-lughawiyyīn wa-l-nuḥāt*. Edited by Muḥammad Abū l-Faḍl Ibrāhīm. 2 vols. Cairo.
al-Timbuktī, Aḥmad Bābā, n.d. *Kitāb nayl al-ibtihāj bi-taṭrīz al-Dībāj*. Beirut.
Urvoy, Dominique. 1993. "Effets pervers du *ḥajj*, d'après le cas d'al-Andalus." In *Golden Roads. Migration, Pilgrimage and Travel in Mediaeval and Modern Islam*, edited by I. R. Netton, 43–53. Wiltshire.
——. 1990. *Pensers d'al-Andalus. La vie intellectuelle à Cordoue et Sevilla au temps des Empires Berberes (fin XIe siècle - début XIIIe siècle)*. Toulouse.
Vallejo Girvés, Margarita. 2010. "Archivo Gráfico de España y la Península Ibérica (IV): Heraclio y la recuperación de la Santa Cruz." *Boletín de la Sociedad Española de Bizantinística* 7:2–9.
——. 2006. "Sensaciones bizantinas: las dos caídas de Jerusalén en la literatura del siglo VII." *Erytheia: Revista de estudios bizantinos y neogriegos* 27:43–72.

——. 1999. "Sobre la Península Ibérica y el Mediterráneo bizantino: efecto de la rebelión de Heraclio en la contingencia visigodo-bizantina (a. 602–610)." In *El mundo mediterráneo (siglos III-VII). Actas del III Congreso Andaluz de Estudios Clásicos*, edited by Julián González Fernández, 489–499.

——. 2012. *Hispania y Bizancio: una relación desconocida*. Madrid.

Walzer, Richard. 1985. *Al-Farabi on the Perfect State*. Oxford.

al-Yaʿqūbī. 1980. *Taʾrīkh*. 2 vols. Beirut.

Zakkār, Suhayl, ed. 1992. *Dhikr al-ghazawāt al-ḍāmina al-kāfila wa-l-futūḥ al-jāmiʿa al-ḥāfila al-kāʾina fī ayyām al-khulafāʾ al-ūlā al-thalātha* by Abū l-Qāsim ʿAbd al-Raḥmān Ibn Ḥubaysh. 2 vols. Beirut.

al-Ziriklī. 1980. *al-Aʿlām*. 8 vols. Beirut.

Zuckerman, Constantin. 2013. "Heraclius and the return of the Holy Cross." In *Constructing the Seventh Century. Travaux et mémoires*, 197–218. Paris.

“Ziyād ibn ʿĀmir al-Kinānī”: Andalusī Muslim Crusade Literature

David A. Wacks
University of Oregon

“MUSLIM CRUSADE LITERATURE” sounds like an oxymoron. However, in the tale of Ziyād ibn ʿĀmir al-Kinānī, we have just such an example. Our hero, Ziyād, unites aspects of the chivalresque heroes of crusade narratives with those of the heroes of medieval Arabic heroic narratives. Like the protagonist of a twelfth-century chanson de geste, he defeats the evil pagan astrologer-king in single combat, and subsequently converts the vanquished armies en masse to the one true faith – in this case Islam. We have in our Ziyād a curious example of a Muslim hero who demonstrates many characteristics typical of the chivalric heroes of the age of Crusade. This would be particularly strange if our author hailed from the East, but coming from Granada or the Maghreb in the thirteenth century, as we will see, it is a logical product of circumstances unique to the region.

Written before the mid-thirteenth century by an anonymous author, and inedited until 2009, “Ziyād ibn ʿĀmir al-Kinānī” is the tale of the adventures of the eponymous hero.[1] The work is set in a flashback at the court of the Abbasid caliph Harun al-Rashid, where the hero is being held captive. Ziyād has been summoned by the caliph to regale him with stories of his own adventures, in a narrative frame consciously derived from the setting of *1001 Nights*. The text narrates the adventures of Ziyād ibn ʿĀmir, drawing equally on the literary conventions of the Arabic and Romance traditions of heroic and chivalric narrative.

Just as many medieval works written in French and other Romance

1. The tale of “Ziyād ibn ʿĀmir al-Kinānī” (ca. 1250) exists in a unique manuscript housed in the Escorial library (MS Árabes 1876). It does not appear in Michael Casiri’s catalog of the Arabic manuscripts of the Escorial, but Braulio Justel Calabozo does mention it in his (1981, 38–39). It is a plain manuscript written in a clear Maghrebi hand with red rubrics and no miniatures. In 1882, Spanish Arabist Francisco Fernández y González published a Spanish language translation of the text, giving it the title *Zeyyad ibn Amir el de Quinena*. 1882. I have so far been able to find only two mentions of the text in modern criticism, the first in Menéndez y Pelayo’s *Orígenes de la novela* (2008, 1:xliii-xlv), and the second in Ángel González Palencia’s *Historia de la literatura arábigoespañola* (1945, 346). With the exception of the 2009 Arabic edition of al-Shenawī, the text has almost completely evaded the scholarly gaze.

languages deal with crusading themes, or describe situations in which the hero converts entire communities of non-Christians to Christianity, Ziyād likewise is responsible for the conversion of an entire kingdom of pagans to Islam. His feat echoes scenes from semi-historical Arabic narratives that fancifully relate the expansion of Islam and the victories of Muslim heroes against Christian or pagan foes, but at the same time builds a storyworld that flows directly from the chivalric fiction of the Latin West, in which Christian knights of the crusading period defeat and sometimes convert their Muslim enemies en masse. "Ziyād ibn ʿĀmir al-Kinānī" also resonates with the reality of living in the last Muslim state in Iberia, now reduced to a client state of Castile-León. Substituting pagans for Christians, the story of Ziyād ibn ʿĀmir al-Kinānī is a kind of fictional wish fulfillment by which the author represents a triumphant Islam in a fictional world borrowed in part from the Christian court dominating Granada.[2] In so doing, it turns the crusading narrative on its head, subverting one of the most popular genres of the Christian ruling class while cultivating a hybrid fiction that speaks directly to the cultural life of the Andalusī elite under Castilian hegemony.

"Ziyād" and Arabic Literary History

Much as the chivalric Romances in the Western Latin tradition are linked to earlier chansons de gestes and classical epic material,[3] "Ziyyad ibn ʿĀmir" is likewise in some ways an evolution of narratives of Islamic expansion and the popular Arab epic, beginning with the *Ayyām al-ʿArab*, literary accounts of the some of the first battles of Muslim expansion protagonized by Muḥāmmad and his companions.[4] By the thirteenth century, a second generation of *siyar*, or tales, develops, one that recounts tales of later heroes of Islamic expansion and their struggles with enemies in the Islamic world, Byzantium, and against the Franks (Latin crusaders). These *siyar* of-

2. By the mid-thirteenth century, conquests of Andalusī territory by northern Christian kingdoms had reduced Granada to a small client state of Castile that paid tribute to the King of Castile. This state of affairs contrasted sharply with the heyday of the Andalusī caliphate in the late tenth century, when Cordova was the seat of a powerful state that stretched from Gibraltar to the Ebro Valley. In the first half of the thirteenth century, Granada paid Castile tribute that was economically crippling, amounting to a full half of the Emir's rents. They were later reduced, but Granada remained politically and militarily subject to Castile until its conquest in 1492. Viguera Molins 2000, 87; Ladero Quesada 1989, 86–87, 217.

3. Brownlee Scordilis 2000, 254; Fuchs 2004, 39.

4. On the *Ayyām al-ʿArab*, see Mittwoch 2002; Jones 2016; Ramírez del Río 2002; Galmés de Fuentes 1975. Elsewhere, Galmés de Fuentes notes that the first literary recension of the *Ayyām al-ʿArab* was by the Andalusī author Ibn ʿAbd al-Rabbihī. 1978, 1:36–37.

ten adapted material and themes from the earlier *Ayyām al-ʿArab* tradition.[5] These include the *Sīrat Dhāt al-Himma* and *Sīrat al-Zāhir Baybars*, which flourished in Arabic during the time when "Ziyād" appeared.[6]

These *siyar* were largely popular oral epic traditions that produced little in the way of literary manuscripts until modernity.[7] This is an important fact in understanding the relationship of "Ziyād" vis-à-vis the medieval French romance (and later, the Spanish *novelas de caballería*). While the chivalric romance has its roots in oral epic traditions, it evolves into a courtly literary tradition during the twelfth century, while the Arab epic does not. While the vernacular became an important vehicle for courtly literary expression in the Latin West, the same did not happen in the Islamicate West. Though it is true that Andalusī authors were great experimenters with the use of vernacular language in literary compositions, with the possible exception of the twelfth-century Andalusī poet Ibn Quzmān, authors typically did not compose entire texts in the vernacular.[8] Neither was it the case that literary manuscripts of Arabic epics were entirely vernacular; rather they employed a kind of middle register of Arabic that was a far cry from the formal pyrotechnics typical of learned rhyming prose narrative of the times, and from the type of classical Arabic that was considered fit for courtly audiences.[9]

The other Andalusī popular literary texts of the time, such as the *101 Nights* were, like the eastern *1001 Nights*, set at court, but were in no way part of a courtly literature. Rather, they reflected the values of mercantile society, and populated the court of Harun al-Rashid with merchants, artisans,

5. According to Eugen Mittwoch, "similar subject-matter to that found in the *Ayyām* often recurs in later popular romances, drawn out, it is true, in legendary fashion" (2002) (he then cites an example from the *Sirat Banī Hilāl*, also mentioned in this essay).

6. Heath 2008, 327–328.

7. The earliest manuscript of *Sīrat ʿAntar* dates to the mid-fifteenth, but the vast majority are from the eighteenth century or later. Heath 1996, 232–239.

8. Ibn Quzmān made it amply clear in the prologue to his *Diwān* that he was using a colloquial register of Arabic and not, as some have claimed, a kind of Middle Arabic. In fact, he criticizes earlier authors of vernacular *zajal* poetry for using classical Arabic vowel endings (case markers) in their compositions. Monroe 1990. On the question of the literary vernacular in al-Andalus more generally, see Monroe 1990; López-Morillas 2000, 6; Buturovic 2000, 295.

9. In the post-classical period, "authors displayed more and more willingness to write in a colloquial style." Reynolds 2006, 256. For this they were condemned by the likes of the eleventh-century Andalusī writer Ibn ʿAbd al-Rabbihī (author of the definitive courtly manual *al-ʿIqd al-Farīd*, the "*Unique Necklace*"), who identified popular fiction as the "idle talk" referred to in Qurʾan 23:3. Reynolds 2006, 253. Similarly, the fourteenth-century historian Ibn Kathīr (d. 1373) refers to popular *sīrat* as "lies, falsehood, stupid writings, complete ignorance, and shameless prattle which is only in demand by fools and lowly ignoramuses." Reynolds 2006, 260.

and other members of the middle class.[10] "Ziyād" shares popular linguistic features with the *101 Nights*,[11] but shows us a world populated with knights and ladies and the occasional slave, a world that more resembles that of the French chivalric romance than the *1001 Nights*, with the key exception of its being set in the Muslim East. In this way, "Ziyād" is a sort of hybrid of the Arab narratives of conquest, Arab popular epic, the chivalric novel, and the popular Arabic narrative *Nights* tradition.

In order to develop this analogy between "Ziyād" and the chivalric romance, a few words about Arab narratives of conquest and popular epic are in order. The *Ayyām al-ʿArab* is a literary account of some of the major battles of early Islamic expansion, parts of which are reworked in later, narrative traditions such as the *Siyar Banī Hilāl*, which recounts the exploits of the tribe of the *Banī Hilāl*, primarily in North Africa.[12] The popular epic *Sīrat ʿAntar* likewise centers on North Africa and features a popular hero who begins life in humble circumstances as the son of a black slave woman, but who rises to prominence and power by dint of his strength of character, intelligence, and military skill.[13] The *Sīrat ʿAntar* is the latest of the three traditions, and like its Romance counterparts in the vernacular prosifications of epic chronicles, places great emphasis on the vicissitudes of the protagonists' love life, in this case the romantic relationship between ʿAntar and Abla.[14]

The Practice of Arabic Narrative in al-Andalus

Arabic narrative found enthusiastic practictioners in al-Andalus going back to the tenth century, when Andalusī authors became very much concerned with proving their Arab bona fides.[15] During this time Andalusī Muslims began to certify their Arab lineages and became conspicuous practitioners of traditional Arabic literary culture.[16] Ramírez del Río lists fifty Andalusī scholars (ninth-twelfth centuries) who were expert in the *Ayyām al-ʿArab* tradition. He writes that these writers scrupulously followed Eastern tradition, in an effort to "Orientalize" Andalusī courtly culture. Several of these authors versified Andalusī history, including the feats of non-Arab Andalusīs

10. Sallis 1999, 1; Ott 2012, 260.

11. On Andalusī linguistic features of the text of the *101 Nights*, see Ott 2012, 266–267; Fudge 2016, xxxvi.

12. Reynolds 2006b.

13. Kruk 2006.

14. On the *Sīrat ʿAntar*, see Kruk 2006, 296.

15. Emilio González Ferrín points out that the proliferation of treatises on Arab lineages coincides perfectly with Ibn Ḥazm's projection of Arab-ness onto Andalusī literary culture. 2016, 93–94.

16. Galmés de Fuentes 1978, 37.

of Berber or Iberian origin, in the style of the Eastern *sīrat* laced with allusions to the narrative traditions of early Islam.[17] The Andalusī tradition of the *Ayyām al-ʿArab* survived well into late Spanish Islam as is attested by its *aljamiado* (Romance language in Arabic characters) translation, the *Libro de las batallas.*[18]

While "Ziyād" does consciously demonstrate continuity in some respects with the popular Arabic epic tradition that in the words of Remke Kruk, "evokes a glorious Arab past,"[19] it shows us a very different social world. That of the later *sīrat* maintains the values of the earlier *sīrat* in which heroes of lower social class, such as ʿAntar, son of a black slave woman and an Arab knight, overcome social barriers to achieve great success and renown.[20] This class difference creates conditions that require the hero to prove over and over again his military and moral superiority, and is particularly characteristic of popular literature.[21] By contrast, Ziyād ibn ʿĀmir is born a prince, and no such barriers stand in his way. Indeed, in "Ziyād" the enemy is black, as opposed to *Sīrat ʿAntar* where the hero is black. The popular tendency to celebrate the underdog, while not completely absent (there is a slave character who is depicted as noble and heroic), is much tempered in "Ziyād" in comparison to the *Sīrat* and even the *Cantar de Mío Cid.*

Ziyād is more like the heroes of the chivalric novel in that his excellence is a reflection of his aristocratic background, and as such reinforces the current social order. This is perfectly logical when one considers the authorship and audiences of these texts: the popular *sīrat* were composed and transmitted orally, and have very few medieval manuscript witnesses. The same can be said for the Castilian epic *Cantar de Mío Cid*, which is thought by many critics to be of popular origin.

Ziyād's relationship to Arabic epic parallels in some sense the relationship between the chivalric novel, the chansons de geste and Iberian epic traditions. Just as one of the functions of the chivalric romance is to effect a sort of *translatio narrationis* from classical antiquity to modernity,[22] the Arabic *sīrat* and "Ziyād" likewise ground the fictional worlds they create in the more

17. Ramírez del Río 2002, 92–109. Ibn Ḥayyān reports two specific (but no longer extant) tenth-century Andalusī epic poems describing the Muslim conquest of al-Andalus, one by al-Ghazāl in *rajaz* that was in his time widely diffused. The other is by Tammām ibn ʿAlqama, also in *rajaz*, narrating the conquest of al-Andalus and listing the first governors and caliphs, from Tariq to the last days of Abd al-Rahman II. Ribera 1928, 106.

18. Reynolds 2006a, 258; Ramírez del Río 2002; Galmés de Fuentes 1975.

19. Kruk 2006, 292.

20. Heath 2008, 238.

21. Heath 1996, 38.

22. Agapitos and Mortensen 2012, 6.

authoritative storyworlds of the classical period of Islam.[23] The protagonist of the *Sīrat ʿAntar*, for example, is traditionally identified with the pre-Islamic poet ʿAntara, author of one of the seven pre-Islamic odes or *Muʾallaqāt* that were once suspended from the Kåba in Mecca.[24] Other *sīrat* are set in the world of the early years of Islamic expansion, historical fictions meant to mobilize the authority of the textual world of classical Islam in new fictional narratives.[25] In "Ziyād," the Princess Sadé is daughter of Tarīq al-Hilālī, making her the descendent of the famed tribe of the Banū Hilāl, heroes of the eponymous Arab epic set in the age of Islamic expansion.[26]

The themes of conquest and conversion that propel the early Arabic *sīrat* in their retellings of the great battles of early Islamic expansion, their accounts of the conversion of idolators and the subjugation of populations of Jews and Christians, are inflected in an Andalusī key with the addition of Andalusī linguistic, cultural, and geographic details. This is contemporaneous with the projection of crusading ideals, motifs, and texts on the Christian Iberian world. Arabic epic had, since the *Ayyām al-ʿArab*, depicted the conflicts between the *ʿUmmah* and non-Muslims, and these representations always took care to link later conflicts with those of early Islam. *Sīrat Dhāt al-Himma* narrates conflicts with Byzantines, and *Sīrat al-Zāhir Baybars* shows us Sultan Baybars' crushing defeat of the Knights Hospitallers at Antioch, a defeat from which the crusader movement would never recover.[27] "Ziyād" is a sort of ahistorical continuation of this trend, representing the Christian foes of Granada as pagans much the same way (and as we discuss below) that French texts represent their Muslim foes as idol-worshipping pagans. This (veiled) representation of Christians is well in keeping with the times, in which Muslim writers did not hesitate to describe Christians as *mushrikūn*, or idol worshippers.[28]

23. José Ramírez del Río argues that just as Menéndez Pidal demonstrated that Castilian historiography relied heavily on *cantares de gesta*, so Andalusī historiography relied earlier Arabic *siyar* such as the *Banī Hilāl* (2003).

24. Kruk 2006, 292.

25. Heath 2008, 328.

26. Ziyād eventually is crowned king of the Banū Hilāl ("Beni-hilel") tribe. Fernández y González 1882, 15. The image of the *Banī Hilāl* as fierce fighters reflected in epic and here in popular prose responds not only to tradition but also to the actual political reality. The expansion of Sevilla under the Almohads required expansion of the defensive perimeter (city wall) and increased military presence in the area to defend inhabitants from local Arab clans claiming descent from the Banū Hilāl. Ramírez del Río 2014, 280. See also Fernández y Gonzalez's comments on the legacy of the tribe of Kinān in al-Andalus (1882, 4). This trope has its parallel in heroes of later Iberian romances who are crowned emperor. Rodilla León 2009, 307–308.

27. Heath 2008, 328.

28. Lapiedra Gutiérrez 1997, 158–175; Serrano Ruano 2012, 739. Ibn Ḥazm of Córdoba (d. 1064) criticized the doctrine of the Trinity as "'the most fatuous' (*ahmaqu shirk*) of idolatries,"

Andalusī-Castilian Acculturation

This harkening to the mythic-historical Arab past of the *sīrat* blends with a certain acculturation to the culture of the dominant Castilian state that had subordinated Granada in the course of the thirteenth century. Writing from North Africa, Ibn Khaldūn observed in the fourteenth century that nations who are dominated politically by their neighbor tend to imitate the cultural practices of the dominant kingdom:

> a nation dominated by another, neighbouring nation will show a great deal of assimilation and imitation. At this time, this is the case in Spain [al-Andalus]. The Spaniards [Andalusīs] are found to assimilate themselves to the Galician nations [Galicia, Asturias, Leon, Castile, Navarra] in their dress, their emblems, and most of their customs and conditions.[29]

This idea is born out by other evidence in the plastic arts and to a lesser extent in literary sources. Some forms of Andalusī literary culture in the thirteenth and fourteenth centuries demonstrate the kind of assimilation described by Ibn Khaldūn. Granadan author al-Azdī's "*Maqāma* of the Fair" begins to converge stylistically with works by authors writing in Castilian and French,[30] and Cynthia Robinson has described the thirteenth-century Andalusī narrative *Hadith Bayad wa-Riyad* as a kind of Andalusī *roman idyllique*.[31] This trend extends to the plastic arts and architecture; chivalric themes from the Arthurian imaginary even penetrated the Alhambra itself, as Cynthia Robinson demonstrates in her study of the ceilings of the Hall of Justice.[32] That this exchange of Arthurian themes and chivalric sensibilities should pass from France to Castile to Granada in the thirteenth century supports Ibn Khaldūn's assertion that the Granadans of his day were assimilated, to some extent, to the culture of the Christian North.[33] The Hebrew literature of the time likewise begins to assimilate techniques and habits of thought from vernacular Romance literary practice, with authors such

on the basis that the "deification of Jesus ... postulates the existence of a a second God." Behloul 2013, 475.

29. Ibn Khaldūn 1978, 116.

30. Wacks 2007, 186 n 84.

31. Robinson 2007, 172–182.

32. Robinson 2008.

33. At the same time "Ziyād" also represents practices, such as kissing the stirrup of a superior, that are well documented in the Arab world in both historical and literary representations. Fernández y González 1882, 7, 19, 29, 31. The practice is also amply attested in *Sīrat ʿAntar*. Hamilton 1819, 35, 121, 125, 280. On the practice of kissing the stirrup, see Qurashī 2013, 243; Sanders 1994, 20.

as Judah al-Ḥarīzī and Jacob ben Eleazar (both thirteenth century, Toledo) blending Andalusī and vernacular Romance literary materials and styles in their work.[34]

These borrowings and transformations of literary styles and modes of representation take place in a specific political and ideological context. The Arabic *sīra* tells the story of the Islamic expansion and the growth of the *ʿUmmah* that is meant to justify the political order of the Islamic societies of the ninth century that produced them, not faithfully reproduce events of the seventh century. They cannot be taken as historically accurate or objective accounts of events.[35] Neither can we read French crusade chronicles and epic songs as empirically correct accounts; their authors quite openly sought to justify the current political order and root this justification in (their own personal flavor of) revelation.[36]

Part of the role of fiction – and we may include medieval chronicles and epic in this category, inasmuch as they lack the type of empiric objectivity to which modern historiography would pretend – is to narrate the fears and desires of a society. Someone (it might have been V. I. Lenin or Bertolt Brecht, though the attribution is contested) famously observed that "art is not a mirror held up to reflect reality, but a hammer with which to shape it." As an art form, narrative fiction does both: it reflects the material, social, and ideological realities of the communities it serves, and also serves to shape them by putting ideological and political goals in service to the emotional cathexis generated by the stories narrated.[37] Narrative tells truths that did not necessarily happen, but that we still hold to be true. For many medieval Andalusī, French, and Spanish readers, narrative genres that today would have to pass empirical litmus tests were judged by different standards, by their capacity to communicate values or bear witness to events as they were *believed* to have happened, for reasons that resonated with the values of the community, even if they would come to be at odds with the empirical assessments of modern historians.[38]

34. On the influence of Romance literature on medieval Sephardic authors, see, for example, Schirmann 1962, 295; Schirmann 1949, 177; Wacks 2010.

35. In a similar vien, Boaz Shoshan describes traditional Arabic historiographical texts as "a reflection of the state of mind and agenda of their creators and transmitters, and a response to the interests of the milieu of their consumers" (2015, 6).

36. Querol Sanz 2000, 21.

37. This is not the place for a full accounting of the nature of fictionality, or even for a proper discussion of the political uses of fictional narratives. However, we can agree with Walsh that it is helpful to understand fiction as a rhetorical device that is more poetic than empiric, and that expresses truths that may not correspond to events as they actually occurred. See, for example, Richard Walsh 1992, 14; Cohn 1999, 788; White 1987, 10–28; Agapitos and Mortensen 2012, 18.

38. Mehtonen 1996, 89; Green 2002, 28.

In the case of "Ziyād ibn ʿĀmir al-Kinānī," the author borrows literary forms associated with two different ideological positions and adapts them to serve his own: the *sīra* narrates the triumph of Islam in the region, while the crusader narrative (whether chronicle or epic song, or some mix of the two) narrates the triumph of Christianity. How can a narrative serve two masters? It does not have to. What the author of "Ziyād" takes from the crusader narrative is not a specific ideological position such as the *Chanson de Roland*'s famous "Christians are right! Pagans are wrong!"[39] but rather a mode of representation, and certain heroic and aesthetic values that gained a measure of prestige in Granada due to the geopolitics of the region. Christian Iberian elites were avid consumers of Andalusī science, military technology, and architectural style. Once Castile had subordinated Granada politically, influence also flowed in the other direction. Ziyād's "crusaderness" (and by this I mean the measure in which he acts, talks, and *feels* like a crusader from a French or Castilian narrative), is an aesthetic choice, but not an ideological statement. It is a form of acculturation, one that is put in the service of a literary vision of Islamic triumphalism very much politically at odds with the crusading culture it seeks to emulate. To us Ziyād as a Muslim crusader seems a paradox, or at best highly ironic. But to our author and thirteenth-century audiences it was likely a fashionable representation of a hero of Islam, who righted wrongs and brought the erring pagan into the House of Islam, for his own good. If Christian writers fantasized of repeating the success of the First Crusade, or later, the restoration of a Christian Constantinople, we should not wonder that Granadans might fantasize about converting infidels en masse, like the heroes of the stories so popular with the region's dominant élites.

Pagans and Saracens

Islamic tradition regarded the region's pagans as *mushrikūn*, or idolators who did not form part of the *ʿAhl al-kitāb*, the People of the Book, and whose beliefs were not to be tolerated. The Qurʾan makes specific mention of the cults of Allāt and Al ʿUzzā. Among the Arabs of Central Arabia, Allāt was the solar goddess, patroness of the Thāqif tribe, whose sanctuary was at Tāʾif. Al-ʿUzzā was associated with Venus and was the patroness of Muḥammad's tribe, Quraysh.[40]

39. Tolan 2002, 105; Kinoshita 2006, 15.

40. Her shrine was in Hourad on the road from Mecca to Baghdad. Ryckmans 1951, 15. The ninth-century writer Abū-l-Mundhir Hishām ibn Muḥāmmad ibn al-Sāʾib ibn Bishr al-Kalbī (d. 206/821–822) of Kufa cataloged a series of references to Allāt and al-ʿUzzā from the pre-Islamic poets. Ibn al-Kalbī 1952, 15–29. In North Arabia, the cult of Atarsamain was associated with Allāt, who under Hellenistic influence was the avatar of either Venus, or according to Herodo-

Later sources mention groups that worship stars, fire, and various other cults with which Islam came into contact, particularly in Persia, the Balkans, and what is today Hungary. However, the Arabic epics and other traditions upon which the author of "Ziyād" draws spend little time on paganism, and are more concerned with conflicts between Muslim factions or with the region's Christians and Jews. Ziyād's mass conversion of the defeated pagans is therefore far more characteristic of medieval Christian literature than it is in Arabic narratives by Muslim authors, who frame the *jihad* of the crusader period as a defensive war. Nonetheless, Muslim propagandists responded (if not directly) to Christian crusade chroniclers in kind, lionizing leaders such as the Mamluk Sultan Baybars, hero of the eponymous *sīra*, as mighty champions of *jihad* against the infidel Frankish invaders.[41]

Medieval Christian sources (especially chronicles of the First Crusade, written before the crusaders had an opportunity to get to know Islam up close and personal as they did once they settled in the Levant) often represented Islam as a pagan religion and its adherents as pagans.[42] This was rooted in Western Latin Christians' identification with early Roman Christians vis-à-vis the pagan Roman state (this is of course referring to the period before Constantine's conversion). Medieval Christians likened themselves to the (good) apostles, while their (bad) Muslim counterparts played the (bad) Romans. By this logic, they represented Muslims as pagans who prayed to statues of Muḥammad.[43] The converse was also true: Christian sources referred to idols by "the name of Muḥammad in various corrupted forms (Mahomet, Mahon, Mahoum, Mawmet)."[44]

Conversions of Saracens, especially women in twelfth-century French chansons de gestes, represent the desire to manage and control the Muslim other in the context of Christian society. Sharon Kinoshita has written on the *Prise d'Orange*, a twelfth-century chanson de geste narrating Guillaume of Nîmes' conquest of the city of Orange and his seduction and conversion of the Saracen queen of Orange, Orable. According to Kinoshita, the mapping of the political struggle between Christian and Muslim polities onto the seduction of the Muslim Orable by the Christian Guillaume lends the erotic story a special charge that "makes standard tales of courtly love seem like

---

tus, Aphrodite Urania (the Phoenician Astarte). The people of Edessa (today Syria) worshipped the morning star, Venus, as a female personification of Mars. Teixidor 1977, 68–69; Hawting 1999, 130.

41. Hillenbrand 2000, 255–259.

42. On later crusaders' intimate familiarity with Islam and Eastern culture, see Kinoshita 2011.

43. Tolan 2002, 109–112.

44. Tolan 2002, 127.

stylized, depoliticized repetitions."[45] It is also noteworthy that Guillaume's interest in Orable is not exoticizing; he is attracted by her superlative beauty and character, and Orable is described in precisely the same terms as any French beauty of the times, with pale skin and fair hair. Her otherness is not physical, but rather religious, linguistic, and cultural.[46]

The Iberian imagination took a slightly different approach to converting the Saracen enemy that reflected (up to a certain point) local policies and practices. While French jurisprudence tended to restrict the rights of Muslim spouses of Christians and their offspring, Alfonso X's *Siete partidas* (II.29.7) expressly grants rights of inheritance to children of a Christian knight who, while held captive in al-Andalus, has children by a Muslim woman.[47] The mid-twelfth-century *Siège de Barbastre* features a Muslim woman who seeks conversion and marriage to the Christian hero.[48] We can read her as an allegory for the Christian desire to conquer and dominate the East (or in this case, al-Andalus). Later thirteenth-century narratives such as *Floire et Blancheflor* and *Aucassin and Nicolette* reflect Christian disillusionment with the failing crusader movement. Their depictions of the far-flung journeys of their Christian-Muslim protagonists are wish fulfillment and confusion over the role of interreligous contact in Christian society.[49]

Conversion of Pagans in "Ziyād"

While the majority of Ziyād's enemies and conquests are ostensibly Muslim, his final conquest is of the kingdom of a villainous astrologer-king who is a pagan. Once Ziyād's wife, Khāṭifat al-Ḥurr, comes to her husband's aid to defeat the pagan ruler, the astrologer-king accepts Islam along with the fealty he now owes to Ziyād. Here the pagan king is a curious mix of Islamic traditions about star-worshipping pagans and literary pagan astrologers drawn from the pages of French and Castilian literature. When he faces Ziyād, he makes the following speech:

> I have learned that you are Ziyād ibn ʿĀmir al-Kinānī. I am an astrologer, who has been waiting a full year for you in this place.

45. Kinoshita 2006, 48.

46. Kinoshita 2006, 53–54.

47. Ramey 2001, 58–59.

48. Ramey 2001, 56–58. In the *Siete Infantes de Lara* there is also the case of Garcia Gómez's marriage to the sister of Almanzor while he is in captivity in Cordoba, though she does not convert to Christianity. Their son Mudarra eventually does so after going on a "roots trip" to find his Christian father in Castile. Menéndez Pidal 1934, 220–221, 262; Mirrer 1996, 17–18; Barton 2015, 139–41.

49. Ramey 2001, 5.

> Know that I am an astrologer, [*rajul munajjim*], who has been waiting for you here, scheming against you, until the moment arrived to get my hands on you. Now I swear to you by the Goddesses Allāt and al-ʿUzzā, as well as by all mighty idols, by fire, and by the Tree of Colors [*shajarat al-alwān*], that I will make an example of you that will become proverbial among the tribes of the Arabs.[50]

Here the king claims to be a worshipper of the pre-Islamic goddesses Allāt and al-ʿUzzā. He also swears by "fire," a reference to Islamic authors' traditions about the cult of fire in Persia, the Balkans, and among the Magyars in the early period of Islam, and by the "Tree of Colors."[51]

The pagan astrologer king is a very curious figure in this context, and therefore bears a bit of discussion of perceptions of astrology and astrologers in Arabic and Western Latin tradition. Astrology (or astronomy, for in the thirteenth century there was as yet no hard and fast distinction made between the disciplines) is not typically identified with villainy in Islamic sources. In popular Arabic literature, astrologer is synonymous with wise man, or man of the court. Numerous references to astrologers in the *1001 Nights*, for example, support this idea.[52] In fact, astrologer seems to be a kind of shorthand for "wise man."[53] However, a star-worshipper, one who *worships* stars and planets, rather than God, as opposed to the astrologer who *studies* them, certainly falls into the category of *mushrik*, or idolator, and is worthy of opprobrium in an Islamic context. In short, Islamic society in general did not view astrology or its practitioners in a negative light–in fact, they were considered scientists and were valued members of court elites. Nonetheless, certain forms of astrology that attributed natural events and/or human behavior to the influence of stars, or straight-out star *worship*, was problematic, and viewed as a form of idolatry going back to the cults of Allāt and al-ʿUzzā in the Qurʾan.

50. Al-Shenawi 2009, 105; Fernández y González 1882, 34.

51. The "Tree of Colors" is possibly a reference to the "Lote Tree" mentioned in the Qurʾan (53:16)a described in a *hadith* as being "shrouded in colors." Also, early Muslims believed that pagan Arabs worshipped the goddess al-ʿUzzā (Qurʾan 53:19) in the form of a tree. According to the tradition recorded by Ibn al-Kalbī in his *Kitāb al-Asnam* (*Book of Idols*), Muḥammad ordered Khālid ibn Walīd to destroy the trees thought to be inhabited by al-ʿUzzā. Peters 1994, 237.

52. El-Shamy 2006, 165, 187, 253, 462.

53. Astrology in medieval Islam was a well-regarded discipline, whose practitioners were courtiers, physicians, political advisors, and the like, whose advice was often taking into account in making difficult political decisions (Saliba 1992). In Hawting's study on idolatry in early Islam there is not a single mention of astrology, which suggests that the association of astrology with idolatry and more generally with evil is a later, and probably Christian, development (Hawting 1999).

Christian views of astrology were more mixed. While some forms of astrology were licit, others were viewed as heretical and dangerous.[54] In 1277, Bishop Steven Tempier of Paris condemned a number of Aristotelian teachings connected to astrology as heretical.[55] During the same period, Alfonso X of Castile-León took a more nuanced (and perhaps charitable) stance in the *Siete Partidas*. According to him, as one of the seven liberal arts, astronomy

> is respectable only so long as a recognized scholar studies and practices it; unauthorized persons should avoid it. The other type is that which seers and sorcerers practice. The law contends that they are harmful and deceitful men and are therefore prohibited from residing within the jurisdiction of the law.[56]

Fiction contemporary with the First and Second Crusades exploited the reputation of astrology as a potentially dangerous art by representing Saracen/pagan villains as astrologers, particularly those who are not available for seduction and/or conversion by the Christian protagonist. In French romances, pagan characters are sometimes depicted as astrologers, reflecting at once historical awareness of the status of astrology as a legitimate discipline in the Islamic world and a questionable one in Western Latin Christendom. Some are "good" Saracens (usually women or girls) who come to the aid of the Christian hero, and others (usually older men) are villains. These astrologers are bad not because they are astrologers, but because they are not Christians. One example that is instructive for the astrologer-king in "Ziyād" is the twelfth-century romance *Floovent*, about a war between Christians and Muslims, whose villain is "an old pagan doctor, Jacob, [who possesses] the power of prophecy by reason of his astrological knowledge."[57]

Iberian sources, notwithstanding Alfonso's approval of (certain forms of) astrology, follow this same line. The eponymous hero of the *Poema de Fernán González* claims that

> The Muslims, as you well know, are guided by the stars, not by God, but by the stars, which they have made into another, new Creator. By their power the Muslims see marvels. [58]

54. Tester 1987, 125.

55. Tester 1987, 177.

56. *Partida* VII, Title XXIII, Law I. Alfonso X 1844, 4:335–336; Corry 2005, 82.

57. Wedel 1968, 100–101. Compare with Midrashic (Jewish narrative exegesis) traditions of Abraham as astrologer (Jacobs 1995, 86–88); keeping in mind that *Genesis Rabbah* (a canonical source of Midrash) also depicts God reminding Abraham: "thou art a prophet, not an astrologer" (44:12), ostensibly to distinguish him from his fellow Mesopotamians, who are associated with astrology in Jewish tradition.

58. "Los moros, bien sabedes, que s'guían por estrellas,/ non se guían por Dios, que se

This condemnation of astrology as a form of star-worship coincides (at least in principle) with Islamic bans on star-worship cults of the Arabian region. Elsewhere, Muslim astrologers appear as skilled diviners and counselors, but not as diabolical heretics or sorcerers, such as in the *Gran Conquista de Ultramar*, in which the Muslim Queen Halabra "began to watch the stars and cast lots, because she wished to tell the future."[59] The further we get from the Alfonsine moment, when Christians were still under the spell of a far superior Andalusī astrology (as evidenced by Alfonso's translation of al-Zarkalī's *Tables*), the more strident Christian estimations of astrology become. By the fourteenth century, Pero López de Ayala condemns astrology most forcefully among medieval Hispanic authors in the *Rimado de Palacio*, where he equates it with paganism.[60] The *Ordenanzas Reales de Castilla* promulgated by Juan I in 1386 specifically and in no uncertain terms forbid the practice of astrology.[61]

What all of this means is that the author of "Ziyād" took pains to heed the legacy of Arab epic with respect to religious values (the hero is a good Muslim, the villain is a *mushrik* or idolater), but writes in a sort of modified romance-mode. The evil astrologer pagan king is taken right from the pages of a French romance, but where in the French romance the evil pagan king would be Muslim, here his idolatry is likely a code for Christianity, given the then-current idea among Muslim intellectuals that Christians were, technically, idol worshippers.[62]

The image of Ziyād ibn ʿĀmir as a vanquisher of pagan astrologers and hero of mass conversion owes at least as much to Arthurian chivalric literature and its projections in the literature of the Crusades as it does to the Arabic *siyar* and popular Arabic narratives such as the *1001* or *101* nights. It provides us with a window into the cultural imaginary of thirteenth-century Granada, at once the last redoubt of Islamic polity on the Iberian Peninsula as well as a cultural crossroads where forms popular in the Christian North as well as in the Arab Muslim world came together under the influence of Christian dominance and Granadan acculturation. The result is the Muslim crusader Ziyād ibn ʿĀmir al-Kinānī.

---

guían por ellas,/ otro Criador nuevo han fecho ellos dellas,/ diz que por ellas veen muchas de maravellas." Martínez 1991, 128, st. 477–478; Corry 2005, 148.

59. "... començo mirar las estrellas e echar suertes, porque pensava adevinar las cosas que havía de venir." Cooper 1989, 1:323, cited in Corry 2005, 152.

60. Corry 2005, 163.

61. San Martín 1872, 515–516; Corry 2005, 222 n 68. On the critique of astrology in the Crown of Aragon see Ryan 2011, 55–79.

62. See note 28 above.

Bibliography

Agapitos, Panagiotis A, and Lars Boje Mortensen. 2012. Introduction to *Medieval Narratives between History and Fiction: From the Centre to the Periphery of Europe, c. 1100–1400*, edited by Panagiotis A. Agapitos and Lars Boje Mortensen, 1–24. Copenhagen.

Alfonso X. 1844. *Las siete partidas*, edited by Gregorio López. vol. 4. Barcelona.

Barton, Simon. 2015. *Conquerors, Brides, and Concubines: Interfaith Relations and Social Power in Medieval Iberia*. Philadelphia.

Behloul, Samuel. 2013. "Ibn Hazm's Refutation of Christianity." In *Ibn Hazm of Cordoba: The Life and Works of a Controversial Thinker*, edited by Camila Adang, Maribel Fierro, and Sabine Schmidtke, 457–483. Leiden.

Brownlee Scordilis, Marina. 2000. "Romance at the Crossroads: Medieval Spanish Paradigms and Cervantine Revisions." In *The Cambridge Companion to Medieval Romance*, edited by Marina Scordilis Brownlee and Kevin Brownlee, 253–266. Cambridge.

Buturovic, Amila. 2000. "Ibn Quzman." In *The Literature of Al-Andalus*, edited by María Rosa Menocal, Raymond P. Scheindlin, and Michael Sells, 292–305. Cambridge.

Cohn, Dorrit. 1999. *The Distinction of Fiction*. Baltimore.

Cooper, Louis, ed. 1989. *La Gran Conquista de Ultramar: Biblioteca Nacional MS 1187*. Madison, WI.

Corry, Jennifer M. 2005. *Perceptions of Magic in Medieval Spanish Literature*. Bethlehem, PA.

El-Shamy, Hasan M. 2006. *A Motif Index of* The Thousand and One Nights. Bloomington.

Fernández y González, Francisco, trans. 1882. *Zeyyad ben Amir el de Quinena*. Madrid.

Fuchs, Barbara. 2004. *Romance*. New York.

Fudge, Bruce, ed. and trans. 2016. *A Hundred and One Nights*. New York.

Galmés de Fuentes, Alvaro. 1975. *El Libro de Las Batallas: Narraciones épico-Caballerescas*. Madrid.

——. 1978. *Épica árabe y épica castellana*. Barcelona.

González Ferrín, Emilio. 2016. *Historia general de al-Andalus*. 4th ed. Cordova.

González Palencia, Ángel. 1945. *Historia de la literatura arábigoespañola*. Barcelona.

Green, D.H. 2002. *The Beginnings of Medieval Romance: Fact and Fiction, 1150–1220*. Cambridge.

Hamilton, Terrick, trans. 1819. *Antar: A Bedoueen Romance*. London.

Hawting, G. R. 1999. *Cambridge Studies in Islamic Civilization: The Idea of Idolatry and the Emergence of Islam: From Polemic to History*. Cambridge.
Heath, Peter. 1996. *The Thirsty Sword:* Sirat Antar *and the Arabic Popular Epic*. Salt Lake City.
——. 2006. "Other Sīras and Popular Narratives." In *Arabic Literature in the Post-Classical Period*, edited by Roger Allen and D.S. Richards, 319–329. Cambridge.
Hillenbrand, Carole. 2000. *The Crusades: Islamic Perspectives*. Oxford.
Ibn al-Kalbī. 1952. *The Book of Idols, Being a Translation from the Arabic of the* Kitāb Al-Asnām. Translated by Nabih Amin Faris. Princeton.
Ibn Khaldun, Abu Zayd Abd al-Rahman. 1978. *The Muqaddimah: An Introduction to History*. Translated by Franz Rosenthal. London.
Jacobs, Irving. 1995. *The Midrashic Process: Tradition and Interpretation in Rabbinic Judaism*. Cambridge.
Jones, Alan. 2016. "Ayyām Al-ʿArab." In *EI3*, edited by Kate Fleet, Gudrun Krämer, Denis Matringe, John Nawas, and Everett Rowson Leiden. http://dx.doi.org.ezp1.lib.umn.edu/10.1163/1573-3912_ei3_SIM_0259
Justel Calabozo, Braulio. 1981. *Catalogación del fondo complementario de códices árabes de la real biblioteca de El Escorial*. Madrid.
Kinoshita, Sharon. 2006. *Medieval Boundaries: Rethinking Difference in Old French Literature*. Philadelphia.
——. 2011. "Crusades and Identity." In *The Cambridge History of French Literature*, edited by William Burgwinkle, Nicholas Hammond, and Emma Wilson,93–101. Cambridge.
Kruk, Remke. 2006. "Sirat ʿAntar Ibn Shaddad." In *Arabic Literature in the Post-Classical Period*, edited by Roger Allen and D. S. Richards, 292–306. Cambridge.
Ladero Quesada, Miguel Ángel. 1989. *Granada: Historia de un país islámico (1232–1571)*. 3rd ed. Madrid.
Lapiedra Gutiérrez, Eva. 1997. *Cómo los musulmanes llamaban a los cristianos hispánicos*. Alicante.
López-Morillas, Consuelo. 2000. "Language." In *The Literature of Al-Andalus*, edited by María Rosa Menocal, Raymond P. Scheindlin, and Michael Sells, 33–59. Cambridge.
Martínez, H. Salvador, ed. 1991. *Poema de Fernán González*. Madrid.
Mehtonen, Päivi. 1996. *Old Concepts and New Poetics: Historia, Argumentum and Fabula in the Twelfth- and Early Thirteenth-Century Latin Poetics of Fiction*. Helsinki.
Menéndez Pelayo, Marcelino. 2008. *Orígenes de la Novela*. 2 vols. Madrid.
Menéndez Pidal, Ramón. 1934. *La Leyenda de Los Infantes de Lara*. Madrid.

Mirrer, Louise. 1996. *Women, Jews, and Muslims in the Texts of Reconquest Castile*. Ann Arbor.

Mittwoch, E. 2002. "Ayyām al-ʿArab." In *EI2*, edited by P. Bearman et al. Leiden. http://dx.doi.org/10.1163/1573-3912_islam_SIM_0926.

Monroe, James T. 1990. "Ibn Quzman on *Iʾrāb*: A *zéjel de Juglaría* in Arab Spain?" In *Hispanic Studies in Honor of Joseph H. Silverman*, edited by Joseph Ricapito, 45–56. Newark, DE.

Ott, Claudia. 2012. "Nachwort." In *101 Nacht*, edited by Claudia Ott, 241–263. Zurich.

Peters, F. E. 1994. *Muhammad and the Origins of Islam*. Albany.

Querol Sanz, José Manuel. 2000. *Cruzadas y literatura: El caballero del cisne y la leyenda genealógica de Godofredo de Bouillon: estudio de literatura comparada*. Madrid.

Qurashī, Idrīs ʻImād al-Dīn. 2013. *The Founder of Cairo: The Fatimid Imam-Caliph Al-Muʿizz and His Era*. London.

Ramey, Lynn Tarte. 2001. *Christian, Saracen, and Genre in Medieval French Literature*. New York.

Ramírez del Río, José. 2002. *La orientalización de al-Andalus:* Los días de los árabes *en la Península Ibérica*. Sevilla.

——. 2003. "Notas acerca de un texto épico andalusí." *Anaquel de Estudios Árabes* 14:219–230.

——. 2014. "Documentos sobre el papel de los árabes hilālíes en el al-Andalus almohade: traducción y análisis." *Al-Qanṭara* 35, no. 2:359–396.

Reynolds, Dwight. 2006a. "Popular Prose in the Post-Classical Period." In *Arabic Literature in the Post-Classical Period*, edited by Roger Allen and D. S. Richards, 243–269. Cambridge.

——. 2006b. "*Sīrat Banī Hilāl*." In *Arabic Literature in the Post-Classical Period*, edited by Roger Allen and D. S. Richards, 307–318. Cambridge.

Ribera, Julián. 1928. "Épica andaluza romanceada." In *Disertaciones y opúsculos*, 1:93–150. Madrid.

Robinson, Cynthia. 2007. *Medieval Andalusian Courtly Culture in the Mediterranean:* Hadith Bayad Wa-Riyad. London.

Rodilla León, María José. 2009. "Troya, Roma, y Constantinopla en *El Claribalte*." In *Amadís y sus libros: 500 años*, edited by Aurelio González and Axayácatl Campos García Rojas, 303–311. Mexico City.

Ryan, Michael A. 2011. *A Kingdom of Stargazers: Astrology and Authority in the Late Medieval Crown of Aragon*. Ithaca.

Ryckmans, Gonzague. 1951. *Les religions arabes préislamiques*. 2nd ed. Louvain.

Saliba, George. 1992. "The Role of the Astrologer in Medieval Islamic Society." *Bulletin d'Études Orientales* 44:45–67.

Sallis, Eva. 1999. *Sheherazade through the Looking Glass: The Metamorphosis of the* Thousand and One Nights. Richmond, Surrey.
Sanders, Paula. 1994. *Ritual, Politics, and the City in Fatimid Cairo.* Albany, NY.
San Martín, Antonio de, ed. 1872. *Ordenzanzas Reales de Castilla.* Madrid.
Schirmann, Hayim. 1949. "Isaac Gorni, Poète Hébreu de Provence." *Lettres Romanes* 3:175–200.
——. 1962. "Les contes rimées de Jacob ben Eleazar de Toledo." In *Études d'orientalisme dédiées a la mémoire de Lévi-Provençal*, 285–297. Paris.
Serrano Ruano, Delfina. 2012. "Ibn Al-Idhari Al-Marrakhushi." In *Christian-Muslim Relations: A Bibliographical History, Volume 4, (1200–1350)*, edited by David Thomas, Alexander Mallett, and Juan Pedro Monferrer Sal, 737–742. Leiden,
al-Shenawi, Ali al-Gharib Muhammad, ed. 2009. *Kitāb fīhī hadīth Ziyād ibn ʿĀmir al-Kinānī.* Cairo.
Shoshan, Boaz. 2015. *The Arabic Historical Tradition & the Early Islamic Conquests: Folklore, Tribal Lore, Holy War.* London.
Teixidor, Javier. 1977. *The Pagan God: Popular Religion in the Greco-Roman Near East.* Princeton.
Tester, S. J. 1987. *A History of Western Astrology.* Woodbridge, Suffolk.
Tolan, John Victor. 2002. *Saracens: Islam in the Medieval European Imagination.* New York.
Viguera Molins, María Jesús. 2000. *El reino nazarí de granada (1232–1492): Política, instituciones, espacio y economía.* Madrid.
Wacks, David A. 2007. *Framing Iberia: Maqamat and Frametale Narratives in Medieval Spain.* Leiden.
——. 2010. "Toward a History of Hispano-Hebrew Literature of Christian Iberia in the Romance Context." *eHumanista* 14:178–209.
Walsh, John K. 1992. *Relic and Literature: St Toribius of Astorga and His* Arca Sancta. St. Albans.
Walsh, Richard. 2007. *The Rhetoric of Fictionality: Narrative Theory and the Idea of Fiction.* Columbus, OH.
Wedel, Theodore O. 1968. *The Mediaeval Attitude Toward Astrology.* Hamden.
White, Hayden. 1987. *The Content of the Form: Narrative Discourse and Historical Representation.* Baltimore.

The Expulsion of the Andalusīs in Arab Memory, 1609/1614–2014[1]

Nabil Matar
University of Minnesota, Twin Cities

THE EXPULSION OF THE ANDALUSĪS, those who were derisively called Moriscos or "little Moors," from Spain between 1609 and 1614 was widely recalled in Arabic writings in the seventeenth and eighteenth centuries.[2] In the nineteenth and early twentieth century, the expulsion was forgotten, but from 1948 on, the earlier 1492 expulsion was conflated with the 1609 one, and since 2009 there has been a resurgence in memory and nostalgia across all of the Arabic-speaking world, from Casablanca to Doha and from Tunis to Kuwait. Although al-Andalus and its literary, religious, and musical history continue to inspire Arab writings and scholarship, ranging from celebrations of the glorious past and its *convivencia* to Andalusī influences on the contemporary Arab imagination,[3] the language about the expulsions has changed dramatically from the seventeenth century to the twenty-first century, marking a shift from faith-inspired acceptance to activist nationalism.[4] This essay will examine the 1609–1614 expulsion in Arabic sources and show how the language used to describe the expulsion reflects transformations in ideology.

Even before the 1609 expulsion, while fears were growing and persecution increasing, the Andalusīs had queried jurists in the Arabic-speaking world from the four Sunni schools about the legitimacy or illegitimacy of

1. I am grateful to Professor Mohammad Asfour for his help and comments.

2. The vast majority of European and Arab historians use the term Moriscos. But it is important to note the angry observation made by Professor Jaʿfar ibn al-Hajj Sulamī at the second conference held in Shafshāwan in 1997 on the Moriscos when he asserted: I am a Moroccan of Andalusian ancestry who has "never forgotten the *hijra* and its tribulations." The derogatory term "Moriscos," he emphasized, was never used in any Arabic text in the early modern period (Sulamī 2000, 255). For a study of the Spanish terms used for the expulsion, see Martinez 1999, 193–207.

3. See, for instance, the essays in Doubleday and Coleman 2008; and the studies by Hirschkind 2014 and Shannon 2016.

4. For a short history of the 1609 expulsion, see Harvey 2005, ch. 9. Although García Arenal and Wiegers (2014) studied the expulsion extensively, they did not include the Arabic history.

hijra from the Christian-dominated al-Andalus.[5] The word *hijra* was deliberately used to recall the emigration of the Prophet Muhammad in 622 CE from the Mecca of infidelity to the Yathrib of Islam. In the Qur'an, the association between *īmān* and *hijra*, belief and emigration, is frequently repeated: *āmanū wa hājarū* (they believed and they emigrated). The reply to the query came: only the Hanbalite *fatwa* urged *hijra*, while the other three schools did not. But as Spanish Catholicism forcibly changed the cultural and religious life of the Andalusīs in the course of the sixteenth century, those who did not emigrate began to invent a history of their past to sustain them in their *takhalluf ʿan al-hijra* (deferment of emigration). They composed stories of resistant faith under the leadership of ʿAlī ibn Abī Ṭālib – ʿAli having been the one who had stayed behind in Mecca to facilitate the *hijra* of Muḥammad.[6]

The first description of the reception of the Andalusīs in North Africa appears in a book by al-Muntaṣir ibn al-Murābiṭ Abī Liḥya al-Qafṣī (1551–1622), *Nūr al-Armāsh*, about the Tunisian Sufi leader, Abū al-Ghayth al-Qashshāsh. The author describes the Andalusīs after their arrival in Tunis: for him they were fellow Muslims, emigrating from infidelity: *muhājirūn.* He first saw them near the Zaytouna Mosque after they had received a letter from Sīdī Abū al-Ghayth.[7] They had not been able to read it because they could not read Arabic, only *rūmī* (non-Arabic). Sīdī Abū al-Ghayth had welcomed them to the homes of his father and of his teacher, and he had praised them, having become close friends with one of their elders, Muḥammad ibnʿAbd al-Rafīʿ ibn Muḥammad al-Andalusī, who had fled to Tunis ca. 1596. "You make the earth blossom wherever you go," Abū al-Ghayth addressed them; "you are like rain to the soil." Al-Qafṣī continued by describing how crowded the streets and markets and mosques and stores were with them, and how often they went to Abū al-Ghayth because he distributed bread and couscous, some carob for their animals, and two head of cattle per day.

Abū al-Ghayth was sympathetic to the Andalusīs and so was al-Qafṣī, although with the latter there is an element of confusion and uncertainty. Al-Qafṣī wrote how he dreamt he was standing at the entrance to a mosque in Qafṣa and saw

> three [of them] come out of the *ḥammām* and walk in the direction of the mosque entrance. They had spurs on their feet and as I looked and wondered at them, I soon realized that they were men and dressed in the clothes of men, each in a white caftan, a woolen coat, and a white turban on his head. At first I thought them *murābiṭs* (frontier warriors) from among *al-awliyā'* (holy men), and so I drew near them

5. Van Koningsveld and Wiegers 1996, 133–152.
6. See the translations from *aljamiado* in Faḍl 1989.
7. For an extended study of Andalusīs in Tunisia, see Latham 1957, 203–252.

> and kissed their hands....Then I asked, "By God almighty, who are you?" They said: "We are Andalusīs from our city Granada." I said: "By God, what are your names?" They said: "We will write you our names but we speak only *rūmī*." ... "And where are you going?" They said: "We came to visit." ... They stood at the entrance of the mosque and stretched their hands, and then we all read the *fātiḥa* (the opening chapter of the Qurʾan) together. And then they continued to visit holy sites until they reached Sīdī ʿAlī al-Zartī. I told them to enter and visit him, but they answered: "You visit on your own and we visit on our own. For we are not like you and you are not like us." [8]

While some North Africans like al-Qafsī welcomed the Andalusīs, others calumniated them because the exiles appeared to know less Arabic than Spanish, less of the Qurʾan than of the Bible: after a century of deculturalization, they had lost their Islamic past. It may be because of local opposition to the exiles that Ottoman Sultan Aḥmet I sent a *firman* (royal decree) to the Tunisian bey urging the acceptance of the Andalusīs in the regency. Interestingly, there is no mention of expulsion in the *firman*; it might have been too humiliating to state that Muslims had been defeated. And so the *firman* only states that some people belonging to *ahl al-Islām* (people of Islam) had reached Tunis, God having saved them from the hands of the *mushrikīn* (polytheists) and helped them to *diyār al-Islām* (the lands of Islam).[9] Perhaps encouraged by the *firman*, the new arrivals began to defend themselves against accusations that they were crypto-Christians, and so the above-mentioned al-Andalusī in his *al-Anwār al-nabawiyya fī ābāʾ khayr al-bariyya* recalled how their grandfathers had appealed to the kings of Islam for help, but none had come forth.[10] The enemies of God imposed restrictions on those who remained in their land, he continued, prohibiting the Islamic dress, baths, and Sūfī circles. Those who disobeyed were burned.

After this litany of horrors, however, al-Andalusī asserted how strongly "Arab" the Andalusīs remained, recalling the *ḥadīth* of the Prophet (recorded by ʿAlī) that "only the hypocrite derides the Arabs."[11] He then turned to celebrate the expulsion and joyously announced that all that had happened to the Muslims had been divinely preordained: the expulsion was the fulfillment of God's will and a vindication of His power over the infidels; it was not a defeat but a victory since the Andalusīs had so tenaciously preserved

8. al-Qafṣī 1998, 499–500. See the French translation of this account in Pieri 1978, 128–135.

9. Temīmī 1993, 57–70.

10. The text was begun ca. 1019–1020 AH /c. 1610–1611 CE, finished in 1044/1635, and copied in 1049/1639. The author died in 1052/1642. See Matar 2008, 194–200.

11. See L. P. Harvey, who argues for a sense of Arabism/Arabicity among the emigrés (1985–86, 223–233).

their faith and so frightened the infidels that God had to intervene on their behalf by compelling the infidel kings to expel them to wherever they wanted to go in the lands of "victorious and celebrated Islam." The expulsion of *maʿshar al-Andalus* (the Andalusīs) was thus *luṭf ʿazīm wa raḥma ẓāhir,* (great bounty and evident mercy). How noble a *karāma* (miracle) it was, he added, and how beautiful that *niʿma* (grace of God), recalling the Qurʾanic verse: *wa mā bikum min niʿma fa-min Allah* (Whatever blessings you possess come from God) (Khalidi translation, 16:53). Writing in Tunis, which was under Ottoman rule, al-Andalusī praised the Ottomans and stated specifically that after the Ottoman sultan threatened the kings of France and Spain, they, in fear of his might, expelled the Muslims – thereby fulfilling God's plan for them. The expulsion of the Andalusīs, young and old, was one of the *muʿjizāt* (miracles of the Prophet), a *felix culpa*: out of the lands of infidelity and into the realm of Islam. It was a *fadīla ʿajība* (wondrous act of virtue) done to "our people of al-Andalus" (*fa yā lahā min uʿjūba*) he repeated, "What a wonder, and how great a virtue, and how honorable a magnanimity, and how beautiful a blessing" (*mā aʿzamahā wa min faḍīla [,] mā ashrafahā wā min karāma [,]mā ajmalahā wa min niʿma*).[12]

Such an interpretation appealed to Andalusīs trying to find answers from God, which is why the Grand Mosque in al-Alia includes an Andalusī inscription by earlier escapees/emigrés: it dates to 1607/08 and expresses gratitude to God for deliverance from *al-kufr* (infidelity).[13] Having emigrated before the expulsion, they presented themselves as having sought shelter from infidelity. Other Andalusīs, however, treated the expulsion as an act of exclusion and war and turned to maritime revenge. During his stay in Fez (until 1618), the Algerian-born chronicler of al-Andalus, Shihāb al-Dīn Aḥmad al-Maqarrī witnessed the arrival of the Andalusīs in Salé and their corsairing against their former countrymen. Later historians quoted his description of the Andalusī *mujāhidīn*: how "the sultan of Morocco recruited some of them into his army while those who settled in Salé dedicated their lives to maritime *jihād*, and they grew famous in defending Islam. They fortified Salé and built palaces and baths and houses. Some of them reached Istanbul and Egypt and Sham and other Islamic lands. This is the state of the Andalusīs now."[14] Importantly, and just like the author of *al-Anwār al-nabawiyya*, al-Maqarrī emphasized the mastery of Arabic (*ghayat al-balagha*) among

12. al-Turkī 1967, 23–82.

13. Gafsi Slama 1998, 487–507. See also the same view by an unknown Tunisian Morisco, quoted in Shāshiyya 2015, 1:243.

14. al-Maqarrī, *Nafḥ al-ṭīb*, 280.

the Andalusīs:[15] he wanted to confirm how much the Andalusīs were embedded in their Qurʾanic history. His description in the above lines about their *jihād* was brief in an otherwise massive history of al-Andalus: not untypical of Arab writers, there was little focus on suffering or humiliation,[16] and instead, al-Maqarrī praised the quick adaptation of the Andalusīs and their achievements. Perhaps because he was too close to events, he might not have been able to comprehend fully the meaning of the expulsion and therefore folded it in with the 1492 expulsion. That earlier expulsion, he wrote, had allowed the Andalusīs to preserve their religion with *ʿizz* (pride and glory), without humiliation;[17] for him, expulsion confirmed that Muslims had persevered in their faith and had preferred exile over capitulation.

The Andalusīs continued to defend themselves before the host populations, and they did so in Arabic, in documents as well as in inscriptions on fountains, gravesites, madrasas, and mosques. A school built in Tunis in 1625 celebrated the builders, "*jamāʿa min al-Andalus*" (community of Andalusīs), including "*naqīb shurafāʾ al-Andalūsiyyīn*" (the head of the Sharifean Andalusīs):[18] the use of the term *shurafāʾ* emphasized Arab descent since the term applied to descendants of the Prophet. A dedication to Usṭa Murad in 1644 included the name of the donor as *andalusī* (Andalusī), but *isbanyūl* (Spanish) is used about Murad himself.[19] The Andalusīs wrote to ensure acceptance and integration among their suspicious Muslim hosts. Sometime at the end of the 1630s, the Andalusī escapee Aḥmad ibn Qāsim translated from Spanish into Arabic a book about the use of artillery.[20] It had been written at the beginning of that decade by Aḥmad ibn Ghānim, an Andalusī who wanted to educate his fellow Muslims about Western war technology. Ibn Ghānim wrote (in Ibn Qāsim's translation) about the first expulsion, *al-khurūj al-awwal,* referring to 1571 after the 1568 failed rebellion and the subsequent *ikhrāj* (exodus) of the Andalusīs. The specific word *ikhrāj* recalled the Qurʾanic words:

15. al-Maqarrī, *Azhār al-riyāḍ*, 115. Arabic was also emphasized in the 1580s/90s *Libros Plúmbeos*, see Harvey 1985–86, 229.

16. Actually, there is more about the violence of the 1609 expulsion in contemporaneous English and Dutch Protestant anti-Catholic writings than in the Arabic sources: See Waite 2013, 95–123, and Matar 2009, 132–149.

17. al-Maqarrī, *Azhār al-riyāḍ*, 114. See the study by Chikha 1984, 171–180. By associating the Andalusīs with the *shurafāʾ*, the author confirmed their Arab ancestry through the Prophet Muḥammad.

18. Gafsi Slama 1988, 173.

19. There is another on the Grand Mosque of Zaytouna in Tunis, 1637; and on the gravestone of Yusuf Dey in Tunis, 1639: see Gafsi Slama 1998, 496.

20. Ibn Ghānim 1640, 87. See the study in James 1978, 237–257.

إِنَّمَا يَنْهَاكُمُ اللَّهُ عَنِ الَّذِينَ قَاتَلُوكُمْ فِي الدِّينِ وَأَخْرَجُوكُمْ مِنْ دِيَارِكُمْ وَظَاهَرُوا عَلَى إِخْرَاجِكُمْ أَنْ تَوَلَّوْهُمْ وَمَنْ يَتَوَلَّهُمْ فَأُولَئِكَ هُمُ الظَّالِمُونَ

> Allah forbiddeth you only those who warred against you on account of religion and have driven you out from your homes and helped to drive you out, that ye may make friends of them. Whoever maketh friends of them – (all) such are wrong doers. (Pickthall translation 60:9)

The Qurʾan enjoined believers never to befriend those who drove them out of their homes.

In another work consisting of his memoir of flight from Spain to Morocco at the end of the sixteenth century, but written in the early 1640s, Ibn Qāsim described the life of the Andalusīs in their homeland before the expulsion and was the first author to include a full Arabic translation from Spanish of the edict of expulsion. He explained to the prince of Orange during his mission to Holland in 1611 that Catholic Spain had large numbers of monastic orders and so few men were fathering children. As a result, the number of Andalusīs rose and caused alarm in the kingdom; Ibn Qāsim was the only writer who mentioned this demographic factor, seemingly adopting the Spanish imperial discourse. But, writing his memoir for co-religionists who had asked him for an account of his flight from al-Andalus and his experience of the Christians after his visits to France and Holland, he emphasized that the expulsion had brought *faraj* (relief) for the Muslims who were under "the despotism of the sultan of the land known as Philip III"; it was an emigration, a "*hijra* to God almighty" in which *laṭṭafa Allahu binā wa fakkanā minhum sālimīn* ("God showed kindness to us and manumitted us into safety"). But much as he admitted the presence of God's will in the expulsion, he did not want to mince words: he had witnessed the expulsion of 1609 when thousands arrived in Morocco, after being robbed and humiliated, to an irreversible exile. Writing after about two decades on the expulsion, he could not but repeat the other Qurʾanic words which he had used in his translation: *khurūj* and *ikhrāj*. Now he recalled the Qurʾanic verses about the believers who had been *ukhrijū min diyārihim bi-ghayri ḥaqq* (22:40) ("expelled from their homes unjustly"); also *ukhrijnā min diyārinā* (2:246) ("expelled from our homes"). While he himself had fled with a friend long before 1609, thousands upon thousands had been thrown out, and Ibn Qāsim was eager for them not to forget the rest of the Qurʾanic verses that described those who had been expelled as subsequently going forth to fight in the cause of God: "They said: Why should we not fight in Allah's way when we have been driven from our dwellings with our children? Yet, when fighting was prescribed for them, they turned away, all save a few of them."[21]

21. See the Arabic version in Van Koningsveld, al-Samarri, and Wiegers 1997, 8–12.

Meanwhile, the Andalusīs who were launching maritime *jihād* raided the Spanish mainland – in a kind of reclamation of al-Andalus. For them, al-Andalus had been lost but not defeated: God remained in power and He could bring about change. And so, on visiting cities and villages in al-Andalus that had once been Muslim, travelers repeated the prayer, "May God return them to Islam" (*aʿādaha Allahu ilā al-Islām*). Muḥammad ibn ʿAbd al-Wahhāb al-Ghassānī was an ambassador sent by Mulay Ismāʿīl (r. 1672–1727) to ransom Muslim captives from Spain in 1690/91. In the first part of his account, *Riḥlat al-wazīr fi iftikāk al-asīr* (*Journey of the Vizier to Ransom the Captives*) and while he was in southern Spain, he met with numerous communities that claimed Andalusī origin – even though they had become Christian.[22] He recalled how his own ancestors had been among those that had been expelled and so, eager to show that the expulsion had not been a defeat of his community or of Islam, he used the word *jalāʾ* (evacuation), which recalled the Qurʾanic verse where God decreed the evacuation (*jalāʾ*) of the believers:

وَلَوْلا أَنْ كَتَبَ اللهُ عَلَيْهِمُ الْجَلاءَ لَعَذَّبَهُمْ فِي الدُّنْيَا وَلَهُمْ فِي الآخِرَةِ عَذَابُ النَّارِ

> Had God not ordained expulsion upon them, He would have tormented them in this life, and in the hereafter they shall face the torment of the Fire. (Pickthall's translation 59:3)

The expulsion was God's, not man's, decree, and although al-Ghassānī did not go so far as to call it an act of grace or a miracle, he still situated it within the divine will since the Qurʾanic verse occurs in the chapter on, not inappropriately, *al-Ḥashr* (exile). Importantly, *jalāʾ* had earlier been used in the poem about the 1492 expulsion that had been sent by Andalusīs to Ottoman Sultan Bayezid II (reg. 1481–1512) (and quoted in full by al-Maqarrī in *Azhār al-riyāḍ*).[23] Al-Ghassānī then turned to *baqāyā al-Andalus* (the remnants [survivors] of al-Andalus) whom he met in various cities, from Jerez de la Frontera to Atrira, those who were "of the blood of the last king of Granada," and, rather generously, invited them to cross over to Morocco – as if they were still Muslims living in the land of infidelity. Although *baqāya al-Andalus* had become completely integrated in Christendom, they lived in a Spain that still bore for al-Ghassānī the marks of Islam – which he hoped God would reclaim one day.

Up until the end of the seventeenth century, the expulsion was treated in Arabic sources as an act of God, according to which God sought to preserve the faith of the Muslims by sending them out to the lands of Islam. Interestingly, and unlike in *aljamiado* writings, there was no reference to the

22. al-Ghassānī 1940. See translations of parts of this travelogue in Matar 2003.
23. See the translation in Monroe 2012, 540–546.

expulsion as a punishment of the Muslims for not having abided by their religious codes, as was prevalent in a sixteenth-century tradition of Morisco prophecies.[24] God decreed the expulsion to save Muslims and not to punish them. Writing contemporaneously with al-Ghassānī in the 1690s, the Tunisian chronicler Ibn Abī Dīnār recalled the *nafī* (exile) of al-Andalus by the Spanish ruler but then explained: "*Al-Andalus jāʾat min bilād al-Naṣāra*" ([the people of] al-Andalus came from the lands of the Christians).[25] Although he was the first to use the word *nafī*, a distinctly non-Qurʾanic term, he did not elaborate and, like al-Maqarrī earlier, celebrated the contributions of the Andalusīs in Tunisia: "They now own great cities, having cultivated orchards and olive trees. They built roads, organized travel by coach, and are now considered part of the inhabitants of the land." The violence of the expulsion had receded and the focus was now on the expelled and what they had effected: they have become, he wrote, natives of the land (*ṣārū yuʿaddūna min ahl al-bilād*). Al-Wazīr al-Sarrāj, writing in Tunis a generation later, borrowed from Ibn Abī Dīnār, adding that the Andalusīs built mosques with large endowments, and established twenty cities. In Tunis, they had built a school in 1034/1625 that employed two famous teachers, Shaʿbān the Andalusī, learned in *ʿilm al-kalām* (theology), and Abū Rabīʿ Sulaymān, the Sībawayh (linguist of his age).[26] A contemporary of al-Sarrāj, Moroccan chronicler Muḥammad al-Ṣaghīr al-Ifrānī (d. ca.1742) mentioned nothing about the expulsion but denounced the Andalusīs (*Ahl al-Andalus*) for having colluded with the Spanish Christians against Muḥammad al-ʿAyyāshī, who had fought the Spanish occupiers a century earlier.[27] Muḥammad ibn al-Ṭayyib al-Qādirī, another chronicler of Morocco, wrote in his *Nashr al-Mathānī* about the *khurūj* of the Andalusīs in 1609 and borrowed from al-Maqarrī the description of their settlement in Salé and their maritime *jihad*. He then quoted at length from al-Maqarrī about the fall of Granada in 1492, thereby conflating the two expulsions.

The Andalusīs of the 1609 expulsion were remembered at the end of the eighteenth century in a striking way. Writing in 1780, the Moroccan ambassador Ibn ʿUthmān al-Miknāsī reported in his *al-Iksīr fī iftikāk al-asīr* (*The Elixir in Ransoming the Captive*) what his Spanish hosts had told him during his diplomatic mission in that year: that the

> Turkish king at that time wrote to Philip's vizier urging him to send out (*ikhrāj*) the remnants of the defeated Muslims in the land. The

24. See the reference in Ḥatāmleh 2013, 566.
25. Ibn Abī Dīnār 1983, 228.
26. Sarrāj 1973, 157–158.
27. al-Ifrānī 1998, 382–389.

> vizier told his master that those who were still attached to their religion were high in number and could not be trusted not to rebel again. They had rebelled during the reign of Philip II, the father of that tyrant (*ṭāghiya*). So it was better to evacuate (*yajlū*) this country and go overseas and settle in Berber lands (*berberiyya*). And so they did, except those who had willingly turned Christian.

Al-Miknāsī did not have any information of his own to add: actually, all the histories that he reported came from his hosts. But five years later, in his second travelogue, *Iḥrāz al-maʿālī wa-l-raqīb* (1785–86), and during his return journey from the pilgrimage to Mecca, he stopped in Testour in Tunisia, where the local community came out to welcome him with music and food. And here he actually met the descendants of the Andalusīs who had been expelled over 180 years earlier:

> Most of the inhabitants of this city are from al-Andalus. They are highly urbanized and well-mannered, and continue to inquire about their country, al-Andalus. I had been there when I visited in the year 1193 AH [1779–80 CE]. And so I told them about their country and their land, which caused them to rejoice. Each was telling me: "I am from such and such a city" and then would ask me to describe it. Which I did. They rejoiced as they recalled their cities of origin, especially those who came from major sites such as Cordoba, Seville, and Granada. Many of their scholars assembled around us and we discussed matters of learning. May God help them and assist them to realize their goals.[28]

Nothing similar to this description will appear in later Arabic writings. Actually, in the nineteenth century, there were few references to the expulsion: the Tunisian Aḥmad Ibn Abī Diyāf (1804–74), in his *It-ḥāf ahl al-zamān bi-akhbār mulūk Tūnis wa ʿahd al-amān*, included biographies of numerous Andalusīs but he did not write about the expulsion as such.[29] One of the early publications of the Bulaq press in Egypt in 1856 was Aḥmad ibn Muḥammad Khafajī's (d.1659) *Hādhā kitāb rayḥānat al-alibbā*, which included a poem by Yaḥyā al-Qurṭubī (the Granadan) who had been taken captive in al-Andalus. He wrote to the Muslim rulers for help, especially to the Ottoman Sultan Suleyman, but none responded, and so he lamented the fall of Toledo that had been a house of learning, wondered where Muslims were who would fight for Granada and its Ḥamrāʾ palace, and wept for the fall of Malaga and al-Zahrāʾ and for all the children, mothers, and virgins who were led by infi-

28. al-Miknāsī 1965, 93. Matar 2015, 179.
29. See Ibn Abī Diyāf 2005.

dels to captivity.[30] Less than half a century later, and in the first years of the twentieth century, the Lebanese Jurjī Zaydān, while living in Cairo, wrote the first historical novels in Arabic. Following in the footsteps of Sir Walter Scott, he selected moments of high drama and framed them in fictional narratives, sometimes good, sometimes bad. Two of his novels were about al-Andalus, although not about the expulsions, but about the Muslim battles in Iberia: *Fatḥ al-Andalus* (*The Conquest of al-Andalus*), about Tāriq ibn Ziyād in 711, and *Charles Martel wa ʿAbd al-Raḥmān*, about the Battle of Poitiers in 732. In 1912, and while traveling in America, the Egyptian Prince Muḥammad ʿAlī was reminded of the Moroccan Andalusīs as he examined some of the "Arabian saddles, fully equipped" in a store selling Indian products in Williams, Arizona.[31] But the ongoing Arab *Nahḍa* from the mid-nineteenth century on paid little attention to al-Andalus: from the late 1870s until the early 1950s, a distinguished journal such as the Cairo-based *al-Muqtaṭaf* included only a handful of articles about the history of al-Andalus, none of which were about the expulsion/s; and from 1898 until 1950, the Beirut-based *al-Machriq*, another important journal, included nothing at all. As Arab immigrants to the United States declared in 1898: "Why should not our Andalus be America?" (*Andalusunā Amayrkā?*) [32] While al-Andalus may have survived as a site of memory in the minds of immigrants to the United States, al-Andalus as a historical reality had disappeared from the writings of their compatriots in the Arab World.

The shift in Arabic writings about al-Andalus and the 1609 expulsion occurred after 1948. Although Aḥmad Shawqī, prince of poets (d. 1932), wrote about al-Andalus,[33] it was from 1948 on, after the expulsion of the Arab population of Palestine, that writers began to draw analogies between the latter and the expulsion of the Arab population of al-Andalus. Thus the Syrian poet Nizār Qabbānī wrote to his mistress about Ṭāriq ibn Ziyād, the model redeemer-conqueror, while the Palestinian poet Maḥmūd Darwīsh wrote an elegy on the poet Lorca, and the Egyptian novelist, Raḍwā ʿAshūr, completed her *Thulathiyāt Gharnāṭa* (*Granada Trilogy*) in 1994, perhaps as an Arabic response to Amin Maalouf's highly popular 1986 *Leo Africanus* (in French). In 2004, a study by ʿAbd al-Razzāq Ḥussayn on *al-Andalus fī al-shiʿr al-ʿArabī al-muʿāṣir* (*Al-Andalus in Contemporary Arabic Poetry*) surveyed the writings of over sixty poets who had written about "our lost paradise" (*firdawsunā*

30. Khafajī 1856, 141–143.

31. Pasha 2004, 112.

32. The title of an article in the Philadelphia-based *Al-Hoda* (1 March 1898). Interestingly, and in the novels surveyed in Omri 2010, 279–298, there is no recollection of al-Andalus.

33. He wrote a poem, a *muwasshaḥ*, an elegy, and a prose drama – the last and only work with a historical (medieval) setting: see Maḥfūz 2016, 66–71.

al-mafqūd), a phrase that was used frequently in writings about al-Andalus, evoking Milton's *Paradise Lost*.[34] The author dedicated his book to "*al-ḥabība al-Andalus*" (beloved al-Andalus), and in the unit about "the hope for return" (*al-amal fī-l-ʿawda*), he quotes – which is what he does most of the time in the book, adding brief and sentimental comments – writers from various parts of the Arab world: ʿOmar Abū Rīsha (Syria); Ibrahīm Ṭūqān and Samīḥ al-Qāsim (Palestine), Fawzī al-Maʿlūf (Lebanon) and others from Saudi Arabia, Egypt, and other Arab countries. "Sing to me, O friend," one poem reads, "for my sky is full of storms. Sing to me that I return" – to al-Andalus.[35]

Meanwhile, numerous conferences and academic publications began to focus exclusively on the 1609 expulsion: in 1980 the pioneering work of Muḥammad Qashtilio, *Miḥnat al-Mūriskus fī Isbāniya* (*The Ordeal of the Moriscos in Spain*) appeared, and two years later, a major conference was organized in Zaghouan, Tunisia, by that one-of-a kind Tunisian scholar, ʿAbdjelīl Temīmī, resulting in a multi-volume Arabic and French publication on *Religion, Identity, and Documentary Sources about the Andalusian Moriscos.* A year later, *al-Andalūsiyyūn al-Mawārika* (*The Andalusī Moriscos*) was published in Damascus by ʿĀdil Saʿīd Bishtāwī, about the post-1492 history of the Moriscos, with an extensive examination of the 1609 expulsion.[36] Meanwhile, the Jordanian scholar, Muḥammad ʿAbduh Ḥatāmleh began publishing on *al-tahjīr al-qusri-yy* (the forcible eviction) of the Moriscos under Philip III (culminating in his magnum opus of 2013, *Al-Muriskiyyūn wa maḥākim al-taftīsh fī al-Andalus* [The Moriscos and the Inquisition Courts in al-Andalus]),[37] and in 1989 the Egyptian scholar Ṣalāḥ Faḍl translated the sixteenth-century *aljamiado* epics of the Moriscos into Arabic. As he wrote in the introduction, the "tragedy (*maʾsāt*) of those crushed Moriscos, enduring the bigotry of the Inquisition, made them turn their history into epic."[38] Two years later, another conference was organized by Temīmī's Center for the Study and Research on Ottoman and Morisco History in Tunis about what the London-based *Al-Ḥayāt* newspaper described as the "defeat/fall (*suqūṭ*) of Granada and the Morisco tragedy (*maʾsāt*) – and the aftermath of the Morisco expulsion (*ṭard*)."[39] Aware of the dearth of Arabic scholarship on the Moriscos, the Egyptian Higher Council of Culture, under the directorship of Jābir ʿAsfūr, began in the early 2000s to commission and publish translations from Spanish into Arabic of major

34. Ḥussayn 2004, 9.

35. Ḥussayn 2004, 108.

36. It would be remiss not to mention here the excellent work, *Islam and the West*, by the Lebanese scholar of the University of Minnesota (in English), Anwar G. Chejne.

37. See Ḥatāmleh 1983, 111–124; 1987, 95–124.

38. Faḍl 1989, 6.

39. *Al-Ḥayāt*, 13 December 1991.

historical studies about the Moriscos, including the classic work by Míkel de Epalza, *Los Moriscos antes y después de la expulsión*.[40]

As can be seen, from 1948 and the Arab expulsion from Palestine, the Arabic terminology about the Andalusī expulsion changed dramatically: from the divinely sanctioned or neutral references to the passionate and forceful. No more was the expulsion a result of God's will or a *hijra* (migration) in emulation of the Prophet's; it was now a *maʾsāt* (tragedy), a loss of paradise, a *ṭard* (expulsion), a *suqūṭ* (a fall) (as in *Al-ʿArabī* magazine's *Andalūsiyyāt* collection of 1988), a forcible Christianization of Muslims (*tanṣīr*) (a favorite term of Ḥatāmleh), a chronicle of *al-umma al-shahīda* (martyred nation) (the title of a book by Bishtāwī), and a *miḥna* (ordeal). While early modern writers had appealed to God to destroy the enemy and to reclaim the lost Andalusī homeland, now writers and scholars turned to reproach and recrimination.

The full awakening of memory about the Andalusī 1609 expulsion occurred in 2009. Along with the numerous conferences that were held in Morocco, Algeria, and Tunisia,[41] Al-Jazeerah TV presented in July of that year an extended report on *maʾsāt al-mūriskiyyīn* (the tragedy of the Moriscos), "the first ethnic cleansing in the history of mankind," the first time that the phrase, *taṭhīr ʿirqī* (ethnic cleansing) was used in the context of 1609 and earlier. The Al-Jazeerah report spanned the whole history of the expulsions from al-Andalus, from 1492, to 1502, to 1609. The report included a discussion among a number of distinguished North African scholars, interrupted by dramatic reenactments of the forced Christianization of the Muslims by the Inquisition, and of the subsequent expulsion. Prepared in the international climate of bigoted Western reporting about Islam (in the wake of the horror of 9/11), the program sought to show the cruelty of the Christian past, the brutal expulsion of Muslims by Christians, with repeated reference to *tanṣīr* (forcible conversion) to Christianity. It explained that the Western designs on the Muslim world had continued from then into the twentieth century, with the "*nakba*" (catastrophe) of the Palestinians, who like the expelled Andalusīs, had been driven out of their country, and never allowed to return. Like them, the Andalusīs "built little villages across from

40. Works translated into Arabic as part of this initiative include: García Arenal 1996 (translated by Jamāl ʿAbd al-Raḥmān in 2003); Epalza 2001 (translated by Jamāl ʿAbd al-Raḥmān in 2005) Mercedes García Arenal and Gerard Wiegers 1999 (translated by Mamdūḥ al-Bistāwī in 2005); Guillermo Gonzalbes Busto 1992 (translated by Marwa Muḥammad Ibrāhīm in 2005); Antonio Domínquez Ortiz and Bernard Vincent, *Historia de los moriscos* 2003 (translated by ʿAbd al-ʿĀl Ṣāliḥ in 2007) and others.

41. In May/June 2009, *Saudi Aramco* ran an article on al-Andalus, but completely ignored the expulsion and focused instead on Spanish scholarship about the Andalusī legacy. See Werner and Conde Alaya 2009.

their former homeland and sat waiting to return at any moment. But never did." One of the speakers mentioned how the descendants of the Andalusīs in North Africa still recalled those faraway days with sorrow and despair:

> When we search for our origins and ask our grandparents, they tell us that they came from al-Andalus. They came through that route, to this region, and joined the tribe of ᶜAnjara. We find that many of the villages of that tribe carry names similar to names in al-Andalus, such as Faḥamīn and Bani ᶜItāb....We find that the people of ᶜAnjara retain the hope of returning to their lands because they came here after the expulsion.[42]

A year later, in April 2010, *al-ᶜArabī* magazine, widely distributed from Kuwait, ran an interview with Temīmī in which he lambasted the Arab governments for not supporting research on Morisco history.[43] Seated in his amazing library-cum-conference center in Zaghouan, he also lambasted the Spanish king for not apologizing to the expelled Andalusīs in the manner that he had apologized for the expulsion of the Jews: "The tragedy of the Moriscos," he said, "is a horrible tragedy, one of the most violent in human history, compared in its deep suffering only to the tragedy of the Palestinian people today." But, he continued, proud of his own Andalusī descent, "the civilizational legacy of the Moriscos remains today in Spain, even though it was vanquished by bigotry and intolerance." A year later, Ḥasan Awrīd published a novel in French, *Le Morisque*, which was translated into Arabic as *al-Mūriskiyy* and based on the memoir of Aḥmad ibn Qāsim. He dedicated the book to "Those whose tragedy has been ignored by history – in memory of the Moriscos who have been forgotten."[44] In the introduction he stated:

> The Moriscos were the victims of what can be considered ethnic cleansing ... stemming from a purist reading of Christianity. They were the prelude to what other Muslim peoples would endure in the course of the destruction of Islamic civilization. They were the Palestinians of that age; actually, we can say that the Palestinian tragedy is a repetition of the tragedy of the Moriscos.[45]

In that same year, the new Moroccan constitution included the Andalusīs as part of the fabric of Moroccan identity, along with other population

42. Al-Jazeerah. See the list of Andalusī names that have survived in North Africa in Epalza 1969, 247–327. See also Ḥamrūnī 1998.

43. Fāḍil 2010.

44. Awrīd 2011.

45. Awrīd 2011, 9.

groups: Arab, Islamic, African, Hebrew, and Amazigh. Meanwhile, a center for the study of "Moriscos in Tunisia" was established at the University of Manouba with a website that includes a vast amount of literature, videos, academic studies, translations, and conference information about the history of the Moriscos in Spain and in North Africa.[46]

Then, exactly 400 years after the completion of the expulsion, the first imagining of the 1609 expulsion appeared in Arabic fiction. In October 2014, the Egyptian novelist Ṣubḥī Mūsa (b. 1972) finished his *al-Mūriskiyy al-akhīr* (*The Last Morisco*), a novel of vast intellectual and emotional scope. It spanned events from the sixteenth/seventeenth centuries in al-Andalus, to early nineteenth-century Egypt under Muḥammad ʿAlī, and then to Cairo in 2011.The book was carefully researched, and the narrative moves dramatically, juxtaposing events from those three time periods. The opening chapter featured the last Morisco in Tahrir Square, Murād, staring at the F16s flying above him. He was more afraid than others because he knew, wrote Ṣubḥī, that he belonged to "a dynasty that was about to go extinct, a dynasty that was scattered between Morocco and Syria and the countries of the Old and the New World. The elders traveled far and wide, ever dreaming that they would regroup if even on one meter of earth, one meter that could hold them all."[47]

Mūsā compared the revolt of the Alpujarras (*al-Bishārāt*) in 1568 to the anti-Mubarak revolution of 2011 – although he ended the book with the defeat of the Andalusīs as they staggered from the ships that carried them from the Peninsula to the coast of Morocco. As the novel progressed from 1568 to 1609 in alternate chapters, it also traveled inside 2011 Cairo as Murād searched in the public library, Dār al-Kutub, for the deed of property left to him by his family when they settled in the city in the early 1800s. In the course of his search he came across a manuscript bearing the title, *Miḥnat al-mūriskiyyīn* (*The Ordeal of the Moriscos*), which led him to Morisco relatives in Australia. After they all met, they separated, and Murād was about to lose hope, walking among the Cairene throngs who spoke as "if it were all over, that there was a new road map for the country."[48] Back in his house, he faced the temptation of death – to which his grandmother had succumbed, the woman who had always told him stories about the Moriscos:

> He walked behind her [ghost] like a little bird clinging to a branch of a big tree. When she reached the door separating the stairs from the roof, she turned to him, saying: "Not now, Murād." She opened

46. See "Expulsados 1609, La Tragedia de los Moriscos."
47. Mūsā 2015, 8–9.
48. Mūsā 2015, 288.

> the door and an immense light shone through at which Murād felt he could not open his eyes. He covered his face with his hand to look through his fingers at how his grandmother had gone into that brilliance, as if she were a drop sinking into a mighty river. When he pushed ahead after her, he found the door closed and so, he said the salutation of peace to her and turned to go down. He heard the echo of her voice behind him saying: "And peace be to you, from me."[49]

He returned to his room and opened his email. He found a message about a Morisco conference: "All he had to do was fill out the form delineating his family tree. So he did and with one press of the button, reserved a seat among the attendants." The last Morisco had discovered that he was not the last: the Moriscos were not extinct.

In an interview, the author denounced Arab and Muslim historians for ignoring the "tragedy" (*maʾsāt*) of the Moriscos who were persecuted, expelled, and forcibly made to emigrate (*tahjīr*). What happened to the Moriscos, he concluded, is a blemish on the forehead of mankind's history.[50]

Conclusion

In that same year, 2014, oil was poured on the Andalusī fire of anger when the Spanish government declared its willingness to grant citizenship to the Sephardi Jews who had been expelled in 1492 – but refused to act in the same manner to the Andalusīs when they demanded their "Right of Return."[51] Meanwhile, *Munazamat shaʿb al-Andalus al-ʿālamiyya* (*The World Organization of the People of al-Andalus*), based in Algeria, called for the return of the exiles and adopted the modern Jewish terminology of diaspora (*shatāt*) to describe the condition of the Andalusīs who were deprived of their homeland.[52] The flag of this movement carries the Arabic words of the Alhambra palace in Granada: *Lā ghāliba illa Allah* (God alone is victor) – which, significantly, is the motif in the mausoleum of King Hasan V (d. 1961) in Rabat, too.[53] In the wake of the association between the 1492 Sephardi and the 1609 Andalusī expulsions, a massive study appeared in 2015 by Husām al-Dīn Shāshiyya about the similarities between the histories of expulsion of the two communities: *Al-Safardīm wa-l-Mūriskiyyīn: riḥlat al-tahjīr wa-l-tawṭīn fī bilād al-Maghrib 1492–1756* (*The Sephardim and the Moriscos: Journey of Forcible Expulsion and Settlement in the Maghrib*). The author documented the history of the two exiles, editing

49. Mūsā 2015, 292–293.
50. Shūsha 2014.
51. Kern 2014; Shefler 2014.
52. The word "diaspora" was also used in García Arenal 2014.
53. See Organización mundial del pueblo de al-Andalus.

and translating primary sources from Arabic, Spanish, and Hebrew.

At the beginning of the fifth century after the expulsion, the Andalusīs continue to recall their ancestral homeland. In an interview on May 8, 2016, with Zaghouan professor of history Shāfiya al-Sukhayrī, the septuagenarian of Andalusī descent recalled: "the Moriscos were expelled from Spain but many continue to cling to their customs and traditions. And up till today, the family patriarch congregates and plays the sorrowful composition that reflects the story of the Morisco *tahjīr* and tragedy."[54] During my visit to Tetuan, I was graciously hosted by Professor al-Sulamī, himself of Andalusī descent and a scholar of Andalusī history. As we were entering his house, he pointed to the pomegranates decorating the front gate. "A reminder of our *hijra* from Granada," he explained.

54. Ibn Qāsim 2016.

Bibliography

Anonymous. 1988. *Al-ʿArabī. Andalūsiyyāt* collection. Kuwait.

Anonymous. 1991. *Al-Ḥayāt*. 13 December 1991.

Anonymous. 1898. "Andalusunā Amayrkā." *Al-Hoda* 1 March 1989. Philadelphia.

ʿAshūr, Raḍwā. 1998. *Thulathiyāt Gharnāṭa*. Beirut.

Awrīd, Ḥasan Awrīd. 2011. *Al-Mūriskiyy/ Le Morisque*. Translated by ʿAbd al-Karīm al-Juwayṭī. Rabat.

Bishtāwī, ʿĀdil Saʿīd. 1983. *Al-Andalūsiyyūn al-Mawārika*. Cairo.

——. 2000. *Al-Ummah al-shahīda*. Beirut.

Chachia, H. E. 2016. "Los moriscos de Túnez." http://moriscostunez.blogspot.com/2010/11/1609.html

Chejne, Anwar G. 1983. *Islam and the West: the Moriscos*. Albany.

Chikha, Djemaa. 1984. "Les Morisques dans la poesie andalouse." In *Religion, Identity, and Documentary Sources about the Andalusian Moriscos*, edited by Abdeljelil Temīmī, 171–180. Tunis.

Darwīsh, Maḥmūd. 1964. "Lorca." In *Awrāq al-Zaytūn*, 136–138. Haifa.

Domínguez Ortiz, Antonio and Bernard Vincent (2003), *Historia de los moriscos*, Madrid.

Doubleday, Simon R. and David Coleman, eds. 2008. *In the light of Medieval Spain: Islam, the West, and Relevance of the Past*. New York.

Epalza, Miguel de. 1969. "Moriscos y Andalusíes en Túnez durante el Siglo XVII." *Al-Andalus* 34:247–327.

——. 2001. *Los Moriscos antes y después de la expulsion*. Alicante.

"Expulsados 1609, La Tragedia de los Moriscos." 2010. Los Moriscos de Túnez. http://moriscostunez.blogspot.com/2010/11/1609.html.

Fāḍil, Jihād. 2010. "Wajhan li-wajh." *Al-ʿArabī*. April 2010. Kuwait.

Faḍl, Ṣalāḥ. 1989. *Malḥamat al-maghāzī al-mūriskiyya*. Cairo.

Gafsi Slama, Abdel Hakim. 1988. "Le medersa des Moriscos andalous a Tunis." *Sharq al-Andalus, estudios arabes* 5:69–180.

——. 1998. "Chrétiens convertis et Moriscos-Andalous en tunisie au XVIIe siècle d'après les documents épigraphiques." In *Chrétiens et Musulmans à la Renaissance*, edited by Bartolomé Bennassar and Robert Sauzet, 487–507. Paris.

García Arenal, Mercedes. 1996. *Los Moriscos*. Granada.

García Arenal, Mercedes and Gerard Wiegers, eds. 1999. *Entre el Islam y Occidente: Vida de Samuel Pallache, judío de Fez*. Madrid.

——, eds. 2014. *The Expulsion of the Moriscos from Spain: A Mediterranean Diaspora*. Leiden.

al-Ghassānī, Muḥammad ibn ʿUthmān. 1940. *Riḥlat al-wazīr fi iftikāk al-asīr*. Edited by Alfred Bustani. ʿArāʾish.

Gonzalbes Busto, Guillermo. 1992. *Los moriscos en Marruecos*. Granada.

al-Ḥamrūnī, Ahmad. 1998. *Al-Mūriskiyyūn al-Andalūsiyyūn fī Tunis*. Tunis.

Harvey, L. P. 1985–86. "Pan-Arab Sentiment in a Late (1595) Granadan Text: British Library MS Harley 3507." *Revista del Instituto Egipcio de Estudios Islámicos* 23:223–233.

——. 2005. *Muslims in Spain: 1500-1614*. Chicago.

Ḥatāmleh, Muḥammad ʿAbduh. 1983. "Al-tahjīr al-qusriyy li-l-Mūriskiyyīn khārij shibh jazīrat Ibireia, 1598–1621." *Dirasat* 10:111–124.

——. 1987. "Muriskiyyū Valanciya taḥta waṭʾat al-sulṭa al-dīniyya wa-l-siyāsiyya, 1598–1621." *Dirasat* 14:95–124.

——. 2013. *Al-Muriskiyyūn wa maḥākim al-taftīsh fī al-Andalus*, Amman.

Hirschkind, Charles. 2014. "The Contemporary Afterlife of Moorish Spain." In *Islam and Public Controversy in Europe*, edited by Nilüfar Göle, 227–240. Burlington.

Ḥussayn, Abd al-Razzāq. 2004. *Al-Andalus fī al-shiʿr al-ʿArabī al-muʿāṣir*. Kuwait.

Ibn Abī Dīnār, Muḥammad. 1983. *Al-Muʿnis fī akhbār Ifrīqiya wa Tūnis*. Beirut.

Ibn Abī Diyāf, Aḥmad. 2005. *It-ḥāf ahl al-zamān bi-akhbār mulūk Tūnis wa ʿahd al-amān* (*Consult Them in the Matter*). Translated by L. Carl Brown. Fayetteville.

Ibn Ghānim, Aḥmad. 1640. *Kitāb al-ʿizz w-al-manāfiʿ li-l-mujāhidīn fī sabīl Allah bi-l-madāfiʿ*. National Library, MS Jīm 87. Rabat.

Ibn al-Ṭayyib al-Qādirī, Muḥammad. 1981. *Nashr al-mathānī*. Oxford, UK.

Ibn Qāsim, Rawʿa. 2016. "Zaghouan qiṣat ʿishq." *Al-Quds al-ʾArabi* (Arabic language newspaper published in UK). 8 May, 2016.

al-Ifrānī, Muḥammad al-Saghīr. 1998. *Nuzhat al-ḥādī bi-akhbār mulūk al-qarn al-ḥādī*. Edited by ʿAbd al-Laṭīf al- Shādlī. Casablanca.

James, David. 1978. "The 'Manual de artillería' of al-Raʾīs Ibrāhīm ḅ Aḥmad al-Andalusī with Particular Reference to Its Illustrations and Their Sources." *Bulletin of the School of Oriental and African Studies*, 41:237–257.

Al-Jazeerah TV. 2009. "*Maʾsāt al-mūriskiyyīn*."

Kern, Soeren. 2014. "Muslims Demand 'Right of Return' to Spain." Gatestone Institute. 21 February 2014. https://www.gatestoneinstitute.org/4183/muslim-right-of-return-spain

Khafajī, Aḥmad ibn Muḥammad. 1856. *Hādhā kitāb rayḥānat al-alibbā*. Cairo.

Khalidi, Tarif, trans. 2008. *The Qurʾan: A New Translation*. New York.

Latham, J. D. 1957. "Towards a Study of Andalusian Immigration and Its Place in Tunisian History." *Les Cahiers de Tunisie* 5:203–252.

Maalouf, Amin. 1986. *León l'Africain*. Paris.
Maḥfūz, Hind ʿAbd al-Ḥalīm. 2016. "Riḥlat Shawqī ilā al-Andalus." *Al-ʿArabī* 691:66–71.
al-Maqarrī, Aḥmad ibn Muḥammad. 1939. *Azhār al-riyāḍ fī akhbār ʿIyaḍ*. Edited by Musṭapha al-Saqqā et al., Cairo.
——. 1949. *Nafḥ al-ṭīb min ghuṣn al-Andalus al-raṭīb*. Edited by M.ʿAbd al-Ḥamīd, Muḥammad Muḥyiddīn. Cairo.
Martinez, François. 1999. "L'Expulsion des Morisques: Discours et representations." In *Images des Morisques dans la literature et les arts*, edited by ʿAbdjelīl Temīmī, 193–207. Zaghouan.
Matar, Nabil. 2009. "The 1609 Expulsion of the Moriscos in Early Modern British Thought." *Explorations in Renaissance Culture* 35:132–149.
——. 2008. *Europe through Arab Eyes*. New York.
——, trans. 2003. *In the Lands of the Christians*. New York.
——, trans. 2015. *An Arab Ambassador in the Mediterranean World, The Travels of Muhammad ibn Uthman al-Miknasi*. New York.
al-Miknāsī, Ibn ʿUthmān. 1965. *Al-Iksīr fī iftikāk al-asīr*. Edited by Muḥammad al-Fāsī. Rabat.
Monroe, James. 2012. "A Morisco Appeal to the Ottoman Sultan." In *Medieval Iberia: Readings from Christian, Muslim, and Jewish Sources*, edited by Olivia Constable, 540–547. Philadelphia.
Al-Mūriskiyyūn fī al-Maghrib. 2000. Shafshāwan.
Mūsā, Subḥī. 2015. *Al-Mūriskiyy al-akhīr*. Cairo.
Omri, Mohamed-Salah. 2010. "Representing the Early Modern Mediterranean in Contemporary North Africa." In *Trade and Cultural Exchange in the Early Modern Mediterranean: Braudel's Maritime Legacy*, edited by Maria Fusaro et al., 279–299. London.
Organización mundial del pueblo de al-Andalus. 2017. phpBB (blog). http://andalous.dbzworld.org/.
Pasha, Muḥammad Alī. 2004. *Al-Riḥla al-Amrīkiyya*. Edited by ʿAlī Aḥmad Kanʿān. Abu Dhabi.
Pickthall, Marmaducke, trans. 1938. *The Meaning of the Glorious Qurʾan*. Hyderabad. Quran.com 2016 https://quran.com
Pieri, Henri. 1978. "L'accueil par des tunisiens aux morisques expulses d'Espagne: un temoignage morisque." In *Recueils d'etudes sur les Moriscos andalous en Tunisie*, edited by Miguel de Epalza and Ramón Petit, 128–135. Madrid.
al-Qafṣī, Al-Muntaṣir ibn al-Murābiṭ ibn Abī Liḥya. 1998. *Nūr al-armash fī manāqib al-Qashshāsh*. Edited by Luṭfī ʿIssā and Ḥussayn BūJarra. Tunis.
Qashtilio, Muḥammad. 1980. *Miḥnat al-Mūriskus fī Isbāniya*. Tetouan.

al-Razzāq Ḥussayn ʿAbd. 2004. *Al-Andalus fī al-shiʿr al-ʿArabī al-muʿāṣir*. Kuwait.
al-Sarrāj, Al-Wazīr. 1973. *Al-Ḥulal al-sundusiyya fī al-akhbār al-Tūnisiyya*. Edited by Muḥammad al-Ḥabīb al-Hīla. Tunis.
Shannon, Jonathan H. 2016. "There and Back Again: Rhetorics of al-Andalus in Modern Syrian Popular Culture." *International Journal of Middle East Studies* 48:5–24.
Shāshiyya, Ḥusām al-Dīn. 2015. *Al-Safardīm wa-l-Mūriskiyyīn: riḥlat al-tahjīr wa-l-tawṭīn fī bilād al-Maghrib (1492–1756)*. 2 vols. Abu Dhabi.
Shefler, Gil. 2014. "Spanish Muslims, or Moriscos, seek parity with Jews expelled from Spain." *Washington Post*, 5 June, 2016. https://www.washingtonpost.com/national/religion/spanish-muslims-or-moriscos-seek-parity-with-jews-expelled-from-spain/2014/06/05/3dbf2c78-ece1-11e3-b10e-5090cf3b5958_story.html
Shūsha, Zīzī. 2014. Interview with Mūsā, Subḥī. *Al-Badīl*, 13 March 2014.
Sulamī, M. 2000. *Al-Muriskiyyūn fi-l Maghrib*. Shafshāwin.
Temīmī, ʿAbdjelīl. 1993. "Taṭawwur mawqif sulutāt iyālat Tunis tijāh al-Mūriskiyyīn ʿala ḍawʾ firmān jadīd li-l-sulṭān al-ʿUthmānī." *Al-Majalla al-tārīkhiyya al-maghāribiyya* 69–70:57–70.
al-Turkī, ʿAbd al-Majiī. 1967. "Wathāʾiq ʿan al-hijra al-Andalūsiyya al-akhīra ilā Tūnis." *Ḥawliyyāt al-Jāmiʿa al-Tūnisiyya*, 23–82.
Van Koningsveld, P. S. and G. A. Wiegers. 1996. "Islam in Spain During the Early Sixteenth Century: The Views of the Four Chief Judges in Cairo (introduction, translation and Arabic text)." In *Poetry, Politics and Polemics: Cultural Transfer between the Iberian Peninsula and North Africa*, edited by Otto Zwartjes, Geert Jan van Gelder, and Ed de Moor, 133–152. Amsterdam.
Van Koningsveld, P. S., Q. al-Samarrai, and G. A. Wiegers, eds. 1997. *Kitāb Nāṣir al-dīnʿala al-qawm al-kāfirīn*. Madrid.
Waite, Gary K. 2013. "Empathy for the Persecuted or Polemical Posturing? The 1609 Spanish Expulsion of the Moriscos as Seen in Netherlandic Pamphlets." *Journal of Early Modern History* 17:95–123.
Werner, Louis and Jesus Conde Alaya. 2009. "Al-Andalus." *Saudi Aramco* (May/June).
Zaydān, Jurjī. 1997. *Charles Martel wa ʿAbd al-Raḥmān*. Cairo.
——. 1985. *Fatḥ al-Andalus*, ed. M. Makkī. Cairo.

Contributors

Shamma Boyarin is a professor in the English Department at the University of Victoria, BC. He explores the relationship between Hebrew and Arabic in the Middle Ages - particularly in a literary context - and the interplay between discourses that we identify as a "religious" or as "secular." His scholarship and teaching also look at the way current pop culture engages with the Middle Ages and religion - especially in the complex arena of global Heavy Metal. Both in his work on the Middle Ages and on contemporary matters, he is influenced by scholarly approaches that interrogate what seem like binary oppositions and hard-drawn boundaries between categories.

Olga M. Davidson earned her Ph.D. in 1983 from Princeton University in Near Eastern studies. She is on the faculty of the Institute for the Study of Muslim Societies and Civilizations, Boston University, where she has served as research fellow since 2009. From 1992 to 1997, she was Chair of the Concentration in Islamic and Middle Eastern Studies at Brandeis University. Since 1999, she has been Chair of the Board, Ilex Foundation. She is the author of *Poet and Hero in the Persian Book of Kings* (1994; 2nd ed. 2006; 3rd ed. 2013) and *Comparative Literature and Classical Persian Poetry* (2000; 2nd ed. 2013).

Samuel England is associate professor of Arabic at the University of Wisconsin-Madison. He teaches classical and modern Arabic, Mediterranean cultures, and sub-Saharan African sources. His published research covers classical Arabic poetry and prose, courts in the Middle East and Europe, Crusades literature, Arab nationalist film and drama of the past century, and Romance language treatments of Islam. He is the author of *Medieval Empires and the Culture of Competition: Literary Duels at Islamic and Christian Courts* (Edinburgh University Press, 2017). Currently, he is writing a book about the role of classical Arabic in military regimes from the twentieth century to the present day.

Raymond K. Farrin studied Arabic at the American University in Cairo, and received a Ph.D. in Near Eastern studies from the University of California, Berkeley, under the guidance of James T. Monroe. He is currently professor of Arabic at the American University of Kuwait. His publications include

Abundance from the Desert: Classical Arabic Poetry (Syracuse University Press, 2011), *Tharwa min al-badiya: al-shi'r al-'arabi al-qadim* [Arabic translation of *Abundance from the Desert*] (Beirut: Dar al-Farabi, 2013), and *Structure and Qur'anic Interpretation: A Study of Symmetry and Coherence in Islam's Holy Text* (Ashland: White Cloud Press, 2014).

Maribel Fierro is research professor at the Council for Scientific Research (Madrid). Her research focuses on the political, religious, and intellectual history of al-Andalus and the Islamic West, on Islamic law, the construction of orthodoxy, and on violence and its representation in premodern Islamic societies. She is the author of *Abd al-Rahman III: The First Cordoban Caliph* (2005) and *The Almohad revolution: Politics and Religion in the Islamic West during the Twelfth-Thirteenth Centuries* (2012). She has edited *The Western Islamic World, Eleventh-Eighteenth Centuries*, vol. 2 of the *The New Cambridge History of Islam* (2010), and *Orthodoxy and Heresy in Islam: Critical Concepts in Religious Studies* (2013).

Teresa Garulo is professor of Arabic language and literature at the Universidad Complutense de Madrid. She is the author of *Dīwān de las poetisas de al-Andalus* (1986, 1998) and *La literatura árabe de al-Andalus durante el siglo XI* (1998). Among her recent studies are "Notas sobre *muŷūn* en al-Andalus: El capítulo VII del *Nafḥ al-ṭīb*," *AEA* 26 (2015): 93–120; "Ibn Ḥamdīs y la poesía estrófica de al-Andalus," *Vivir de tal suerte: Homenaje a Juan Antonio Souto Lasala*, Córdoba-Madrid, 2014, 215–32; "Erudición y nostalgia: *Al-Ḥanīn ilà l-awṭān* en el editor de *Al-Faraŷ ba'd al-šidda*," *Al-Qanṭara* XXXIII, 1 (2012): 107–46.

Michelle M. Hamilton is the director for the Center of Medieval Studies and professor of Spanish at the University of Minnesota, Twin Cities. Her scholarship explores the intersection of Arab, Jewish, and Christian cultural production in medieval Iberia. In her recent work, Hamilton investigates medieval material culture and its use in the construction of modern narratives of the past. She is author of two monographs, *Beyond Faith: Belief, Morality and Memory in a Fifteenth-Century Judeo-Iberian Manuscript* (2015), and *Representing Others in Medieval Iberian Literature* (2007), as well as several articles on medieval literature and culture. She is also the co-editor of a volume of essays on Iberia and the medieval Mediterranean *In and of the Mediterranean* (2015).

Manuela Marín is research professor emerita at the Consejo Superior de Investigaciones Científicas, Madrid. She has worked mainly on the cultural and social history of al-Andalus; her main contribution to the field is her book *Mujeres en al-Ándalus* (2000). Among her other interests, she has published several articles on the history of Arab studies in Spain, and is the author of a lengthy study on "Arabismo e historia de España (1886-1944): Introducción a los epistolarios de Julián Ribera Tarragó y Miguel Asín Palacios" (2009).

Nabil Matar is Presidential Professor in the President's Interdisciplinary Initiative on Arts and Humanities, and Samuel Russell Chair in the Humanities. He teaches courses in English, history, and religious studies. His latest work was a translation of selections from the travelogues of the only early modern Arab writer in the Mediterranean basin (Routledge, 2015). His forthcoming book is *The United States through Arab Eyes, 1876-1914* (Edinburgh University Press).

Dwight F. Reynolds is professor of Arabic language and literature, Department of Religious Studies, University of California, Santa Barbara. He is the author of *Heroic Poets, Poetic Heroes: The Ethnography of Performance in an Arabic Oral Epic Tradition* (1995), *Arab Folklore: A Handbook* (2007), co-author and editor of *Interpreting the Self: Autobiography in the Arabic Literary Tradition* (2001), *The Garland Encyclopedia of World Music, Vol. 6: The Middle East* (2002), and *The Cambridge Companion to Modern Arab Culture* (2015), as well as some twenty articles on Andalusian music. He is currently completing a book titled, *The Musical Heritage of al-Andalus.*

David A. Wacks is professor of Spanish in the Department of Romance Languages at the University of Oregon. He is author of *Framing Iberia: Frametales and Maqamat in Medieval Spain* (Brill, 2007) and *Double Diaspora in Sephardic Literature: Jewish Cultural Production before and after 1492* (Indiana University Press, 2015) and co-editor, with Michelle M. Hamilton, of *Wine, Women and Song: Hebrew and Arabic Poetry in Medieval Iberia* (Juan de la Cuesta, 2004). His research focuses on the literary footprint of the confluence of Christianity, Judaism, and Islam in medieval Iberia. He maintains a research blog at davidwacks.uoregon.edu.

Index